Air Transport and Re
Development Metho(

Air Transport and Regional Development Methodologies is one of three interconnected books related to a four-year European Cooperation in Science and Technology (COST) Action established in 2015. The action, called Air Transport and Regional Development (ATARD), aimed to promote a better understanding of how the air transport–related problems of core regions and remote regions should be addressed to enhance both economic competitiveness and social cohesion in Europe.

This book discusses key methodological approaches to assessing air transport and regional development, outlining their respective strengths and weaknesses. These include input-output analysis, cost benefit analysis, computable general equilibrium models, data envelopment analysis, stochastic frontier analysis, discrete choice models and game theory.

Air Transport and Regional Development Methodologies aims at becoming a major reference source on the topic, drawing from experienced researchers in the field, covering the diverse experience and knowledge of the members of the COST Action. The book will be of interest to several large groups. First, it will serve as an authoritative and comprehensive reference for academics, researchers and consultants. Second, it will advise policy-makers and government organizations at European, national and regional levels. Third, it presents invaluable insights to transport companies such as airports and airline operators. Along with the other two books (*Air Transport and Regional Development Policies* and *Air Transport and Regional Development Case Studies*), it fills a much-needed gap in the literature.

Anne Graham is Professor of Air Transport and Tourism Management at the University of Westminster, UK. She has two main research areas: first, airport management, economics, and regulation; and second, the relationship between the tourism and aviation sectors. She has published widely with recent books including *Air Transport: A Tourism Perspective, Airport Finance and Investment in the Global Economy, Managing Airports: An International Perspective, The Routledge Companion to Air Transport Management,* and *Airport Marketing.* She is a previous editor-in-chief of the *Journal of Air Transport Management* and in 2016 was made a fellow of the Air Transport Research Society.

Nicole Adler is Full Professor and Head of the Department of Operations Research and Operations Management at the School of Business Administration of Hebrew University in Jerusalem. Her major research interests include game theory and productivity estimation applied to the field of transportation. Her work has analysed hub-and-spoke airline competition and mergers, public service obligation tenders, and airport productivity, and she recently has utilised game theoretic concepts in order to understand air traffic control markets. Nicole is currently an Associate Editor for *Transportation Research Part B: Methodological*.

Ofelia Betancor is Associate Professor of Economics in the Department of Applied Economics at the University of Las Palmas de Gran Canaria (Spain). She holds an MSc in economics from the University of London, and two doctorate degrees in economics (Institute for Transport Studies-University of Leeds and University of Las Palmas). She has participated in many research projects at the national and international level, and has also collaborated with the World Bank and the Inter-American Development Bank as specialist in air transport and the economic evaluation of projects and transport policies. The results of her works have been published in leading journals in the area of transport economics.

Volodymyr Bilotkach is Senior Lecturer in Economics at the Singapore Institute of Technology, Singapore. His research interests cover various issues in economics of the aviation sector including airline alliances and mergers, airport regulation, and the economics of distribution of airline tickets.

Enrique J. Calderón is a retired professor from the Department of Transport and Territorial Planning in the Polytechnic University of Madrid, Spain. He specialises in urban, regional, and environmental issues at all levels, sustainability assessment, and the integration of environmental concerns into government policies and programmes, notably in regard to transportation.

Gianmaria Martini is Full Professor of Applied Economics at the University of Bergamo, Italy. His research interests are applied econometrics and methods to estimate efficiency in the air transport sector, extended to environmental issues. Recent research activities have covered regional development and aviation, with a specific focus on African countries. He is currently Associate Editor of the *Journal of Air Transport Management* and was the chairman of the organising committee of the 2013 Air Transport Research Society Conference in Bergamo. He has been nominated as vice president for publications of the ATRS.

Hans-Martin Niemeier is Director of the Institute for Transport and Development at Bremen University of Applied Sciences, Germany. He is Chairman of the German Aviation Research Society and member of the Advisory Board of the European Aviation Conference. He chaired the ATARD

COST Action from 2016–2019. From 2014 through May 2019, he was member of the Performance Review Body of the Single European Sky. He has published on privatisation, regulation, and competition of airports, the reform of slot allocation, and airline and airport alliances.

António Pais Antunes is Professor in the Department of Civil Engineering at the University of Coimbra (Portugal). He has been Visiting Fellow at Princeton University, Invited Professor at EPF Lausanne, Visiting Professor at MIT and a visiting researcher at the University of Bergamo. His teaching and research focus on public facility location, urban mobility (notably public transport and vehicle sharing), and air transport planning. He currently acts as Deputy Director of CITTA (Research Centre for Territory Transport and Environment) and as Coordinator of the Doctoral Programs in Spatial Planning and in Transport Systems at the University of Coimbra.

Air Transport and Regional Development Methodologies

Edited by Anne Graham, Nicole Adler,
Ofelia Betancor, Volodymyr Bilotkach,
Enrique J. Calderón, Gianmaria Martini,
Hans-Martin Niemeier, and
António Pais Antunes

Routledge
Taylor & Francis Group
LONDON AND NEW YORK

cost
EUROPEAN COOPERATION
IN SCIENCE & TECHNOLOGY

First published 2021
by Routledge
2 Park Square, Milton Park, Abingdon, Oxon OX14 4RN

and by Routledge
52 Vanderbilt Avenue, New York, NY 10017

Routledge is an imprint of the Taylor & Francis Group, an informa business

British Library Cataloguing-in-Publication Data
A catalogue record for this book is available from the British Library

Library of Congress Cataloging-in-Publication Data
Names: Adler, Nicole, editor. | Niemeir, Hans-Martin, editor. |
Graham, Anne, 1958– editor.
Title: Air transport and regional development methodologies /
edited by Nicole Adler, Hans-Martin Niemeir, Anne Graham,
Ofelia Betancor, Antonio Pas Antunes, Volodymyr Bilotkach,
Enrique J Calderóna and Gianmaria Martini.
Description: 1 Edition. | Boca Raton : Routledge, 2021. |
Includes bibliographical references and index.
Identifiers: LCCN 2020038472 (print) | LCCN 2020038473 (ebook)
Subjects: LCSH: Aeronautics, Commercial. |
Airports–Management. | Regional planning. | Strategic planning.
Classification: LCC HE9776 .A356 2021 (print) |
LCC HE9776 (ebook) | DDC 387.7/1–dc23
LC record available at https://lccn.loc.gov/2020038472
LC ebook record available at https://lccn.loc.gov/2020038473

ISBN: 9780367076498 (hbk)
ISBN: 9780429021855 (ebk)

Typeset in Bembo
by Newgen Publishing UK

Contents

List of contributors   ix

1 Introduction   1
   NICOLE ADLER, HANS-MARTIN NIEMEIER, ANNE GRAHAM,
   OFELIA BETANCOR, ANTÓNIO PAIS ANTUNES, VOLODYMYR
   BILOTKACH, ENRIQUE J. CALDERÓN, AND GIANMARIA MARTINI

2 Regional economic theory and the impact of transport
   investments   9
   STEF PROOST AND SHARON SARMIENTO

3 A review of connectivity utility models and their applications   26
   YAHUA ZHANG AND ANMING ZHANG

4 Wider economic benefits: what they are, how they
   manifest, and an example from network air services   45
   DAVID GILLEN

5 The application of an input-output approach to measuring
   the impact of air transport on the economy: a critical review   66
   SONIA HUDEREK-GLAPSKA

6 Cost-benefit analysis of air transport projects with effects
   on the regions   93
   JAVIER CAMPOS AND OFELIA BETANCOR

7 The use of CGE models in the evaluation of air transport
   policy and large-scale investment: a survey   108
   ERIC TCHOUAMOU NJOYA AND PETER FORSYTH

8 Economic impact analysis, cost benefit analysis, and computable general equilibrium modelling: outline of techniques and where to use them 129
PETER FORSYTH AND HANS-MARTIN NIEMEIER

9 How to estimate the social costs of airport negative externalities: a case study on Milan Bergamo airport 156
GIANMARIA MARTINI, MATTIA GRAMPELLA, AND DAVIDE SCOTTI

10 Econometric approaches to the study of air transport impacts on regional development: main methods and results 175
ANTÓNIO PAIS ANTUNES AND GIANMARIA MARTINI

11 Stated preference and travel behaviour modelling: an application to airport accessibility analysis at regional level 202
ANGELA STEFANIA BERGANTINO AND MARIO CATALANO

12 Entry games for the airline industry 226
CHRISTIAN BONTEMPS AND RAQUEL M. B. SAMPAIO

13 Applying game theory to analyse aviation markets and their impact on regional development with a case study of the EU-Israel aviation agreement 249
NICOLE ADLER

14 Stochastic frontier analysis 269
DAVIDE SCOTTI AND NICOLA VOLTA

15 Data envelopment analysis 286
DAVIDE SCOTTI AND NICOLA VOLTA

Index 307

Contributors

Nicole Adler, Hebrew University, Jerusalem, Israel

António Pais Antunes, University of Coimbra, Coimbra, Portugal

Angela Stefania Bergantino, University of Bari, Bari, Italy

Ofelia Betancor, University of Las Palmas de Gran Canaria, Las Palmas, Spain

Christian Bontemps, Toulouse School of Economics and École National de Aviation Civile, Toulouse. France

Javier Campos, University of Las Palmas de Gran Canaria, Las Palmas, Spain

Mario Catalano, Science Analytics and Toolkits for Emerging Challenges, UK

Peter Forsyth, Monash University Melbourne, Australia

David Gillen, University of British Columbia, Vancouver, Canada

Sonia Huderek-Glapska, Poznań University of Economics and Business, Poznań, Poland

Mattia Grampella, SEA, Milan Airports Operators, Milan, Italy

Gianmaria Martini, University of Bergamo, Bergamo Italy

Hans-Martin Niemeier, Bremen University of Applied Sciences, Bremen, Germany

Eric Tchouamou Njoya, University of Huddersfield, Huddersfield, UK

Stef Proost, University of Leuven, Leuven, Belgium

Raquel Menezes Bezerra Sampaio, Universidade Federal do Rio Grande do Norte, Natal, Brazil

Sharon Sarmiento, Unison Consulting, Inc., Laguna Hills, United States

Davide Scotti, University of Bergamo, Bergamo, Italy

Nicola Volta, Ernst & Young, Brussels, Belgium

Anming Zhang, University of British Columbia, Vancouver, Canada

Yahua Zhang, University of Southern Queensland, Darling Heights, Australia

1 Introduction

Nicole Adler, Hans-Martin Niemeier, Anne Graham,
Ofelia Betancor, António Pais Antunes, Volodymyr
Bilotkach, Enrique J. Calderón, and Gianmaria Martini

The air transport sector is a major contributor to the globalisation of the economy. Its growth has been accompanied, and to a certain extent, caused by liberalisation. The growth in traffic levels has led to congestion at both major airports and in the airspace, and to a lack of services on thin routes, thus affecting both core and remote regions.

A four-year European Cooperation in Science and Technology (COST) Action was established in 2015 and this book is a direct product of this. The Action, called Air Transport and Regional Development (ATARD), aimed to promote a better understanding of how the air transport related problems of core regions and remote regions should be addressed in order to enhance both economic competitiveness and social cohesion in Europe. It had members from a wide variety of professions and backgrounds from 33 countries and organised conferences/workshops in various locations, Ph.D. training schools, and short-term scientific missions of researchers to other academic institutions. The many countries that participated in so many different activities is a testament to the great interest that aviation research and regional development engenders among academics and practitioners.[1]

The area of the Action, namely the relationship between transport and regional development has been widely examined in the literature from a multiplicity of perspectives. However, most research has focused on land transport modes (especially road), whereas air transport research is far from having led to a coherent body of knowledge, despite some publications over the last two decades. Only a few methods have been used to explore the relationship, with attention being placed mostly on the economic dimensions of development. Moreover, it is clear that research on this subject is much more advanced in the United States than in Europe.

This book is one of three inter-related books related to the most important themes that were explored during the four-year COST Action. It will focus on methodologies (known here as ATARD methodological approaches) related to air transport and regional development. The other two books will focus on cases (known here as ATARD case studies) and policy implications (known here as ATARD policies). The three books complement each other in focusing on different aspects of ATARD, but are also stand-alone publications in their own right. The books fill a much-needed gap, presenting a multi-sector (airports, airlines, air navigation services, government organisations) and geographically Europe-wide coverage of both remote and core regions to fully explore all critical issues related to the linkages between air transport and regional development.

They are aimed at becoming a major reference on the topic, within which the main findings of the Action will be condensed. There is no other single source publication that currently covers this topic area in such a comprehensive manner. The books draw on experienced researchers in the field, covering the diverse experience and knowledge of the members of the Action from 33 countries. Many of the chapters in all three books have already been presented and debated at the ATARD conferences and workshops.

The ATARD case studies book is divided into four geographical regions after a general chapter that compares regional air transport connectivity between remote and central areas in Europe. The first region is Northern and Western Northern Europe (case studies related specifically to Norway, Finland, the UK, and Ireland); the second Central and Eastern Europe, (Bulgaria, Bosnia and Herzegovina, and Poland); the third Central Western Europe (France, Germany, the Netherlands, Luxemburg, Austria, Belgium and Switzerland; and finally Southern Europe (Portugal, Spain, and Italy).

The ATARD policies book begins with chapters that generally discuss important policy issues related to air transport and regional development in relation to connectivity and accessibility, dependency, airport governance and regulation, and air traffic control frameworks. This is followed by a number of chapters considering government studies and state aid. The final chapters then focus on other policy implications (tourism development, airport expansion, passenger taxation, and noise control).

This book, ATARD methodological approaches, is divided into four distinct groups of chapters; the first discussing regional economic theory, the second presenting the theory on economic impact assessment, the third describing applied economic methods covering both econometrics and game theory and the fourth and final group debating the use of performance estimation techniques when measuring the impact of aviation on regional development. A summary of the different chapters of this book is provided below. The important links with the other two ATARD books are also highlighted.

Within the first set of three papers, Proost and Sarmiento in Chapter 2 analyse how regional economic theory estimates the effects of changes in air transport infrastructure on regional economic development. Regional economic theory deals with uneven development of economic activity over space. For sectors and regions that have a natural advantage, for example with respect to agriculture and tourism, a decrease in interregional transport costs has obvious implications as the lower costs allow these regions to better use their advantages. On the other hand, a decrease in freight and passenger transport costs also affects the economic activity of regions that were equal at the start. Explanations for growing divergence in economic development are based on increasing returns to scale, initial market size, and better infrastructure between the periphery and the core regions, which may be detrimental for the peripheral regions. European regional policy has invested heavily in improved interregional transport infrastructure but assessments suggest that this policy has had limited success.

In Chapter 3, Zhang and Zhang provide an overview of connectivity measures and present a model to measure connectivity called ConnUM. This model shows how both direct and indirect air connectivity between countries can be calculated, which may be used to test and predict the relationship between air transport and economic activities. For example, the connectivity indices can be compared over years and across regions to evaluate the success of transport policy reforms and to support open skies and free trade agreements. The first step of constructing ConnUM is to assess direct connectivity for an airport considering quality factors such as the availability of seats (capacity) and travel time (velocity). The quality of indirect connections is largely dependent on the quality of transfer, which is dependent on both transfer time and transfer services. An application shows the connectivity levels between China and many countries around the globe and extends the case to a vulnerability study showing the impact of a reduction in a connection on the overall network. In ATARD cases, Martini et al. analyse air transport regional connectivity in Europe and Graham explores developments and challenges related to UK regional airports, including connectivity. In ATARD policy, Lenaerts et al. examine the quality of air transport networks, by considering a topology of connectivity and accessibility metrics, which aims to help decision-makers understand their economic value for overcoming distances.

In Chapter 4, Gillen discusses the concept of wider economic benefits often used to justify transport infrastructure expansion due to increases in access to markets and economic density. Wider economic benefits enhance household utility, firm profitability and macroeconomic (government) factors that have not been included in the standard welfare measures of consumer and producer surplus. Consequently, wider economic benefits are distinct from the catalytic effects utilised in impact assessments because they represent positive externalities that increase social value but have not been internalised in output or factor prices. The empirical component of this chapter examines how different types of air service in the United States affect the multifactor productivity of a range of different industries as a function of market size and reduced access costs. Gillen finds the coefficient of variation to be small in administration and waste management while it is key for the accommodation and food industries. A high coefficient may mean there is more likely to be wider economic benefits since with the variability around markets, not all available benefits may be internalised. In ATARD cases, Wittmer and Noto focus on the intangible effects of regional airports in Switzerland, contributing to the discussion of wider economic benefits.

In the second set of papers focused around economic impact assessments, Huderek-Glapska discusses the input-output approach most frequently utilised in the airport industry in Chapter 5. The input-output model is a quantitative economic technique developed in the 1930s and 1940s of the twentieth century which spread globally mainly due to the relatively simplicity and low cost of conducting such an analysis. In almost all studies, the estimation results for the income and employment effects that are generated by air transport activities are found to be significant and support the policy of developing air transport infrastructure. The input-output model, based on freely available, standardised and consistent input-output tables produced by Statistical Bureaus, is a tool for analysing inter-sectoral dependencies whereby changes in output are distributed between the industries and sectors of the economy in the form of direct, indirect, and induced effects. However, the academic literature has also discussed the inappropriate use of the method and the misinterpretation of the results due to issues with double-counting and problematic assumptions including fixed technological coefficients, constant returns to scale, no resource constraints and the calculation of aggregate rather than marginal effects. Consequently, any approach investigating the effects of air transport on the regional economy should have the versatility to focus on effective resource allocation, wider economic benefits (Chapter 4), micro factors related to airport operations, meso factors focusing on the air transport sector and macro factors considering the national and global socio-economic situation, technological environment in addition to the political, legal, and institutional conditions. In ATARD cases, Halpern applies input-output analysis to estimate the impact of aviation on geographical peripheries by considering the case of Norway and Buyle et al. review input-output analyses from Belgium.

In Chapter 6, Campos and Betancor discuss the application of cost-benefit analysis to estimate the impact of air transport on regional development. When a project involves public investment and/or may have a significant impact on the rest of the society, its economic evaluation needs to transcend a simple comparison of private flows of revenues and expenditures and should be performed instead from a wider social perspective. This is one of the main roles of cost-benefit analysis, a decision tool particularly well-suited for air transport projects and policies because their overall effects on the society can be analysed by using two complementary approaches. On the one hand, Campos and Betancor model a set of technical relationships that can be designed to seek the most efficient use of the available resources, including aircraft, infrastructure, and airspace. On the other hand, they model a set of economic connections among the social agents directly or indirectly participating in these movements, including passengers, airlines, airport managers, and third-party companies. In this context, the chapter discusses new decision criteria to accept or reject air transport projects by comparing the social net present value of carrying out an integration project versus the corresponding alternatives of choosing local projects. The authors provide criteria for the measurement and comparison of benefits and costs in order to facilitate implementation.

Cost-benefit analysis applied to the assessment of aviation related projects with potential effects on multiple regions or across countries may need to consider an alternative option that is preferable for the region as a whole but that might be not considered by individual countries that focus on their own interests. Consequently, the correct identification of such alternative projects is key to maximising the impact of aviation on the entire set of regions. Cost-benefit analysis, which is based on the estimation of changes in social agents' surpluses, may help to identify those who gain and those who may lose by group and nationality, in a similar manner to that of game theory discussed in Chapter 13 of this book. In ATARD cases, Vasallo et al. estimate the socio-economic accounts for the four main interurban transport modes in Spain.

In Chapter 7, Njoya and Forsyth review computable general equilibrium models that model both broad, economy-wide impacts of changes and specific sectors, such as transport markets. Computable general equilibrium models consist of a set of equations describing the behaviour of representative agents and the technological and institutional constraints facing them. The main agents include households, firms and the government that are linked through market equilibrium conditions. More recently, computable general equilibrium models have become a means of evaluating policy options and investments, such as new roads, rail subsidies and tax reforms in terms of their impact on variables such as gross domestic product, consumption and employment. In addition, such models have been used to measure welfare effects similar to cost-benefit analysis discussed in Chapter 5. With respect to aviation, computable general equilibrium models have been applied to estimate the impacts of an air passenger tax, building a new airport and effects of a specific liberalisation package, similar to game-theoretic models (Chapter 13).

In Chapter 8, Niemeier and Forsyth analyse how investments in airports and in air traffic control as well as policy decisions on taxes or subsides for air transport can best be evaluated. They compare and contrast three economic impact techniques, namely economic impact analysis, cost-benefit analysis, and computable general equilibrium models as described in this group of papers (Chapters 5 to 7). Whilst economic impact analyses are heavily criticised in both this and Huderek-Glapska's chapter, there would appear to be a place for both cost-benefit and computable general equilibrium. In fact, as the latter has evolved to include welfare estimates explicitly, the two approaches are attempting to answer similar questions. Both approaches provide a vigorous assessment of specific policies hence estimate net benefits for the region or country. Economic impact studies cannot answer this question despite claiming to measure benefits. In ATARD policy, Mueller provides a case study on the new Berlin International Airport and documents the lack of economic rationality in terms of costs and benefits. In contrast, Devlin discusses how the UK government adheres to economic rationality in their assessment of Public Service Obligations by mandating cost-benefit analysis.

The last chapter in this group discusses the estimation of the costs of negative externalities created at airports, including noise and emissions. In Chapter 9, Martini, Grampella, and Scotti present a methodology that is based on aircraft certification and airport scheduled operations. The method is demonstrated on a specific day of operation at the Milan Bergamo airport. The results suggest that the daily total social costs are equal to about €80,000, of which 76% is due to noise, which translates to a per seat cost of € 2.20. It is noted that such a procedure could be applied to multiple airports and a frontier approach, such as those discussed in Chapters 14 and 15, could help to identify appropriate public policies. In ATARD cases, Buyle et al. review the impact of noise pollution at Belgian airports and in ATARD policy, Morlotti et al. examine noise reduction measures and detail the initiatives adopted at Milan Bergamo airport.

The third group of chapters covers econometric and game-theoretic analyses. In Chapter 10, Antunes and Martini review econometric papers that investigate the relationship between air transport and regional development and their main determinants. Two types of econometrics dominate the literature, namely regression analysis (ordinary least squares and two-stage least squares) and Granger-causality analysis. The main takeaways from the literature review are that air transport impacts regional development with a high degree of probability and is clearly more relevant for the service sector than for the manufacturing sector. Remaining issues include the failure to consider the multidimensional nature of regional development, which may be better considered within productivity estimates (Chapters 14 and 15), and the need to test the impact of airport accessibility and connectivity on regional development. In ATARD cases, based on econometric techniques, Ringbom investigates the relationship between air traffic and economic development in Finland. Todorova and Haralampiev determine causal relationships between regional aviation and economic growth in Bulgaria. Freiria and Antunes evaluate the impact of Oporto Airport on the development of the Norte Region of Portugal and Percoco studies the impact of airport de-hubbing at Milan Malpensa airport in Italy.

In Chapter 11, Bergantino and Catalano review stated preference modelling within the framework of discrete choice approaches, which identify the behavioural responses of individuals to choice situations characterised by alternatives and attribute levels that are not yet available and/or observable in the market and hence cannot be analysed through revealed preference models. A case study of the Apulian region in Italy highlights the technique and how it may be employed in order to support decision-makers planning regional air transport infrastructure.

In Chapter 12, Bontemps and Sampaio review the literature on static entry games and show how they can be used to estimate the market structure of the airline industry. The econometric challenges are presented, in particular the problem of multiple equilibria and some solutions are discussed. They also discuss how complete information setting and incomplete setting models could be estimated from available data on market presence and market characteristics. Finally, they illustrate the modelling approaches by estimating a static entry game on Western European data with heterogeneous firms using simulated maximum likelihood.

In Chapter 13, Adler discusses the application of game-theoretic models in order to understand aviation markets and their potential impact on regional development through social welfare estimations. The chapter presents a mathematical model of network competition in which airlines set airfares, frequencies, and aircraft size with the aim of maximising profit as a best response to their competitors' choices. In order to validate the analysis, Adler attempts to reproduce an existing equilibria which relates to the market situation prior to any impending changes. Subsequently a what-if style of analysis compares the baseline scenario to a series of potential scenarios. As an illustration, the case of a multi-lateral agreement between the European Union and Israel is analysed. The analysis suggests that consumer surplus will increase two-fold under open skies between Israel and Europe. The results of the model show that frequencies may rise significantly and the average ticket price may fall by around 20%, although the price range may increase due to price discrimination. These results have proven reasonably accurate since the full implementation of the agreement in Summer 2018. The bottom line is that the implementation of the Euro-Mediterranean agreement for the Israeli party was estimated to be worth around $440 million annually based on a game-theoretic estimation and second-stage welfare computation that also considers impacts on local employment.

In the fourth and last group of chapters based on frontier analyses, Scotti and Volta discuss stochastic frontier analysis in Chapter 14 and data envelopment analysis in Chapter 15. Each chapter presents the individual approach, with the former based on parametric-based econometrics and the latter based on an a-parametric linear program. In Chapter 14, stochastic frontier analysis is applied to study the effect of aviation on regional gross domestic product using a panel dataset of 270 NUTS2 level European regions over 11 years. Five different models suggest that aviation positively affects the generation of gross domestic product proving the effect to be robust to multiple specifications. In Chapter 15, data envelopment analysis is applied to a similar dataset with discussions of outlier detection, bias corrections, and second-stage approaches. The analysis suggests a positive relationship between efficiency estimates and the quality of human capital and a negative relationship between regional efficiency and unemployment. Furthermore, the generally positive effect of aviation on gross domestic product growth is not homogeneous suggesting that regions with relatively small populations do not gain from such activities. In ATARD cases, Noto and Kansikas benchmark Swiss Airports to a representative set of 112 European airports based on stochastic frontier analysis. In ATARD policy, Niemeier et al. examine airport governance and regulation in a number of European countries with a focus on efficiency incentives which could be estimated using either frontier methods.

Finally, we would like to thank all the contributors to this book for carefully reviewing other chapters and providing helpful comments and suggestions. We are especially indebted to Florian Allroggen, Leo Basso, Christiaan Behrens, Paolo Beria, Doramas Jorge-Calderón, Marina Efthymiou, Frank Fichert, Marc Gelhausen, Wolfgang Grimme, Georg Hirte, Shravan Kumar, Sven Maertens, Benny Mantin, Eric Pels, Kok Fong See and Andreas Wittmer for their extensive review activity. We would also like to thank Shravan Kumar for managing the finances of the ATARD action together with Enrique J. Calderón and Mickael Pero, Science Officer at the COST Association.

Wishing you a pleasant read,

Regards, Nicole and Hans-Martin

Note

1 The ATARD network remains active and continues to organise workshops and conferences. The past workshops are documented on the website as are calls for papers for upcoming workshops at: www.atard-online.com/

2 Regional economic theory and the impact of transport investments

Stef Proost and Sharon Sarmiento

Introduction

In this chapter we analyse what regional economic theory can offer to understand the effects of changes in air transport infrastructure and costs on regional economic development. Regional economic theory deals with uneven development of economic activity over space. Regional economics is spatial economics without land. Each region has its own labour market, and regional interactions take place through export and import of goods and services. It is useful to distinguish regional economics from urban economics (Proost & Thisse, 2019).[1]

Income levels differ sharply not only between countries, but also between regions within one country. Figure 2.1 shows regional income disparities between and within the 27 European Union (EU) countries. Comparing with an EU average index of 100 for gross domestic product (GDP) per capita, the lowest income region has an index of 30 while the highest income region has an index of 300. Several countries show wide internal regional income differences. For example, in the United Kingdom, London has an index that is five times that of the region with the lowest GDP per capita.

Article 158 of the Treaty on European Union states that the Union shall strive to reduce the differences in income between European regions. This is the main goal of the European regional policy. It also ranks at the top of each member state's policies.

Despite many contributions to regional economics since Krugman (1991), the literature still does not adequately explain why some regions are richer than others. Regional income disparities can be due to any number of factors, including those related to transport costs. The first part of the chapter analyses the role of three different economic mechanisms in explaining differences in regional output:

- Governance, which is relevant to all industry sectors
- Natural advantage, which is relevant to tourism and agriculture
- Economies of scale and product differentiation, which are relevant to goods-producing industries and some service-producing industries

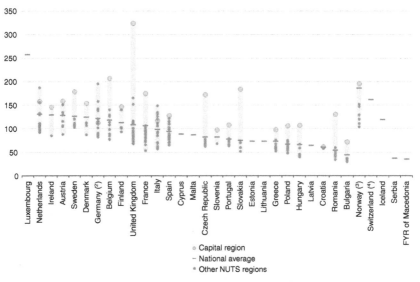

(1) The light purple shaded bar shows the range of the highest to lowest region for each country. The dark green bar shows the national average. The light green circle shows the capital city region. The dark purple circles show the other regions.
(2) Only available for NUTS level 1 regions.
(3) Only available at national level.
(4) 2012.

Figure 2.1 Regional GDP per capita in EU countries.

The second part addresses the role of transport costs in regional economic development and the role of EU regional policy in promoting transportation investments.

Essentially the analysis takes four steps. First, we discuss conventional economic theory, assuming constant returns to scale, to explain how governance and geographic factors can make one region inherently more productive than another. Governance plays an important role in creating an economic environment conducive for growth and promoting investments in transport infrastructure. Geographic factors can create natural advantages for producing certain goods in certain regions, and a decrease in transport costs will promote growth in those sectors that harness a region's geographic advantage. For example, lower air transport costs strongly promoted growth in tourism on Greek and Spanish islands. Second, we discuss modern economic theory to explain why two initially identical regions can develop very differently when transport costs decrease. Here one needs to move away from the traditional assumption of constant returns to scale in favour of less traditional assumptions like economies of scale and product differentiation. The third step focuses on the role of transport costs: we document the long-term changes in interregional transport costs and review empirical studies focusing on the effects of changes in air transport costs on regional development. In the fourth and final step, we return to the role of the European Regional policy and finally conclude.

How natural advantage and governance can explain differences in regional economic development

To depict the production potential of a region, we use a production function relating the total regional product in a given sector to the sum of production factors employed in sector i and region j, assuming constant returns to scale. Output Y_{ij} can be represented as a function of the level of technological progress t_{ij}, the quality of governance of the region g_j, the region's specific natural advantage a_{ij} (climate, soil, and landscape), labour input L_{ij}, capital input K_{ij}, and energy and intermediate inputs E_{ij}:

$$Y_{ij} = t_{ij}.g_j.a_{ij}.P(L_{ij}, K_{ij}, E_{ij}) \qquad (2.1)$$

The production function determines the maximum output a given set of inputs can produce. Given fixed quantities of labour and capital inputs, a region with more or higher quality labour inputs can produce more when capital supply follows.

Imagine a world where capital moves freely, labour is homogenous, other production inputs are the same across all regions, and there are constant returns to scale in production. In this world, international trade theory provides a clear result: capital will be allocated among regions until the marginal product of labour is equal across regions. Regional output per capita will also become equal across regions if the proportion of working population is the same in all regions. The outcome is an economic system where every region is self-sufficient; there is no interregional trade and therefore no role for transport. Clearly this is not what we observe. Using traditional economic theory, two factors can explain differences in regional output: the quality of governance and differences in natural advantages – factors g_j and a_{ij}, respectively, in the production function.

Governance stands for the quality of institutions. Institutions represent all organisational aspects of an economy: the political system, the legal system governing property rights, corporate law, and less formal elements like social norms. Institutions determine how production processes are organised. They influence firms' access to capital and establish property rights, thereby increasing or decreasing the output one can produce with a given input of production factors. Acemoglu and Robinson (2012) demonstrate the importance of institutions by comparing areas that have identical geographical conditions, but show large differences in economic performance. They provide the example of two border towns, one located in Mexico and the other in Texas, which share the same natural advantage factors like climate and soil. Yet their average incomes differ by a factor of three due to different institutional environments. Within the EU, institutions differ between countries, but not so much between regions within an EU country. Hence governance alone cannot explain regional income inequality within EU countries.

Under the same governance, some regions can be more productive than others in certain sectors when they have a natural advantage. In the production function, natural advantage (a_{ij}) is sector specific, while governance (g_j) is not. Geographic factors like soil quality, landscape, and climate can allow one region to produce more output than another region with the same input of labour and capital. For example, hotels located in places with nice beaches and good weather do not need to incur the high costs of building and maintaining an indoor swimming pool. If the output of the sector enjoying a natural advantage is too costly to transport to other regions, the result is mostly a reallocation of production and consumption within the region. Allow transport costs to decrease, regions will specialise and trade with other regions. For the Greek and Spanish islands, the arrival of cheaper flights has been a game changer. The same holds true for the tropical flower industry that relies on fast transport over long distances that only air transport can offer. Decreases in interregional transport costs have allowed regions to specialise in industries in which they have a natural advantage and trade with other regions.

When there are no differences in natural advantage and governance, one starts with a level playing field. This is the case in most manufacturing sectors and service sectors (except tourism) in most EU regions. Yet EU regions have very different regional products per capita. A suitable theory to explain these differences is still evolving, and we summarise the elements of theories that have taken on the challenge.

Explaining differences in regional economic development in the absence of differences in natural advantage and governance

The theoretical framework to explain unequal regional development is complex and is still developing. As we observe in most EU countries, natural advantage and governance do not sufficiently explain regional differences in productivity in manufacturing sectors and service sectors. In this section, we identify other factors that may generate regional differences in output, drawing from modern economic theory.

Proost & Thisse (2017, 2019) review the main theoretical developments in regional and urban economics and we mainly rely on their surveys. Their work is centred on five concepts: (1) imperfect competition due to increasing returns to scale, (2) home market effect, (3) core-periphery model (4) input-output linkages, and (5) increasing spatial fragmentation of firms and the role of communication costs. We discuss each of them here very briefly.

Imperfect competition due to increasing returns to scale

When there are constant returns to scale in production, there is no advantage to consolidating production in fewer regions. Consider production function (2.1), which is an aggregate over constant returns to scale production units. For instance, if one always needs for one unit of output one unit of labour L, two regions with the same governance and the same natural capital will have the same output per worker in every sector. Assume a firm's production is given by L^2 rather than by L, then total production by that sector is no longer given by total input of L in the region but by the allocation of labour over firms.

Increasing returns to scale in one region tends to limit the number of firms in each sector as average costs are decreasing, giving rise to imperfect competition. This holds within every region and affects neighbouring regions. If two regions have the same number of employees in one sector and transport costs decrease significantly, in equilibrium, only one region will end up producing the good. This is a very simple case where transport cost decreases can generate net welfare gain. Output per unit of labour now shifts to only one region and doubles: $(2L)^2/L = 2(L^2/L)$. Although output doubles with the same inputs, output is re-allocated to only one region. We note that many empirical studies find that a decrease in transport costs, for example from improved airport infrastructure and advances in aircraft technology, increases output in one region as a result of a reallocation of output among regions. This is not necessarily bad from a global point of view. Concentration of production in one region can still generate a welfare gain when the other region concentrates production in another sector. In this example, cheaper transport allows the doubling of total production.

Home market effect

To avoid full concentration of production in one region, one needs either high interregional transport costs or product differentiation. Product differentiation allows firms to cover fixed costs and generate profits when there are no transport costs. When there are increasing returns to scale, two forces are at work: firms like the concentration of customers in a large market as this allows them to sell their product at a large scale, known as *agglomeration force*, but firms also like to be protected against competition by avoiding too many competitors around them. These two forces give rise to the *home market effect,* a crucial concept in regional economics.

The home market effect generates regional inequality. Consider two regions (North and South) with immobile labour but mobile capital. Let λ, θ represent the share of firms and of workers in one region. Suppose one of the two regions (say North) is slightly larger ($\theta > 0.5$), as it has more workers. When trade between the two regions becomes possible, there will be a proportionally larger number of firms in the North region ($\lambda > \theta$).

How does a decrease in interregional transport costs affect this result? On the one hand, lower transport costs make exports to the smaller market cheaper, allowing firms to exploit their scale economies more intensively by locating in the North. On the other hand, lower transport costs reduce the advantages of geographical isolation in the South that provided them protection from competition. These two effects push toward more agglomeration, implying that, as transport costs decrease, the smaller region becomes deindustrialised to the benefit of the larger region. Therefore the home market effect has unexpected implications for transport policy. By making the transport of goods cheaper in both directions, the construction of new infrastructure may induce firms to pull out of the smaller region. In other words, connecting lagging regions to dynamic urban centres may weaken their industrial base. This result is also known as *highways run both ways*. In the review section, we note that there is solid empirical evidence for this mechanism.

Of course the world is more complicated. We discuss a few complicating but more realistic features. There is a lot of heterogeneity among the firms. Following the home market effect reasoning, one can expect that the most efficient firms locate in the larger regions, and the less efficient firms seek protection in the smaller region via interregional transport costs. This results in even larger regional productivity differences.

Core-periphery model

The third feature is the mobility of workers. Having more workers has a different effect from having more capital, because workers spend their income locally while the return on capital is not necessarily consumed locally. Workers tend to follow higher real incomes. In the EU, differences in language and culture limit workers' mobility, but labour migration does occur and the EU encourages it.

The setting with both capital and labour mobility is known as the *core-periphery model* due to Krugman (1991). In his setting, both regions have immobile farmers and mobile workers. Farming has constant returns to scale. Assume that the North becomes slightly bigger than the South, how will this affect the equilibrium? First, this increase in market size leads to higher demand for manufactured goods. The home market effect implies that the number of firms grows proportionally more than the increase in market size, leading to an increase in nominal wages. But the presence of more firms means more varieties offered locally and more competition. This means that in the North, not only nominal wages increase but also real wages (corrected for product variety). Higher real wages attract more workers from the other region, increasing product demand. Workers' mobility leads to an even greater expansion of the North. The manufacturing sector would concentrate in the North (*the centre*), leaving the South (*periphery*) behind.

This story is highly simplified and other outcomes are possible. We are mainly interested in the possible role of a decrease in interregional transport costs in this equilibrium process. When transport costs are sufficiently high, there will be very little interregional shipment of goods, firms will focus on their home markets, and the two regions will have the same sectoral composition. When transport costs are sufficiently low, manufacturing will concentrate in the North. The South will supply only the agricultural good and will become the periphery. Firms will exploit increasing returns by selling more in the larger market without losing much business in the smaller market. Lowering trade costs will foster agglomeration of economic activities, and changes in interregional transport costs will produce regional asymmetric development, reinforced by economies of scale in the transport costs themselves.

Input-output linkages

Agglomeration of economic activity in one region can also result from *input-output linkages*. When the final goods industry is more concentrated in one region, the production of intermediate goods can also become concentrated in the same region because of economies of scale. The reverse also works: concentration of the intermediate goods industry may trigger concentration of the final goods industry.

The four factors we discussed up to now all point to an increased inequality in regional development as a result of lower transport costs. What stops this process? When labour supply cannot move to the high growth region, real wages will increase in the high growth region. When transport costs are sufficiently low, some activities may relocate to the lower growth region that has lower real wages. So a progressive decline in transport costs may give rise to more concentration initially. But as this process continues, it may also give rise to more dispersion of economic activity.

Increasing spatial fragmentation of firms and the role of communication costs

Firms tend to become multinational or multiregional, locating different components of the supply chain in different countries and different regions based upon production cost differences. This requires low transport costs and low communication costs. Low communication costs allow the concentration of the coordination function at headquarters. Lower interregional passenger costs facilitate dispersion of production and concentration of management. In the review section, we will find that empirical studies have demonstrated the important effect of a decrease in air transport costs on the coordination costs of multinationals.

As we intend to look into the role of transport costs and more specifically air transport costs on regional development, the next section reviews the development of interregional transport costs. In the review section we return to empirical evidence on the impact of transport costs on regional income.

Long-term developments in the costs of trade and transport

Changes in freight costs are better documented than changes in passenger transport costs. The costs of interregional export and import of goods and services, also called trade frictions, include several components. Pure transport costs are only one minor component. Exports to another country face many other costs, such as custom duties, inspection delays, communication costs (language and cultural differences), and the costs of adapting a product to foreign standards. Anderson and Van Wincoop (2004) estimate that total trade costs can be 170 per cent of the mill price of manufactured goods, although there is a high variance in this estimate. Within the EU, total trade costs are much lower because there are no custom duties; there is a harmonisation of technical product requirements, and most EU member countries speak one national language.

Several sources report significant decreases in freight transport costs. Glaeser and Kohlhase (2004) find that, in the last 100 years, freight costs in the United States have decreased by a factor of 10, leading to significant changes in the importance of regions specialising in rail and harbour operations.

Since World War II, interregional transport has benefited mainly from an improvement in the road infrastructure in the US and the EU. An extensive network of highways, the abolition of border controls in the EU, and liberalisation of road freight have led to a significant decrease in freight costs and a massive increase in road freight transport. Looking at longer distance transport costs, Hummels (2007) also found that the improvements in aviation technology, including the introduction of jet engines, avionics, and materials, led to a decrease in air freight costs by a factor of 10 since 1955. Over the same period, Hummels found that ocean shipping costs decreased only by a factor of three, mainly due to containerisation.

Interregional passenger transport costs have also decreased. For road transport, the motorway network is probably the main factor partially replacing rail transport in Europe. The relative shares of long-distance passenger rail and air transport are very different in the EU and the US. The EU relies more heavily on High Speed Rail (HSR), while the US relies more heavily on car and air transport (Eurostat, 2017). In the EU, people travel only 1,000 km per year by air and 200 km by HSR, while Americans travel some 3,000 km per year by air.

For air transportation, two technological changes have had a dramatic impact: the arrival of the jet engine in the 1950s and the introduction of ultra-long haul aircraft in 1989–1995 with the Boeing 747-400, Airbus A330, Airbus A340, and the Boeing 777 (Campante and Yanagizawa-Drott, 2018). These ultra-long haul aircraft allowed non-stop flights for 12 hours, covering 6,000 miles with a limited crew. This technological change created a discontinuity in passenger transport cost for trips to airports beyond 6,000 miles requiring stopovers and flight connections. We will return to the role of this development in the review section when we discuss the effects of globalisation on regional development.

Finally, interregional freight and passenger transport are themselves characterised by economies of scale – also called economies of density. When there is a larger volume of freight to be transported, one can use larger ships and offer more frequent service. This applies to both point-to-point service and hub and spoke networks. The same holds for passenger air transport where one can use larger aircraft and increase flight frequency.

Empirical assessment of the effects of transport costs on regional development

Assessing the effect on regional development of transport infrastructure investments and the associated decreases of transport costs is difficult both ex ante and ex post. Ex ante, it is difficult because transport investments have a multitude of effects. They reduce trade barriers and affect the pattern of trade for both goods and services (via lower coordination costs for business and tourism trips). The assessment may be tractable for goods and services where there is a natural advantage like agriculture and tourism, but it is difficult for all the other sectors and regions where economic activities are increasingly footloose.

Ex post assessing the development impact of transportation is difficult because there is no obvious counterfactual. Decision makers tend to locate transport investments where they expect the largest returns, for instance because they expect the region to be growing strongly. This introduces an endogenous element in the explanatory factor breaking the causality we are looking for: is the region growing more strongly because of the transport investment, or is the transport investment simply correlated with the high growth in that region? We need causation not correlation.

The dominant conclusion of the surveys of the empirical work on the link between transport infrastructure and regional growth (Redding & Turner, 2015) is that many transport investments reallocate economic activities between regions but do not lead to a significant increase in total product. This is in line with our increasing returns to scale driver discussed previously: the decrease in transport costs concentrates production hence decreasing production costs but this effect is much less important than the spatial reallocation of production.

In this section we focus on the role of air transport costs on regional activity. We distinguish two types of empirical work: (1) economic impact studies that measure the direct and multiplier effects of airport investment and activity on the regional economy, and (2) econometric studies investigating correlation and causality between air transportation and regional development. Economic impact analysis measures the economic contribution of airports and air transportation in terms of job creation, income generation, and contribution to regional product, while econometric analysis tests for causal effect of changes in air transport costs on regional output. Some of the empirical works confirm the theories discussed previously.

Economic impact studies

The most common empirical studies that measure the economic contributions of the air transport industry and airports in particular employ economic impact analysis. Economic impact analysis estimates the economic repercussions of changes in final demand – purchases of goods and services by final users – arising from an economic activity via the concept of the multiplier. The multiplier accounts for the economic effects of subsequent rounds of spending resulting from an initial expenditure.

There are two key inputs to economic impact analysis: an estimate of the exogenous economic stimulus and a model of the economy that produces estimates of the multiplier effects. There are three basic categories of models used to derive regional multipliers for estimating total economic impact: (1) economic base models, (2) econometric models, and (3) input-output models (Pleeters, 1980), all discussed in individual chapter of this book.

Nearly all economic impact studies done for the air transport industry and airports use multipliers derived from input-output models. A few exceptions use regional econometric models and survey methods.

In economic impact analysis, an economic activity's total economic impact encompasses direct, indirect, and induced impacts. Direct economic impacts are the outcomes of the initial round of transactions generated by the economic activity. These initial transactions generate multiplier effects throughout the local economy in two ways: (1) when businesses buy intermediate inputs from other businesses, creating indirect impacts; and (2) when their employees spend their earnings on various purchases (housing, food, groceries, services, and other things), creating induced impact.

There are four measures of economic impact: employment, earnings, output, and value added. Output is the most popular and broadest measure, but it is criticised for overstating economic impact. Output is an aggregation of business revenues (sales); it double-counts the value of intermediate inputs used in pro-duction or delivery of services. Value added avoids double counting and is a better measure of contribution to gross regional product.

Double counting is not the only problem of economic impact estimates based on input-output multipliers (Niemeier, 2001). Other problems are the neglect of constraints on the availability of production factors, the mechanical nature of the effects, neglecting the market context and finally the focus on the effect on one region. The input-output framework is based on at least six restrictive assumptions (US Bureau of Economic Analysis, 2015):

i.   Backward linkages: an increase in the demand for output increases the demand for inputs.
ii. Fixed-purchase patterns: industries do not change the relative mix of inputs used to produce output, so that doubling output requires a doubling of input.
iii. Industry homogeneity: all businesses in an industry use the same produc-tion process.
iv. Unlimited supply: input-output models assume fixed prices, so that businesses can use as many inputs without facing higher prices or without taking resources away from other uses.
v.   No regional feedback: input-output models ignore any feedback that may exist among regions.

vi. No time dimension: input-output models do not consider the time it takes for economic impacts to be realised. There can be a long lag between the time when initial final demand changes are made and the time when the multiplier effects are realised fully.

Unsurprisingly there are numerous studies estimating the economic impact of airports, often commissioned by airport associations and individual airport authorities to tout the airports' significant contributions to the regional development and to gain political and community support to airport development and expansion. Robertson (1995) looks at airport economic impacts from a different angle, focusing on the potential of airports to aid regeneration of depressed areas. Airports not only create employment, providing opportunities for less skilled workers and significant numbers of local unemployed workers, but also help attract business investment and promote tourism into the region by providing air service. While the great majority of impact studies have been done using economic impact assessment models, there are now some studies which use a computable general equilibrium, approach, which, if done correctly, avoid the problems of impact assessments, as discussed in Chapter 15.

Hansman and Ishutkina (2009) use a series of case studies at the global level to study the impact of air transport activity on economic activity. They also consider the specific role of governance of the air transport sector. The International Air Transport Association (IATA) estimates the economic impact of aviation by world region. Of particular interest for us is the effect of air transport developments on the role of the naturally advantaged sector, that is tourism. For Europe, it counts for 36 per cent of the GDP impact. Again, the GDP impact that is shown here, gives an idea of the value added of the aviation sector. It does not mean that GDP would be lower when there is less aviation. This statement would require a causal analysis.

Although economic impact studies are commonly used to justify the positive contribution of airport investments on the regional economy, they are not suited to show a casual link between investment and regional output.

Table 2.1 Economic impact of aviation by world region

World region	Total GDP supported by aviation ($ billion)	Tourism-catalytic GDP supported by aviation ($ billion)	Jobs supported by aviation (million)
Africa	44.8	$35.9	6.2
Asia–Pacific	684	$287.8	30.2
Europe	823	$293.6	12.2
Latin America and the Caribbean	156	$64.7	7.2
Middle East	130	$66	2.4
North America	$844	$149.7	7.3

Sources: IATA (www.iata.org/policy/promoting-aviation/Pages/value-for-regions.aspx) and ATAG (2019).

Econometric studies on the effects of air transport on economic development

Do airports stimulate economic growth? Empirical studies, mostly employing regression modelling techniques with corrections for endogeneity, confirm airports' positive contributions to regional economic growth. As Redding and Turner (2015) point out, most studies of the effects of transport investments show mainly a reallocation effect of economic activities between regions. This is in line with the regional economic theory exposed previously where we pointed to the economies of scale factor that pushes for a concentration of certain production activities in one region. This may generate a significant gain in regional product for one region but the sum of effects over regions will be much smaller and is often not studied at all. For interregional air transport costs, we expect this effect to play a role mainly for the service sectors, for the tourism sector, and for coordination and management activities.

Bilotkach (2015) uses panel data on commercial passenger air traffic at all primary airports in the United States to evaluate the impact of traffic volume and number of destinations served with non-stop flights on the key indicators of regional economic development. The results confirm the positive contributions of air transport to growth in employment, number of business establishments, and wage levels on the regions affected.

Baker, Merkert, and Kamruzzaman (2015) claim empirical evidence for bi-directional short- and long-run causality between regional air transport and economic growth based on an analysis of a panel data of 88 regional airports in Australia. They use total airport passenger movements to represent the level of airport activity and real aggregate taxable income to represent economic growth. They use Granger causality and find significant short and long-run effects of airport activity on regional incomes. Local passenger numbers and local taxable income are jointly determined.

Based on multiple regression analysis of cross-section data on US metropolitan areas, Florida, Mellander, and Holgersson (2015) find that airports contribute significantly to regional development, measured as economic output per capita. Passenger air service is more important than air cargo service in promoting regional development. The impact of airports on regional development varies with their size and scale. There is no real test of causality.

Sheard (2014) also employs cross-section data on US metropolitan areas to analyse the relationship between air traffic volume and employment. He finds airport size has a positive effect on the employment share of tradable services, controlling for overall local employment, but no measurable effect on manufacturing or most nontradable sectors. The effect of airport size on overall local employment is practically zero, suggesting that airports lead to specialisation but not growth at the metropolitan-area level.

Earlier studies on the effect of air transport on employment include Brueckner (2003), Green (2007), and Button and Yuan (2013). Brueckner finds that a 10 per cent increase in passenger enplanements yields a 1 per cent increase in service sector employment. Green (2007) uses cross-section data from 100 largest US airports and finds that a 10 per cent increase in passenger enplanements per capita leads to 3.9 per cent higher population growth and 2.8 per cent increase in employment growth over the 1990–2000 period in the regions affected. Button and Yuan (2013) find that air cargo drives local economic development. They link air freight volume to metropolitan-area income and employment using data on 35 airports from 1990–2009.

Bel and Fageda (2008) use European data to analyse whether the number of non-stop intercontinental flights determines location of large firms' headquarters. They find support for this hypothesis that is in line with the theory put forward on the importance of communication costs for multinational firms.

None of the mentioned empirical studies show that a decrease in air transport costs improved regional output not only in the region concerned but also in all the regions, including the neighbouring or substitute region. So these studies cannot really show there is a more global welfare gain.

IATA (2007) examines the relationship between a country's level of connectivity to the global air transport network and labour productivity and economic growth using regression analysis of a panel data of 48 countries over a 10-year period, 1996–2005. This study uses a measure of aviation connectivity that reflects the range and economic importance of destinations, the frequency of service and the number of onward connections available through each country's aviation network. The study finds a positive link at the country level between connectivity and productivity – a 10 per cent rise in connectivity boosts labour productivity by 0.07 per cent. The relationship between connectivity and productivity is nonlinear, suggesting that investment in air transport capacity has a much larger impact on productivity and economic growth in developing or transition countries than in relatively developed countries.

Two empirical studies focus in particular on estimating the causal effect of air transport costs on regional economic development, exploiting exogenous changes in airline costs.

Blonigen and Cristea (2015) exploit the airline deregulation in the United States as a quasi-natural experiment leading to an increase in air traffic. They examine the impact of deregulation-induced change in passenger air traffic on long-term growth rates in over 300 US metropolitan areas. Their most conservative estimates find that a 50 per cent increase in an average city's air traffic growth rate generates an additional stream of income over a 20-year period equal to 7.4 per cent of real GDP. Their study confirms the positive impact of air service on regional growth, with the magnitude of this effect differing across the metropolitan areas. Campante and Yanagizawa-Drott (2018) exploit the discontinuity in air transport costs at 6,000 miles. With the arrival of the long-range aircraft in the period 1989–1995, many more city pairs can be connected with a direct flight. They show that better connectivity for city pairs with airports improves local economic activity. Economic activity is measured by satellite measured night light. Better passenger connections generate business links and capital flows between better-connected cities. The effect is clearly positive in the vicinity of the cities that are better connected, but this can be partly a reallocation effect from cities that miss this better connection. Given the range of the connections (above 6,000 miles), this study implies that the major hubs in Europe have been the major beneficiaries of the decrease in the long-range air transport costs by attracting headquarters of large firms and specialised services. This confirms the positive effects of air transport costs on the internal organisation of firms.

European regional policy

In the EU, transport policy has two main objectives. The first is to decrease trade costs, as the goal of transport policy is to strengthen the EU internal market. The second objective is to promote the economic development and structural adjustment of lagging regions. This second objective is also the first objective of EU regional policy. The main idea is that the larger EU market would provide opportunities to poorer regions that are often at the periphery. Arbitrage possibilities arising from competition and factor mobility are expected to generate greater-than-average growth in lagging regions. Because the EU's federal competence is limited, its regional policy has emphasised subsidies for trans-frontier transport investments that improve the links between member countries. Other regional economic aspects of this EU policy are discussed more thoroughly by Puga (2002).

In the late 1990s, the EU selected a priority list of transport investments – the Trans European Network investments – whose total value accounted for some €600 billion. These investment projects are the first that should receive European subsidies. These investments were selected using as criteria that they should solve the missing links between countries and benefit the poorer regions. The majority of the projects were freight transport projects; the other projects were mainly HSR projects. To assess the benefits of the 22 priority freight projects, Bröcker et al. (2010) developed a model in the tradition of the home market theory discussed above with 260 European regions. In this model, firms produce a differentiated good and operate under increasing returns and monopolistic competition; interregional trade is costly while capital and labour are immobile. A particular transport investment decreases transport costs between specific regions, which translates into changes in production activities, trade patterns, and ultimately the welfare level of consumers residing in different regions. To assess the HSR projects Adler, Nash, and Pels (2010) developed a network model where passengers can choose between the HSR network and the air transport network. Both operate under imperfect competition, but endogenous trade effects were not taken into account.

There are three main findings from a cost-benefit assessment of this first round of EU transport priority projects (Proost et al., 2014). First, only 12 of the 22 freight projects pass the cost-benefit analysis test at the EU scale. The cost-benefit test made use of the home market theory mentioned above by modelling the trade links between 260 regions. Second, most projects benefit only the region where the investment takes place, so that the EU value added, or the *positive spill over argument*, does not seem to warrant the investment. Finally, the projects do not systematically favour the poorer regions. The same conclusion holds for the HSR projects – most of them do not pass the cost-benefit test. Of course, it is difficult to assess interregional transport investments, and economic models fail to take all factors into account. But this holds for the decision maker, as well as for the economist assessing the projects ex post.

Assessments of EU investment projects illustrate that the selection of these highly subsidised projects is heavily influenced by political dealing. This is not that different from the United States where, according to Knight (2004), the allocation of federal highway funds in the United States was highly inefficient. For every two dollars invested, one dollar was wasted.

Reconsidering the EU experience of subsidising interregional transport investment, Proost & Thisse (2017) offer two general thoughts. First, it may be that inequality in regional development is the price to pay for high overall growth: there is an efficiency-equity trade-off. Second, what matters is the income inequality among individuals not among regions. Helping poor regions through transport investments will not necessarily help the poor in those regions. Member states have progressive income taxes to redistribute income within their country but the EU cannot raise taxes so they are forced to use very indirect instruments to redistribute incomes over EU regions.

Conclusions

In this chapter we analysed what regional economic theory can offer to understand the effects of changes in transport costs on regional products, and more specifically what the role is of changes in the air transport infrastructure and costs.

For sectors and regions that have a natural advantage (agriculture and tourism), a decrease in interregional transport costs has obvious implications as the lower costs allow these regions to use their advantage. But a decrease in freight and passenger costs also affects the economic activity of regions that were equal at the start. Regional economics offers a complex theory to explain this. The theory uses an increasing returns to scale setting and small differences in initial market size to explain a growing divergence in the economic development of regions. The theory also shows that better infrastructure between the periphery and the core regions may be detrimental for the peripheral regions.

Interregional freight and passenger costs have decreased significantly over the last 70 years. This holds also for aviation costs where the arrival of more efficient aircraft has allowed faster, cheaper, and longer distance flights.

Regions that received airports and better connections have seen their economic product increase but the causal link remains difficult to establish. An increase in the regional product is often at the expense of the economic activity in the neighbouring regions.

The European regional policy has invested heavily in better interregional transport infrastructure but assessments show that this policy had limited success.

Note

1 Urban economics deals with a smaller spatial scale where there is one labour market and commuting within the urban area is important. Although the mechanisms playing at the urban and regional levels are different, it is clear that a region with one or more prosperous urban areas will be a prosperous region.

References

Acemoglu, D., and J. Robinson. 2012. *Why Nations Fail: The Origins of Power, Prosperity, and Poverty*. Crown Business.

Adler, N., E. Pels, and C. Nash. 2010. High-speed rail and air transport competition: Game engineering as tool for cost-benefit analysis. *Transportation Research Part B: Methodological* 44(7): 812–833.

Baker, D., R. Merkert, and M. Kamruzzaman. 2015. Regional aviation and economic growth: cointegration and causality analysis in Australia. *Journal of Transport Geography*, 43, 140–150.

Bel, G., and X. Fageda, 2008. Getting there fast: globalization, intercontinental flights and location of headquarters. *Journal of Economic Geography* 8(4): 471–495.

Bilotkach, V. 2015. Are airports engines of economic development? A dynamic panel data approach. *Urban Studies* 52(9): 1577–1593.

Blonigen, B.A., and A.D. Cristea. 2015. Air service and urban growth: evidence from a quasi-natural policy experiment. *Journal of Urban Economics* 86(2): 128–146.

Bröcker, J., A. Korhenevych, and C. Schürmann. 2010. Assessing spatial equity and efficiency impacts of transport infrastructure projects. *Transportation Research Part B* 44(7): 795–811.

Brueckner, J. 2003. Airline traffic and urban economic development. *Urban Studies* 40: 1455–1469.

Button and Yuan. 2013. Airfreight transport and economic development: an examination of causality. *Urban Studies* 50: 329–340.

Campante F., and D. Yanagizawa-Drott. 2018, Long-range growth: economic development in the global network of air links. *The Quarterly Journal of Economics*, 1395–1458.

Florida, R., C. Mellander, and T. Holgersson. 2015. Up in the air: the role of airports for regional economic development. *The Annals of Regional Science* 54(1): 197–214.

Green, R.K. 2007. Airports and economic development. *Real Estate Economics* 35(1): 91–112.

Hansman, R.J., and M. Ishutkina. 2009. Analysis of the interaction between air transportation and economic activity: a worldwide perspective, MIT Thesis Ishutkina_ICAT-2009-2.pdf

Hummels, D. 2007. Transportation costs and international trade in the second era of globalization. *Journal of Economic Perspectives* 21(3): 131–154.

Florida R., Mellander C., and Holgersson T., 2015. Up in the air: the role of airports for regional economic development. *The Annals of Regional Science* 54(1): 197–214.

International Air Transport Association. 2007. Aviation Economic Benefits. *IATA Economics Briefing No. 08*, www.iata.org/publications/economic-briefings/aviation_economic benefits.pdf

Knight, B. 2004. Parochial interests and the centralised provision of local public goods: Evidence from congressional voting on transportation projects. *Journal of Public Economics* 88(3–4): 845–866.

Krugman, P.R. 1991. Increasing returns and economic geography. *Journal of Political Economy* 99(3): 483–499.

Niemeier, H.-M. 2001. On the use and abuse of Impact Analysis for airports: a critical view from the perspective of regional policy. In W. Pfähler (ed.), *Regional Input-Output Analysis*. Baden-Baden: Nomos, pp. 201–220.

Pleeter, S. 1980. Methodologies of economic impact analysis: an overview. In S. Pleeter (ed.), *Economic Impact Analysis: Methodology and Applications, Studies in Applied Regional Science*, Vol. 19. Boston, MA: Martinus Nijhoff, pp. 7–31.

Proost, S., and J-F Thisse. 2017. Regional disparities and efficient transport policies. In L. Matyas, R. Blundell, E. Cantillon, B. Chizzolini, M. Ivaldi, W. Leininger, R. Marimon, and F. Steen (eds.), *Economics Without Borders: Economic Research for European Policy Challenges*. Cambridge: Cambridge University Press, pp. 324–361

Proost S., and J.F. Thisse, 2019. What can be learned from spatial economics? *Journal of Economic Literature* 57(3): 575–643.

Proost, S., F. Dunkerley, S. van der Loo, N. Adler, J. Bröcker, and A. Korzhenevych. 2014. Do the selected trans European transport investments pass the cost benefit test? *Transportation* 41(1): 107–132.

Puga, D., 2002, European regional policies in light of recent location theories, *Journal of Economic Geography*, 2, 373–406.

Redding, S.J., and M.A. Turner, 2015. Transportation costs and the spatial organization of economic activity. In G. Duranton, J.V. Henderson, and W. Strange (eds.), *Handbook of Regional and Urban Economics*, Vol. 5. Amsterdam: Elsevier, pp. 1339–1398.

Richardson, H. 1972. *Input-Output and Regional Economics*. Trowbridge: Redwood Press.

Sheard, N. 2014. Airports and urban sectoral employment. *Journal of Urban Economics* 80: 133–152.

U.S. Bureau of Economic Analysis. 2015. Regional Multipliers from the Regional Input-Output Modeling System (RIMS II): A Brief Description.

3 A review of connectivity utility models and their applications

Yahua Zhang and Anming Zhang

Introduction

A safe and well-connected transport network is vital for our economy (Zhu et al., 2019a). The intertwined relationship between air transport and economic development has been examined and evidenced in numerous studies, such as Brueckner (2003), Bannò, and Redondi (2014), Zhang and Findlay (2014), Van De Vijver et al. (2014), and Matsumoto et al. (2016) (see, e.g., Zhang, 2012, for a literature survey). For example, Blonigen and Cristea (2015) show that a 50 per cent increase in an average city's air traffic growth could result in an additional 7.4 per cent increase in real GDP in the United States. Baker et al. (2015) reveal a significant bi-directional relationship between regional economic growth and regional air transport services in Australia. Liu et al. (2013) find that cities with a higher level of air connectivity are appealing to globalised business service firms, which in turn can stimulate the development of aviation connections. Campante and Yanagizawa-Drott (2017) show that air links increase business links and that the movement of people induces the movement of capital.

Researchers have used different definitions for air connectivity. Traditional approaches to measuring air connectivity include the number of destinations, flight frequencies, seat capacity, seat-kilometres, cargo-hold capacities, passenger and cargo traffic volumes, and market shares (OECD/ITF, 2018). These simple measures are easy for the general public to understand and can offer insights into the development of the air transport network. However, the OECD/ITF (2018) warns that these simple metrics are not particularly useful for policy or business analysis as they sometimes provide misleading information. One example, as illustrated in OECD/ITF (2018), is that if we use transfer share as a measure of hub connectivity, we may observe that over time, this metric is decreasing at some airports when the total number of passengers handled there is increasing, although the (absolute) number of transfer passengers is actually increasing at these airports. Relying on a single-metric may result in a wrong conclusion.

A review of more sophisticated air connectivity measures can be found in Burghouwt and Redondi (2013), Calatayud et al. (2016), Zeigler et al. (2017), and OECD/ITF (2018). One type of the air connectivity measure is based on flight schedule data (Zeigler et al., 2017). The NetScan model developed by Veldhuis (1997), Burghouwt and Veldhuis (2006), and Burghouwt et al. (2009) is an example. It is a network quality model that considers air flight-level data that allow the calculation of both direct and indirect connections as well as hub connections. The quickest path length model developed in Malighetti et al. (2008) is another network quality model based on the flight schedule data. A time-dependent minimum path approach is used to calculate the minimum travel time between each pair of airports in the network, with a consideration of flight times and waiting times. A recent study by Cattaneo et al. (2017) uses this approach to analyse the number of quickest connections and the share of indirect quickest paths that remained un-managed for a period from 2006 to 2016. However, this approach was criticised for not accounting for route frequencies, making it inadequate for assessing connectivity implications of policy changes (OCED/ITF, 2018). It is worth noting that the NetScan model and many other connectivity models only measure a single transport mode's connectivity (e.g., Alderighi et al., 2007; Malighetti et al., 2008; Paleari et al., 2010; Hossain and Alam, 2017), and have not been extended to measure possible multi-modal connections.

Another stream of measures is based on actual passenger traffic data. This kind of approach explores the topological properties of the air transport network with various measure indices for network structure (the configuration of a network), centrality (the relative importance of a node within a network), and degree correlation (a node's degree related to the average degree of its neighbours) as discussed in Wang et al. (2011). The Global Airport Connectivity Index proposed in Cheung et al. (2020) is an example that combines degree, closeness, and eigenvector topological indicators and two volumetric indicators.[1] However, Otiso et al. (2011) note that standard airline data only show individual legs of a given trip rather than the trip as a whole. Therefore, if a passenger makes a transfer at a hub, the route is collected twice in the database: from the origin point to the hub and from the hub to the destination. This may lead to an inaccurate calculation of the hub connectivity. For this reason, we prefer the flight schedule-based connectivity measure, and our connectivity measure presented in this chapter is supply-based with a consideration of multiple quality factors, such as the capacity and velocity of a connection. These quality indicators are closely associated with air passengers' travel utility. Therefore, this measure was named the Connectivity Utility Model (ConnUM), which has been developed in Zhang et al. (2017), Zhu et al. (2018), and Zhu et al. (2019a, 2019b). This model creates a network metric to measure the direct and indirect, single- and multi-modal connections of a city, region, or country, and shows how they are accessible to the outside world.

There has been a large family of connectivity measures that capture one or more of the following four components: travellers, transport system, land use, and temporal change (Geurs and Van Wee, 2004; Taylor, 2008; Matisziw and Grubesic, 2010). In recent years, researchers have continued to develop new connectivity measures based on these components for different purposes. For example, a similar connectivity measure to our ConnUM is the Global Connectivity Index (GCI) developed by Allroggen et al. (2015). It is also a quality-weighted connectivity measure with an emphasis on the connection frequency of directness. A novel aspect of the GCI is the consideration of the destination quality, i.e., the level of potential economic interaction to which a destination airport provides access. Compared with GCI and other similar measures, our ConnUM considers more quality elements including the capacity and speed of the travel vehicles, which implies that this measure can be used to aggregate the connectivity of different transport modes. This is important in a number of countries, and especially China, where high-speed rail (HSR) has been well developed and become a good substitute for air transport (e.g., Zhang and Zhang, 2016; Zhang et al., 2019). The following sections will present a review and demonstration of this connectivity measure.

A review of the Connectivity Utility Model

The construction of the direct air connectivity measure

The first step of constructing the ConnUM is to develop direct connectivity for an airport. This has been described in Zhang et al. (2017), in which the connectivity of 69 Chinese airports was calculated. The quality factors considered include the availability of seats (capacity) and travel time (velocity). More specifically, in Eq. (3.1) below, k represents a unique connection between origin airport c and destination airport j. Every flight linking airport i and airport j is regarded as a unique connection, even for the connection with the same flight number on a different date, as a different type of aircraft might be used. This implies that the frequency for every connection is always one (Zhu et al., 2019a). The connectivity (Connectivity$_{ijk}$) of flight k from airport i to airport j is calculated by multiplying the velocity discount factor and capacity discount factor in Eq. (3.1):

$$\text{Connectivity}_{ijk} = D_{Cap_{ijk}} \times D_{Vel_{ijk}} \tag{3.1}$$

where $D_{Cap_{ijk}}$ represents the capacity discount for connection k between airports i and j. $D_{Vel_{ijk}}$ represents the velocity discount.

To calculate the capacity discount, we need to decide on a benchmark capacity Seat$_0$. Seat$_0$ is a general term for the benchmark for the capacity of a transport vehicle. This variable can vary in different studies for different purposes. In Zhu et al. (2018), the capacity of a Boeing 747 with 434 seats was chosen as the benchmark. This can be changed to any other aircraft type however, and the connectivity (a unitless index) results will only change in scale, with relative ranking remaining unchanged, as long as the same capacity benchmark is applied for all flights. If we denote the capacity of flight k from airport i to airport j as $Seat_{ijk}$, the capacity discount $D_{Cap_{ijk}}$ can be expressed as:

$$D_{Cap_{ijk}} = \sqrt{\frac{Seat_{ijk}}{Seat_0}} \qquad (3.2)$$

Most of the existing schedule-based connectivity measures, including the NetScan, adopt a linear form for the quality factors, which may fail to account for the nature of diminishing returns of the benefit of the quality factors. For example, passengers usually prefer larger aircraft, but the marginal benefit of having a larger aircraft with more seats diminishes. After a certain point, the extra benefit of adding another flight is larger than having a larger aircraft. Therefore, the ConnUM employs a concave function (square root).

The velocity discount factor is calculated based on the following system of equations:

$$Duration_{Adjusted_{ijk}} = T_{landing_{ijk}} - T_{takeoff_{ijk}} + t_{airport_{ijk}} \qquad (3.3)$$

$$Velocity_{ijk} = \frac{Distance_{ij}}{Duration_{Adjusted_{ijk}}} \qquad (3.4)$$

$$D_{Vel_{ijk}} = \sqrt{\frac{Velocity_{ijk}}{Velocity_0}} \qquad (3.5)$$

where $Duration_{Adjusted_{ijk}}$ is the adjusted time length (duration) of flight k from airport i to airport j. The scheduled flying time between two airports is the difference between the scheduled arrival and departure times. It is worth noting that the actual flying time might be shorter than the published estimated flying time as these days, airlines tend to pad the schedules to increase their punctuality statistics. This is especially so for flights to and from big cities, which can lead to inaccurate results for the connectivity indices. This is a shortcoming for using the scheduled data. $t_{airport_{ijk}}$ is included to account for the extra time needed at departure and arrival airports for check-in, security check, and baggage collection. Normally 100 minutes for domestic flights and 180 minutes for international flights are required. Similar to the capacity benchmark, a velocity benchmark, $Velocity_0$, can be selected. The speed of a flight varies depending on the type of aircraft used. Statista (2018) suggests that a major commercial jet aircraft cruises at about 420–500 knots or 778–926 km/h. Therefore, Zhang et al. (2017) assume that the average speed is 900 km/h.

The connectivity due to the unidirectional flights from airport i to airport j is the aggregation of the connectivity of all k flights from airport i to airport j.

The connectivity of airport i is calculated by aggregating the connectivity due to the flights between airport i and airport j of both directions. The illustration of the airport direct connectivity calculation has been detailed in Zhang et al. (2017). This chapter uses this direct connectivity measure to quantify the air connectivity between China and the rest of the world at the country level.

The construction of indirect air connectivity measure

Zhu et al. (2019a) have detailed this approach. To construct the indirect connection measure, the connectivity of flight k from airport i to airport j is modified as:

$$\text{Connectivity}_{ijk} = D_{Cap_{ijk}} \times D_{Vel_{ijk}} \times D_{Trans_{ijk}} \tag{3.6}$$

where $D_{Trans_{ijk}}$ is the transfer discount. Eq. (3.3) needs to include the time spent at the transfer airport and thus becomes:

$$\text{Duration}_{Adjusted_{ijk}} = T_{arrive_{ijk}} - T_{depart_{ijk}} + p_T \times t_{transfer_{ijk}} + t_{airport_{ijk}} \tag{3.7}$$

where extra time needed at the transfer airport is denoted as $t_{airport_{ijk}}$. As with de Wit et al. (2009), the extra penalty for transfer time p_T is set at 50 per cent.

For simplicity, this study and previous studies concerning the ConnUM only consider the case of one transfer. This is actually a reasonable assumption. Take the market of Beijing-Sydney as an example. In 2005, 54.89 per cent of the passengers flew on direct flights from Beijing to Sydney (only Air China provided direct services between 2005 and 2016) and 45 per cent undertook one transfer; the share of those who made two or more transfers was only 0.1 per cent. In 2016, these three figures were 47.81 per cent, 52.14 per cent, and 0.04 per cent, respectively. In the Shanghai-Sydney market (China Eastern, Air China, and Qantas provided direct services), these three percentages were 84.41 per cent, 15.56 per cent, and 0.02 per cent in 2005, and 73.84 per cent, 26.13 per cent and 0.03 per cent in 2016.

The quality of indirect connections is largely dependent on the quality of transfer. Transfer time and transfer service constitute two significant aspects of the quality of transfer (Choi et al., 2019). Different lengths of transfer time provide significantly different transfer experiences for passengers. An ideal way to determine the transfer time quality function is through a large-scale passenger experience survey. For illustration purpose, we assume that the relationship between the transfer time and the transfer time quality is captured by a function illustrated in Figure 3.1. The horizontal axis denotes the time difference between the transfer time and the minimum connection time (MCT) required by an airport. When the transfer time is equal to the MCT, passengers have a good chance of catching the connecting flight, but the risk of missing

Figure 3.1 Transfer time quality.

the connecting flight still exists if there is a slight delay for the incoming flight. Therefore, the quality is set as 0.2. In fact, most passengers would prefer a transfer time longer than the MCT, so it is reasonable to assume that a transfer time that is 30 minutes longer is most desirable, so its value is one. However, if the transfer time is too long (more than three hours), the long wait will result in lower transfer quality, and thus a value of 0.7 is assigned.

Although different airlines have a different MCT at every airport, the same MCT for all airports and all airlines is assumed for simplicity. The MCT standards are listed in Table 3.1.

The service quality for transfers is mainly decided by the relationship between the airlines operating the two flight segments. Zhu et al. (2019) set different service values to each situation as shown in Table 3.2. In general, when both flights are operated by the same airline or by airlines in the same alliance, the transfer service quality is generally better than the situation where the two segments are operated by two separate airlines without any cooperation agreement. In the case where one flight is operated by an LCC, the service quality would be relatively less desirable. It should be acknowledged that the assignment of the values is arbitrary and the connectivity values will depend on the values assigned to the time and service qualities. Future studies can consider using survey data to elicit more accurate values for these parameters. In addition, code-sharing outside the alliance is not accounted for in this study, which should be addressed in future studies.

The transfer discount can be expressed as:

$$D_{Trans_{ijk}} = q^T_{ijk} \times q^S_{ijk} \tag{3.8}$$

Table 3.1 MCT (minimum connecting time) for all possible transfers

First flight segment	Second flight segment	Whether at the same terminal	MCT (minutes)
Domestic flight	International flight	Yes	120
Domestic flight	International flight	No	160
International flight	Domestic flight	Yes	120
International flight	Domestic flight	No	160

Note: Transfers at the same airport but at different terminals are considered, while transfers at different airports in the same city are not considered in this research. The latter cases are rather small in number in our sample.

Table 3.2 Transfer service quality

Transfer types	Service value
Transfer with the same airline	1
Transfer between two airlines in the same airline alliance	0.9
Transfer between two full-service airlines from different alliances	0.3
Transfer with the same low-cost carrier	0.3
Other	0.1

where q_{ijk}^T is the time quality for the transfer of indirect connection k from airport i to airport j, and q_{ijk}^S represents the service quality of transfer for indirect connection k from airport i to airport j.

It should be noted that for indirect connections from airport i to airport j transferring at airport h, some direct connections from airport i to airport h and from airport h to airport j will be calculated more than once. For example, in the case shown in Figure 3.2, connections k2, k3, and k4 take off from airport h 40, 60, and 90 minutes after the landing of connection k1, respectively. k1+k2, k1+k3, and k1+k4 are all feasible indirect connections between airport i to airport j. Therefore, there are three indirect connections between airport i to airport j, but there is only one connection between airport i and airport h.

When multiple indirect connections (e.g., k1+k2, k1+k3, and k1+k4) share one flight segment (e.g., connection k1), the capacity of these indirect connections is constrained by the capacity of the shared connection. The example shown in Figure 3.2 shows that first segment of an indirect connection is shared. In fact, the second segment can also be shared. Therefore, we add an upper limit for indirect connectivity, which can be expressed as:

$$\sum_{\forall k \text{ with } s_k^1} D_{Cap_{i(h)jk}} \leq D_{Cap_{ih(j)s_k^1}} \tag{3.9}$$

$$\sum_{\forall k \text{ with } s_k^2} D_{Cap_{i(h)jk}} \leq D_{Cap_{ih(j)s_k^2}} \tag{3.10}$$

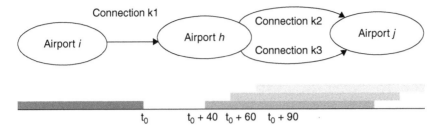

Figure 3.2 Example for repeated calculation.

where $s_{k'}^1$ denotes the first segment of indirect connection k'; $s_{k'}^2$ denotes the second segment of indirect connection k'; $D_{Cap_{i(h)jk}}$ denotes the capacity discount of indirect connection k from airport i to airport j transferring at airport h; $D_{Cap_{ih(j)s_{k'}^1}}$ denotes the capacity discount of the first segment of indirect connection k', which is from airport i to airport h and is connected by a second connection from airport h to airport j; $D_{Cap_{(i)hjs_{k'}^2}}$ denotes the capacity discount of the second segment of indirect connection k', which is from airport h to airport j and connects to the first connection from airport i to airport j. The left-hand side of Eq. (3.8) sums up the capacity discount of all indirect connections taking the route $i{\rightarrow}h{\rightarrow}j$ sharing a common segment, i.e., the first segment of indirect connection k'. The right-hand side of Eq. (3.8) gives the capacity discount of the first segment of indirect connection k' $(i{\rightarrow}h)$. Likewise, Eq. (3.9) shows that the capacity of indirect connections is constrained by the capacity of the second segment of the indirect connection. If Eqs. (3.8) or (3.9) are not satisfied, the capacity of the commonly shared segment is assigned to the indirect connection with the highest velocity discount and transfer discount.

The directional connectivity from airport i to airport j is the connectivity of route $i{\rightarrow}j$, which is the aggregate connectivity for all connections (direct and indirect) on the route:

$$\text{connectivity}_{ij} = \sum_k \text{connectivity}_{ijk} \tag{3.11}$$

The connectivity of airport i is the aggregate of the connectivity for all routes starting or ending at airport i, which can be expressed as:

$$\text{connectivity}_i = \sum_j \text{connectivity}_{ij} + \sum_j \text{connectivity}_{ji} \tag{3.12}$$

For a hub airport, its hub connectivity or centrality is the total of connectivity of all indirect connections with a transfer at that airport. The connectivity of a city, a region, or a country is the aggregate connectivity of all airports that contribute to the city, region, or country's transport services.

The link connectivity between airport i to airport j of an airline is the sum of the connectivity of all the flights of this airline between airport i and airport j in both directions. In the same fashion, we can obtain the link connectivity of all airlines between two countries.

The construction of a multi-modal connectivity measure

Most cities rely on multiple transport modes. In countries with a large land area such as China, rail plays an important role in the country's transport system. Zhu et al. (2018) attempt to incorporate both rail and air in their connectivity measure. However, their study only develops a direct connectivity measure without considering indirect and hub connectivity. A more comprehensive multi-modal connectivity measure is developed in Zhu et al. (2019b). They considered six types of connections in the extended multi-modal ConnUM covering direct connections such as from airport to airport, and from railway to railway, and indirect connections such as making a transfer at an airport, railway station, or both.

The basic ideas of the extended multi-modal ConnUM are the same as that of the simple ConnUM. A novel innovation in the multi-modal connectivity measure is the use of various radiation functions that not only help to aggregate the overall connectivity of different transport modes' terminals (e.g., rail terminal and airport terminal) in a city, but also capture their contribution to neighbouring cities' connectivity. For example, Shanghai's two airports not only contribute to its own air connectivity, but also increase its neighbouring cities' air connectivity. Suzhou is a city 50 km west of Shanghai. People living in Suzhou can easily access Shanghai Hongqiao airport in 20 minutes by HSR. Even though there is no airport within the administrative area of Suzhou, its air connectivity is high thanks to the presence of HSR. This is also the case for Wuxi that is 140 km west of Shanghai and has its own airport, although many Wuxi citizens choose to travel to Shanghai via HSR and use Shanghai's airports for flying. The existence of Shanghai airports and the HSR link greatly improve its neighbouring cities' overall connectivity. Therefore, the connectivity contribution from *terminal$_i$* to *city$_a$* can be assumed to be a function of *terminal$_i$*'s connectivity and the relative location of *terminal$_i$* against *city$_a$*. The connectivity of *city$_a$* can be expressed as:

$$connectivity_a = \sum_i f(terminal_i, location_{ia}) \tag{3.13}$$

To capture the impact of a terminal on a city's connectivity, various forms of functions could be adopted for formula (5). The impact of a terminal is smaller when the distance between the terminal and the city becomes greater. Zhu et al. (2019b) name this consideration radiation discount, which can be illustrated in Figure 3.3. Eq. (3.13) is an example of the radiation function. However various forms can be used as long as they show a non-linear inverse relation between the distance and the radiation discount. This is quite similar

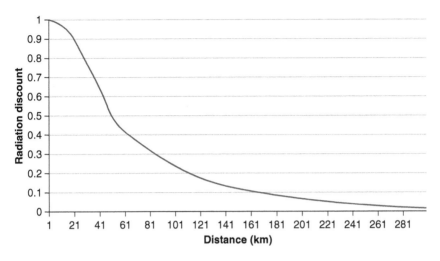

Figure 3.3 An example of radiation discount distance.

to the decay function in the destination quality model presented in Allroggen et al. (2015).

$$e^{-\frac{d_{ia}}{70}}, d_{ia} > 50$$

$$\frac{\cos(\frac{d_{ia}}{31.84}) + 1}{2}, 0 \leq d_{ia} \leq 50 \tag{3.14}$$

Applications of the Connectivity Utility Model

China's direct air connectivity with other countries/economies

The simple direct connectivity measure is used to examine how China is connected with the outside world with only direct connections considered. We examine a period from 2005 to 2016. For each year, two weeks' flight information was collected: 10–16 April and 10–16 November. All the direct flight information was extracted from IATA AirportIS database. The flight data include flight number,[2] number of seats, origin airport, destination airport, take-off time, and landing time. The time zone is then matched to every airport, and airline block time is calculated in minutes.

Table 3.3 ranks the 20 best connected economies/economies with China in 2016. Much information can be observed from the table. First, most of China's top 20 trading partners such as the United States, Hong Kong, Japan, Korea, Vietnam, Germany, India, Singapore, Taiwan, Russia, Malaysia, Australia, and Thailand are in Table 3.3, reflecting a close link between international trade and

Table 3.3 The best connected countries/economies with China (direct connectivity)

Ranking	Country	2004	2005	2006	2007	2008	2009	2010	2011	2012	2013	2014	2015	2016
1	Korea	964	1,173	1,475	1,935	1,861	738	1,665	1,735	1,913	2,165	2,629	3,056	3,108
2	Japan	1,531	1,673	1,706	2,029	2,085	956	1,924	1,806	1,950	1,771	1,990	2,666	3,026
3	Thailand	346	421	454	484	436	193	514	644	805	1,142	1,513	2,202	2,767
4	Hong Kong	1,697	1,988	2,192	2,119	2,095	944	1,959	2,117	2,147	2,370	2,450	2,369	2,370
5	Taiwan	0	0	0	0	33	376	826	1,070	1,407	1,462	1,775	1,847	1,759
6	Singapore	451	515	514	578	625	281	622	736	868	891	880	889	994
7	Malaysia	238	222	243	265	369	183	399	425	440	539	553	549	727
8	US	304	411	472	535	574	276	382	427	451	489	533	617	665
9	Macau	248	349	346	352	329	113	217	279	322	420	477	511	465
10	Vietnam	98	112	140	151	174	90	222	247	225	263	229	304	459
11	Russia	128	145	143	183	178	78	203	294	302	308	316	336	390
12	UAE	42	70	69	100	157	79	207	222	253	240	267	294	334
13	Philippines	67	96	102	115	118	67	136	178	185	256	234	232	275
14	Indonesia	44	46	102	94	70	32	85	86	99	123	176	188	274
15	Germany	173	198	264	262	275	129	229	261	256	237	259	268	268
16	Australia	77	121	130	130	131	62	129	182	232	220	205	217	240
17	Cambodia	25	46	45	51	68	33	78	87	101	147	196	228	234
18	France	132	151	152	153	175	87	174	178	187	198	203	224	231
19	Canada	68	83	97	99	101	42	91	113	101	118	127	133	155
20	India	21	40	43	54	96	37	102	120	128	169	134	132	147

air connectivity. Hong Kong, Macau, Taiwan, Thailand, Japan, Vietnam, Korea, Singapore, and the United States are the top ten destinations for Chinese tourists that are also included in Table 3.3, suggesting a close association between the provision of air services and tourism.

Second, air connections with China experienced remarkable increases for all the economies listed in Table 3.3. However, the negative impact of the 2008–2009 global financial crisis on the direct connectivity was real and substantial, indicating the strong association between air transport and macroeconomic conditions.

Third, Hong Kong was the most connected place with China in 2004, but in 2016, it was in the fourth place as Hong Kong experienced the slowest growth from 2004 to 2016 among the economies listed in Table 3.3. Hong Kong was a gateway to China for many decades. Its hub status in terms of attracting mainland Chinese passengers seems to have weakened in the last decade. For example, according to Zhu et al. (2019a), Hong Kong was the number one transfer hub between China and Australia measured by hub connectivity in 2008. However, in 2016, it was in fourth place. Guangzhou has a far greater hub connectivity in the China-Australia market today.

Fourth, Korea was in third place in 2004, but surpassed Japan in 2013 and Hong Kong in 2014, becoming the best connected country with China in 2015 and 2016. Korea has been actively negotiating open skies agreement with China to strengthen Seoul's hub status. Korean airlines have operated air services to many medium-sized Chinese cities and transport many Chinese passengers to many international destinations via Seoul by offering very competitive prices.

Air connectivity between countries has significant policy implications. For example, there has been much discussion about the establishment of an integrated aviation market in Northeast Asia in recent years. Negotiations on a free trade agreement (FTA) in this region has progressed well. However, air transport as a key infrastructure in facilitating the flows of goods and people is not part of the proposed FTA. The strong air connectivity between China and Japan and Korea suggests that it is worth exploring the possibility of forming a single aviation market in this region. Table 3.3 also shows that Southeast Asia, North America, and the EU are key destination markets for Chinese passengers. Each of them have had quite liberal aviation arrangement. These markets are also important to Japan and Korea, implying that if the three countries can form a single aviation market and act as one in negotiating air services agreements with other countries or blocs, the centre of gravity of the air transport will shift from the western hemisphere to this region. In addition, by using the ConnUM, we can also generate route-level connectivity and reveal each individual airline's network to inform airline management and decision makers about the likely winners and losers when a regional open skies agreement applies. This can be a future research topic.

China's overall connectivity (the sum of direct and indirect connectivity)

To illustrate the methodology of calculating indirect connectivity, we use the flight schedule data from the IATA AirportIS database for a period between 4 and 26 October 2016 to calculate the air connectivity scores. Table 3.4 reports the results of the overall connectivity including both direct and indirect connections. For indirect connection, only one transfer is assumed. In addition, we restrict the total distance of the indirect connection to less than twice of the direct distance between the origin and destination airports. The time at the transfer airport is limited to between 30 minutes and 24 hours.

Interestingly, as can be seen in Table 3.4, the US becomes the best connected country with China, followed by Thailand, Japan, and Korea. The connectivity of the United States with China is more than double that of the second and third country. Germany, Australia, Canada and Russia are among the top ten, indicating their close economic ties with China. Australia and Canada are the main migration destinations for Chinese citizens, which may suggest a close relationship between immigration and air transport.

These connectivity indices represent the existing air transport infrastructure between countries, which are useful in international trade and tourism studies where transport is regarded as a key impediment for the flows of goods and people. Many proxies have been used for the availability and quality of the overall transport infrastructure. Our ConnUM, particularly the extended

Table 3.4 Connectivity of foreign countries/economies with China (top 20)

Ranking	Country	Connectivity
1	USA	130,906.82
2	Thailand	52,889.50
3	Japan	50,977.87
4	Korea	28,980.19
5	Germany	25,483.90
6	Australia	23,274.81
7	Malaysia	21,973.46
8	Canada	20,092.10
9	Indonesia	19,340.50
10	Russia	19,184.89
11	Taiwan	17,166.97
12	Italy	16,077.64
13	Singapore	15,955.22
14	UK	15,069.49
15	France	14,328.14
16	India	13,463.61
17	Vietnam	13,063.69
18	United Arab Emirates	11,298.23
19	Spain	10,073.00
20	Turkey	9,535.90

ConnUM, can provide a comprehensive measure, which is a good representation of the transport infrastructure.

Using the extended ConnUM for vulnerability analysis

This section will use the calculated connectivity values to conduct a vulnerability analysis for China's transport network.[3] Any kind of incidents taking place in a city's transport network will affect the connectivity of the city. Train breakdowns, electrical failures, road construction, air traffic control, etc., would result in a connectivity decrease. In extreme situations such as war or a natural disaster it is possible to lose an entire route, terminal, or even a city. Vulnerability, which is defined by Berdica (2002) as the degree of susceptibility of a network to certain incidents that may lead to reduced service or accessibility levels, is critical under these circumstances. When a city has a disaster-resistant transport network, which means that it will remain functional under extreme situations, it brings flexibility and ease for the government, private sector, and individuals to rebuild and restore the city. Therefore, it is important to analyse the vulnerability of a city's transport services.

There has been much research concerning how to define, evaluate, and handle the vulnerability of a region's transport systems (Berdica, 2002; Taylor, 2008; Taylor, 2012; Rodríguez-Núñez and García-Palomares , 2014). In this research, the characteristics of the incidents are not considered. The focus is on the consequence in terms of connectivity, when the incident has already happened and affected a terminal, route, or city.

We consider two kinds of vulnerability here. The first one is city impact, which is the loss of overall network connectivity when a city's transport links with other cities are suddenly disrupted as a result of an incident. When a city is impacted by such an incident, not only is its connectivity affected but also is that of other cities connecting with it. City impact represents the importance of the city in the network. Figure 3.4 presents the impact of the top 25 cities in terms of overall connectivity and direct connectivity. Shanghai, Beijing, Guangzhou, and Nanjing are the top four cities in overall city impact. When Shanghai is affected by an incident, 9.6 per cent of the overall connectivity and 15.1 per cent of the direct connectivity of the country's transport systems will be lost. Nanjing surpasses Guangzhou to be the third most important city in direct connectivity with respect to city impact. If Nanjing is isolated from other cities, 10.0 per cent of the direct rail and air connectivity of China will be lost. Hangzhou, Wuhan, Zhengzhou, Changsha, Tianjin, and Xuzhou also rank higher in terms of direct city impact than in overall city impact, meaning that these cities play an important role in forming direct connections in China's rail and air networks.

The second vulnerability considered is city resistance, which is the loss of a city's remaining connectivity when a certain number of top-ranking routes connecting it are lost. If a city is only well connected with one city, it will be disconnected from the world when the only route is destroyed. However, if a

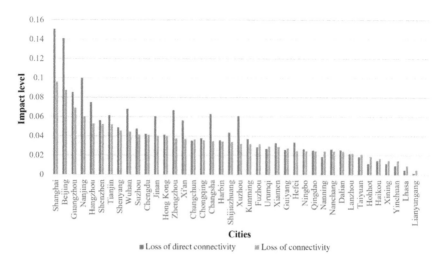

Figure 3.4 City impact of Chinese cities.

city is well connected with multiple cities, the city will still be well connected when one route is lost. Figure 3.5 presents a city's remaining connectivity when up to the top 20 routes connecting the city are lost. Only cities ranking in the top five and the bottom five are presented. It is observed that Hong Kong, Shanghai, Beijing, Hangzhou, and Ningbo are the most resistant to route losses. Hong Kong is the leader, keeping 88.94 per cent of its original connectivity without the top 20 routes, while Lhasa would keep only 59.05 per cent of its connectivity if the top 20 routes were cut.

Conclusions

This chapter has discussed the methodology of constructing a connectivity measure, the ConnUM. This measure was developed in several papers and each paper focused on a specific area with its broad usefulness not being spelled out. The purpose of this chapter is to integrate the different versions and show that this model can generate results of significant policy implications at country levels. For example, previous studies only use this model to look at the connectivity of an airport or a city. This chapter shows that the direct and indirect air connectivity between countries can be calculated, which can be used to test and predict the relationship between air transport and economic activities. They are particularly useful for trade and tourism studies that need a good proxy for transport infrastructure. In addition, the connectivity indices can be compared over years and across regions to evaluate the success of transport policy reforms, and to support open skies and FTA negotiations. It is ideal that such indices can be complied at the city, regional, and country levels and updated each year for policy makers and industry practitioners.

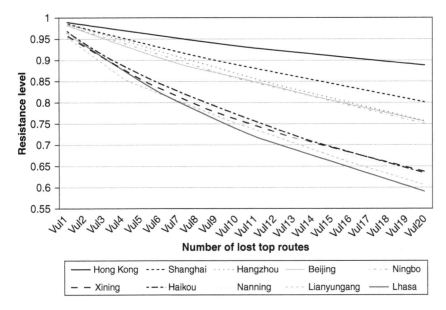

Figure 3.5 City resistance of Chinese cities.

This chapter also conducted a vulnerability analysis for China's air and rail transport network. The vulnerability analysis suggests that if Shanghai were affected by an incident, 9.6 per cent of the overall connectivity and 15.1 per cent of the direct connectivity of the country's transport systems would be lost. This again shows that the connectivity values calculated from the ConnUM have significant policy implications as they can be used to test the robustness of the exiting transport network and guide future infrastructure construction.

However, it should be acknowledged that although the word 'utility' is included in the name of ConnUM, this connectivity measure is not derived from a utility model, and is actually a physical node-to-node measure. This measure ignores the fact that different passenger groups (business and leisure passengers) place different values on travel time (Burghouwt, 2017). More importantly, air-fare, a significant choice parameter for passengers, is not included. For a utility-based connectivity measure, readers may want to refer to the one developed by Mandel et al. (2017) based on the path aggregation theorem (PATH). This utility-based measure captures passengers' monetary cost and the value of travel time. The utility weights of this measure are derived from the actual path choice model estimates, and the actual path utilities between the departure and destin-ation points are measured with logit models. It is not surprising to see that the physical network measure and the utility-based measure produce quite different rankings for the European airports (Mandel et al., 2017). Thus, when policy makers use connectivity measures to make decisions, they should be clear of the limitations of each measure and choose the most appropriate one that suits their needs.

Notes

1 Relatedly, O'Connor, K. (2003) and Wong et al. (2019) examine whether a spatial dispersal trend dominates the development of the global aviation industry by considering the aviation network at both the airport level and the airport–city level, with a city consisting of one or more airports.
2 For code-sharing flights, only the operating flights are retained.
3 Li et al., (2019) have also conducted a vulnerability analysis for China's air and rail transport network by using a different methodology.

References

Alderighi, M., Cento. A., Nijkamp, P., & Rietveld, P. 2007. Assessment of new hub-and-spoke and point-to-point airline network configurations. *Transport Reviews*, 27, 529–549.

Allroggen, F., Wittman, M. D., & Malina, R. 2015. How air transport connects the world – a new metric of air connectivity and its evolution between 1990 and 2012. *Transportation Research Part E: Logistics and Transportation Review*, 80, 184–201.

Baker, D., Merkert, R., & Kamruzzaman, M. 2015. Regional aviation and economic growth: cointegration and causality analysis in Australia. *Journal of Transport Geography*, 43, 140–150.

Bannò, M., & Redondi, R. 2014. Air connectivity and foreign direct investments: economic effects of the introduction of new routes. *European Transport Research Review*, 6(4), 355–363.

Berdica, K. 2002. An introduction to road vulnerability: what has been done, is done and should be done. *Transport Policy*, 9(2), 117–127.

Blonigen, B. A., & Cristea, A. D. 2015. Air service and urban growth: evidence from a quasi-natural policy experiment. *Journal of Urban Economics*, 86, 128–146.

Brueckner, J. K. 2003. Airline traffic and urban economic development. *Urban Studies*, 40, 1455–1469.

Burghouwt, G. 2017. Influencing air connectivity outcomes. International Transport Forum Discussion Paper 2017–24. SEO Amsterdam Economics, Amsterdam, the Netherlands.

Burghouwt, G., & Veldhuis, J. 2006. The competitive position of hub airports in the transatlantic market. *Journal of Air Transportation*, 11, 106–130.

Burghouwt, G., de Wit, J., Veldhuis, J., & Matsumoto, H. 2009. Air network performance and hub competitive position: evaluation of primary airports in East and South-East Asia. *Journal of Airport Management*, 3(4), 384–400.

Burghouwt, G., & Redondi, R. 2013. Connectivity in air transport networks: an assessment of models and applications. *Journal of Transport Economics and Policy*, 47(1), 35–53.

Calatayud, A., Palacin, R., Mangan, J., Jackson, E., & Ruiz-Rua, A. 2016. Understanding connectivity to international markets: a systematic review. *Transport Reviews*, 36(6), 713–736.

Campante, F., & Yanagizawa-Drott, D. 2017. Long-range growth: economic development in the global network of air links. *The Quarterly Journal of Economics*, 133(3), 1395–1458.

Cattaneo, M., Malighetti, P., Paleari, S., & Redondi, R. 2017. Evolution of the European network and implications for self-connection. *Journal of Air Transport Management*, 65, 18–28.

Cheung, T. K. Y., Wong, C. W. H., & Zhang, A. 2020. The evolution of aviation network: global airport connectivity index 2006–2016. *Transportation Research Part E: Logistics and Transportation Review*, 133, 101826.

Choi, J. H., Wang, K., Xia, W., & Zhang, A. 2019. Determining factors of air passengers' transfer airport choice in the Southeast Asia-North America market: Managerial and policy implications. *Transportation Research Part A: Policy and Practice*, 124, 203–216.

Geurs, K. T., & Van Wee, B. 2004. Accessibility evaluation of land-use and transport Strategies: review and research directions. *Journal of Transport Geography*, 12, 127–140.

Hossain, M. M., & Alam, S. 2017. A complex network approach towards modeling and analysis of the Australian Airport Network. *Journal of Air Transport Management*, 60, 1–9.

Li, T., Rong, L., & Yan, K. 2019. Vulnerability analysis and critical area identification of public transport system: a case of high-speed rail and air transport coupling system in China. *Transportation Research Part A: Policy and Practice*, 127, 55–70.

Liu, X., Derudder, B., & García, C. G. 2013. Exploring the co-evolution of the geographies of air transport aviation and corporate networks. *Journal of Transport Geography*, 30, 26–36.

Malighetti, P., Paleari, S., & Redondi, R. 2008. Connectivity of the European airport network: 'Self-help hubbing' and business implications. *Journal of Air Transport Management*, 14(2), 53–65.

Mandel, B., Gaudry, M., & Ungemach, D. 2017. Europe-wide aviation connectivity measures and the PATH theorem. Université de Montréal, Agora Jules Dupuit, Publication AJD-161, 21.

Matisziw, T. C., & Grubesic, T. H. 2010. Evaluating locational accessibility to the US air transportation system. *Transportation Research Part A: Policy and Practice*, 44(9), 710–722.

Matsumoto, H., Domae, K., & O'Connor, K. 2016. Business connectivity, air transport and the urban hierarchy: a case study in East Asia. Journal of Transport Geography, 54, 132–139.

O'Connor, K. 2003. Global air travel: toward concentration or dispersal? *Journal of Transport Geography*, 11(2), 83–92.

OECD/ITF 2018. Defining, measuring and improving air connectivity. International Transport Forum, OECD, Paris.

Otiso, K. M., Derudder, B., Bassens, D., Devriendt, L., & Witlox, F. 2011. Airline connectivity as a measure of the globalization of African cities. *Applied Geography*, 31(2), 609–620.

Paleari, S., Redondi, R., & Malighetti, P. 2010. A comparative study of airport connectivity in China, Europe and US: which network provides the best service to passengers? *Transportation Research Part E: Logistics and Transportation Review*, 46(2), 198–210.

Rodríguez-Núñez, E., & García-Palomares, J. C. 2014. Measuring the vulnerability of public transport networks. *Journal of Transport Geography*, 35, 50–63.

Statista 2018. Cruising speeds of the most common types of commercial airliners (in knots). Available at www.statista.com/statistics/614178/cruising-speed-of-most-common-airliners/. Accessed 30 December 2018.

Taylor, M. A. 2008. Critical transport infrastructure in urban areas: impacts of traffic incidents assessed using accessibility-based network vulnerability analysis. *Growth and Change*, 39(4), 593–616.

Taylor, M. A. 2012. Remoteness and accessibility in the vulnerability analysis of regional road networks. *Transportation Research Part A: Policy and Practice*, 46(5), 761–771.

Van De Vijver, E., Derudder, B., & Witlox, F. 2014. Exploring causality in trade and air passenger travel relationships: the case of Asia-Pacific, 1980–2010. *Journal of Transport Geography*, 34, 142–150.

Veldhuis, J. 1997. The competitive position of airline networks. *Journal of Air Transport Management*, 3(4), 181–188.

Wang, J., Mo, H., Wang, F., & Jin, F. 2011. Exploring the network structure and nodal centrality of China's air transport network: a complex network approach. *Journal of Transport Geography*, 19, 712–721.

Wong, W. H., Cheung, T., Zhang, A., & Wang, Y. 2019. Is spatial dispersal the dominant trend in air transport development? A global analysis for 2006–2015. *Journal of Air Transport Management*, 74, 1–12.

Zeigler, P., Pagliari, R., Suau-Sanchez, P., Malighetti, P., & Redondi, R. 2017. Low-cost carrier entry at small European airports: low-cost carrier effects on network connectivity and self-transfer potential. *Journal of Transport Geography*, 60, 68–79.

Zhang, A. 2012. Airport improvement fees, benefit spillovers, and land value capture mechanisms. In Gregory K. Ingram and Yu-Hung Hong (eds.), *Value Capture and Land Policies*, pp. 323–348, Cambridge, MA: Lincoln Institute of Land Policy.

Zhang, A., Wan, Y., & Yang, H. 2019. Impacts of high-speed rail on airlines, airports and regional economies: a survey of recent research. *Transport Policy*, 81, A1–A19.

Zhang, Y., & Findlay, C. 2014. Air transport policy and its impacts on passenger traffic and tourist flows. *Journal of Air Transport Management*, 34, 42–48.

Zhang, Y., & Zhang, A. 2016. Determinants of air passenger flows in China and gravity model: deregulation, LCCs, and high-speed rail. *Journal of Transport Economics and Policy*, 50(3), 287–303.

Zhang, Y., Zhang, A., Zhu, Z., & Wang, K. 2017. Connectivity at Chinese airports: the evolution and drivers. *Transportation Research Part A: Policy and Practice*, 103, 490–508.

Zhu, Z., Zhang, A., & Zhang, Y. 2018. Connectivity of intercity passenger transportation in China: a multi-modal and network approach. *Journal of Transport Geography*, 71, 263–276.

Zhu, Z., Zhang, A., Zhang, Y., Huang, Z., & Xu, S. 2019a. Measuring air connectivity between China and Australia. *Journal of Transport Geography*, 74, 359–370.

Zhu, Z., Zhang, A., & Zhang, Y. 2019b. Measuring multi-modal connections and connectivity radiations of transport infrastructure in China. *Transportmetrica A: Transport Science*, 15, 1762–1790.

4 Wider economic benefits

What they are, how they manifest, and an example from network air services

David Gillen

Introduction

Much has been claimed regarding the value of public or private investments in generating spinoffs, additional impacts that may not to be included in conventional benefit-cost assessments (see discussion in OECD, 2016). A difficulty with including such wider economic benefits (WEBs) is they should be a net addition to welfare that has not been internalised in any markets that currently are considered in the benefit-cost assessment. An expansion of infrastructure will potentially alter downstream market access with subsequent effects on prices and, perhaps, service quality. Such effects have been internalised and would therefore not be counted as a WEB. However, if the investment also leads to increases in variety to improve consumer welfare due to more choice, this is most likely a WEB. In some instances we observe proponents of a new investment counting gross-value-added as a benefit to be included but these can easily be transfers rather than net gains. This would be inappropriate and would fall in the category of what have been termed 'catalytic' effects. These effects and WEBs are different and have a different underlying modelling structure. Catalytic effects are best considered as part of Impact Analysis whereas WEBs as part of benefit-cost analysis are firmly grounded in welfare theory and measurement.

The literature discussing and assessing wider economic benefits really began with the investigation of macroeconomic variable relationships; how public expenditure affects economic growth. This public capital literature soon evolved to consider more micro relationships and in particular how expenditures on public capital could enhance or replace (substitute for) other factors of production or lead to rearrangements in the supply chain (e.g. inventory and warehouse location strategy). This chapter explores the evolution of the literature and illustrates how WEBs might be considered for changes to the design, size, and use of an aviation network. We provide a detailed, but not exhaustive, description of the evolution of the literature of transportation investments. It covers the public capital and economic growth literature, examines the mechanisms of WEBs and WEBs versus catalytic effects. Then we look more closely at the relationship between WEBs and aviation followed by a discussion of the aviation infrastructure service as it provides access to economic mass and spillover effects. This section provides an empirical example of aviation network change using multifactor productivity as an impact metric. Subsequently, we describe the data, models, and empirical results as well as illustrating the values associated with changes to a network.

Literature evolution

Public capital and economic growth

A substantial research effort has focused on how much public capital, generally represented in terms of infrastructure, has contributed to economic growth. This initially had been stimulated by two factors. First, public capital spending in the United States as a proportion of GDP had fallen through the period 1971–1990 and second, the decrease in public capital spending in the United States was claimed to have contributed to the productivity slowdown which occurred in the 1970s and 1980s. Using U.S. data for 1949–1985 Aschauer (1989) found the elasticity of aggregate multifactor productivity with respect to increases in the public capital stock to be 0.4; a 10 per cent increase in the stock of public capital would increase multifactor productivity by 4 per cent, an enormous impact. Early in this literature studies using aggregate data found similarly large impacts to Aschauer but such large impacts were found to be fraught with problems (see Gramlich, 1994).

In a 1998 survey that examined the relationship between public capital and economic growth, Sturn et al. (1998) found a wide range of estimates in the literature. In some cases, the marginal product of public capital was found to be [much] higher than private capital (Aschauer, 1989), about equal to the marginal product of private capital (Munnell, 1990), in some cases values were well below the return on private capital (Eberts, 1986) and there were instances in the literature where the return on public capital was negative, (Hulten and Schwab, 1991). This literature focused on macro measures and generally treated public capital as entering the aggregate production function. It could do so by entering directly or by affecting multifactor productivity $\phi(G_t)$; where G_t is some measure of public capital stock at time t. Therefore, in equation 1 Q_t is some measure of aggregate output, K_t is a measure of non-residential private capital stock, and L_t is a measure of labour input.

$$Q_t = \phi(G_t)h(K_t,L_t,G_t) \tag{4.1}$$

This specification treats public capital symmetrically with other inputs, private capital, labour, and perhaps transportation, a special type of public capital.

This literature evolved to consider the *flow of services* from the capital stock rather than focus on the stock itself. If transportation infrastructure is separated from other public capital, the transportation services would be a function of the available capacity of infrastructure and the capacity of vehicles, generally private, utilising it. Technology could enter either as factor neutral or factor augmenting. This characterisation would be represented as:

$$Q_t = \sum q_i = h_i \phi^i \left[K_i, L_i, T_i \left(MV_i, G \right) \right] \tag{4.2}$$

where q_i is the output of industry i, transportation services (T_i) in industry i are a function of motor vehicle capacity (MV_i) and public capital infrastructure capacity (G) and h_i is Hicks neutral technological change in industry i; see Nadiri and Mamuneas (1996) and Fernald (1999).

The locational aspect of public capital was the next evolution, recognising transportation public capital was part of a network industry. Companies manufacturing hard goods (e.g. textiles, electronics, fabricated metals) had a transportation/inventory strategy that would include accumulation as well as distribution centres which may be located in adjacent jurisdictions.[1] Therefore, the amount of transportation public capital available in the adjacent jurisdiction should enter the relationship to account for spillover effects; see Cohen and Morrison Paul (2004), Gillen et al. (2004), Garrison et al. (2003) and Gillen (1997). Thus (4.2) could be adjusted as:

$$Q_t = \sum_{i=1}^{n} \sum_{k=1}^{m} q_{i,k} \, h_i \phi^i \left[K_i, L_i, T_i \left(MV_i, G_k, G_j \right) \right] \tag{4.3}$$

where $Q_{i,k}$ is the output of industry i in location k and it is impacted by, among other factors, the amount of public capital capacity in location k and in adjacent or near adjacent location j.

The 'public capital' literature continued to expand along a number of paths. The way in which public capital was defined, how to calculate the public capital stock and the difficulty of measuring public capital across countries due to differences in prices across countries; how a project is financed or if it is a public-private partnership will affect how efficient the investment is. Pritchett (1996), for example, claims a public capital stock constructed on the basis of cumulative investment will be overvalued.

The production function and cost function approaches are described in Gillen (1996, 2000), Sturm et al. (1998) and Romp and de Haan (2000). The production function approach was driven in part by data availability but it had a number of significant problems. First, there was an issue of reverse causation on both the demand and supply side; potential feedback between income and capital stock and the feedback between income and the demand for infrastructure. The solution seemed to be in ramping up the sophistication of the econometrics as various authors tried estimating panel or simultaneous equation models or using instrumental variables; see Romp and de Haan (2000) for a detailed survey. The shift to a cost function approach was motivated in part by greater opportunity to use more sophisticated functional forms with the attractive feature that the substitutability between factors could be explored. This was important in establishing whether public capital drove out private capital and whether public capital was enhancing employment or not. Cohen and Morrison Paul (2004) provide an excellent illustration of cost function estimation using data for 48 contiguous states over the period 1982–1996. The modelling includes spillovers by considering both intra and inter-state effects; interestingly, in their work, they measure the impact of public capital ignoring spillovers which results in a cost elasticity of -0.15 but including spillovers it increases to 0.21.

An important conclusion from the literature on public capital is that there is heterogeneity in terms of impacts; the effect of public capital will differ across regions and sectors. Not unsurprisingly, the impact will depend on how much public capital is available and whether changes are incremental and how technology is affected – consider how smart roads might affect the returns to road capital. It is the two features of network effects or spillovers and the differences in services that stimulate this chapter.

Mechanisms of WEB

WEBs may create opportunities for agglomeration economies resulting from combining market density and market size. Venables (2016) identifies such circumstances as giving rise to clusters which result in spillover effects or externalities. Suppliers may not be able to capture all of the gains in the form of producer surplus because of indivisibilities or scale effects. Users may benefit from greater product variety which may not be fully captured in measures of willingness to pay. Whether they could be wider economic benefits depends on whether they have been internalised. If markets are working efficiently all value should be fully reflected in standard economic welfare measures. The trouble it appears is not identifying them but rather measuring them.

Investments in infrastructure potentially change proximity; I refer to 'infrastructure' in the discussion but the ideas apply to any type of capital investment whether it is social, human, physical, institutional, or operations processes.[2] A proximity change with transport infrastructure could be represented by a change in the generalised cost of travel or more generally a change in the generalized cost of transacting. Household would have potential for high utility with such value being reflected in higher willingness to pay (WTP) and if not, a WEB is manifest. Firms may gain higher profit with changes in productivity resulting from a complementarity between the infrastructure investment and other factors of production. For example, the opportunities for a broader use of land may shift the production opportunity function with a consequent improvement in overall output opportunities. Governments may gain through improvements in labour markets or labour market participation. In each of the impacts identified there are no obvious imperfections that would lead to a failure to fully capitalise value added into factor prices, product prices or profit (surplus) such that the price system will equate marginal value and marginal cost.

WEBs occur when economic agents other than the original investor benefit for whatever reason: classic externalities. Agglomeration is a good example where an investment by one agent may have spillover effects due to a combination of cost economies (scale) and market density (see Rosenthal and Strange, 2004). Agglomeration shifts cost functions down due to improvements in productivity and shifts demand functions up due to quality and agglomeration rests on specialisation – products, skills, and service. The degree to which we will get specialisation in the supply chain will depend on the underlying economic characteristics of the product and this will in turn define the extent to which we realise clusters. Note clustering can result in lower costs due to specialisation but also possibly higher costs due to upstream and downstream dependency. Setting aside the issue of which way costs may move, if cost economies dominate or if there are indivisibilities (Melo et al. 2013) and the market is large enough there are going to be spillovers to all cluster participants.

Wider economic benefits vs catalytic effects

Over the last several years there has been significant discussion of what have been termed wider economic benefits and/or catalytic effects of transport improvements (however they might arise). The development of this literature seems to be driven by studies analysing competing locations for new airports (Heathrow vs Gatwick), ports (London) and headquarters locations (e.g. Amazon), for example. There are some papers that use the terms 'wider economic benefits' synonymously with 'catalytic effects', while others claim they are different (see for example, Forsyth and Niemeier, 2016).

The UK Airports Commission's take on wider economic impacts is they consider four things: increased productivity through trade (likely excluding foreign direct investment (FDI)), agglomeration effects, increased tax revenues and increased output in imperfectly competitive markets. In the results for the different options proposed for airport capacity expansion, the trade effect was thought to be in the range of 60–75 per cent of the total wider economic impacts. Overall, the Airports Commission were very cautious about these figures and did not use them in their formal assessment of which was the better scheme. The UK Department of Transport subsequently published an updated appraisal in which they were even more sceptical about using these measures (see Department of Transport (UK), June 2018). However, they did link such WEBs to a benefit-cost framework.

Regarding WEBs, it is certainly the case that WEBs encompass a wider range of potential impacts than intended when we talk about catalytic effects. We tend to think of the latter as the long-run macroeconomic impacts of airport infrastructure, or strictly the connectivity the infrastructure facilitates. The theoretically pure way of trying to address these is, of course, the CGE model: modelling the impact of increased access (reduced generalised travel costs) on demand and the feedback loops through the economy.

There is some debate as to what constitutes WEBs and what are catalytic effects. I consider that each is grounded in a particular evaluation methodology. WEBs are identified with benefit-cost models and computable general equilibrium (CGE) models.[3] A catalyst is an event, material or person causing a change or acceleration of a change. A report for ACI – Europe (2004) defines a catalytic impact as 'employment and income generated in the economy of the study area by the wider role of the airport in improving the productivity of business and in attracting economic activities such as inward investment and inbound tourism'. Defined in this way these are economic impacts and not wider economic benefits. However, Cooper and Smith (2005) who state catalytic impacts are composed of consumer surplus to users, economic spillovers, and environmental and social impacts resulting from tourism and trade (demand side) and long-run contribution to productivity and GDP growth (supply side). However, I disagree. These are wider economic impacts in my view and catalytic impacts are simply external effects that would not have been included in traditional impact models. But here is the point: catalytic impacts are associated with economic impact analysis (EIA) which provides no notion of economic welfare. There is no notion of markets or of equilibrium and there is no consideration for costs. EIA measures how much more (or less in the case of a demand or investment withdrawal) employment, income, output, and tax revenue, taken to an extreme that could make the economy worse off rather than better off. WEBs are the antithesis of catalytic effects.

When new technology is introduced there are generally two outcomes: we can do old things better and we can do new things. When I say 'technology' I include new infrastructure, new services, new policy, or new management strategies, for example. All of these cases provide opportunities for improvement and opportunity to combine different technologies to provide something brand new. Both cases might be included in the concept of Wider Economic Benefits (WEB). WEBs generally involve a shift in a function. They have the effect of being able to do new things not just existing things better which should be fully internalised by markets. A transportation investment or policy change or operational decision may result in some technological change, such as information spillovers that are not intermediated through a market.

Venables (2016) sees wider economic benefits (WEBs) as benefits that add social value over and above user benefits, that is over and above consumer and producer surplus. Essentially WEBs are those portions of social value going to either consumers or producers that have not been fully internalised due to a market failure of sorts and are therefore externalities. WEBs are additional social benefit or cost not captured by user benefits and should reflect a general equilibrium net value meaning a benefit in i is not displacing a benefit in j and they should be measurable.

Wider economic benefits (WEBs) and aviation

The aviation mode has attracted a sizable literature as to the economic value of both air transport liberalisation and the opportunities that increased connectivity, net of liberalisation, brings about; see, for example, Oum, Fu, and Zhang, 2010; Kincaid and Tretheway, 2015; Burghouwt, 2017 and Burghouwt and Redondi, 2013. Connectivity is often measured in terms of numbers of direct and indirect flight frequencies and the number of routes to which they apply (Burghouwt, 2017). However, this treats connectivity as a homogeneous measure of service quality irrespective of market segments, business values frequency, and minimum correct time as well as numbers of routes whereas leisure passengers, for the most part, value choice of destinations or access measured by numbers of routes.

Burghouwt and Redondi (2013) provide a comprehensive survey of eight air connectivity models and examine them empirically in a European context. They point out that connectivity measures for an airport can be separated along the lines of, what they term, accessibility versus centrality. The former measures the number of direct and indirect connections taking account of the amount of time penalty an indirect connection might take. The latter measure considers the number of flight opportunities at a (hub) airport which counts both flight frequency and number of destinations.

These two measures, centrality and accessibility, could be encompassed in a generalised travel cost measure whether couched in utility or productivity terms. It is the transactions costs that effect the amount of overall utility or trade (change in GDP) that are affected by connectivity. This is what underlies the wider economic benefits and in some cases catalytic effects. The international trade literature has traditionally treated distance as a form of barrier to trade but a supply chain perspective is much richer. Connectivity encompasses not just the transport mode but the way in which logistics is organised and carried out. It is not simply a matter of airport to airport; it is origin to destination that matters. In this regard there are airport access and egress costs that enter the overall transactions cost. It is this supply chain model that can aid in distinguishing catalytic effects from wider economic benefits. It is the changes in the supply chain which may represent externalities which are the WEBs as possible changes in connectivity that may not be internalised by markets; if the economic benefits are internalised, counting these impacts as WEBs would constitute double counting.

Aviation infrastructure service: access to economic mass and spillover effects (WEBs)

The importance of market density and clusters of activities for improving productivity has been well documented (Glaeser, 2011). Access to economic mass and linking to productivity can be established using a measure of economic distance (Venables, 2016), from an economic concentration (employment for example) and from establishing how each of these factors or the combination of distance and mass can affect productivity. The empirical example used here is to examine aviation networks and how the way in which air services are delivered over these networks affect 'economic distance' and how economic mass might offer a separate influence, market size or density.

The empirical example explores the contribution of air service as applied over a network to change economic distance to local, regional, and national economies. This network is a key component of transportation infrastructure that allows business travellers to meet existing and new customers, expand markets, and generate efficiencies in terms of scale, scope, and agglomeration economies. Improvements in the connectivity widen the available markets and may lead to greater market density and clustering. The objective was to understand how changes in air service connectivity between airports, regions, or countries would affect the level of economic output, specifically how changes in airline network connectivity improve productivity and hence the ability of the economy to increase real output. An additional question was whether connectivity affected industries in the same way.

Productivity is measured in terms of many or multiple factors, such as labour, raw materials, energy, and capital, termed multifactor productivity (MFP), which is a comprehensive measure of productivity. The approach used here was to use a measure of MFP for different industries and link this to different measures of air service connectivity as well as other standard economic variables that would be expected to affect MFP. A sample of 11 industry sectors was analysed for 20 metropolitan areas[4] and at four points in time (1995, 2000, 2005, 2010).[5] The selection of metropolitan regions was designed to capture different types (hubs vs non-hubs) of airports as well as different sizes and types of markets with a variety of industrial makeups. Cumulatively, these regions represented 21 per cent of the US population and 23 per cent of the US gross domestic product (GDP) in 2010. The linkages explore how the change in air service connectivity affects productivity, in this case multifactor productivity, and how the change in productivity in turn increases real GDP which serves as a measure of the value provided by the airline network.

The air service variables were chosen to measure the level of air traffic activity at each airport as well as provide different measures of airline network connectivity and to distinguish between domestic and international connectivity. Models also included population, GDP, and employment data for each of the metropolitan areas.

The specification of the estimation model was generally:

$$MFP_j = \emptyset\left(CN', Z'\right)$$

which states that multifactor productivity growth in industry j is a function of a vector of connectivity measures and a vector of other economic factors, Z.

The particular specification was:

$$lnMFP_j = \alpha + \sum \beta_i lnCN_i + \sum \gamma_k lnZ_k + \epsilon$$

where the CN_i are the different measures of connectivity and included variables that captured frequency of flights, destinations served, hub access, and percentage of the world GDP served. The connectivity variables that were statistically significant were: number of airlines, domestic non-stop departures, domestic airline hubs served, domestic non-stop destinations, number of markets with two or more non-stop domestic flights, number of markets with five or more non- stop domestic flights, number of international non-stop departures, number of non-stop international destinations, percentage of the world GDP served by non-stop flights and the per centage of the world's GDP served by two or more daily non-stop flights.

The variables included in the Z_k vector were labour productivity index for a given SMSA, labour productivity index for industry in a given SMSA, population, aggregate output for an SMSA (measured by GDP), dummy time variables for 2000, 2005, and 2010. These variables were designed to capture factors that can influence the MFP growth in a given industry. The model was estimated for each industry using generalised least squares; variable descriptions are contained in Appendix C.

Table 4.1 and Table 4.2 list the results of the regressions for the 11 industry sectors across the 20 regions in the sample. Coefficients included in the table are statistically significant at least at the 90 per cent confidence level; adjusted R^2 and log-likelihood values are shown in the bottom rows. The degree of explanatory power ranges from a low of 64 per cent for the Arts, Entertainment, and Recreation sector to a high of 92 per cent for the Information sector.

The set of variables of most interest is those that measure the effect of air service connectivity. There are several categories of variables that sought to reflect both domestic and international connectivity. These included the number of departures, the frequency of non-stop flights in different markets, and the degree of connection of each region to the world economy. The important result from the table is that aviation networks connect different industries in different ways and the relative effect of improvements in connectivity on MFP varies across industries as well. For example, increasing the number of domestic non-stop destinations has more than twice the effect on MFP for manufacturing as for wholesale trade, with a model coefficient (elasticity) of 0.034 versus 0.015. We can see from the statistically significant coefficients that service frequency and having direct flights to a large number of destinations have a statistically significant effect on productivity in most industry sectors examined. The number of domestic airline hubs served has a statistically significant effect on productivity in the Information, Finance, and Insurance, Professional, Scientific, and Technical Services, Management of Companies and Enterprises, and Arts,

Table 4.1 Estimation results for multifactor productivity regressions

Variable	MFG	Wholesale	Info	Finance and insurance	Real estate	Professional, scientific, and technical services
Ln Regional Population (market size)	0.0037	0.0015				
Ln Number of Airlines	0.0439	0.0215		0.0433	0.0252	
Ln Domestic Non-stop Departures	0.0237	0.0257		0.0479	0.0213	0.0182
Ln Airline Hubs Served –Domestic			0.0151	0.0716		0.0361
Ln Domestic Non-stop Destinations	0.0344	0.0152			0.0397	
Ln Two or More Daily Non-stop Domestic Flights	0.0991		0.0121	0.0312	0.0406	
Ln Five or More Daily Non-stop Domestic Flights						
Ln International Non-stop Departures	0.0479					
Ln International Non-stop Destinations					0.0532	0.0262
Ln Per cent of the World GDP Served Non-stop			0.0257	0.0107		
Ln Per cent of the World GDP Served re Daily		0.0214				0.0491
Ln Per cent of the World GDP Served Twice or More Daily	0.0157					
Adjusted R^2	0.74	0.79	0.92	0.89	0.84	0.81

Notes:
Ln – Natural Logarithm
MFG – Manufacturing
Info. – Information

Table 4.2 Estimation results for multifactor productivity regressions

Variable	Management companies enterprises	Administration and waste management	Art, entertainment, and Recreation	Accommodation and food service
Ln Regional Population (market size)	0.0185	0.0004	0.0113	0.0529
Ln Number of Airlines				
Ln Domestic Non-stop Departures		0.0104		0.0001
Ln Airline Hubs Served – Domestic	0.0106		0.0093	
Ln Domestic Non-stop Destinations	0.0321		0.0132	0.0229
Ln Two or More Daily Non-stop Domestic Flights				
Ln Five or More Daily Non-stop Domestic Flights			0.0197	
Ln International Non-stop Departures	0.0091	0.0211		
Ln International Non-stop Destinations	0.0227	0.0877		
Ln Per cent of the World GDP Served Non-stop	0.0203	0.0472		
Ln Per cent of the World GDP Served Daily			0.0399	0.0222
Ln Per cent of the World GDP Served Twice or More Daily	0.0779			
Adjusted R^2	0.85	0.71	0.64	0.74

Entertainment, and Recreation sectors, while the number of airlines affects productivity for only two sectors: Manufacturing and Wholesale Trade.

In all cases the estimated coefficients for the regional population are positive and generally significant indicating that the size of the market has an impact on multifactor productivity. The coefficients for the dummy year variables are positive except in two cases (the values for which are not statistically significant) and generally significant. The values for 2010 are not always larger than for 2000 and 2005 showing that productivity growth has varied significantly across industries as well as over time.

The coefficients can be interpreted as elasticities As an example, the results for the Manufacturing sector show that a 1 per cent increase in the number of airlines serving a region would lead to a 0.044 per cent increase in MFP, while a 1 per cent increase in the number of domestic non-stop flight departures would increase MFP by 0.024 per cent and a 1 per cent increase in the number of non-stop domestic and international destinations served would increase MFP by 0.082 per cent (0.034 per cent for domestic destinations plus 0.048 per cent for international destinations). These results assume that the air service variables are continuous (or have large enough values to be effectively continuous), so it is meaningful to assume a 1 per cent increase. Of course, in practice some variables, such as the number of airlines or the number of airline hubs served, generally have relatively small values and can only be increased in discrete increments.

Table 4.3 and Table 4.4 illustrate how the change in economic distance or access can be used to measure the impact on economic output; measured by the change in value added, for the year 2010. The values contained in Table 4.3 and Table 4.4 are for the impact on only the 11 industries contained in the data set and for only the 20 regions considered in the analysis and for the 2010 base year. The results have not been scaled to reflect the impact on the entire US economy. The values in each row for each of the industries were changed by 1 per cent (in the case of number of airlines variable it was an integer value) from their mean value, holding the economic variables included in the regression at their mean value. The values in each cell in Columns 2–6 of Table 4.3 and 1–6 of Table 4.4 illustrate the impact on the respective industry for a 1 per cent change in the value of the respective variable. The first column (Output over 20 regions) provides a measure of the change in aggregate value-added output if each aviation connectivity variable were to change by 1 per cent times the mean value of the variable. The changes for each connectivity variable are summed to yield the values in Column 1.

These results reveal which connectivity/access measures appear to have the strongest effect on economic output for different industries. The number of airlines is ranked relatively low on average across industries in terms of the effect on productivity based on the average elasticity values, but this measure has a fairly strong effect on the output of the manufacturing sector, which forms a large proportion of total GDP, accounting for the third largest increase in value added for this sector ($157 million) of all the air service measures, as shown in the row for this sector. Similarly, the number of domestic airline hubs served non-stop, strongly affects the finance and insurance sector, accounting for the highest amount of value added for this sector ($226 million) of all the air service measures.

Conclusions

Wider economic benefits are distinct from what are called catalytic effects. The latter imply relationships that have no theoretical foundation nor empirical support and are generally identified in an economic impact framework which itself does not measure net welfare changes. WEBs are [positive] externalities that increase social value and are not internalised in output or factor prices. The WEB literature is an outgrowth of the research investigating the contribution

Table 4.3 Impact of changes in different connectivity measures on industry output (2010 $M)

Industry	Output over 20 regions ($Million)	Number of airlines	Domestic non-stop departures	Domestic airline hubs served non-stop	Domestic non-stop destinations	Domestic destinations with two or more daily non-stop flights
Manufacturing	$358.86	$157.54	$85.05		$123.45	$355.63
Wholesale Trade	$199.96	$42.99	$51.39		$30.39	
Information	$158.16			$23.88		$19.14
Finance and Insurance	$315.88		$151.30	$226.17		$98.55
Real Estate and Rental and Leasing	$444.51		$94.68		$176.47	$180.47
Professional, Scientific, and Technical Services	$311.42		$56.68	$112.42		
Management of Companies and Enterprises	$80.04			$8.48	$25.69	
Administration and Support and Waste Management Services	$108.78		$11.31		$32.74	
Arts, Entertainment, and Recreation	$34.21			$3.18	$4.45	
Accommodation and Food Services	$87.11		$0.09		$19.95	
Other**	$734.24		$2.94		$272.40	
Total	$2,833.17	$200.53	$453.44	$374.14	$685.55	$653.79

Source: Data from Moody's Analytics, Inc.

Note: See Appendix B for complete listed of industries.

Table 4.4 Impact of changes in different connectivity measures on industry output (2010 $M)

Industry	Domestic destinations with five or more daily non-stop flights	International non-stop departures	International non-stop destinations	Per cent of the world GDP served non-stop	Per cent of the world GDP served daily	Per cent of the world GDP served twice or more daily
Manufacturing						
Wholesale Trade	$63.59		$171.89			$56.34
Information		$38.59	$38.19		$6.40	
Finance and Insurance		$41.70	$22.77		$40.65	
Real Estate and Rental and Leasing	$48.90				$33.80	
Professional, Scientific, and Technical Services		$81.59	$236.48		$152.91	
Management of Companies and Enterprises		$7.28	$18.17	$16.25		$14.33
Administration and Support and Waste Management Services		$22.95	$95.40	$51.34		
Arts, Entertainment, and Recreation	$6.74				$13.65	
Accommodation and Food Services					$19.34	
Other			$99.86		$94.72	
Total	$119.22	$192.11	$682.77	$67.59	$361.46	$70.67

of public capital to productivity and economic growth which began in the early 1990s as discussed in the Introduction.

WEBs will enhance household utility, firm profitability, and macroeconomic (government) factors and do not get counted in the standard welfare measures of consumer and producer surplus. WEBs are generally manifest as productivity improvements or increases in household access to goods or improvements in quality of goods and services.

WEBs have been most often associated with evaluating investments in infrastructure which can serve to increase access to markets, or economic density (Venables, 2016). In a private setting WEBs may serve as an indicator of under-investment since the private investor cannot reap the rewards. In a public setting WEBs may be important to make the case for and achieving, with a given probability, a particular net benefit.

The empirical component of this chapter examined how different types of air service affect the MFP of a range of different industries. We were interested in how both market size and reduced access cost might have influenced different industries. We found the impact of market size as measured by the elasticity MFP with respect to market size had a mean of 0.015 across industries but a coefficient of variation of 1.35 indicating a large amount of dispersion about the mean; market size did not matter at all for Administration and waste management while it was key for the Accommodation and Food Industry. On the other hand, we found different means of reducing access costs were more or less important across industries. The most important factor on average was domestic destinations with two or more services with an average elasticity of 0.09 and second was international non-stop destinations with an elasticity of 0.038. After this, four factors had average elasticities of 0.28 and another group had elasticities of 0.18. Thus, productivity in a given industry was affected differently by different access costs changes and the same access cost had a different impact across industries. The coefficient of variation across the differing access cost strategies varied from 0.41 to 0.95 with some impacts clearly showing significant variation across industries while others show substantially less.

The value in the empirical example is that it distinguishes the importance of scale versus lowering the cost of distance in affecting productivity It may also indicate where WEBs might be more likely to occur or be more or less important. If the coefficient of variation is small meaning little variation of the elasticity, this stability may mean few if any WEBs because the market will be stable and capitalise impacts. On the other hand, a high coefficient may mean there is more likely to be WEBs since with the variability around markets they may not internalise all the available benefits since the same strategy will vary across industries and different strategies will vary within the same industry.

Notes

1 In terms of the air mode, such an adjacent jurisdiction may be in another country.
2 The ideas developed here are a generalization of Venables (2016) discussion Figure 1.

3 The problems with CGE are, of course, that you get a massive black box calculator that nobody can verify, and, realistically all of this is built on heroic assumptions about the whole economy in order to assess the impact of changing one small bit of it. Our method was always to take a rule of thumb to this – looking at the potential impact of reduced generalized travel costs in business travel, the role business travel plays in facilitating trade and FDI, and then the impact of greater economic openness on productivity.

4 See Appendix A for a complete listing of metropolitan areas and airports included in the data set.

5 See Appendix B for complete listed of industries.

References

Airports Commission (2015), Economy: Wider Economic Impacts Assessment (available at www.gov.uk/government/organisations/airports-commission)

Arnaud, B., J. Dupont, S-H. Koh, and P. Schreyer (2011), *Measuring Multi-Factor Productivity by Industry: Methodology and First Results from the OECD Productivity Database*, Organization for Economic Cooperation and Development (OECD), Paris.

Aschauer, D.A. (1989), Is Public Expenditure Productive? *Journal of Monetary Economics* 23, 177–200.

Burghouwt, Guillaume (2017), *Influencing Air Connectivity Outcomes* (Discussion Paper No. 2017–24, International Transport Forum, OECD).

Burghouwt, Guillaume and Renato Redondi (2013), Connectivity in Air Transport Networks: An Assessment of Models and Applications, *Journal of Transport Economics & Policy* 47(1), 35–53

Cohen, J.P. and C.J. Morrison Paul (2004), Public Infrastructure Investment, Interstate Spatial Spillovers, and Manufacturing Costs, *Review of Economics and Statistics* 86, 551–560.

Cooper, A. and Phil Smith (2005), *The Economic Catalytic Effects of Air Transport in Europe*, EEC/SEE/2005/004, Eurocontrol Experimental Centre, Brussels.

Department of Transport (UK), Addendum to the Updated Appraisal Report: Airport Capacity in the South East-Moving Britain Ahead (June 2018) at www.gov.uk/government/publications/airport-expansion-updated-cost-and-benefits-appraisal

Eberts, R.W. (1986), Estimating the Contribution of Urban Public Infrastructure to Regional Growth, Federal Reserve Bank of Cleveland Working Paper No. 8610.

Fernald, John G. (1999), Roads to Prosperity? Assessing the Link between public Capital and Productivity, *American Economic Review*, 89, 3 (June), 619–638.

Forsyth, Peter and Hans Niemeier, *Wider Economic Benefits or Catalytic Effects of Air Transport: How to Asses Airport Investments?* Paper presented at the Technical University of Berlin, June 2–3, 2016.

Forsyth, Peter, Hans-Martin Niemeier, and Eric Tchouamou Njoya (2019), Economic Evaluation of Investments in Airports: Old and New Approaches (mimeo Monash University

Garrison, Williamson, David Gillen and Chris Wiliges (2003), On the Processes Generating Impacts from Transportation Improvements. In *The Economics of Disappearing Distance*, edited by Ake. E. Anderson, W.P. Anderson, and B. Johansson. Farnham: Ashgate, Chapter 12

Gillen, David (1997), Evaluating Economic Benefits of the Transportation System. Transportation and the Economy, Public & Research Symposium Series, Public Policy Program, UCLA, Lake Arrowhead, California, December 7–9.

Gillen, David. (2000), Public Capital, Productivity and the Linkages to the Economy: Transportation Infrastructure. In *Public Capital in Canada*, edited by John Richards and H. Vining. C.D. Howe Institute.

Gillen, David (2019), *Airport Infrastructure, Network Air Services and the Economic Benefits of Air Transport*. Paper presented at the American Economics Association Annual Meeting, Atlanta, Georgia, January 2019.

Gillen, David, Elva Chang, and Doug Johnson (2004), Productivity Benefits and Cost Efficiencies from ITS Applications to Public Transit: The Case of AVL, *Research in Transportation Economics*, 8, 549–567.

Gillen, David, Geoff Gosling, and Steven Landau (2015), Measuring the Relationship Between Airline Network Connectivity and Productivity, *Transportation Research Record (TRR), Journal of the Transportation Research Board* 250, 66–75.

Glaeser, E.L., (2011), *The Triumph of the City*, New York: Penguin.

Glaeser, E.L. and J. D. Gottlieb (2009), The Wealth of Cities: Agglomeration Economies and Spatial Equilibrium in the United States. *Journal of Economic Literature* 47(4), 983–1028.

Graham, D. (2007), *Agglomeration Economies and Transportation Investment*, Discussion Paper No. 2007–11, OECD-International Transport Forum, Paris, December.

Gramlich, E.M. (1994), Infrastructure Investment: A Review Essay. *Journal of Economic Literature* 32, 1176–1196

Hulten, C.R. and R.M. Schwab (1991), Is There Too Little Public Capital?, American Enterprise Institute Conference on Infrastructure Needs.

Hulten, C.R. (1996), Infrastructure Capital and Economic Growth, How Well You Use It May Be More Important Than How Much You Have, NBER Working Paper No. 58.

Hulten, C.R. (2001), Total Factor Productivity: A Short Biography. In *New Developments in Productivity Analysis*, edited by C.R. Hulten, E.R. Dean, and M.J. Harper. Chicago: University of Chicago Press for the National Bureau of Economic Research.

InterVISTAS Consulting, Inc. (2015), *Economic Impact of European Airports: A Critical Catalyst to Economic Growth*, Report prepared for ACI Europe (January).

Keeler, T. and J. Ying (1988), Measuring the Benefits of Large Public Investments: The Case of the US Federal-Aid Highway System. *Journal of Public Economics* 36, 69–85.

Kincaid, Ian and Michael Tretheway (2016), Economic Impact of Aviation Liberalization. In *Liberalization in Aviation: Competition, Cooperation and Public* Policy, edited by Hartmut Wolf, Peter Forsyth, David Gillen, Kai Huschelrath and Hans-Martin Niemeier. Abingdon: Taylor and Francis, Chapter 19.

Mackie, P., D. Graham, and J. Laird (2011), The Direct and Wider Impacts of Transport Projects: A Review. In *A Handbook of Transport Economics*, edited by A.R. De Palma, Lindsey, E. Quinet, and R. Vickerman . Cheltenham: Edward Elgar.

Melo P.C., D.J. Graham, and R. Brage-Ardao (2013), The Productivity of Transport Infrastructure Investment: A Meta-Analysis of Empirical Evidence. *Regional Science and Urban Economics*, 43, 695–706.

Munnell, A.H. (1990), How Does Public Infrastructure Affect Regional Economic Performance? *New England Economic Review* (September/October), 11–32.

Nadiri, M. Ishaq and Theofanis Mamuneas (1996), *Contributions of Highway Capital to Industry and National Productivity Growth*, September 1996, Final Report, FHWA Work Order BAT-94-008.

OECD (2016), *Quantifying the Socio-Economic Benefits of Transport,* International Transport Forum Roundtable Summary and Conclusions Report (April 2016), Discussion Paper 2016-06

Oum, Tae, Xiaowen Fu, and Anming Zhang (2010), Air Transport Liberalization and its Impact on Airline Competition and Air Passenger Traffic. *Transportation Journal* 49(4), 371–390.

Pritchett, L. (1996), Mind Your P's and Q's: The Cost of Public Investment is Not the Value of Public Capital, World Bank Policy Research Paper No. 1660.

Romp, Ward and Jakob de Haan (2007), Public Capital and Economic growth: A Critical Survey, *Perspektiven der Wirtschaftspolitik* 8 (Special Issue), 6–52.

Rosenthal, S.S. and W.C. Strange (2004), Evidence on the Nature and Sources of Agglomeration Economies, In *Handbook of Regional and Urban Economics,* vol 4., edited by J.V. Henderson and J.F. Thisse. Amsterdam: Elsevier, pp. 2119–2171.

Shirley, C., and C. Winston (2004), Firm Inventory Behaviour and Returns from Highway Infrastructure Investment. *Journal of Urban Economics* 55, 398–415.

Sturm, J.E., G.H. Kuper, and J. de Haan (1998), Modelling Government Investment and Economic Growth on a Macro Level: A Review. In *Market Behaviour and Macroeconomic Modelling,* edited by S. Brakman, H. van Ees, and S.K. Kuipers. London: Macmillan.

Venables, A.J. (2016), *Incorporating the Wider Economic Impacts within Benefit-Cost Appraisal,* Discussion Paper 2016-05, International Transport Forum OECD.

Appendix A   Metropolitan regions and airports included in Data

Code	Airport/region	Multi-airport regions
SF Bay	San Francisco Bay Area	SFO, OAK, SJC
Chicago	Chicago metropolitan region	ORD, MDW
ATL	Hartsfield–Jackson Atlanta International Airport	
CVG	Cincinnati/Northern Kentucky International Airport	
STL	Lambert-St. Louis International Airport	
PIT	Pittsburgh International Airport	
RDU	Raleigh-Durham International Airport	
DEN	Denver International Airport	
Phoenix	Phoenix metropolitan region	PHX, AZA
SLC	Salt Lake City International Airport	
Boston	Boston metropolitan region	BOS, MHT, PVD
PHL	Philadelphia International Airport	
DTW	Detroit Metropolitan Wayne County Airport	
SAN	San Diego International Airport	
PDX	Portland International Airport	
TPA	Tampa International Airport	
MCI	Kansas City International Airport	
TUL	Tulsa International Airport	
SAT	San Antonio International Airport	
BNA	Nashville International Airport	

	Airports in the Four Multi-Airport Regions	
SFO	San Francisco International Airport	
OAK	Oakland International Airport	

Appendix A Cont.

Code	Airport/region	Multi-airport regions
SJC	Mineta San Jose International Airport	
ORD	Chicago O'Hare International Airport	
MDW	Chicago Midway Airport	
PHX	Phoenix Sky Harbour International Airport	
AZA	Phoenix-Mesa Gateway Airport	
BOS	Boston Logan International Airport	
PVD	Theodore Francis Green State Airport (Providence)	
MHT	Manchester–Boston Regional Airport	

Appendix B Industry sectors included in the analysis

NAICS code	Sector	Specific sector model	"Other" sector model
11	Agriculture, Forestry, Fishing and Hunting		11
21	Mining, Quarrying, and Oil and Gas Extraction		11
22	Utilities		11
31–33	Manufacturing	1	
42	Wholesale Trade	2	
44–45	Retail Trade		11
48–49	Transportation and Warehousing		11
51	Information	3	
52	Finance and Insurance	4	
53	Real Estate and Renting and Leasing	5	
54	Professional, Scientific, and Technical Services	6	
55	Management of Companies and Enterprises	7	
56	Administrative and Support and Waste Management and Remediation Services	8	
61	Educational Services		11
62	Health Care and Social Assistance		11
71	Arts, Entertainments, and Recreation	9	
72	Accommodation and Food Services	10	
81	Other Services (except Public Administration)		11
92	Public Administration		11

Appendix C Variable names, descriptions, and definitions

Variables

Number of Airlines
Flights by Dominant Carrier
Domestic Non-stop Departures
Transborder Non-stop Departures
International Non-stop Departures

Airline Hub Served – Domestic
Domestic Non-stop Destinations
Transborder Non-stop Destinations
International Non-stop Destinations
Percent of World GDP by Non-stop Flights
Percent of World GDP by At Least Daily
Percent of World GDP by Two or More Daily
Enplaned Domestic
Enplaned Transborder
Enplaned International
Deplaned Domestic
Deplaned Transborder
Deplaned International
International Hub At Least Daily
Three or More Daily Non-stops
Total Passengers Domestic
Total Passengers Transborder
Total Passengers International
Two of More Daily Non-stop Domestic
Five or More Daily Bon-stop Domestic

Variable	Description	Units
City	20 Cities including Cincinnati, St. Louis, Pittsburgh, Raleigh, Denver, Phoenix, Salt Lake City, Boston, Philadelphia, Detroit, San Diego, Portland, Tampa, Kansas City, Tulsa, San Antonio, and Nashville	
Year	1995, 2000, 2005, 2010	
SMSA Employment	SMSA Employment, thousand; seasonally adjusted by NAICS	000s
SMSA Wage	SMSA Wage and salary disbursements, million $ (nominal) by NAICS	Million$-nominal
SMSA Gross Product	SMSA Gross Product, million $ (nominal) by NAICS	Million$-nominal
NAICS	NAICS codes (31–33, 42, 51, 52, 53, 54, 55, 56, 71, 72 and other)	
SMSA Population	SMSA Population of each city (number of people) (not by NAICS)	Number
National Output ($s)	National value of production, billions of current dollars by NAICS	Billion$s Nominal
National MFP Index	National MFP Index by NAICS	
National Output/ Hour Index	National Labour Productivity	
CPI	CPI by city and year	
SMSA Real Gross Product	SMSA Real Gross Product (calculated as (SMSA Gross Product*1000000)/(CPI/ 100)), in $ (real)	$ (real)

Variable	Description	Units
SMSA Labour Productivity	SMSA Labour Productivity (calculated as ((SMSA Gross Product*1000000)/(CPI/100))/(SMSA Employment*1000))	$ (real)
SMSA Labour Productivity Index	SMSA Labour Productivity Index (calculated as SMSA Labour Productivity/SMSA Labour Productivity at base year 2005*100)	$ (real)
SMSA MFP Index	SMSA MFP Index (calculated as SMSA Labour Productivity Index/ National Output per Hour Index* National MFP Index)	

5 The application of an input–output approach to measuring the impact of air transport on the economy

A critical review

Sonia Huderek-Glapska

Introduction

The input-output model is a quantitative economic technique developed in the 1930s and 1940s, and is used to measure the quantity of input factors required to produce a given set of outputs. Through the use of this tool, one can calculate the response of the economy to changes caused by the project or policy modification. Input-output analysis is one of the oldest and most popular methods for measuring the effects of air transport services on regional and national economies. Up to now almost all hub airports and numerous of regional airports have conducted airport economic impact studies through the application of the input-output approach; mainly in the United States and Europe but also in Asia, Africa, the Middle East, and South America. Such economic impact studies have spread around the world mainly due to the relatively simplicity of their application and the relative low cost of conducting an analysis. In almost all studies, the estimation results for the income and employment effects that are generated by air transport activities are found to be significant and support the policy of developing air transport infrastructure. The size of airport production, expressed in the number of aircraft operations and the number of passengers and goods handled, is found to be positively correlated with the level of economic impact. However, there are reports in the literature about the inappropriate use of the input-output method and the misinterpretation of analysis results.

The aim of this chapter is to critically review the input-output method as a tool in the process of measuring the relationship between air transport and the economy; to discuss the factors that affect this relationship, such as the level of regional development and the maturity of the air transport market, and to call for a more holistic approach.

Air transport and regional development

Transport infrastructure creates conditions for the proper development of the entire economy and stimulates its development. The improvement of transport infrastructure leads, among other things, to higher productivity of private production factors and changes in their location. Conversely, the lack of appropriate transport infrastructure acts as an obstacle to the development of the economy, and may even constitute a barrier to growth.

Research on the relationship between transport infrastructure and economic development has a long tradition, but only from the mid-1980s attempts were made to more accurately recognise and verify the effects created by the construction and modernisation of transport infrastructure and its impact on the surrounding area. Throughout the evolution of the new theory of growth, which emphasised endogenous growth factors, econometric estimates of public capital productivity began to appear in the literature as the main methods of studying the relationship between infrastructure and regional development. At that time, the studies of Heggie (1972), Biehl (1986), Nijkamp (1986), Aschauer (1989), Rietveld (1989), and Munnel (1992) emerged. The results of the studies indicated a positive relationship between infrastructure expenditure and the level of growth and productivity of private capital and labour. The elasticity of the productivity of private capital in respect to public capital, which included transport infrastructure, among other things, varied between 0.15 and 1.16. Nevertheless, according to Romp and De Haan (2007), the marginal productivity of each additional infrastructure investment can decrease, and the problem arises in modelling the relationship between the direction of causality that occurs between transport infrastructure and economic growth. The reason is that the growth of economic activities and increasing incomes lead to an increase in demand for transport services. More intensive use of communication networks can be an impulse for the undertaking of new infrastructure investments that will be aimed at meeting growing transport needs. Thus, the increase in the demand for infrastructure services has an impact on the size of infrastructure investments.

From a transport policy point of view, questions about the net effect of infrastructure investments and the optimal level of equipping a given area with infrastructure facilities seem to be relevant. Much work on the effects of transportation projects focuses on the impact of new public infrastructure investments on economic growth, neglecting the effects of public expenditure on the maintenance of existing infrastructure facilities. New investment projects are more politically attractive and more spectacular than expenditure on infrastructure maintenance. Nevertheless, neglecting existing infrastructure objects and promoting new infrastructure investments can reduce the productive capacity of the economy. Research by Kalaitzidakis and Kalyvitis (2005) indicate that relocating part of the funds for investment expenditures, primarily allocated for new infrastructure projects, to the maintenance of existing infrastructure facilities may bring positive effects and contribute to economic growth.

Since the main source of finance for public infrastructure investments are taxes, promoting the policy of using public investments to stimulate regional development has its natural limitations. Affluent regions that pay high taxes automatically have more opportunities to finance infrastructure investments, while regions with low income and thus with limited funds for investments have difficulties in achieving a level of development similar to affluent regions. Thus, the problem of the relationships between air transport infrastructure and economic development has gained particular importance in making decisions regarding the implementation of projects in European Union countries. Actions in the field of infrastructure investments are one of the most important tools in the community's regional development policy. The main objective of the development of transport infrastructure is to promote social and economic cohesion, increase the accessibility of peripheral regions, and, at the same time, improve development opportunities for less developed areas.

According to Rietveld and Bruinsma (1998), the basic classification of transport infrastructure effects is a division into the effects resulting from the supply of infrastructure and those resulting from the use of infrastructure facilities. At the same time, these effects are interrelated and in practice it is difficult to distinguish which changes in the economy are the result of supply and which changes are the result of the use of infrastructure. The first effects are related to investments in transport infrastructure and appear in the phase of investment implementation (*construction effects*). They mainly stimulate the demand for labour and capital and can usually be investigated directly. The main changes in economic activities due to transport infrastructure investments occur over a long period and are related to the operation and maintenance of the infrastructure. These effects appear on the supply side (*programme effects*) of the economy and are much more challenging to identify and measure. While the demand effects are related to the functioning of a given infrastructure object, the supply effects refer mainly to the changes in the mobility of people, goods, and capital, facilitated by the presence of an infrastructure object. This is due to the fact that infrastructure improvements increase regional accessibility, lead to savings in time and costs of transport, as well as stimulate the flow of passengers, goods, and capital. This, in turn, affects the performance of companies and households located in the areas under the influence of transport infrastructure. In addition, due to growth in regional accessibility, the investment attractiveness and competitiveness of a given region increases.

An airport is a specific example of transport infrastructure, which generates numerous effects and direct benefits to users, mainly by shortening travel time and reducing travel costs. Additionally, the construction and operation of transport infrastructure create indirect effects by stimulating, among other things, income and employment in the surrounding area. The demand effects (increases in employment and income) related to the investment in airport infrastructure will occur regardless of the usage of this new infrastructure. However, airport infrastructure investments will not contribute to economic growth and development in the long term if the airport is not operating. Without airlines, there is no airport. The effects created by an airport are part of the overall impact generated by the aviation industry, which is defined as those activities that are directly dependent on transporting people and goods by air; covering primarily airport and airline operations but also air traffic control, aircraft maintenance, ground handling services, and other things. Additionally, there are numerous activities that support airport operations and air transport services. Not all of these activities necessarily take place at an airport or in the surrounding area; however, they contribute to the overall socio-economic impact of the air transport sector. Therefore, there is a need to investigate the impact of the whole air transport sector on economic development.

The multifaceted criteria for the influence of air transport on the economy are reflected in the diversity of methods used to measure these effects. In the literature, there are many theoretical approaches and empirical applications that have been applied for estimating the economic impact of proposed transportation projects. Among the variety of methods, the most widely applied is an economic impact analysis based on the input-output model.

Economic evaluation of air transport infrastructure

The first airport economic impact studies (EIS) probably occurred in the late 1970s in the United States, where the world's most extensive airport system was and where there was a large federal investment in it (Niemeier 2001; Graham 2013). It was also a time when regional economic impact analyses were used as a tool in estimating the regional impacts of policies, programmes, and projects (Drake 1976). The emergence of input-output models that examined the flow of capital among product suppliers and buyers in the industry was enabled by new technological possibilities. In the 1970s and 1980s computer simulation models facilitated the evaluation and forecast of the regional economic consequences of transportation projects (Weisbrod 2006). At the beginning of the 1980s, a regional input-output modelling system (RIMS II) was constructed, which became the basis for estimations of the economic effects of infrastructure projects.

Butler and Kiernan in their reports 'Measuring the Regional Economic Significance of Airports' (1986) and the updated version 'Estimating the regional economic significance of airports' (1992) under the auspices of the Federal Aviation Administration, established the guidelines for modelling the economic significance of an airport. These works were prepared in response to the requests from the public airport community to justify the importance of airport operations in the competition for funds with other governmental activities. The reports were designed to support the decision to maintain and develop the infrastructure of public airports and/or balance the negative effects resulting from airport operation, namely aircraft noise and air pollution. The assumptions underlying the guidelines were to propose an approach to the measurement of the economic significance of airports that would not be time and cost intensive, and that the results of the analysis could be easily understood by a wide audience in order to gain public support.

Butler and Kiernan (1992) recognise two main indicators as evidence of an airport's importance, precisely transportation benefits and economic impact. Transportation benefits result directly from the service that a local airport makes available to the inhabitants and organisations in its surrounding area.

These benefits include time and cost savings and other advantages such as improvements in transportation safety. Airport economic impact is defined as regional economic activity, the employment as well as the consumption of goods and services that can be attributed, directly and indirectly, to the operation of a local airport.

At the same time, the European branch of the Airports Council International made a recommendation for conducting airport impact studies, based on the recognition of the direct and indirect, as well as induced, tangible, and intangible catalytic effects of airport operations. The study called 'Airports – Partners in Vital Economies' (ACI Europe, 1992) stated that airports are important regional assets offering considerable economic and social benefits to their surrounding areas. The results of economic impact analyses undertaken by the airports themselves and by ACI Europe have been presented in more in-depth studies (ACI Europe 1998, 2000, 2004). About 60 small and large airports in Europe, accounting for more than 60% of the workload units at European airports, conducted economic impact analyses on the basis of the methodology and definitions from the ACI Europe reports. In European studies (ACI Europe 1992, 1998, 2000, 2004) and later industrial reports (AOA 2005; ATAG 2005; OEF 2006; ATAG 2008), as well as in US studies (Butler and Kiernan 1986, 1992; TRB 2008; FAA 2016; The Industry High Level Group 2017), the applied methodology considers the overall economic impact of airports as the sum of direct, indirect, and induced impacts. Up to now, almost all hub airports and numerous regional airports have conducted airport impact studies; mainly in the United States and in Europe, but also in Africa (Luke and Walters 2010), the Middle East, South America and Asia (Industry High Level Group, 2017).

Economic impact studies are conducted at various spatial levels and include an analysis of the airport's effects on the local (Kazda et al. 2017), regional (L'Envoi Spécial 2002), national (Gillingwater et al 2009), and international (Button and Taylor 2000) economy. Estimations of aviation's contribution to regional development have been provided by numerous of institutions, such as universities and research centres (Batey et al. 1993; Gillen and Hinsch 2001; Hakfoort 2001; Heuer et al. 2005; Dusek and Lukovic 2011), consultancy agencies (OEF 1999, 2006; SQW 2008), national government bodies (TRB 2008; FAA 2016), as well as airport operators and owners (Aéroport Nantes Atlantique 2005).

A positive correlation is observed between the need to justify airport expansion and the number of airport impact studies (Forsyth and Niemeier 2012; Huderek-Glapska et al. 2015). In particular, the number of airport impact analyses coincides with the period of the air transport market liberalisation (Figure 5.1). This is mainly because increasing air traffic, being a consequence of opening up the aviation market, requires infrastructure improvements leading to airport expansion – which may cause disagreements with the local community and environmentalists. The first wave of airport economic impact studies occurred in the 1980s in the United States, when the liberalisation of air transport had increased air traffic and new airport capacity was needed (Graham

2013). The second wave of airport impact studies was in Europe in the 1990s, after gradual market deregulation and congestion problems at main airports. The input-output approach was used among others in the mediation process for developing the infrastructure of Frankfurt airport (Hujer and Kokot 2001). Similarly, in the first decade of the twenty-first century, regional airports in Europe experienced the need to extend their capacity due to the extensive activity of low-cost carriers (Forsyth and Niemeier 2012). In 2011, and then updated in 2017, Oxford Economics, together with IATA and ACI, prepared more than 60 country reports worldwide on the economic benefits from air transport (IATA and OE 2017). The estimation of aviation benefits was based on the calculation of added value and jobs, supported by an economic activity called in the report's 'aviation economic footprint', through the use of the input-output model approach. In 2008 the US Transportation Research Board in the Synthesis Airport Economic Impact Methods and Models considered that the traditional method used in airport economic impact studies which focuses on applying multipliers to airport jobs and visitor spending might be inadequate today (TRB 2008). However, the 2016 Federal Aviation Administration study estimated the economic impact of civil aviation in the United States through the use of a standard input-output analysis (RIMS II) (FAA 2016).

The aim of this chapter is to present and critically evaluate input-output analysis as a method for conducting an economic impact analysis of the aviation sector. The state of knowledge on the relationship between air transport and regional development is presented in the Introduction. In the second section, the input-output analysis is described as a tool in the measurement of the socio-economic effects of an airport, and the concept of airport economic impact analyses is presented. Next, based on the review of the scientific literature and industrial reports, numerous examples of the application of input-output

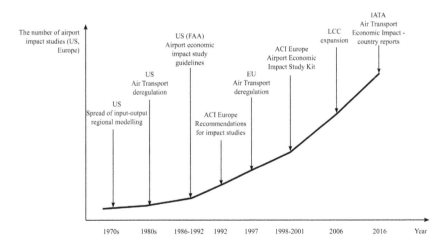

Figure 5.1 The expansion of airport impact analyses

analyses are demonstrated. In the third section, the limitations of input-output analysis are considered. The factors affecting the relationship between the air transport sector and the economy, as well as concluding remarks on input-output analyses and recommendations for a more holistic approach, are given at the end.

Input–output model as a tool in the measurement of the socio–economic effects of an airport

In the literature there are a variety of methods used to estimate the socio-economic impact of airport construction and operation. The three main types of approaches (Pfähler ed. 2001; TRB 2008) are input-output models (I-O), cost-benefit analyses (CBA) and methods measuring catalytic effects. Other methods and models applied to measure the effects created by the development and use of airport infrastructure include econometric analyses with a production function (Allroggen and Malina 2010), regression models (Benell and Prentice 1993), and general equilibrium models (Madden 2004).

Among the methods listed above, the most widespread analysis is the input-output model for which detailed guidelines in its application to the process of measuring the economic impact of airports have been developed both in the United States and in Europe. The input-output method is most often used by both airport operators and government institutions preparing reports on the impact of aviation on the economy.

Input–output approach

An input-output model is a way of describing the economic relationship between producers and suppliers in an economy. This is a quantitative economic technique developed in the 1930s and 1940s and is used to measure the number of input factors required to produce a given set of outputs. The fundamentals of the input-output method were created by Leontief (1936, 1986) and were a simplified version of the classical theory of general equilibrium. The economy is presented as a system of interconnected branches and the flow of goods between them connects all sectors of the economy. On the one hand, this flow presents the successive stages of production; on the other, generated values. Therefore, the data provided by the balance of inter-branch flows is useful for assessing changes taking place in the economy. Through the use of an input-output model one can calculate the response of the economy to changes caused by a project or policy changes.

An input-output model is constructed from the observed data for a particular economic area – a country, a region, or even a complex company (Miller and Blair 2009). The starting point in an input-output analysis is the construction of the input-output table, in which the production expenditures for a given sector and the results achieved from such production are expressed in monetary values. The input-output table shows how the output of each industry is distributed among other industries and sectors of the economy. The values in the columns represent purchases made from other sectors, and the values in the rows illustrate the values of goods and services sold to other sectors.

Assume there is a system (economy) with n-sectors, and each sector produces x_i units of a single, homogeneous good. Assume that the *jth* sector, in order to produce one unit of a particular good, must use X_{ij} units of good from sector i. Each sector sells some of its output to other sectors, called intermediate output, and sells some of its output to final consumers (final demand). The relationships between the various sectors of the economy can be represented by the matrix:

$$X_{11} + X_{12} .... + X_{1n} + Y_1 = X_1$$

$$X_{i1} + X_{ij} .... + X_{in} + Y_i = X_i \tag{5.1}$$

where the total output of branch (i), marked as X_i, is the sum of the intermediate production X_{ij} of branch (i) and used by industry (j), and the final demand Y_i. If we incorporate a_{ij} as the input-output coefficients which express the intermediate requirements from sector i per unit of output of sector j, then the matrix can be written:

$$a_{11}X_1 + a_{12}X_2 .... + a_{1n}X_n + Y_1 = X_1 \tag{5.2}$$

The input-output model which describes the relationship between global product and final product can be written as a matrix equation:

$$\underline{AX} + \underline{Y} = \underline{X} \tag{5.3}$$

Assuming $(I-A) \neq 0$, the gross output is given by the matrix:

$$\underline{X} = (\underline{I} - \underline{A})^{-1} \star \underline{Y} \tag{5.4}$$

where the element $(I-A)^{-1}$ is called the Leontief-inverse and describes the amount the production units of industry (i) must increase to achieve an increase of one unit in the final product of sector (j) with unchanged final products for the other branches. Hujer and Kokot (2001) argue that in a simple input-output model, all components of the final demand are treated as exogenous. The additional income generated in the production process is partly used to purchase additional goods and services. The increase in the final demand will be higher than the initial increase in income. This effect is sometimes called the induced impact. An extended input-output model aims to capture this additional increase in gross production by treating the consumption expenditures as endogenous. The incorporation of a Keynesian consumption function into the standard extended input-output model was presented in the early work of Miyazawa (1960), Pischner and Staglin (1976), and then Hujer and Kokot

(2001). The explanation of input–output model formulated below is based on the work of Hujer and Kokot (2001).

Extended input-output models, in which the changes in the output ΔX caused by changes in the final demand ΔY can be written as follows:

$$\Delta \underline{X} = (\underline{I} - \underline{A})^{-1} \star \Delta \underline{Y} \tag{5.5}$$

The changes in the final demand ΔY have an impact on the changes in revenue across all sectors of the economy. Assuming that vector b contains the input coefficient for the income generated in each sector of the economy, the element $b_j = W_j/X_j$, where W_j is the income distributed to private households (wages and profits) and X_j is the gross output of sector (j). ΔW_o is the total of the first round income changes across all industries as a result of changes in the final demand ΔY.

$$\Delta \underline{W}_o = \underline{b} \star (\underline{I} - \underline{A})^{-1} \star \Delta \underline{Y}_o \tag{5.6}$$

Indirect income effects of an infrastructure project can be calculated according to equation 5.7.

$$\Delta \underline{X}_{indir} = \{(\underline{I} - \underline{A})^{-1}\} \star \Delta \underline{Y} \tag{5.7}$$

Regarding the relationship to airport operations, the indirect effects can be defined as the additional final demands resulting from the activities of suppliers to enterprises located on-site at an airport. An extended input-output model can capture changes to both income and employment levels. In order to assess the income level ΔW_{indir}, the indirect effect ΔX_{indir} is multiplied by the diagonal matrix $\underline{B}$, which both have the sectoral income coefficients as diagonal elements. Income effects are reflected by the fact that the income shares are taken into account.

$$\Delta \underline{W}_{indirect} = \{\underline{B} \star (\underline{I} - \underline{A})^{-1}\} \star \Delta \underline{Y} \tag{5.8}$$

The indirect employment effects are calculated using a sectoral coefficient of labour $(AK_j) = E_j/X_j$ which is the ratio of the number of employees in sector j to the gross output X_j produced by sector j.

$$\Delta \underline{E}_{indirect} = \underline{AK} \star (\underline{I} - \underline{A})^{-1} \star \Delta \underline{Y} \tag{5.9}$$

Induced effects include the income created by the spending of employees in entities directly and indirectly related to the airport's operation. The induced impacts are a multiplier effect on the sum of direct and indirect impacts. In order to calculate the induced effects of an airport one should determine the consumption function and incorporate it into the input-output model. The matrix multiplier consumption is expressed by a reverse matrix $(\underline{I}-\underline{V})^{-1}$.

The sectoral final demand ΔY_{dir} is the sum of wages and salaries earned by the airport employees and multiplied by the marginal consumption propensity and the sectoral consumption coefficients. The relationships of direct effects and indirect effects to induced effects are represented in equations 5.10 and 5.11, respectively (Hujer and Kokot 2001):

$$\Delta \underline{X}^{dir}{}_{induced} = \{(\underline{I} - \underline{A})^{-1} \star (\underline{I} - \underline{V})^{-1}\} \star \Delta \underline{Y}_{dir} \tag{5.10}$$

$$\Delta \underline{X}^{indir}{}_{induced} = \{(\underline{I} - \underline{A})^{-1} \star [(\underline{I} - \underline{V})^{-1} - I]\} \star \Delta \underline{Y}_{indir} \tag{5.11}$$

Induced effects are calculated using the same interdependencies in the economy that occur in indirect effects. The data on the flow of intermediate goods, which are a direct incentive to the creation of indirect effects, are then used in the evaluation of induced effects. In order to avoid double counting in equation 5.11, indirect effects were excluded from the induced effects (Hujer and Kokot 2001). The problem of double counting has been clearly addressed by Jensen and West (1980).

The overall induced effect is the sum of the partial results:

$$\Delta \underline{X}_{induced} = \Delta \underline{X}^{dir}{}_{induced} + \Delta \underline{X}^{indir}{}_{induced} \tag{5.12}$$

The induced employment (5.13) and income effects (5.14) can be calculated accordingly:

$$\Delta \underline{E}_{induced} = \underline{AK} \star \Delta \underline{X}_{induced} \tag{5.13}$$

$$\Delta \underline{W}_{induced} = \underline{B} \star \Delta \underline{X}_{induced} \tag{5.14}$$

The empirical applications of input-output models led to the estimations of multipliers. The calculation of multipliers is based on the assumptions that income and employment in a sector are linearly dependent on the output (Jensen and West 1980). According to Hujer and Kokot (2001) the employment multiplier (15) can be defined as the additional workers that are being employed in the surrounding area of an airport per worker employed on-site at the airport.

$$m^E = (\text{indirect employement} + \text{induced employment})/\text{direct employment} \tag{5.15}$$

The income multiplier (5.16) gives the additional income that is earned in the surrounding area per unit of income earned by employees on-site at an airport.

$$m^W = (\text{indirect income} + \text{induced income})/\text{direct income} \tag{5.16}$$

The multiplier (M) approach has been extensively used in the economic impact studies of public and private projects, with the intention of reducing the dimensionality of the results (Hujer and Kokot 2001) as well as due to its relative simplicity in calculating the total economic impact. However, there is confusion in the literature about the proper application and understanding of the multiplier approach and its relationship to induced effects. This is the main source of misinterpretations regarding input–output model results and leads to an overestimation of results (so-called double counting). This happens when the multiplier effect is misinterpreted as an induced effect rather than as a total income effect (ΔY^{total}), and as a result, the combined direct and indirect effects ($\Delta Y^{direct+indirect}$) are counted twice (Pfähler 2001).

$$\Delta Y^{total}=M\star \Delta Y^{direct+indirect} \tag{5.17}$$

$$\Delta Y^{induced}= \Delta Y^{total} - \Delta Y^{direct+indirect} \tag{5.18}$$

According to the input–output method, the total economic impact is the sum of direct, indirect and induced effects. Pfähler (2001) argues that in the interpretation of total effects, care must be taken with respect to the persistence of these effects. Income and employment will be stimulated by the project only if the project implies a continuous increase in the initial expenditure level. The construction of a new project will create direct, indirect, and induced effects; however, after the completion of the project, income and employment would return to the previous level.

The definitions of input–output effects are fairly homogenous; however, in some studies these effects are calculated differently. Batey et al. (1993) argue there is a discrepancy in the usage of indirect (second-round effects) and induced effects in the literature.

The aim of the input–output analysis is to provide numerical estimates for short-run, nominal, demand effects from building and/or operating a public expenditure project (Pfähler 2001). The short-term demand effects result from not including productivity, price, factor-reallocation and growth effects in the analysis. Since in a standard static IO-analysis the price effect is excluded, all demand effects are reported in nominal terms, not in real terms.

The indicators that are most often measured through the application of input–output models, as the benefits of project implementation, are income and employment. Earnings and fiscal effects are expressed in monetary terms and flow in the economy being stimulated by changes in the size and structure of production. Employment effects result from changes in physical resources, and technical and technological changes are supposed to be included in the calculation of the employment effect. The results of an input–output analysis refer to a certain period of time; most often one year. The input–output analysis can be conducted ex-ante and ex-post. An ex-ante study gives predictions regarding the effects of investment that have not been completed, and as such, can justify as a proposed project. For this reason, policymakers are usually more interested in ex-ante projects. In some cases, ex-post studies may be used for ex-ante purposes. However, every project has its unique nature; therefore, it is not easy to predict its effects based on past experience (Rietveld and Bruinsma 1998).

Input-output models have a long history of being applied to measure the effect of exogenous injections on regional economies (Battey et al. 1993). Considering the relationship between air transport and the economy, by using Leontief's demand-driven input-output model, one can estimate the degree to which changes in the air transport industry influence changes in the economy.

Airport economic impact model

The idea of an airport economic impact model is the recognition and estimation of direct, indirect, and induced effects resulting from airport operations (Butler and Kiernan 1992; ACI 1998):

- *The direct impact* of airport operations results from the economic activities carried out at the airport by entities directly involved in aviation (airport operators, airlines, ground handling agents, and others) or activities that are an immediate consequence of airport economic activity. This comprises the employment, income/value added, output and tax revenues wholly or largely related to the operation of an airport and generated either on-site or in the surrounding area. The direct impact should represent economic activities that would not have occurred in the absence of an airport.
- *The indirect impact* is the economic effect (employment, income/value added, output, and tax revenues) created by the chain of suppliers of goods and services to direct activities at the airport. These activities include services provided by travel agencies, hotels, and restaurants. Indirect impact originates outside the airport. In the calculation of the indirect impact of an airport, only those effects that result from aviation sector activities should be considered.
- *The induced impact* is the economic effect (employment, income/value added, output and tax revenues) generated by the expenditure of those employed by companies, directly and indirectly, related to airport operations and services. Induced impact is the multiplier effect of the direct and indirect impacts. The selection and application of the proper multiplier should include the structure and characteristic of the local and regional economy. The more economically self-sufficient the region, the higher the multiplier is. This is because in the more economically independent regions the expenditures of those directly and indirectly involved in airport operations keep turning over within the region, creating additional effects with each new round of spending.

An ACI study (1998) recognises the fourth type of airport economic impact, namely the *catalytic impact* which is the productivity growth resulting from airport operation. In some studies the catalytic impact is recognised as wider economic benefits (InterVISTAS 2015).

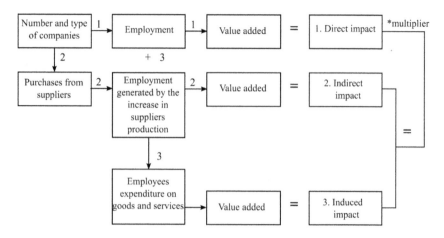

Figure 5.2 Airport economic impact model.

The catalytic impact is also called a *spillover effect* and includes the impact of air transport on the performance of other industries, the effects on consumer welfare due to the increased availability of travel, as well as the impact on the environment (Britton et al. 2005). The spillover effect, like spending of tourists in the country, is a part of tangible effects of airport operation and services. The total economic impact of aviation is the sum of the direct, indirect, induced, and catalytic impacts (Figure 5.2).

The direct impact is usually calculated by the estimation of income and employment effects generated by the airport and aviation related businesses that are located on or near the airport site. These data can be obtained directly from airport operators or an average estimation can be applied. The most often used criterion for estimating the level of employment is passenger throughput. According to ACI study (2004) the average direct employment (on-site) per 1 million handled passengers is 950 workplaces. However, the level of on-site employment may vary at airports due to differences in employment productivity (Figure 5.3). According to Andrew and Bailey (1996), economies of scale apply to labour productivity. The increase in air traffic due to the usage of larger aircraft or the expansion of airport infrastructure may require only a small number of additional staff due to the increase in their productivity. Other factors that affect the number of on-site employees include the aviation industry legal framework impacting, among other things the number of security-related employees, as well as differences in cost levels and the traffic structure at the airport. The number of average direct work places is higher at small airports handling up to 1 million passengers per year. This is due to the fact that small airports are not able to achieve economies of scale and a certain level of employment is necessary for airport operations.

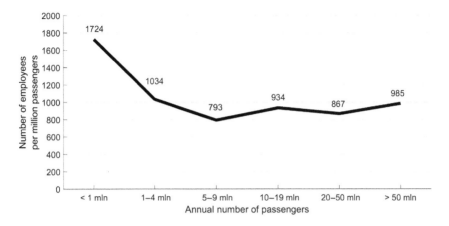

Figure 5.3 Economies of scale in labour productivity – direct employment at the airport.
Source: (ACI Europe and York Consulting 2000).

Within the category of direct employment, there may be some changes in the structure that do not necessarily affect the level of direct employment. Gillen and Hinsch (2001) found that the level of airport labour productivity may increase with the rise in the number of both flights and passengers. This may be explained by a shift from airport employees to contracting services (outsourcing). The offset to demands for a reduction in airport employment is an increasing demand for other categories of labour like concessions (restaurants, shops, car hire), airline services (repair, maintenance, fuel) and others (banks, travel agents, public services).

Direct employment is related to the type of airport. Hub airports, where a feeder carrier has its base, have higher direct employment due to work places generated by the airline's headquarters, including maintenance. At Budapest Airport the number of workers employed by Malev constituted one third of all direct employment in 2009 (Dusek et al. 2011). Therefore, the collapse of Malev significantly reduced the level of direct employment, and Wizz Air did not pick up the slack, mainly due to operating a different business model.

The definitions of direct impact are relatively homogenous among studies; however, the calculations for the employment and income effects differ. According to Statistical Office or industrial classification definitions, air transport covers only the activities of airlines, namely the carriage of cargo and passengers. The activities of airport operators as well as traffic control and ground handling companies are included in the category of other activities supporting air transport. Airlines, airport operations, and air traffic control provide the baseline definitions for air transport direct employment. Many air transport economic studies add an additional employment group defined as 'other air transport activities' intended to include airport retail, catering, and hotels. Additionally, some studies extend the term direct employment by adding

Table 5.1 Calculation of direct employment in different air transport economic impact study reports in the UK

Economic study report	Airlines, airport, ATC, operators	Retail, catering, hotels	General aviation	Civil aerospace
OEF 1999	Y	Y	Y	
ACI 2004	Y	Y		
AOA 2005	Y	Y		
ATAG 2005	Y	Y	Y	Y
OEF 2006	Y	Y	Y	
BAA 2007	Y	Y		
ATAG 2008	Y	Y	Y	Y
BHC 2000	Y	N		
Bon and Wit 2005	Y	?		

Source: (Gillingwater et al. 2009).

general aviation (OEF 1999, 2006; ATAG 2008) or civil aerospace manufacturing (ATAG 2005, 2008), see Table 5.1. Since the level of direct employment is the starting point for the economic impact modelling of airport operations, the discrepancies that occur at this stage of analysis may seriously hinder the total results.

Butler and Kiernan (1992) conclude that in the calculation of direct impact only such employment should be considered as an airport's contribution to local economic activity that would not have occurred in the absence of the airport. Only such work places that are generated by airport activities should be calculated as the economic contribution of aviation (net effects). However, the authors admit that the base-case scenario may be challenging to recognise.

Direct impacts are consequences of economic activities carried out at airports by airport operators, airlines, ground handling agencies, and other companies directly involved in the aviation sector. Creating work places, purchasing goods and services, and paying taxes are examples of airport activities that generate a direct impact. The calculation of the number of work places supported by airport operations and aviation related companies, is the starting point for further estimations of direct impact. Based on the employment level, the creation of income due to airport operations can be estimated. In the case of a lack of data to calculate the income effect, it is usual practice to take the average value added per employee in a given sector. According to various estimates, air transport contributes to the creation of 0.90% to 2.4% of the national Gross Domestic Product and the direct contribution is on average 1.1% of GDP (Gillingwater 2009).

The indirect (second-round) impact of airport operations is calculated through the use of different approaches. In some studies, the term indirect effect is used differently from most mainstream and input-output research (Batey et al. 1993). Apart from using the input-output table or applying the multiplier to estimate the indirect effects, the impact created by the spending of passengers travelling to the region through the airport is calculated and interpreted as indirect impact (Aéroport Nantes Atlantique 2005; SQW 2008). In other studies (Malina et al. 2006; Dusek et al. 2011), passenger spending is calculated as a separate impact. However, not all studies recognise the net value of tourism expenses. Malina et al. (2006) argue that apart from foreign passenger spending in the region, the spending of the region's residents abroad should be taken into account.

The induced impact is usually calculated as the sum of expenditures on goods and services of workers employed in the companies directly or indirectly involved in airport operations. There are two main but different approaches for measuring induced effects. The most widely used method is the multiplier approach, based on the simple demand-side model of the macro-economy for goods and services. The induced effect is obtained by multiplying the combined direct and indirect effects by the multiplier. The higher the combined direct and indirect effects are and/or the larger the multiplier is the higher the induced effect. Induced demand effects are not project-specific, unlike direct and indirect effects. Any other project that yields the same direct and indirect income effects would have the same demand effects (Pfähler 2001).

Indirect (second-round) impact, being the economic effects created by the chain of suppliers of goods and services to the direct activities at the airport, is calculated through the use of various approaches. In some studies (Dusek et al. 2011; Malina et al. 2006), passengers' expenditure on goods and services is calculated as a separate impact. However, not all studies recognise the net value of tourism expenses. Malina et al. (2006) argue that it is not only foreign passengers' spending in the region that should be taken into account but also the expenditure of the region's residents abroad.

Table 5.2 presents the results of selected research on the economic impact of regional airports in Europe. Depending on the interpretation of the components of the input-output method and the adopted multiplier, the final values of employment and income effects are on different levels. Additionally, some studies do not take into account induced impact (Glasgow, Charleroi, Nantes), and though the economic impact analysis refers to one year. In some studies (Dusek et al. 2011), the ex-post study formulates the basis for the projection of future effects. The various analyses are conducted at different spatial levels with different sizes of the region under consideration. The larger the region of the study, the larger the indirect and induced impacts are. Bearing in mind the above, a direct comparison of the different results of airport impact studies appears to be difficult and may not deliver robust results.

Apart from the direct, indirect, and induced impacts in the recognition and calculation of the importance of air transport on regional development, the catalytic effects are identified. Both the definition of these effects and the methodology of the study vary depending on the type of analysis. The catalytic effect is most often associated with the supply side of the economy and is related to the creation of a favourable environment for business development in the long term. The supply, catalytic effects result from the potential to influence changes

Table 5.2a Economic impact studies – results from selected European airports – employment effects

Airport	Study	Year of analysis	Pax (mln)	Number of on-site companies	Employment effects				Multiplier
					Direct	Indirect	Induced	Total	
Bologna	(Gualtieri, 2010)	2009	4.7	141	2248	1008	1746	5002	1.2
Budapest	(Dusek et al. 2011)	2009	8.9	120	6822	2100	2300★	11222	n.a
Charleroi	(Kupfer and Lagneaux 2009)	2006	2.1	34	922	1065	n.a.	1987	1.16
Dortmund	(Malina et al. 2006)	2005	1.7	n.a.	1531	2070	628	4229	1.8
Frankfurt Hahn	(Heuer et al., 2005)	2003	2.4	n.a.	2315	2233	968	5516	n.a.
Glasgow Prestwick	(SQW Consulting 2008)	2008	2.4	n.a.	645	1717	n.a.	2386	n.a.
Katowice	(Huderek-Glapska 2011)	2009	2.3	58	1954	832	46	2832	0.45
Cologne/ Bonn	(Booz Allen Hamilton, Prognos, Airport Research Center, 2008)	2006	9.8	n.a.	12460	21412	3220	37092	1.98
Nantes	(Aéroport Nantes Atlantique 2005)	2005	2.1	76	1752	n.a.	n.a.	1752	n.a.
Poznań	(Huderek-Glapska 2011)	2009	1.2	82	1076	1070	59	2205	1.05
Warsaw	(Huderek-Glapska 2013)	2011	9.3	198	14115	4076	1158	19349	n.a.

Source: Own compilation based on the literature.

Table 5.2b Economic impact studies – results from selected European airports – income effects

Airport	Study	Year of analysis	Pax (millions)	Number of on-site companies	Income (million EUR)				Multiplier
					Direct	Indirect	Induced	Total	
Bologna	(Gualtieri, 2010)	2009	4.7	141	297,7	99,1	167,5	564,3	1.2
Budapest	(Dusek et al. 2011)	2009	8.9	120	303,5	88	964,1★	1355,7	1.3
Charleroi	(Kupfer and Lagneaux 2009)	2006	2.1	34	67,2	87,3	n.a.	154,5	1.3
Dortmund	(Malina et al., 2006)	2005	1.7	n.a.	121	129	35	286	1.8
Frankfurt Hahn	(Heuer et al., 2005)	2003	2.4	n.a.	109	118,9	46	274	n.a.
Glasgow Prestwick	(SQW Consulting 2008)	2008	2.4	n.a.	20,8	46,7	n.a.	67,5	n.a.
Katowice	(Huderek-Glapska 2011)	2009	2.3	58	38,2	17,2	1	56,4	0.81
Cologne/Bonn	(Booz Allen Hamilton, Prognos, Airport Research Center, 2008)	2006	9.8	n.a.	800	854	171	1825	1.28
Nantes	(Aéroport Nantes Atlantique 2005)	2005	2.1	76	135	120	510	765	2
Poznań	(Huderek-Glapska 2011)	2009	1.2	82	22	21,4	1,3	44,9	1.83
Warsaw	(Huderek-Glapska 2013)	2011	9.3	198	404	95	27	527	n.a.

in the quantity of the resources used and changes in the efficiency with which those resources are employed. The supply-side effects include the following (Britton et al. 2005):

- impact on investments, location decisions of enterprises, technology transfer;
- impact on labour supply, the ability to attract a highly qualified workforce (Button et al. 1999);
- impact on productivity by increasing the mobility of production resources, and their more efficient allocation;
- impact on market structures and innovation, by increasing market access, by broadening the potential market, as well as by encouraging competition leading to greater efficiency and specialisation in areas of comparative advantage;
- impact on congestion and local business costs.

On the other hand, demand-side catalytic effects consist of the following:

- impact of tourist traffic through the expenditure of non-resident passengers in the region where the airport is located; estimation of the net inflow of tourism spending and its contribution to changes in the value added;
- impact on the trade in goods caused by changes in the value added through net changes in the inflow of goods.

The supply-side effects, namely the impact on investments, location decisions of enterprises and technology transfer, the impact on labour supply and firms' productivity refer to tangible effects of air transportation. Where the impact on the market structure and innovation as well as impact on congestion and local business cost are intangible catalytic supply-side structural effects. The network, image, and competence effects are among the latter.

Application of input–output methods in economic impact analyses for the aviation industry – areas of concern

There are reports in the literature about inappropriate use of the input–output method and the misinterpretation of analysis results in the estimation of airport economic impacts (Montalvo 1998; Niemeier 2001). Recognising the problems of the input–output approach could help identify the areas of concern and lead to improvements in the identification and assessment process regarding the effects of air transport activity on regional development and contribute to the better application of other methods.

Rietveld and Bruinsma (1998) identify general problems arising in the evaluation process of transport infrastructure projects: namely the proper recognition and definition of the effects to be analysed; appropriate selection of the valuation approach; as well as dealing with the uncertainty about infrastructure costs that tend to be underestimated, and about infrastructure effects resulting from the long life of transportation projects combined with the fact that some effects of infrastructure only materialise after a long period.

In the case of applying the input-output approach to the measurement process of the economic impact of air transport activities the main areas of concerns are related to the limitations of the input-output method, problems with the correct use of the input-output approach, as well as with the correct interpretation of the results of the input-output analysis.

Limitations of the input-output method

The first difficulty arises in the data collection stage. Not all national statistical offices provide input-output tables at the regional level. In the case of lack of regional input-output data, researchers are forced to adopt certain assumptions and thus reduce the accuracy of the analysis results.

Traditional input-output analysis is static. The results of the impact analyses are usually based on data collected in the selected year. Air transport is particularly sensitive to changes in the local and global economic environment. Impact analyses conducted during a peak year may overstate the results; and conversely, conducting an economic impact study during a recession may underestimate the size of the effects (Montalvo 1998). The static nature of the results causes them to be quickly outdated. According to Rietveld and Bruinsma (1998), the more stable the environment the easier it is to apply models based on earlier years for ex-ante purposes. Conversely, in a dynamic environment forecasts based on input-output analysis results are of limited value (Niemeier 2001). However, in the literature, there are examples of dynamic input-output models (Duchin and Szyld 1985; Leontief and Duchin 1986) that imply capital accumulation due to the usage of goods occurring not in the current period but subsequent ones. This improvement may decrease the drawbacks resulting from not including time in the standard input-output approach.

The core point of interest in the input-output analysis is processes triggered by exogenous stimuli (air transport infrastructural projects for example) in which only quantity reacts. Price changes are not included in the traditional input-output method as it takes time and money to change them. However, there are extensions of the input-output approach which help in quantifying changes in prices as a result of exogenous changes in wages or rents on capital (Huderek-Glapska et al. 2015). To the best knowledge of the author, there is a lack of studies that apply dynamic and price extensions in airport economic impact research.

The input-output method calculates aviation impact in terms of gross value (called economic impact as it is produced – AIIP) (Montalvo 1996). Butler and Kiernan (1986) consider measuring only those activities that would not have taken place if the airport did not exist. This problem is related to resource allocation. In the absence of the airport, the resources would be used in other sectors of economy.

One concern which is raised is about the degree of resource utilisation and thus the productivity of labour and capital. The input-output analysis does not address the problem of the efficient use of resources. Moreover, the results of input-output studies promote more inefficient projects and employ more resources (i.e. workers) in the production process. In the long run this solution may have a negative impact on regional development (Niemeier 2001). Input-output analysis does not address the problem of the opportunity cost of other projects nor the marginal cost of additional effects (i.e. generating work places or income). Gillingwater (2009) argues that it would be suitable to calculate the marginal changes, namely the changes in employment related to an increase in passenger numbers.

The aim of airport impact studies based on the input-output method is to provide evidence of economic benefits in terms of employment and income generation due to airport operation and/or infrastructure development. Each study provides a positive result since direct, indirect, and induced impacts will always take positive values. The input-output method does not take into account other effects created by project implementation, namely negative environmental effects, as well as the cost of implementing a particular project and many others. Airport impact analysis estimates only a part of the total impact of an airport on its surroundings.

Moreover, the input-output analysis does not resolve the issue regarding the causality of the relationship between economic development and changes in the air transport market. The socio-economic regional profile affects the operation and development of an airport. The increase in the output provided by the air transport market affects the level of employment and income in the region.

Problems with the correct application of the input-output method

Differences in defining and calculating direct, indirect, and induced effects result in difficulties in drawing a conclusion and comparing results. Most variations in the method are related to the calculation of indirect and induced effects. In a large number of US studies, indirect effect is estimated on the basis of non-residents expenditure in the region, in contrast to Europe and Canada where the indirect effect is estimated using input-output multipliers. In some studies, the expenditure of passengers is calculated as a separate aviation impact. These discrepancies in the method applied mainly result from difficulties in data gathering and/or eagerness to reduce both the time and cost of conducting an analysis. The application of the traditional input-output approach would help to reduce the problems that occur through correctly using economic impact analysis. Incorrect calculation of the total impact led to an overestimation of the analysis results (Jensen and West 1980). The issue of double counting is the main flaw of the input-output method.

The other issue is the definition of the area under an airport's influence. The larger the area of impact under analysis, the more diffuse the effects are and the larger are the indirect and induced impact values. On the other hand, a broad area of analysis makes the income and employment effects appear to be small compared to the entire employment and the entire production of the region. Andrew and Bailey (1996) argue that broadening the geographical scale of airport impact studies make the analysis more complex, and as the scale of an economic impact study increases, the benefits become less tangible. According to Butler and Kiernan (1986), the more economically self-sufficient a region, the higher the value of the multiplier is because the region is less dependent on regional imports and more reliant on the spending and re-spending in the area.

Problems with the correct interpretation of the input-output analysis results

The effects captured by an input-output analysis are related to the demand side of the economy. In particular, the impact on employment and income is calculated. However, employment may not be a good indicator of the sector's contribution to the economy, because in the case of airport closure, the workers would be employed in other sectors. Additional, changes in the Gross Domestic Product caused by air transport market activities are wrongly interpreted as welfare measures (Forsyth and Niemeier 2012). Consumer and producer surpluses are more accurate indicators of welfare maximisation.

The employment, income, and even fiscal revenue impacts are short-term, demand effects. In the meantime, a variety of effects from airport operations and their infrastructure developments occur over the long term, because it may take a long time for different actors to adjust to the possibilities and challenges implied by infrastructure utilisation. This uncertainty about the effects of airport infrastructure projects results from the long life of infrastructure objects and from the difficulties in forecasting consumers' and firms' behaviour in the long term.

The other problem with the correct interpretation of input-output analysis results is a question about the resources available for an induced effect (Niemeier 2001). In the case of full or near full employment in a region, some employees may be drawn away from other sectors. This means that airport operations affect the distribution of labour among sectors. It is important to distinguish between local value added components of expenditures and the regional import component. Therefore, there is a need to pay attention to and properly discriminate between generative and distributive effects. Similarly, there is a question about the most effective use of resources.

There are also concerns about the spatial extent of airport economic impacts. It often happens that the construction of infrastructure objects is carried out by companies from outside the region, so the employment and income effect is generated outside the area in which the airport is located.

The fundamental issue is that induced impact is not project-specific, which means that any other project that requires similar amounts of income to be spent would stimulate the economy by the expenditure of those employed by companies, directly and indirectly, involved in the project. The value of the induced effect is determined by the propensity to consume. Therefore, only if the airport project is related to a higher propensity to consume than other expenditure projects will the induced effect differ from those of other projects (Pfähler 2001; Niemeier 2001).

Conclusions

The input-output model, being based on a freely available, standardised, and consistent input-output table, is an accurate tool for analysing intersectoral dependencies. Any change of the output is distributed among the other industries and sectors of the economy in the form of direct, indirect, and induced effects. The input-output model provides the foundation for airport impact analysis – up to now the most popular approach in measuring the contribution of air transport to regional development. Numerous airport impact studies have been conducted, mainly by the aviation industry, however, among such economic impact analyses, there are discrepancies in the definitions and estimations of direct, indirect, and induced effects. Over the decades the input-output model has undergone evolution and some limitations can be reduced to cope with double counting, introducing price changes, and dynamics. However, the underlying assumptions remain unchanged: fixed technological coefficients; constant returns to scale; no constraints on resources; not addressing the problem of the efficient use of resources; and the calculation of short-term, demand, aggregate (not marginal) effects. The results of input-output studies promote projects that are more inefficient and employ more resources (i.e. workers) in the production process. According to Niemeier (2001), this solution may have a negative impact on regional development in the long run.

The input-output method has not been used correctly in most airport economic impact studies – the results have not been interpreted correctly, but first and foremost the method is not suitable for the process of identifying and estimating the relationship between air transport and regional development. The problem of the total impact of aviation on the local, regional, and national economy is beyond the scope of the input-output method. There is increasing concern about certain externalities that occur in the air transport market (i.e. noise, pollution, congestion) not being captured by input-output analysis.

Only estimating a project's positive effects, which are beyond the scope of welfare maximisation and ignore the efficient use of resources, makes the input-output method an inappropriate tool for policy decision making. The input-output model could be used for identifying the local structure of industries around airports, and in this sense can provide useful information for the planning process of the business location. However, in terms of the process of recognising and calculating the relationship between air transport and regional development, there is a call for a more holistic approach that would include wider economic benefits including intangible effects.

Any approach used in the investigation of the effects that air transport has on the economy should have the versatility to focus on effective resource allocation, include both positive and negative effects resulting from airport operations, but foremost focus on wider economic benefits. It is suggested that the formulation of the research method, the application and interpretation of analysis' results, should discuss the factors affecting the relationship between air transport and regional development. These factors could be divided into three levels: namely micro – related to airport operations; meso – focusing on the air transport sector and the characteristics of the region; and macro – considering the different macro-environmental aspects. Among the micro-level factors, one can distinguish the type of airport, the life cycle of an airport, the size of an airport, the form of ownership, organisational structure, investment conditions, level of resources used, and the financial situation. Factors related to the air transport market include the maturity of the air transport market, market structure, market competition, and the dynamics of change. Among the important regional characteristics that influence the relationship between air transport and economic development are geographical location, socio-economic characteristics (i.e. population, income, labour force), the structure of the regional economy, the stage of development, and economic agglomeration. Macro factors include the national and global socio-economic situation; the technological environment; as well as the political, legal, and institutional conditions.

References

ACI Europe (1992). *Airport – Partners in Vital Economies.* ACI Europe.

ACI Europe (1998). *Creating Employment and Prosperity in Europe – A Study by ACI Europe of the Social and Economic Impact of Airports.* ACI Europe, 1998.

ACI Europe, York Aviation (2004). *The Social and Economic Impact of Airports in Europe.* ACI Europe.

ACI Europe, York Consulting (2000). *Creating Employment and Prosperity in Europe: an Economic Impact Study Kit.* ACI Europe.

Aéroport Nantes Atlantique (2005). *Impact économique de l' Aéroport Nantes Atlantique.* Aéroport Nantes Atlantique.

Airport Operators Association (AOA) (2005). *The Economic and Social Impact of Airports.* AOA.

Air Transport Action Group (ATAG) (2005). *The Economic and Social Benefits of Air Transport.* ATAG.

Air Transport Action Group (ATAG) (2008). *The Economic and Social Benefits of Air transport.* Geneva: Air Transport Action Group.

Allroggen, F. and Malina, R. (2010). *Casual Relationship between Airport Provision, Air Traffic and Economic Growth; An Economic Analysis.* 12th WCTR, Lisbon.

Andrew, A. and Bailey, R. (1996). *The Contribution of Airports to Regional Economic development.* Luton: University of Luton.

Aschauer, D.A. (1986). Is public expenditure productive? *Journal of Monetary Economics* 23, 177–200.

Batey, P.W., Madden, M., and Scholefield, G. (1993). Socio-economic impact assessment of large-scale projects using input-output analysis: a case study of an airport. *Regional Studies* 27 (3), 179–191.

Benell, D. and Prentice, B. (1993). A regression model for predicting the economic impacts of Canadian airports. *Logistics and Transportation Review* 29 (2).

Berkeley Hanover Consulting (BHC) (2000). *The Impacts of Future Aviation Growth in the UK.* London: Berkeley Hanover Consulting.

Biehl, D. (1986). *The Contribution of Infrastructure to Regional Development.* Luxemburg: European Communities.

Boon, B. H. and Wit, R.C.N. (2005). *The Contribution of Aviation to the Economy: Assessment of Arguments Put Forward.* Delft: Report 05.7997.35, CE Solutions for Environment, Economy and Technology.

Booz Allen Hamilton, Prognos, Airport Research Center (2008). *Der Koln Bonn Airport als Wirtschafts – und Standortfaktor.*

British Airport Authority (BAA) (2007). *Economic Benefits of Heathrow Airport.* London: BAA.

Britton, E., Cooper, A., and Tinsley, D. (2005). *The Economic Catalytic Effects of Air Transport in Europe.* Oxford Economic Forecasting. European Transport Conference Proceedings.

Butler, S.E. and Kiernan, L.J. (1986). *Measuring the Economic Impact of Airport.* Washington, DC: Federal Aviation Administration.

Butler, S.E. and Kiernan, L.J. (1992). *Measuring the Regional Economic Significance of Airports.* Washington, DC: Office of Airport Planning and Programming, Federal Aviation Administration.

Button, K., Lall S., Stough, R. and Trice, M. (1999). High-technology employment and hub airports. *Journal of Air Transport Management* 5 (1), 53–59.

Button, K. and Taylor, S. (2000). International air transportation and economic development. *Journal of Air Transportation Management* 6 (4), 209–222.

Drake, R.L. (1976). A short-cut to estimates of regional input–output multipliers: methodology and evaluation. *International Regional Science Review* 1 (2), 1–17.

Duchin, F. and Szyld, D. (1985). A dynamic input-output model with assured positive output. *Metroeconomica* 37, 269–282.

Dusek, T., Lukovics, M., and Bohl, P. (2011). *The Economic Impact of Budapest Airport on the Local Economy.* ERSA Conference Papers ersa11p1228. Barcelona: European Regional Science Association.

Federal Aviaiton Administration (FAA) (2016). *The Economic Impact of Civil Aviaiton on the U.S. Economy.* Washington, DC: Federal Aviaiton Administration.

Forsyth, P. and Niemeier, H-M. (2012). *The Good, the Bad and the Future: Economic Assesment of Airports and Air Transport Liberalization.* Berlin: GARS Workshop.

Gillen, D. and Hinsch, H. (2001). Measuring the economic impact of liberalization of international aviation on Hamburg airport. *Journal of Air Transport Management* 7 (1), 25–34.

Gillingwater, D., Mann, M., and Grimley, P. (2009). *Economic Benefits of Aviation – Technical Report.* OMEGA Study 40, Loughborough University.

Graham, A. (2013). *Managing Airports: An International Perspective,* 4th ed. Abingdon: Routledge.

Gualtieri, G. (2010). *L'aeroporto come motore di sviluppo per il terrirorio: l'Aeroport di Bologna, L'economia cresce con gli aeroporti,* Bologna.

Hakfoort J., Poot T., and Rietveld P. (2001). The regional economic impact of an airport: the case of Amsterdam Schiphol Airport. *Regional Studies* 35 (7), 595–604.

Heggie, I.G. (1972). *Transport Engineering Economics.* Maidenhead: McGraw-Hill.

Heuer, K., Klopphaus, R., and Schaper, T. (2005). *Regionalökonomische Auswirkungen des Flughafens Frankfurt Hahn für den Betrachtungszeitraum 2003–2015.* Bierkenfeld: Zentrum für Recht und Wirtschaft des Luftverkehrs (ZfL)

Heuer, K., Klopphaus, R., and Schaper, T. (2005). *Regionalökonomische Auswirkungen des Flughafens Frankfurt Hahn für den Betrachtungszeitraum 2003–2015.* Bierkenfeld.

Huderek-Glapska, S. (2011). Oddziaływanie portu lotniczego na gospodarkę region. In Rekowski, M. (ed.), *Regionalne porty lotnicze, charaktersytka i tendencje rozwojowe.* Poznań: Wydawnictwo Uniwersytetu Ekonomincznego w Poznaniu.

Huderek-Glapska, S. (2013). The employment and income benefits of airport operation on the country in transition. *LogForum* 9 (1), 27–34.

Huderek-Glapska, S., Inchausti-Sintes, F., and Njoya, E. (2015). Modeling the impact of air transport on the economy – practices, problems and prospects. *LogForum* 12 (1), 47–61.

Hujer, R. and Kokot, S. (2001). Frankfurt Airport's impact on regional and national employment and income. In Pfähler, W. (ed.), *Regional Input-Output Analysis.* Baden-Baden: Nomos Verlagsgesellschaft.

Industry High Level Group (IHLG) (2017). *Aviation Benefits.* Available from www.iata.org/policy/Documents/aviation-benefits-%20web.pdf (accessed 30 September 2018).

International Air Transport Association (IATA), Oxford Economics (OE). (2017). *Value of Aviation.* Available from www.iata.org/publications/economics/pages/index.aspx?menu=Public%20Policy%20Issues&cat=Value%20of%20Aviation%20-%20Country%20Reports (accessed 0 October 2018).

InterVISTAS (2015). *Economic Impact of European Airports, A Critical Catalyst to Economic Growth,* prepared for ACI Europe, January.

Jensen, R.C. and West, G.R. (1980). *The effect of relative coefficient size on input-output multipliers, Environment and Planning A* 12, 659–670.

Kalaitzidakis, P. and Kalyvitis, S. (2005). 'New' public investment and/or maintenance in public capital for long-run growth? The Canadian experience. *Economic Inquiry* 43 (3), 586–600.

Kazda, A., Hromádka, M., and Mrekaj, B. (2017). Small regional airports operation: unnecessary burdens or key to regional development. *Transportation Research Procedia* 28, 59–68.

Kupfer, F. and Lagneaux, F. (2009). *Economic Importance of Air Transport and Airport Acitvities in Belgium,* National Bank of Belgium, 158.

L'Envoi Spécial. (2002). *Impact Economique – Le journal d'Information – Aéroport de Bordeaux,* Bordeaux.

Leontief, W.W. (1936). Quantitative input and output relations in the economic system of the United States. *Review of Economics and Statistics* 18 (3), 105–125.

Leontief, W.W. (1986). *Input-Output Economics,* 2nd ed. New York: Oxford University Press.

Leontief, W. and Duchin F. (1986). *The Future Impact of Automation on Workers.* New York: Oxford University Press.

Luke, R. and Wlaters, J. (2010). The economic impact of South Africa's international airports, *Journal of Transport and Supply Chain Management* 4 (1), 120–137.

Madden, J. (2004). *Assessing the Regional Economic Impact of an Airport: A dynamic Mulitregional CGE Study of Melbourne Airport,* Fourth Biennial Regional CGE Modelling Workshop, Melbourne.

Malina, R., Wollersheim, C., and Peltzer, S. (2006). *Die regionalwirtschaftliche Bedeutung des Dortmund Airport, Industrie – und Handelskammer zu Dortmund*, Dortmund.

Miernyk, W.H. (1965). *The Elements of Input-Output Analysis*. London: Random House.

Miller, R.E. and Blair, P.D. (2009). *Input-Output Analysis: Foundations and Extensions*. Cambridge: Cambridge University Press.

Miyazawa, K. (1960). Foreign trade multiplier, input-output analysis and the consumption function. *Quarterly Journal of Economics* 74 (1).

Montalvo, J.G. (1998). A Methodological Proposal to Analyze the Economic Impact of Airports. *International Journal of Transport Economics* 25, 181–203.

Munnell, A.H. (1992). Policy watch: Infrastructure investment and economic growth. *Journal of Economic Perspectives* 6 (4), 189–198. DOI: 10.1257/jep.6.4.189

Niemeier, H.-M. (2001). On the use and abuse of impact analysis for airports: a critical view from the perspective of regional policy. In Pfähler, W. (ed.), *Regional Input-Output Analysis*. Baden-Baden: Nomos Verlagsgesellschaft.

Nijkamp, P. (1986). Infrastructure and regional development: a multidimensional policy analysis, *Empirical Economics* 11 (1), 1–21.

Oxera (2009). *What is the Contribution of Aviation to the UK Economy?* Final report prepared for Airport Operators Association, Oxera.

Oxford Economic Forecasting (OEF) (1999). *The Contribution of the Aviation Industry to the UK Economy*. Oxford: Oxford Economic Forecasting.

Oxford Economic Forecasting (OEF) (2006). *The Economic Contribution of the Aviation Industry in the UK*, Oxford: Oxford Economic Forecasting.

Pfähler, W. (2001). Input-output analysis: A user's guide and call for standardization. In Pfähler, W. (ed) *Regional Input-Output Analysis*. Baden-Baden: Nomos Verlagsgesellschaft.

Pischner, R. and Stäglin, R. (1976). Darstellung des um den Keynes'schen Mulitiplikator erweiterten offenen statischen Input-Output-Modells. *Mitteilungen aus der Arbeitsmarkt- und Berufsforschung* 9(3), 345–349.

Rietveld, P. (1989). Infrastructure and regional development. *The Annals of Regional Science* 23 (4), 255–274.

Rietveld, P. and Bruinsma, F. (1998). *Is Transport Infrastructure Effective? Transport Infrastructure and Accessibility: Impacts on the Space Economy*. Berlin: Springer-Verlag.

Romp, W. and de Haan, J. (2007). Public capital and economic growth: a critical survey. *Perspektiven der Wirtschaftspolitik* 8 (1), 6–52.

SQW, (2008). *Economic Impact of Glasgow Prestwick Airport*. Prestwick: SQW Consulting.

The Industry High Level Group, (2017). *Aviation Benefits*, The Industry High Level Group.

Transportation Research Board, (TRB) (2008). *Airport Economic Impact Methods and Models*. Washington, DC: Airport Cooperative Research Program, Synthesis 7.

Weisbrod, G. (2006). *Evolution of Methods for Assessing Ecoonomic Development Impact of proposed Transporttion Projects*, 3rd International Conference on Transportation and Economic Development (TED2006).

6 Cost-benefit analysis of air transport projects with effects on the regions[1]

Javier Campos and Ofelia Betancor

Introduction

When private investors make their decisions about implementing a project, they consistently and systematically confront their expected private benefits and costs to summarise them into a few values that simplify the existing alternatives and more easily, lead to an 'accept' or 'reject' answer. However, when the project involves public investment and/or may have a significant impact on the rest of the society, its economic evaluation needs to transcend a simple comparison of private flows of revenues and expenditures and should be performed instead from a wider social perspective.[2]

This is one of the main roles of cost-benefit analysis (CBA), a decision tool particularly well-suited for air transport projects and policies because their overall effects on the society can be analysed by using two complementary approaches. On one hand, they can be modelled as a set of technical relationships that can be designed seeking the most efficient use of the available resources (planes, infrastructure, crews, airspace…) to move people and cargo across different places. On the other hand, they can be figured out as a set of economic relations among the social agents directly or indirectly participating in these movements (passengers, airlines, airports managers, handling companies, cargo owners…), that can be also organised looking for the highest welfare (De Rus *et al.*, 2010).

Whether a society gets or not an air transportation system which adequately optimises its needs will be determined by the integration of both approaches, performed through different air transport markets where the agents that demand and supply infrastructure and/or services, interact within the set of exchange opportunities provided by the existing technologies and the institutional framework governing their relationships. The result of these interactions is a particular allocation of resources, in the form of certain levels of provision and usage of the infrastructure and services, which in turn also leads to an overall level of social welfare. This initial equilibrium in each market evolves over time, either endogenously through the agents' behaviour, or – more interestingly – as a result of an external intervention, that is, a 'project' that affects the existing resource allocation (e.g. by building or expanding an airport) or their current organisation (e.g. by changing pricing policies or safety regulations), yielding a set of new equilibria over time.

Thus, from the point of view of CBA, the socioeconomic evaluation of an air transport project consists in identifying, measuring, and incrementally comparing, the subsequent net changes in *all* the agents' welfare (and, therefore, in the aggregate level of social welfare, *SW*) between the corresponding 'without project' and 'with-project' situations in *all* the affected markets, during the whole time span in which these effects are in place (from $t = 1$ to T). If the sum of changes in these social benefits (ΔSB) is greater than the sum of changes in the social opportunity costs (ΔSC), then it can be asserted that the project effectively contributes to increasing social welfare, as usually summarised into a positive *social net present value* (*SNPV*) expression, where r represents the social discount rate:

$$SNPV = \sum_{t=1}^{T} \frac{\Delta SW_t}{(1+r)^t} = \sum_{t=1}^{T} \frac{\Delta SB_t - \Delta SC_t}{(1+r)^t} > 0.$$

This procedure is not only useful *ex ante*, but also once the project is running (*in medias res*), or even when it has been completed (*ex post*). The assessment, in the latter case, is not about deciding whether or not to carry out the project, but whether it should be amended (provided the new available information), or about extracting lessons that could improve future projects. In all three cases the focus of the evaluation remains on achieving the most efficient resource allocation and, in this sense, the main purpose of CBA is to assist decision makers in prioritising socially-relevant projects according to their computable contribution (in money terms) to social welfare.

However, it is clear that any resource reallocation resulting from an air transport project also modifies the income distribution collected by the owners of those resources. This implies that the consequences of – for example, expanding an airport terminal or restricting night flights – may substantially differ across social groups with different income levels (business travellers vs. tourists, with different time values) or social agents located in different areas (firms and residents nearby, affected by noise and congestion). Project evaluation in these cases might be sensitive to its effects on personal and spatial income redistributions, although the lack of consensus about the overall treatment of equity issues in economic analysis often makes the efficiency criterion prevail (Thomopoulos et al., 2009).

This discussion about the ultimate objectives of cost-benefit analysis is particularly relevant in the assessment of air transport projects which may have an impact on regional development. Two particular issues are necessarily raised in this debate. The first one relates to the adequate definition of the 'society' which is affected by the project. In standard CBA the decision-maker usually does not compute benefits and/or costs accrued by agents outside the relevant society.[3] Thus, in the previous example of evaluating the expansion of an airport terminal, if the project is only financed by national funds, its effects on foreign economic agents (e.g. tourists) are usually not considered, since the society whose welfare matters is only the one whose resources are committed in the endeavour. On the contrary, when the project has cross-border effects, affecting two or more countries (or regions in the same country) and its funding involves all of them, the 'society' (and the corresponding social welfare) must be defined in a wider sense in order to be properly assessed.[4]

Precisely, the second issue relates to the correct identification of the regional development effects.[5] Standard CBA generally focuses on 'direct effects' (in the primary market where the external intervention occurs). However, there are also may be 'indirect effects' (in secondary markets related to the first one), and additional 'wider economic impacts' in the economy as a whole.[6] Regional development effects – sometimes also referred to as 'integration effects' – are usually argued as the main justification for many projects which may have an impact on particular regions. Although they may exist, an adequate measurement is required, since in many cases they are just indirect effects or WEIs, and sometimes only the result of double counting.

There is an extensive literature on cost-benefit analysis, and even on the assessment of air transport projects.[7] The evaluation of projects with regional effects is more recent and still limited. In Europe, transport projects considered within the Trans-European Transport Network (TEN-T) are a good example of the type of projects with regional effects worth considering.

TEN-T projects have two layers: a comprehensive network that covers all European regions, and a core network containing most important connections. The objectives of the TEN-T were revised in 2013, establishing that

> The trans-European transport network shall strengthen the social, economic and territorial cohesion of the Union and contribute to the creation of a single European transport area which is efficient and sustainable, increases the benefits for its users and supports inclusive growth... .

Therefore, there are four basic objectives for projects included in the network: cohesion, efficiency, sustainability and users' benefits. It is also pointed out that projects should be economically viable taking into account their socioeconomic costs and benefits, which includes environmental impacts. The European Parliament has also insisted in the selection of projects according to its European added value, and on the need to quantify its socioeconomic profitability by applying a harmonised methodology.

At the European level, the DG for Regional and Urban Policy uses as a reference the 'Guide to Cost-Benefit Analysis of Investment Projects (2014)'. This guide provides a common CBA methodology to assess projects funded by the Cohesion Fund and the Regional Development Fund. This is a manual referring to a diverse set of projects (transport, energy, telecommunications, environment, etc.), and very detailed with respect to the financial analysis of projects. However, there are no specific recommendations for the evaluation of TEN-T projects with regional effects, but for the fact that the evaluation should focus just on the specific part of the network for which there are different alternatives available (see page 69 of this manual).

On the other hand, the European DG for Mobility and Transport refers to the guide 'Developing Harmonised European Approaches for Transport Costing and Project Assessment (2006)'. These transport specific guidelines were developed within the HEATCO project. This manual specifically mentions trans-border effects and the need to adequately localise them. Actually, it is one of the few works that gives particular recommendations for the value of travel time savings (VTTS) and vehicle operation costs for these types of projects.

Finally, also at an institutional level in Europe, the European Investment Bank has produced the document 'Economic Appraisal of Investment Projects at the EIB (2013)', a manual for the evaluation of very different projects, using CBA as the main approach, but also cost-effectiveness and multi-criteria analyses. In this manual, multinational projects are not mentioned, but in a case study of road transport projects (see page 181).

Outside Europe, the Asian Development Bank (ADB) applies the methodology of the manual 'Cost-Benefit Analysis for Development: a Practical Guide (2013)', and more recently, the 'Guidelines for the Economic Analysis of Projects (2017)'. The first one contains important recommendations in relation to regional projects, and points out the need to modify the conventional methodology used in national projects in order to estimate the net economic benefits for the region as a whole and the net gains to each participating country. The expectation is that, the regional NPV (for a group of countries), must be equal to, or greater than, the sum of the national economic NPVs. Regional projects should create such benefits based on variants of one or more of the following effects: (1) attraction of external funding that would not be forthcoming for national projects; (2) capture of economies of scale and efficiency gains; (3) creation of external effects that accrue outside the boundaries of one individual country. This ADB manual also mentions examples of such types of projects and makes very interesting methodological recommendations for their assessment (see pages 306–310).

Also outside Europe, the Inter-American Development Bank has recently published a specific methodological note for regional projects (Campos and Betancor, 2018), that is the main reference for the work contained in this chapter.

After this introduction, the remaining sections of this chapter are organised as follows. First, we focus on methodological issues, studying in detail what characteristics determine an infrastructure investment project to be pursuing a 'regional development' objective, identifying the factors that make them differ from other – more general – projects. In this section we will also define the acceptability criteria for these projects in order to decide whether their contribution to social welfare make them acceptable or not from a regional development perspective. Then we will move on to the explicit measurement of benefits and costs in regional projects, and the hands-on implementation of

CBA. Finally we briefly summarise the main contributions of this chapter and provide some practical hints on the CBA of air transport projects for regional development.

Methodological issues for the assessment of regional projects

From the point of view of socioeconomic evaluation, as discussed above, any air transport project which may have effects on the regions, can be viewed as an external intervention in a market which entails costs and benefits for social agents located in two or more regions, directly or indirectly affected by the project. These effects may appear in the primary market, in secondary markets, or even spread over the rest of the economy, and all of them should be properly recognised and identified. The use of a CBA methodology to assess such effects requires a prior discussion on some specific issues related to the proper definition of the project, the precise identification of the sources of integration effects, and adequate criteria to accept or reject them (with regard to the 'society' of reference).

Project definition and the existence of regional effects

Following Jenkins and Kuo (2006), a *sine qua non* condition for a project to have regional (multinational) effects is that (at least) some of its consequences can be described as cross-border effects, even though the intervention does not take place near the border or even the affected regions do not share a border (e.g. an airport which provides international services). Lakshmanan (2011) argues that this circumstance does not invalidate the assumptions and procedures of standard cost-benefit analysis. On the contrary, it makes it more relevant to define the precise nature of the project and the underlying problem it intends to solve with the intervention (e.g. lack of capacity), since it may have consequences on a wider set of social agents, whose incentives may be in conflict. For this reason, it is of particular relevance for these regional projects to disaggregate the costs and benefits borne by each region, as well as their exact contribution in terms of money and other resources, since any relevant asymmetry on the distribution of these items may condition the overall acceptability of the project.

From an institutional point of view, as described in the previous section, a major feature of the evaluation of projects with regional effects is that they are always associated with a more complex institutional design and more elaborate management procedures, sometimes including pre-selection criteria based on non-economic rules (for example, the prioritisation of projects in less-developed regions). As a result, even in areas with a high degree of political integration such as the European Union, there is no guarantee that all projects that may potentially improve social welfare will be finally chosen, or that those which finally are selected, are actually the best ones. As an additional drawback, there is an implicit incentive to exaggerate regional integration effects, whose exact identification and measurement constitutes another of the particular methodological issues in the CBA of these projects (Venables, 2003).

Identification and measurement of regional integration effects

The level of integration between two regions generally stems from three dimensions: geographic, economic, and institutional. The first one is related to the physical and social links that determine their current level of communication; the second refers to the functioning of the markets of products and services across them (including labour and capital markets), while the third one refers to the depth of political integration, including rules, institutions, and other cooperation mechanisms.

Although these three dimensions have been extensively studied in the literature, few of the existing contributions have specifically considered their implications for CBA. In most cases (see Puga and Venables, 1998, or Limão and Venables, 2001), it is broadly stated that there is a negative relationship between lack of integration and economic activity, empirically observing that when there are obstacles to factors mobility (for example, due to high transport costs to/from isolated areas), the economic activity is less intense and tends to spread throughout the territory; while when these costs are reduced (by an improvement in air transport connectivity, for example) there is a propensity to concentrate activities in places that benefit from increasing returns (e.g. agglomeration economies, measured within the wider economic impacts). However, these benefits are seldom immediate and do not always appear in the same way: sometimes their net effects are even negative because the integration may also incentivise the reallocation of workers and firms from economically weaker to stronger regions.

In fact, Rodrik *et al.* (2004) argue that the initial conditions of the integrating regions can significantly determine the results of any integration project or policy, and that the main specific benefits traditionally argued in favour of projects that promote regional integration (changes in trade flows and in mobility conditions in factors markets) will be always ultimately transferred to the consumers and producers of the primary and secondary markets, where they can be measured when they really exist. With regard to the quantification of the so-called 'non-traditional' benefits of economic integration (associated, for example, to institutional changes, reputation effects, and other aggregate gains for society),[8] their effects should not be incorporated into the CBA if they cannot be properly measured and identified.

This finally implies that it cannot automatically be assumed that the mere existence of cross-border effects from a project will always imply positive or symmetrically distributed effects on the integrating regions: they should be analysed using a 'case-by-case' rule, and the decision criteria used to accept or reject them ought to be explicit about the distribution of welfare gains and losses across the regions.

Decision criteria for projects with regional effects

The analysis of these decision criteria constitutes the last methodological issue regarding the CBA of air transport projects with potential effects on the regions. As stated before, from an efficiency point of view, the economic evaluation of a project adds benefits and costs over time with reference to an initial (without project) equilibrium. When these decisions are formulated from the point of view of the society as a whole – once it has been properly defined given the scope of the project and the potential existence or not of cross-border effects – the comparison is summarised into the already defined *social net present value (SNPV)*. Alternatively, if the project were to be evaluated by private investors (financial analysis), only changes in private benefits (ΔB) and private costs (ΔC) would be compared into a purely financial *NPV*, with *r'* being the corresponding private discount rate:

$$NPV = \sum_{t=1}^{T} \frac{\Delta B_t - \Delta C_t}{(1+r')^t} .$$

Whereas the socioeconomic evaluation addresses the question of whether the project should be accepted or rejected with regard to its contribution to social welfare, the financial evaluation only assesses the project's ability to cover its costs. The answer to this second question is crucial not only to determine the potential degree of private involvement in the project, but also the consequences for the taxpayers (when public funding is used for non-profitable projects) and for other alternative projects (also competing for limited public support).

As depicted in Figure 6.1, the decision criteria in standard CBA (when projects do not have regional integration effects and there is no uncertainty) use a relatively simple combination of *SNPV* and *NPV* values, which results in three different cases. First, when both the social and financial net present values are positive, the project should be accepted (assuming it is the best option among feasible alternatives) because it does not only increase social welfare, but it is also desirable from the point of view of private investors. On the contrary, a project whose social net present value is negative should not be carried out under its current definition, since it is not welfare-enhancing, regardless of the sign of the financial net present value. Finally, when a project is socially desirable (positive *SNPV*) but not attractive for private investors (negative financial *NPV*), the society should accept it only if there are no relevant budget restrictions. If they exist, the project should be redefined (or delayed) to increase revenues or reduce costs.

Even if financial restrictions are ignored, the corresponding decision criteria become much more complex when the project affects two or more regions, since both the existing alternatives for each of them and their respective changes in social welfare must be explicitly taken into account. To illustrate these ideas, consider for example, as shown in Figure 6.2, a project for improving air

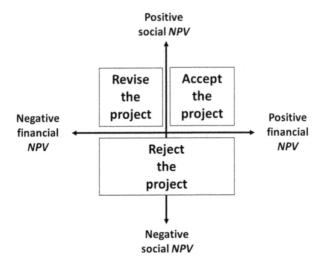

Figure 6.1 Decision criteria for projects without regional effects.

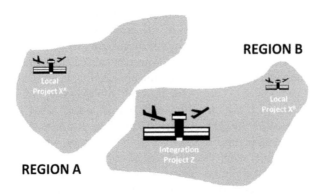

Figure 6.2 A project with regional effects: an example.

connectivity across two neighbouring regions, *A* and *B*.There are two possibilities: either each of them invests in improving their existing (smaller) airports (local projects X_A and X_B, respectively) or they may collaborate, jointly building a larger airport (integration project *Z*), that would provide services to both regions.

In principle, the situation could be addressed using standard CBA to evaluate each of the local options, using the corresponding $SNPV_A^{X_A}$ and $SNPV_B^{X_B}$ to assess the individual changes in social welfare. However, the potential existence of cross-border effects makes it also possible to analyse the regional effects through the social net present value of the integration project,

$SNPV_{A+B}^{Z} = SNPV_{A}^{Z} + SNPV_{B}^{Z}$, defined as the sum of the welfare changes that project Z separately provides to each region. Using this notation, it is now possible to state three conditions that should be fulfilled in order to accept a regional integration project.

First of all, it is required (*Condition 1*) that the integration project makes a relevant contribution to regional development; otherwise, the local options would be preferable. This requirement can be stated as $SNPV_{A+B}^{Z} > SNPV_{A}^{X_A} + SNPV_{B}^{X_B}$, and should be viewed just as a pre-qualification criterion, often imposed in the project definition itself.

An additional condition (*Condition 2*) is that the integration project makes a relevant contribution to aggregate social welfare, $SNPV_{A+B}^{Z} > 0$, which is equivalent to the positive $SNPV$ requirement showed in Figure 6.1. This condition leads the rejection of projects where $SNPV_{A+B}^{Z} \leq 0$, although this does not mean that the integration project cannot individually increase the social benefit; it just states that the gains in one region are not enough to compensate the losses in the other. This suggests that the distribution of gains and losses and the potential existence of compensation mechanisms play a significant role in the socioeconomic evaluation of regional integration projects as compared to standard CBA.

Condition 3 builds on this idea by distinguishing two additional sub-cases when *Condition 2* is fulfilled. First, if the project effects are asymmetric (e.g. $SNPV_{A}^{Z} > SNPV_{B}^{Z}$) its acceptability will necessarily be conditioned to the existence of distribution criteria in which the winner region (A) compensates the loser (B). This is feasible because *Condition 1* is met, although it will be harder to implement the smaller the value of $SNPV_{B}^{Z}$, particularly if it is negative. Finally, if the effects are more evenly distributed ($SNPV_{A}^{Z} \approx SNPV_{B}^{Z}$) the integration project is not only socially desirable from an aggregate point of view, but the presence of compensation mechanisms will not be required. Figure 6.3 provides a final graphic summary of all these criteria.

Measurement of regional benefits and costs

Projects affecting several regions, let us assume multinational projects, have an important feature: their effects on the region's welfare may be greater than the sum of impacts at the individual country level. This result is linked to the definition of the problem that requires a solution (e.g. lack of airport capacity), and the alternatives that allow it to be solved. Both can differ depending on the perspective adopted, either regional or from the individual country view.

To illustrate this idea, let us consider again a project that affects two countries (A and B) and the following relevant options X_A, X_B, Z, where:[9]

- *option* X_A, or infrastructure investment conducted by country A, that maximises its individual social welfare ($SW_A^{X_A}$),
- *option* X_B, or infrastructure investment conducted by country B, that maximises its individual social welfare ($SW_B^{X_B}$),

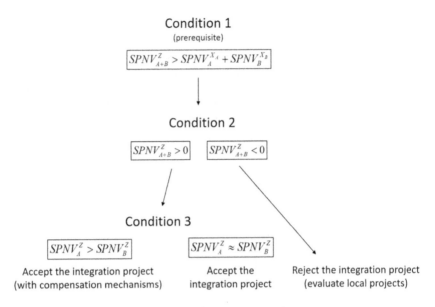

Figure 6.3 Decision criteria for regional integration projects.

- *option Z*, or joint infrastructure investment carried out by both countries (*A* and *B*) that maximises the joint social welfare, such that, $SW^Z_{A+B} = SW^Z_A + SW^Z_B > 0$.

Formally, for the existence of relevant regional effects, the following condition should be fulfilled:

$$SW^Z_{A+B} = SW^Z_A + SW^Z_B > SW^{X_A}_A + SW^{X_B}_B \qquad (6.1)$$

Therefore, there is an investment option (project *Z*) that is superior from the point of view of the group of countries. Each country considers different options (projects X_i), and maximises their welfare by choosing an alternative that neither considers its impact on the rest of the region, nor what their neighbours might do. Hence, options from the individual country perspective, X_i, are independent and might consist in 'doing nothing'.

Above notation can be generalised for the case of *n* countries, and hence equation (6.1) can be now expressed as:

$$\sum_{i=1}^{n} SW^Z_i > \sum_{i=1}^{n} SW^{X_i}_i \qquad (6.2)$$

And using the operator Δ to denote changes:

$$\sum_{i=1}^{n} \Delta SW_i^{Z-X_i} = \sum_{i=1}^{n} SW_i^{Z} - \sum_{i=1}^{n} SW_i^{X_i} > 0 \qquad (6.3)$$

According to expression (6.2) and (6.3), the evaluation of a multinational pro-ject would consist in estimating the impact on social welfare of the integration project Z when the reference base case is given by (the sum of) each of the non-integrated projects, X_i.

As another algebraic alternative we can always compare each project against the situation *without project (wp)* or counterfactual. Under this approach changes in social welfare for projects Z and X_i would be also assessed in relation to a base case. Therefore, when comparing Z with a situation *wp*, this is referred to a base case from the perspective of the whole set of countries (Z^{wp}), whilst for individual options X_i the without-project case is defined considering the indi-vidual countries views (X^{wp}).

Consequently:

$$\sum_{i=1}^{n} \Delta SW_i^{Z} > \sum_{i=1}^{n} \Delta SW_i^{X_i} \qquad (6.4)$$

$$\sum_{i=1}^{n} (SW_i^{Z} - SW_i^{Z^{wp}}) > \sum_{i=1}^{n} (SW_i^{X_i} - SW_i^{X_i^{wp}}) \qquad (6.5)$$

$$\sum_{i=1}^{n} SW_i^{Z} - \sum_{i=1}^{n} SW_i^{Z^{wp}} > \sum_{i=1}^{n} SW_i^{X_i} - \sum_{i=1}^{n} SW_i^{X_i^{wp}} \qquad (6.6)$$

That finally reduce to expressions (6.2) and (6.3) above for the particular case where $\sum_{i=1}^{n} SW_i^{Z^{wp}} = \sum_{i=1}^{n} SW_i^{X_i^{wp}}$. Therefore, regional projects might be assessed either by following the approach as given by equation (6.3) or equation (6.6). Both are equivalent in terms of final results, though the latter is richer regarding the information provided, which can be of great help for the negotiation pro-cess among countries.

As a summary, when feasible, it is advisable to follow the approach as given by equation (6.6). This is to estimate the incremental impact of project Z with respect to the counterfactual *without project* Z^{wp}, and further, to compare this result with the incremental impacts of individual projects (X_i), with respect to them without project situations (X_i^{wp}).

Apart from proving that Z is a better option for the region than X_i, regional multinational projects should also disaggregate welfare impacts by groups of interest taking into account the nationality or residence features. This identification will serve as a basis for future likely compensations among countries. The approach that estimates social welfare as given by the sum of economic agents' surpluses is very adequate for this purpose.[10]

Besides, it is convenient to distinguish between direct, indirect, and wider economic impacts. Direct impacts are those that occur in the market where the intervention takes place or primary market (*P*), whilst the rest of effects, indirect and wider economic impacts, will happen at other secondary markets (*S*). Again by using Δ to indicate changes as results of a project (e.g. option *Z* with respect to Z^{wp} or, alternatively *Z* against individual projects X_i), and having in mind that these changes will appear at primary and secondary markets in two countries *A* and *B*, and assuming that there is not double counting of effects:[11]

$$\Delta SW = \Delta SW_A + \Delta SW_B = [\Delta SW_A^P + \Delta SW_A^S] + [\Delta SW_B^P + \Delta SW_B^S]$$

From the perspective of regional integration, a benevolent planner would be interested in promoting the whole welfare of the region (*A* and *B*). However, the traditional CBA approach for a project promoted for country *A*, will concentrate on the estimation of component ΔSW_A^P, that is, those changes in welfare arising at primary markets that exclusively affect national agents. In such a case the common assumptions are:

1. The planner wishes to maximise country *A* nationals' welfare, and hence does not consider components ΔSW_B^P and ΔSW_B^S.
2. Secondary markets are perfectly competitive and free of market failures and distortions ($\Delta SW_A^S = 0$).

On the contrary, when the project to assess is option *Z*, we should consider effects in both countries, in primary and secondary markets when justified.

Conclusions

Deciding whether to build or expand airport capacity or to substantially change any other factor that determines the current equilibria in air transport markets, always poses a difficult challenge for social decision makers. When, in addition, the effects of these projects spread over two or more countries or regions, the standard assessment techniques provided by cost-benefit analysis (CBA) must be adapted in order to consider two new features. First, the society must be defined in a wider sense, including all the economic agents affected by the project regardless of their place of residence or nationality. Second, the mere existence of cross-border effects does not necessarily justify the project by itself; such effects must be identified and adequately measured in all the markets (primary and secondary) where they take place.

In this context, the main contribution of this chapter has been to discuss several methodological issues that allow a seamless translation of standard CBA to the evaluation of projects with effects on different regions and, in particular, regarding how these effects ought to be measured. More interestingly, we have developed new decision criteria to accept or reject these projects by comparing the social net present value of carrying out an integration project versus the corresponding alternatives of choosing local projects. We have also provided criteria for the measurement and comparison of benefits and costs in order to facilitate the implementation of this methodology.

As a final summary, some useful hints may be of interest for those involved in the economic assessment of projects with potential effects on the regions:

1. In the case of projects affecting different regions and countries it can be the case that, not only those countries are not interested in cross-border effects. Furthermore, they do not consider the same projects. In this regard, an option (Z) may exist that is better for the region as a whole, but that might be not considered by individual countries that focus their interest on other individual options (X_i).
2. The correct identification of the integration project (Z), and of the best project options from the individual country's point of view (X_i), is key to the evaluation. Options X_i may consist in 'doing nothing'.
3. For the assessment of these types of projects, the CBA approach based on estimations of changes in social agents' surpluses can be of help, as it allows the identification of the winners and losers by group and nationality.
4. The assessment of regional projects should prove that option Z is superior to individual country options X_i, otherwise there are no regional integration effects.
5. Trans-border effects may appear at primary and secondary markets. The analysis of welfare changes in secondary markets should be conducted only if justified (not double counting of effects).

Notes

1 This chapter is based on a larger work published by the Inter-American Development Bank. All the details of the analysis are available at: https://publications.iadb.org/ es/evaluacion-socioeconomica-de-proyectos-de-infraestructura-de-integracion-regional
2 Harberger and Jenkins (2002) or Boardman *et al.* (2006) provide classical references on these ideas. For an approach with more examples on the transport sector see De Rus (2010).
3 This practice may be controversial, particularly for projects where a real 'boundary' barely exists.
4 For a detailed discussion of this issue see, for example, Johansson and de Rus (2015).
5 From now on, the term 'regional' and the related expressions may both refer to regions within the same country or two or more countries considered within a wider geographic context (e.g. Southern Europe).
6 For additional discussion, see Vickerman (2013).
7 See for example, Jorge-Calderón (2014).

8 See Fujita *et al.* (2004), for example.
9 Alternatives X_A, X_B, and Z are assumed to have the same temporal horizon, or alternatively, are compared in terms of the equivalent annual net benefits (De Rus, 2010).
10 The surpluses considered are those of relevant economic agents affected by the project: consumer surplus, producer surplus, taxpayers surplus, and the rest of the society surplus (see De Rus, 2010).
11 In what follows it is assumed that changes in welfare are discounted values throughout the project's life.

References

Boardman, E.A., D.H. Greenberg, A.R. Vining, and D.L. Weimer (2006). *Cost-Benefit Analysis: Concepts and Practice*, 3rd edition. Mahwah, NJ: Prentice Hall.

Campos, J. and O. Betancor (2018). *Evaluación Socioeconómica de Proyectos de Infraestructura Multinacionales con Efectos sobre la Integración Regional*. Report for the Inter-American Development Bank. Washington DC. Available at https://publications.iadb.org/es/evaluacion-socioeconomica-de-proyectos-de-infraestructura-de-integracion-regional

Campos, J., T. Serebrisky, and A. Suárez-Alemán (2015). *Time Goes By: Recent Developments on the Theory and Practice of the Discount Rate*. Technical Note IDB-TN-861. Washington, DC: InterAmerican Development Bank.

De Rus, G. (2010). *Introduction to Cost-Benefit Analysis: Looking for Reasonable Shortcuts*. Cheltenham: Edward Elgar.

De Rus, G., O. Betancor, C. Campos, J.L. Eugenio, M.P. Socorro, A. Matas, J.L. Raymond, M. González-Savignat, R. Brey, G. Nombela, and J. Benavides (2010). *Economic Evaluation of Transport Projects Handbook*. Madrid: Ministerio de Fomento CEDEX. Available at www.evaluaciondeproyectos.es/EnWeb/Results/Manual/PDF/EnManual.pdf.

Fujita, M., P. Krugman, and A.J. Venables (2001). *The Spatial Economy*. Cambridge MA: MIT Press.

Harberger, A.C and G. Jenkins (2002). *Cost-Benefit Analysis for Investment Decisions*. Kingston, ON: Queen's University.

Jenkins, G.P. and C-Y. Kuo (2006). Evaluation of the benefits of transnational transportation projects, *Journal of Applied Economics*, IX (1): 1–17.

Johansson, P.O. and G. de Rus (2015). On the treatment of foreigners and foreign-owned firms in Cost–Benefit Analysis. FEDEA Working Paper – 2015/13. Available at www.fedea.es.

Jorge-Calderón, J.D. (2014). *Aviation Investment: Economic Appraisal for Airports, Air Traffic Management, Airlines and Aeronautics*. Farnham: Ashgate.

Lakshmanan, T.R. (2011). The broader economic consequences of transport infrastructure investments. *Journal of Transport Geography* 19: 1–12. https://doi.org/10.1016/j.jtrangeo.2010.01.001

Limão, N. and A.J. Venables (2001). Infrastructure, geographical disadvantage and transport costs. *World Bank Economic Review* 15: 315–343.

Puga, D. and A.J. Venables (1998). Agglomeration and economic development: Import substitution vs. trade liberalization, CEP Discussion Paper No. 377, London.

Rodrik, D., A. Subramanian, and F. Trebbi (2004). Institutions rule: the primacy of institutions over geography and integration in economic development. *Journal of Economic Growth*, 9: 131–165.

Thomopoulos, N., A. Grant-Muller, and M.R. Tight (2009). Incorporating equity considerations in transport infrastructure evaluation: current practice and proposed methodology. *Evaluation and Program Planning*, 32(4): 351–359.

Venables, A.J. (2003). Winners and losers from regional integration agreements. *The Economic Journal*, 113: 747–761.

Vickerman, R. (2013). The wider economic impacts of mega-projects in transport. In H. Priemus and B. van Wee (eds.), *International Handbook on Mega-Projects*, Cheltenham: Edward-Elgar Publishing, pp. 381–397.

7 The use of CGE models in the evaluation of air transport policy and large-scale investment

A survey

Eric Tchouamou Njoya and Peter Forsyth

Introduction

Computable general equilibrium (CGE) models have an established place nowadays in the modelling of both broad economy-wide impacts of changes, as well as the modelling of specific parts of the economy, such as transport markets, where it is important to analyse not just the market itself, but also the impacts on other markets. Their original use was to analyse the effects of a shock, such as 9–11, a mining boom or a crisis on variables such as GDP, GNP, employment, consumption, welfare, tax policies and individual industries such as energy, services, and manufacturing (see Shoven and Whalley, 1972). More recently, they have become a means of evaluating policy options and investments, such as new roads, rail subsidies, and tax reforms in terms of their impact on variables such as GDP, consumption, and employment. In short, they can measure impacts. However, many models can also be used to measure welfare effects, or whether a country gains or loses, for example, if it invests in a new road. In this respect, it can be used to estimate the net benefits of a change, such as an investment or a policy change in the same way that cost benefit analysis (CBA) has been used. Thus CGE models can be used to analyse both the *impacts* question and the *welfare or net benefit* question (see Broecker and Mercenier, 2011).

CGE models can be used to analyse air transport questions. For example, they can be used to:

- Estimate the impacts of an air passenger tax;
- Estimate the net benefits of building a new airport, and
- Estimate the impacts and benefits of a specific air transport liberalisation.

With regard to measuring the economic impact and or benefits a proposed air transport project or proposed air transport policy change, Economic Impact Analyses (EIA), Cost Benefit Analysis (CBA), and Computable General Equilibrium (CGE) models are the most used techniques. Forsyth et al. (2020) have examined this issue, reviewing existing techniques and their capacity to capture the economic impacts and benefits of airport investments. EIA and

CBA have historically been the most widely used techniques to evaluate air transport policies and projects. EIA, on the other hand, takes into account the interdependencies between different sectors and agents in the economy. However, its underlying assumptions are too restrictive and unrealistic. For instance, EIA assumes linear responses and highly elastic supplies of resources. The limitations of these models have been well documented (Forsyth et al. 2020; Dwyer et al., 2004).

CBA is a partial equilibrium technique and if all markets are perfect and there are no distortions, only local externalities, and income distribution is not an issue, it will yield the same answer as a CGE study. CGE models are general equilibrium, and this means that they are able to address several of the qualifications of CBA. Thus, they can assess how important the distortions to markets (e.g. market power and monopoly) are, they can show light on ultimate incidence, and they can measure widely spread externalities, such as carbon emissions. There are several limitations which can be present. Typically there are more aggregative, though this can be addressed by the use of sub-models which analyse particular sectors (e.g. the sectors of the air transport industry) within the context of an economy-wide model. They involve more computational effort, though in many cases, it is rarely necessary to build a new model from scratch, and existing models can be adapted to address the specific problem at hand. If the evaluation problem is to assess a medium to a large project, and there is some chance that there are distortions and externalities present, there is a case to undertake a CGE study.

CGE models have emerged as a promising analytical tool for capturing the economic impacts of air transport policy or projects. Although CGE models have been used since the 1960s to study issues related to trade and taxation among others (Shoven and Whalley, 1972; Harris, 1984; Cockburn et al., 2008), their application to air transport is in its infancy. However, despite the limited use of CGE models to the economic evaluation of air transport policies and projects, the literature has been growing rapidly over the past decade (reviews of their application to the economic assessment of airports are provided by Forsyth et al. (2020)).

Along with the growth of CGE modelling, there has been a growing interest in the separate question of the 'wider economic benefits' and 'wider economic impacts' of transport investments and policies. There is a growing body of work pointing to the role of wider economic impacts in transport appraisals (Vickerman, 2007; Graham and Melo, 2011; Knowles and Ferbrache, 2016). Investments in transport infrastructure or changes in air transport policy can generate wider economic impacts, defined as indirect impacts which are additional to transport user benefits (Department for Transport, 2014). According to the UK Department for Transport (2014), transport investment can generate wider economic impacts that can arise due to market failures in non-transport markets, such as the impact of economies of scope and density, imperfect competition benefits, connectivity, and agglomeration effects. Wider impacts are considered to be an important part of the benefits of air transport investment and should therefore be part of the transport appraisal (Forsyth et al., 2020). While these factors have been identified and discussed in the literature the key challenge is how to measure them (Mackie, 2014; Banister and Thurstain-Goodwin, 2011).

CGE modelling can help meet this challenge. For example, one source of wider economic benefits and impacts which has been recognised is the effects of taxes, such as taxes on labour income. This creates a distortion, and potentially a benefit or disbenefit. If a CGE model embodies details on the tax structure in a country, it can be used to estimate the wider economic benefit which might come about as a result of additional incomes generated by investments, such as an airport investment. For example, Venables (2007) uses a CGE model to measure some of the wider economic benefits of ground transport. If changes in air transport policies give rise to agglomeration, a CGE model may not be able to estimate the agglomeration effect itself, but it can be useful in measuring the impacts of agglomeration and any benefits from it. In short, CGE modelling cannot estimate all of the wider economic benefits from an investment, but it can be of use in estimating some of the wider economic benefits and impacts of policy changes and investments.

In this chapter we examine the contribution of CGE modelling to the quantification of the economic impacts and benefits of air transport infrastructure and policies, focusing primarily on the structure, overall operation, strengths and weaknesses of existing air transport focused CGE models. The remainder of the chapter is organised as follows. A brief presentation of CGE modelling and its applications is provided first, followed by a review of their application to transport in general and air transport specifically. Finally, we outline ways of improving the modelling of air transport services before concluding.

CGE modelling and applications

A CGE model can be defined as a set of equations describing the behaviour of representative agents and the technological and institutional constraints facing them (Thissen, 1998). The main agents in a CGE model include households, firms, and the government. Households allocate time to employment and leisure, and income to consumption and saving to maximise utility, while producers combine productive factors to maximise profits. The government collects taxes to finance expenditure and redistribute income, and address externalities. The equations are linked to one another by market equilibrium conditions and accounting identities and are solved to find prices at which quantity supplied equals quantity demanded across all markets.

CGE models rely on the Walrasian general equilibrium structure (Walras, 1874) and the contributions made by Arrow and Debreu (1954), Harberger (1962), Scarf (1967; 1973) and Arrow and Hahn (1971). Since the pioneering work of Johansen (1960), who developed a Norwegian multisectoral CGE model, numerous CGE models have been developed to investigate, for example, development issues (Adelman and Robinson, 1978; Dervis et al., 1982) and taxation and international trade (Shoven and Whalley, 1972; 1973; de Melo and Tarr, 1990), energy policy (Hudson and Jorgenson, 1974. Since these early applications, CGE models have been widely employed in among others trade, tourism, transport, agriculture and environment. CGE models have been used by various institutions including the World Bank, the European Commission, the Organisation for Economic Cooperation and Development, the Bank of England, Her Majesty's Revenue and Custom (UK), and the Australian Government to assess the impact of policy changes and support trade negotiations.

Models can be distinguished by their treatment of time and the level of spatial detail. With regards to time, CGE models can be split into two broad categories: static and dynamic CGE models. Static models do not contain any explicit time dimension, comparing the economy with a given policy change and the economy without the policy change at two distinct points in time. Dynamic models on the other hand can be separated into two categories, namely recursive and intertemporal dynamic models. Unlike recursive (sequential) dynamic models, where decisions about production, consumption, and investment are made on the basis of past and current values of variables, intertemporal (forward-looking) are based on future values, where the behaviour of economic agents is characterised by perfect foresight (Diao and Thurlow, 2012). The level of spatial detail refers to the treatment of geographical spaces, such as regions of a country. Models that explicitly model spatial aspects of economic policies are called spatial CGE models.

CGE models are designed to establish a numerical framework for empirical analysis and evaluation of policy issue and various shocks. They can be applied to a wide range of 'what if' questions. Unlike EIA, CGE models make it possible to control for nonlinear responses, resource constraints, and price changes when analysing the economic impacts of various shocks. They are capable of capturing indirect impacts of a wide range of possible transport policy changes or transport infrastructure investment without excessive simplification and aggregation. Furthermore, CGE models can incorporate distributional and welfare measures to estimate the 'net benefit' of a policy change or a project (Dwyer et al., 2010; Broecker and Mercenier, 2011). CGE models can be tested for sensitivity of results to elasticity parameter values and the assumptions can be varied, providing researchers and policy makers with an analytical tool for identifying the economic impacts of particular types of economic shocks.

Transport in CGE models

There has in recent years, been continued expansion in the use of CGE models for transport policy and infrastructure appraisal. Examples of application of CGE transport infrastructure projects and policies include: the welfare effects of transport subsidies (Tscharaktschiew and Hirte, 2012); the efficiency of the speed limit policies (Nitzsche and Tscharaktschiew, 2013); the economic impact of highway projects (Kim et al., 2004); the impact on the urban economy of changes in the price of gasoline (Anas and Hiramatsu, 2012) or the effects of transport cost reductions due to infrastructure investments on market structure and welfare (Bröcker, 1998; Bröcker et al., 2010).

The most recent surveys of these models are provided by Robson et al. (2018) and Shahrokhi Shahraki and Bachmann (2018). Transport-focused CGE models have been developed at different spatial levels, including single country, single region, multi-region, and multi-nation (Broecker, 2008). In a single country or single-region CGE model, trading of goods and migration cannot be dealt with explicitly. Thus, the transportation sector is treated like other sectors, namely as intermediate inputs by firms and consumption by households and government. In multi-nation or multi-region models on the hand, transport is handled as an activity transferring goods and people between locations (Broecker, 2008). The behaviour of the transport sector and regional price differentials resulting from transport cost are the unique characteristics of Spatial Computable General Equilibrium (SCGE) model. Tavasszy et al. (2011) indicate that SCGE models are able to assess (dis)economics of scale, external economies of spatial clusters of activity, factor and energy input substitution and consumption goods substitution. CGE models with a spatial dimension have been applied to transportation infrastructure appraisal by several authors since the 1990s (examples include Buckley, 1992; Broecker 2001; Lofgren and Robinson, 2002; Ivanova, 2003; Miyagi, 2006; Kim et al., 2004; Bröcker et al., 2010; Tscharaktschiew and Hirte, 2012).

Tavasszy et al. (2011) document the challenges of implementation of SCGE models for transport appraisal and indicate that one of the main challenges in applying SCGE models remains the specification of the interaction between the transport network and the spatial economic system of production, consumption, and trade. Other challenges include the modelling of transport costs and irrational agglomeration effects. Clearly, existing models vary greatly in the ways the transport sector is modelled. Some spatial CGE models such the model by Broecker et al. (2004) have used the iceberg transport cost model of Samuelson (1954), whereby transport costs are expressed in units of the product transported. Thus, transport costs are modelled by assuming that a fraction of the goods shipped melt away during transportation. Although the iceberg-type transport cost approach does not pose a problem in a macro SCGE model, as the macroeconomic output implicitly includes transport output, it is inappropriate for evaluation in multisector spatial CGE models because it leads to an underestimation of the output effects in the non-transport sectors (Bunditsakulchai and Hitomi, 2009).

An alternative model of transport costs is to define a transport service which is used to ship goods and people between locations (Ivanova et al., 2002; Sebestyen, 2017). Thus, the interaction between regions is represented by trade costs, which, in turn, are dependent, among others, on the state of the infrastructure (Bröcker et al., 2010). Broecker and Mercenier (2011) point out that transport-related sectors can be differentiated by transport object (passengers versus freight, bulk versus container), by distance class (short versus long) or by mode (rail, sea, air). They further indicate that at least three aspects of transport need a specific treatment: time needed for travel or freight; negative externalities within the transport sector such as congestion, noise; and transport as derived demand. While most CGE models adopt generalised costs (monetary and time costs), congestion is often determined exogenously (Broecker et al., 2010; Tscharaktschiew and Hirte, 2012). In fact, integrating congestion would require a fully integrated modelling framework that combines SCGE model with the transport network.

There has been over the past decades a dramatic increase in studies linking CGE models to detailed transport models, where transport decisions are explicitly optimised (see Anas and Yu, 2007 Anas and Liu 2007; Robson et al., 2018, Shahrokhi Shahraki and Bachmann, 2018). These models can explore choices of floor space, land and labour markets and link them into road networks and commuting decisions. Anas and Hiramatsu (2012) use an integrated SCGE model of the Chicago MSA (Metropolitan Statistical Area), with congestion determined endogenously, to assess the impacts of changes in the price of gasoline on aggregate gas consumption, vehicle miles travelled, and on-the-road fuel intensity.

Truong and Hensher (2012), for instance, show how discrete choice and continuous demand models can be used in such an integrated fashion in a Spatial Computable General Equilibrium model to investigate the wider economic impacts of a transport investment project. Both methods are useful for the study of policy measures which require a detailed analysis of individual behavioural decisions, such as decisions on mode choices in the transport sector, while at the same time examining economy-wide impact of these decisions. Similarly, Kim et al. (2004) investigate the economic growth and regional economic equity effect of a highway project in Korea using a framework combining a transport model and a multi-regional CGE model. While the transport model estimated the accessibility of the highway project, the CGE model measures the wider economic impacts of the investment. The authors identify two channels by which transport infrastructure affects economic sectors, namely through construction investment and transportation capital stock, and changes in the spatial accessibility level (determined by minimum travel distances and the levels of activities at the origin and destination).

Zhang and Peeta (2011) on the other hand indicate that most transport CGE models do not consider the network structure and spatial characteristics of the infrastructure systems, modelling each infrastructure system as a single node or sector in the economy. They propose a generalised modelling framework capable of estimating the network characteristic of infrastructure systems and addressing the spatial impacts of risks and disruptions (SCGE). Kulmer et al. (2014) link a multi-region CGE model with a transport forecast model to analyse the interlinkage of spatial planning and transport pricing strategy. In their approach, the CGE and transport models are complementary, with the former illustrating residential choice between urban and rural regions, and the latter depicting the transport implications thereof, in terms of overall transport volume, number of trips, and modal split. In like manner, a CGE model might be linked into a model of airline networks and passenger choices, though we are not aware of any attempts to do this as yet.

CGE models of air transport

CGE models have recently been used in air transport economics and policy formulation. A summary of the use of CGE models in the evaluation of investments in airports is provided by Forsyth et al. (2020). This section provides an overview of the air transport studies that have been undertaken using CGE models (see Table 7.1). It adds to the existing literature by critically examining how air transport is modelled in the existing studies. Air transport focused CGE models reviewed in this section are classified by their policy focus.

Evaluation of air transport infrastructure projects

CGE models have been used in Australia to analyse the economic impacts of an additional runway at Brisbane Airport (Brisbane Airport, 2007) and the impact of a new airport for Sydney (Joint Study, 2012). The model used for several airport evaluation studies in Australia is the MMRF (MONASH Multi-Regional Forecasting) model, a dynamic multi-regional Computable General Equilibrium (CGE) model of Australia's six State and two Territory economies. Each region is modelled as an economy in its own right, with region-specific prices, region-specific consumers, and region-specific industries. MMRF determines regional supplies and demands of commodities through optimising behaviour of agents in competitive markets. The model recognises margin commodities (e.g., retail trade and road transport freight) which are required for each market transaction (the movement of a commodity from the producer to the purchaser).

The primary MMRF database recognises four single product industries producing transport services. The four transport modes are road, rail, water, and air. An MMRF add-in allows for substitution between road and rail freight (intermodal substitution). The usage of road and rail freight margin will depend on: 1. the quantity of goods being transported from the point of production to some user (which varies according to the good and the user); and 2. the relative prices of road and rail freight. (Adams et al., 2010).

Yamaguchi et al. (2001) assess the social welfare of deregulation and airport capacity expansion of Tokyo International Airport (Haneda) using both partial and general equilibrium approach. Using a two-stage least squared approach the authors computed incremental effects of both deregulation and airport capacity expansion. The authors then develop a CGE model to evaluate the effect of double/triple tracking,[1] fare deregulation, expansion of aviation network/ Haneda slots. Transport services comprise road, railway, and aviation. The time resource constraint is the sum of leisure time, working time, and time spent on trips and must equal available time. Transport markets are assumed to be perfectly competitive. Technology is composed of labour inputs, passenger transport services (road, rail, and air) and road freight transport services. It is assumed that the accumulation of the stock of transportation infrastructure reduces travel time and improves the availability of transportation service for all households and private firms in the economy. The authors modified the generalised cost of transportation service so that the accumulation of the stock of transportation infrastructure is reflected. They employ the total network length of the expressway, the total length of the network of high-speed railway lines, and the total length of the airport runway as a proxy for infrastructure stock.

Their analysis shows that deregulation and expansion of Haneda airport resulted in an increase in incremental users' 'benefit' in the period from 1985 to 1999. The authors indicate that further study is deemed important in modelling the oligopolistic nature of the aviation market as well as to identify current and future bottlenecks in airport capacity.

Ueda et al. (2005) develop a spatial CGE model that covers the entire nation of Japan to assess the impacts of expanding the capacity of Haneda airport in Tokyo. Each of the nine regional economies consists of seven industrial sectors. The transportation sector provides passenger transportation service to households and industries. Freight transportation, interregional migration, and capital flows are not incorporated into the model. All markets in the economy are assumed to be in long-run competitive equilibrium.

The level of transportation service is estimated by the price of service and travel time using an aviation network model. The aviation network model describes the airline's behaviour as profit maximisation, the user's behaviour as a multi-stage discrete choice, and equilibrium as a Nash-type non-cooperative game. The model also considers connecting passengers to express the role of a hub airport. The authors input the capacity of Haneda for both cases with and without expansion in the aviation network model. The service levels outputted by the model were then transferred to the SCGE model. The price of transport services is set as part of the policy scenario as well as physical improvement of transport infrastructure.

The results showed that slot increases led to the rescheduling of flight plans and changes in levels of service. The increase in the levels of service measured by the frequency of flights, waiting time, or average travel time is brought about by increased airline competition. The expansion of Haneda can bring a large amount of benefit to all regions in Japan, particularly peripheral regions. They also affect the spatial structure of Japan owing to the hub function of the airport, and the central position is occupied within the domestic aviation network.

One of the most recent applications of CGE to airport infrastructure is the study by PWC for the London Airports Commission of the options for new runways in London Heathrow and Gatwick airports (Airports Commission, 2015). Using a spatial computable general equilibrium model, this study estimates the GDP effects of proposed airport capacity increases at Gatwick and Heathrow. The changes in airport capacity are expected to impact on air fares, the frequency of flights, and destinations available with knock-on effects for the demand for travel and international trade, which are interpreted in the model

Table 7.1 CGE studies of air transport

Studies	Year	Country	Scale	Purpose
Harback et al.	2015	USA	Multisector representative household	Air transport congestion
PWC	2013	UK	Multisector representative household	Abolition of Air Passenger Duty
Yamaguchi et al.	2001	Japan	Multisector representative household	Air transport liberalisation and airport investment evaluation
Ueda et al.	2005	Japan	Multisector representative household	Airport investment evaluation
Njoya	2019	Egypt	Multisector including an air transport sector. Representative household	Air transport liberalisation
Airports Commission	2015	UK	Multisector representative household	Airport investment evaluation
Chen and Haynes	2013	USA	Multisector representative household	Expansion of public air capital stock

Simulations/air transport modelling	Macroeconomic and factor closures	Welfare	Dynamic	Spatial
Changes in congestion incorporated into the CGE framework as decreasing return to scale	Not applied	Present value of additional consumption with next generation	No	No
Scenarios built into a standard model to capture growth effects of airline sectors expansion. E.g. productivity gain of 0.2% for every increase in business air usage assumed.	Applied though it is unclear how investment and savings are treated in the model	Yes (deadweight loss using GDP)	Yes	No
Changes in air fares resulting from aviation policy and airport capacity expansion are estimated using an econometric approach and incorporated into a CGE model to assess their welfare implications. Explicit modelling of transportation costs.	Not applied	Equivalent variation	No	No
Explicit modelling of the links between the flow of passenger trips and consumption or production of non-transport services and commodities. Price of service and travel time by an aviation network model used to estimate the level of transportation service.	Not applied	Equivalent variation	No	Yes
Modelling of mark-up price imperfect competition; improvement in efficiency; reduction in tariff equivalent protection	Not applied	Not applied	No	No
Wider economic impact of airport expansion through impact on GDP, visitor spending, trade and productivity	Sensitivity of the model to the labour market assumption tested	Direct welfare benefit of export expansion	Yes	Yes
A 10% increase in public air capital	Not applied	Equivalent variation	No	No

as interpreted as a shock to productivity across all sectors of the economy. The model results show that expansion at either Heathrow or Gatwick would have a significant positive impact on the air passenger transport and freight sector, and could raise GDP significantly (a welfare measure is also reported, though it is not clear how this was derived). Despite the merits of this study, the lack of a specific treatment of the spatial perspective, i.e. the differences between Heathrow and Gatwick localities, cannot be overlooked. Another weakness of this study is its treatment of the transport sector which is not modelled explicitly and therefore does not explain how expansion affects transport costs.

Air transport policies

The impact of air transportation congestion has been studied using a CGE model. Harback et al. (2015) modify the US Applied General Equilibrium model to incorporate air transportation congestion using a technology variable which functions as the output of the air transportation industry. Congestion is viewed as a technological deterioration that causes decreasing returns to scale (DRTS) in the production of air transport. Thus, as more transportation is produced, congestion increases and the resources needed to produce a unit of air transportation also increase (Harback et al., 2015). Moreover, congestion is approximated by a relatively simple queuing model (following Kamble, 2005) and integrated into the CGE model. The authors document how to translate the output of the air transportation industries as viewed by the air traffic control system (i.e. flights) to the output of these industries in economic terms and how to convert seconds of delay per flight into dollars of cost to air carriers. In order to integrate the model of congestion with the economic model, the number of flights is written as a function of the output of air transportation (RPM) and the price of RPMs in the base year. The model is then used to examine the economy-wide impact of the Next Generation Air Transportation System (NextGen) initiative underway in the United States.

The results show that NextGen would lead to a decrease in prices of air transportation by 2 per cent, while the output of the industry would increase approximately by $10 billion, cumulatively. Several industries, such as tourism and computers, are noticeably simulated by NextGen. Furthermore, US GDP and consumer welfare can be expected to increase from the introduction of NextGen.

Aviation regulation

Taxation

The benefits of the abolition of air passenger tax in the UK and in Germany has been studied using CGE models using a multi-regional, dynamic CGE model for Europe (PWC, 2013; 2017). The model is able to capture each country of interest individually, with all other countries combined into 'Rest of Europe' and 'Rest of EEA' regions. To simulate the impact of changes to the tax system, the database was modified to include an aviation sector, separated from the general trade and transport sector account. The study, commissioned by airline operators, concluded that abolishing UK's and Germany's air passenger tax would boost the country's economy. One of the strengths of this model is its ability to capture productivity benefits. Yet, this model is not a transport-focused model, but rather a standard model with an aviation account and an explicit modelling of the links between the studied countries and selected regions.

Forsyth et al. (2014) estimate the flow and expenditure effects of the recent increase in Australia's Passenger Movement Charge (PMC), as well as its economic impacts on the Australian economy and the tourism industry. They also estimate the welfare effects of the charge – i.e. whether the nation gains or loses from imposing the tax. They conclude that, overall, there is a welfare gain.

Subsidies

The costs and benefits of subsidies to airports using a multi-regional CGE model of the Australian economy have been developed by the Sustainable Tourism Cooperative Research Centre, Centre for Tourism Economics and Policy Research (Forsyth, 2007). It is a model with two regions, New South Wales and the Rest of Australia, and extensive detail on the tourism sector. The results show that a region is likely to enjoy economic gains as a result of an airport subsidy, while the economic impacts in regions other than the host region is likely to be negative. The regional airport subsidies are likely to be positive for the nation as a whole if the region offering the subsidies is relatively depressed and other regions are not. Like the aforementioned model, there is no explicit treatment of the air transport sector in this model, which can be described as a tourism-focused model.

Curfews

One of the earliest applications of CGE models to air transport was the study of the benefits of Melbourne Airport's curfew-free status (Melbourne Airport, 2003). The authors examine the economic consequences of the hypothetical introduction of a curfew of the same type as that operating at some other major Australian airports. They simulate a 9.2 per cent reduction in flights to and from Melbourne Airport in the year in which the hypothetical curfew is assumed to be imposed. The introduction of a curfew is modelled as a restriction on the number of seats available for travelling to and from Melbourne. Results show that the curfew has only a small negative effect on the national economy. While the state of Victoria loses activity and employment, the resources released are taken up by activities in other states. A slight term of trade deterioration is projected through the period, leading to a slight negative deviation in national real household consumption. This model is very close to the model presented in the previous section with no specific treatment of the air transport sector.

Liberalisation

There is very little understanding of the wider economic impact of air services liberalisation, with most on the impact of liberalisation relying on partial equilibrium techniques. The first attempt at applying CGE models to assess the effect of liberalisation is the work by the Centre for International Economics (CIE, 1988). This study examined the impact of liberalisation sufficient to achieve a 20 per cent reduction in airfares to Australia. It was quickly followed by an examination, using the same model, the Australian ORANI model, of similar issues done by the Australian Government's economic adviser, the Industries Assistance Commission (IAC, 1989). Since this work, there has not been much analysis of aviation liberalisation using CGE models. A more recent study is that by Yamaguchi et al. (2001. This study, like most of the other studies, suffers from limitations in its theoretical basis and its treatment of air transport. Moreover, in all models air transport is characterised by constant returns to scale (CRTS), and perfect competition, assuming firms are price-takers. The role of market and industry structure has not been given enough attention in the existing literature. The air transport, like business services (Balistreri et al., 2008) is a service sector characterised by oligopolistic competition, product variety, increasing returns to scale. The ability of CGE models to capture the wider economic impact of infrastructure investment and aviation policies may be enhanced if these features are incorporated.

The liberalisation of air transportation is expected to increase competition both in price and in-service quality attributable to either new entry or increased price competition among the incumbent airlines (Marin, 1995). Regulations distort prices and quantities and raise entry costs and limit the entry of foreign enterprises in the domestic market, hampering competition and supporting market power of domestic firms. Marin (1995) argues that under regulation, firms behave as in an oligopoly with perfect collusion and have few incentives to increase efficiency. Liberalisation permitting entry is expected to expand production and increase variety, bringing about more competitive market structure, lowering costs in the domestic market because of the international competition and lowering the presence of market pricing power by individual firms. How these features can be modelled is well documented (Dixit and Stiglitz, 1977; Balistreri et al., 2008; Konan and Marcus, 2006; Konan and Van Assche, 2007; Abayasiri-Silva and Horridge, 1998; Harris,1984; Elbehri and Hertel, 2004; Roson, 2006). Existing models do not take specific account of these features.

Modelling imperfect competition involves specifying how monopoly rents are generated and distributed (Davies and Seventer, 2006; Konan and Van Assche. 2007). Restrictions on foreign market entry are modelled as tariff-equivalent price wedges. In contrast, barriers on foreign ownership are modelled as both monopoly-rent distortions arising from imperfect competition among domestic producers, on the one hand, and, on the other hand, as inefficiency costs arising from a failure of domestic service providers to adopt least-cost practices (Davies and Seventer, 2006; Konan and Van Assche. 2007). Thus, imperfect competition is introduced as a mark-up on the price received for domestic sales of air transport. This interposes a wedge between the domestic sales price and the demander price, on top of any existing trade and transport margins.

Economies of scale can be introduced using fixed costs, assuming that firms make fixed payments for the use of some resources for their operation irrespective of their production, in addition to the usual input costs of intermediate input and composite factor. In building an empirical model, we have to assume in which cells of the social account matrix the payments of funds corresponding to fixed costs are included and their values. Fixed costs can be specified as a fixed share of the total capital service payment (see Hosoe et al., 2010).

Departing from the standard perfect competition framework, a recent study (Njoya, 2019) has investigated the tourism and wider economic impacts of price-reducing reforms in air transport services in Egypt using a CGE model with imperfect competitive sectors, along the lines of Dixit and Stiglitz (1977). The simulation results indicate that removing distortions arising from imperfect competition, tariff-equivalent protection, and inefficiency costs would benefit the economy as a whole, though the direct impacts of the reforms would be negative for some agents. A possible improvement of this study could be achieved by endogenising transport costs. This would require adding transport costs generated in the transport sector to the Dixit-Stiglitz approach (Behrens et al., 2009).

Issues of CGE models of air transport sector

There are several ways in which CGE models of air transport can be improved to give more accurate results. Further development of CGE models can be oriented towards taking account of these.

One of the limitations of existing CGE models applied to air transport is their failure to address some of the critical issues that CGE models can handle such as distributional impacts of air transport policy and large-scale investment. Most CGE models, which have been applied to transport in general, and air transport in particular, share the same structure involving a highly aggregated transport sector and factor inputs, and a representative household (see Table 7.1). While the degree and nature of the household, sectoral and factor disaggregation is determined by the existing social accounting matrix, it is essential that the model captures the important characteristics of the transport mode considered and the structure of the economy concerned. Using a highly aggregated model may seriously bias the economic evaluation of investments in transport infrastructure or reform in transport policies. Employing a representative household CGE model for evaluation transport infrastructure and policy, it is difficult to examine correctly their distributional effects across various groups within the society, an issue that CGE models can handle, which CBA cannot. The specification of the structure of factor endowments across the household group is useful in that is allows studies of the transmission channels of changes to transport infrastructure to household income. Detailed attention should be paid to the transport sector disaggregation, particularly if different modes of transport are affected differently by a transport policy. Furthermore, changes to transport policies and infrastructure create benefits and costs that are unevenly distributed across different income groups and areas of a city or region (Pereira, 2018).

Another issue observed in existing models concerns the treatment of closure. While most CGE models have examined the welfare impact of transport investments or policies, the treatment of closure is largely neglected in existing models. Taylor (2016) indicates that while the disaggregation of sectors, factors, and households is central to CGE analyses, the outcome of the model depends strongly on its closure. Moreover, a careful examination of the assumptions employed in CGE models regarding closure rules has been recognised as particularly useful in evaluating findings (Adelman and Robinson, 1988). For instance, De Maio et al. (1999) show that the welfare and distributional outcomes are sensitive to macro closure rules.

As already mentioned, a recent development in transport-related CGE models has been the combination of a CGE model and a transport model into one framework. Linking both models in a technically consistent way allows the modelling of the impact of transport policies on the behaviour of agents in the transport system in terms of transport choices, while at the same time estimating their wider economic implications. Thus, the transport model is suitable for the estimation of the generalised cost of transport and agents' behaviour in using transport networks, such as modal choice. CGE models, on the other hand, enable the quantification of the general equilibrium impacts of a proposed transport policy or project. For purposes of simulation of the wider economic impacts of air transport investment and policy issues, an expansion of existing models in this direction is particularly relevant. Moreover, merging airline network models with CGE models, the behaviours of air transport and economic systems and interdependences can be captured comprehensively. Such an approach offers the opportunity to amend the shortcomings of both CGE model and airline network modelling. For example, for a proposed air transport policy or project, airline network models are able to capture the resulting changes in the costs of travel and airlines' routes choices, while SCGE models can assess their macroeconomic and distributional impacts.

Conclusions

This chapter has provided an overview of CGE models and their application to air transport. While documenting the use of CGE models for the quantification of the wider economic impacts of air transport infrastructure and policies the chapter has also discussed different approaches for modelling transport services. It has been shown that although transport-focused CGE models have developed rapidly over the last decades, their use for air transport policies and large-scale investment analysis is not yet widespread, though their use is becoming more common.

Some of the studies referred to are impact studies, seeking to measure the impacts (e.g. on GDP or employment) if policies or investments (e.g. Melbourne Airport, 2003). For these, a CGE approach is appropriate. Others seek to evaluate whether policies or investments increase welfare. For these, both CBA and CGE studies can be used. One can ask whether the additional effort in producing a CGE study is worthwhile. For very small projects, this may not be the case. Medium to large CBAs of medium to large projects are not necessarily cheap. It is possible to use existing CGE models cheaply. However, if additional detail is required, it will be necessary to adjust the model, possibly by developing sub-models of key aspects of the project – this will add to the cost.

We have noted several limitations of the CGE models we have discussed. Some of these are as follows:

Several have been vague or inaccurate about the modelling of the air transport sector and, in some cases, the way they measure welfare. Several have been very aggregative and are not able to show the detail about their estimates. While several studies are very transparent, providing extensive documentation, others provide little other than overall results (something which is said about many CBAs). Finally, most CGE studies of air transport have assumed perfect competition, modelling trade relationships using the Armington assumption (Armington, 1969) that goods are differentiated by country of origin.

The chapter has further demonstrated that existing models have not satisfactorily modelled the characteristics of the air transport market, with most models using a standard general equilibrium model and assuming perfect competition. This approach does not allow for the analysis of the role of strategic behaviour characteristic of the air transport market. A properly specified air transport-focused CGE model incorporates features required to capture various market structures and imperfect competition into the standard model. So this has not been done, but it would be a logical next step in the use of CGE models in the study of air transport.

Note

1 i.e. the level of passengers set by the Ministry of Transport for the route in which two airlines or three airlines could operate.

References

Abayasiri-Silva, K. and Horridge, M. (1998). Economies of scale and imperfect competition in an applied general equilibrium model of the Australian economy. *Increasing Returns and Economic Analysis* (pp. 307–334). London: Palgrave Macmillan.

Adams, P., Dixon, J., Giesecke, J., and Horridge, M. (2010). MMRF: Monash Multi-Regional Forecasting Model: A Dynamic Multi-Regional Model of the Australian

Economy. General Paper No. G-223. The Centre of Policy Studies, Monash University.

Adelman, I. and Robinson, S. (1978). *Income distribution policy in developing countries: A case study of Korea* (No. 10121, p. 1). Washington, DC: The World Bank.

Adelman, I. and Robinson, S. (1988). Macroeconomic adjustment and income distribution: Alternative models applied to two economies. *Journal of Development Economics* 29(1), 23–44.

Airports Commission (2015) Economy: Wider Impacts Assessment, London, PwC/Airports Commission November.

Anas, A. and Liu, Y. (2007). A regional economy, land use, and transportation model (relu-tran©): formulation, algorithm design, and testing. *Journal of Regional Science* 47(3), 415–455.

Anas, A. and Yu, L. (2007) A regional economy, land use and transportation model (RELU-TRAN©): formulation, design and testing. *Journal of Regional Science* 47(3), 415–455.

Anas, A., and Hiramatsu, T. (2012). The effect of the price of gasoline on the urban economy: From route choice to general equilibrium. *Transportation Research Part A: Policy and Practice* 46(6), 855–873.

Annabi, N., Cockburn, J., and Decaluwe, B. (2006). Functional forms and parametrization of CGE models. PEP MPIA Working Paper. Poverty and Economic Policy Research Network.

Armington, P. S. (1969). A theory of demand for products distinguished by place of production. *Staff Papers* 16(1), 159–178.

Arrow, K. J. and Debreu, G. (1954). Existence of an equilibrium for a competitive economy. *Econometrica* 22, 265–290.

Arrow, Kenneth J. and Hahn, Frank (1971). *General Competitive Analysis*, San Francisco: Holden-Day.

Balistreri, E. J., Rutherford, T. F., and Tarr, D. G. (2008). *Modeling Services Liberalization: The Case of Kenya*. Washington, DC: The World Bank.

Banister, D. and Thurstain-Goodwin, M. (2011). Quantification of the non-transport benefits resulting from rail investment. *Journal of Transport Geography* 19(2), 212–223.

Behrens, K., Gaigné, C., and Thisse, J. F. (2009). Industry location and welfare when transport costs are endogenous. *Journal of Urban Economics* 65(2), 195–208.

Brisbane Airport (2007). Volume A: Background and Need, Chapter 2 Need for the Project The Environmental Impact Statement (EIS) and Major Development Plan (MDP), by Sinclair Knight Merz.

Bröcker, J. (1998). *Spatial effects of transport infrastructure: the role of market structure* (No. 5/98). Diskussionsbeiträge aus dem Institut für Wirtschaft und Verkehr. Available at www.econstor.eu/bitstream/10419/48511/1/253525543.pdf

Bröcker, J. (2001). Spatial effects of transport infrastructure: the role of market structure. In J. Roy and W. Schulz (eds.), Theories of Regional Competition (pp. 181–193). Baden-Baden: Nomos.

Bröcker, J., Meyer, R., Schneekloth, E., Schuermann, C., Spiekermann, K., and Wegener, M. (2004). Modeling the socio-economic and spatial impacts of EU transport policy. IASON Deliverable 6, Working paper.

Bröcker, J. (2008). Computable general equilibrium analysis in transportation. In D. A. Hensher, K. J. Button, K. E. Haynes, and P. R. Stopher, *Handbook of Transport Geography and Spatial Systems* (pp. 269–289). Bingley: Emerald Group.

Bröcker, J. and Mercenier, J. (2011). General equilibrium models for transportation economics. In A. de Palma, R. Lindsey, E. Quinet, and R. Vickerman, *Handbook in Transport Economics* (pp. 21–45). Northampton, NH: Edward Elgar.

Bröcker, J., Korzhenevych, A., and Schürmann, C. (2010). Assessing spatial equity and efficiency impacts of transport infrastructure projects. *Transportation Research Part B: Methodological* 44(7), 795–811.

Bröcker, J., Korzhenevych, A., and Schürmann, C. (2010). Assessing spatial equity and efficiency impacts of transport infrastructure projects. *Transportation Research Part B.* doi:10.1016/j.trb.2009.12.008.

Buckley, P. H. (1992), A transportation-oriented interregional computable general equilibrium model of the United States. *The Annals of Regional Science* 26, 331–348.

Bunditsakulchai, P. and Hitomi, K. (2009). Alternative Approach for Incorporating Transport Cost into Spatial CGE Model. www.shiratori.riec.tohoku.ac.jp/~takita/ARSC2009/Paper/ARSC2009_01.pdf

Centre for International Economics, (1988) *Tourism Report: Economic Effects of International Tourism*, Canberra: Centre for International Economics.

Chen, Z. and Haynes, K. (2013). Public Transportation Capital in the US: A Multimodal General Equilibrium Analysis. Available at www.gtap.agecon.purdue.edu/resources/download/6518.pdf

Cockburn, J., Decaluwé, B., and Robichaud, V. (2008). Trade liberalization and poverty: A CGE analysis of the 1990s experience in Africa and Asia. Poverty and Economic Policy (PEP) Research Network.

Davies, R., and van Seventer, D. E. N. (2006). The economy-wide effects of price-reducing reforms in infrastructure industries in South Africa. Available at http://ecommons.hsrc.ac.za/handle/20.500.11910/6411

De Melo J. and D. Tarr (1990), Welfare costs of U.S. quotas in textiles, steel and autos. *Review of Economics and Statistics* LXXII, 489–497.

De Maio, L., Stewart, F., and Van Der Hoeven, R. (1999). Computable general equilibrium models, adjustment and the poor in Africa. *World Development* 27(3), 453–470.

Department for Transport, 2014. WebTAG: TAG unit A2-1 wider impacts. Available at www.gov.uk/government/publications/webtag-tag-unit-a2-1-wider-impacts.

Dervis, K., de Melo, J., and Robinson, S. (1982). *General Equilibrium Models for Development Policy.* New York: Cambridge University Press.

Diao, X. and Thurlow, J. (2012). A recursive dynamic computable general equilibrium model. In Diao X., J. Thurlow, S. Benin and S. Fan (eds.), Strategies and Priorities for African Agriculture: Economywide Perspectives from Country Studies. Washington DC, USA: IFPRI, 17–50.

Dixit, A. K. and J. E. Stiglitz (1977). Monopolistic competition and optimum product diversity. *American Economic Review* 67, 297–308.

Dwyer, L., Forsyth, P. and Dwyer, W. (2010) Tourism Economics and Policy. Cheltenham: Channel View Publications.

Dwyer, L., Forsyth, P., and Spurr, R. (2004). Evaluating tourism's economic effects: new and old approaches. Tourism Management 25(3), 307–317.

Dwyer, L., Forsyth, P., Spurr, R., and Van Ho, T. (2003). Tourism's contribution to a state economy: a multi-regional general equilibrium analysis. *Tourism Economics* 9(4), 431–448.

Elbehri, A. and Herte, T. (2004). A Comparative Analysis of the EU–Morocco FTA vs. Multilateral Liberalization. GTAP Working Paper. No. 1643. Indianapolis, US: Center for Global Trade Analysis.

Forsyth, P (2007). Estimating the costs and benefits of regional airport subsidies: A computable general equilibrium approach. Mimeo May.

Forsyth, P., Dwyer, L., Spurr, R., and Pham, T. (2014). The impacts of Australia's departure tax: Tourism versus the economy?. *Tourism Management 40*, 126–136.

Forsyth, P., Niemeier, H-M., and Njoya, E. (2020). 'Economic Evaluation of Investments in Airports: Old and New Approaches', Monash University, mimeo.

Graham, D. J. and Melo, P. C. (2011). Assessment of wider economic impacts of high-speed rail for Great Britain. *Transportation Research Record* 2261(1), 15–24.

Harback, K., Martin, S., Wojcik, L., Tsao, S., Welman, S., Dixon, P., and Rimmer, M. (2015). Incorporating Air Transport Congestion into a Large CGE Model of the US Economy. Available at www.gtap.agecon.purdue.edu/resources/res_display.asp?RecordID=4757

Harberger, Arnold C. (1962). The incidence of the corporation income tax. *Journal of Political Economy* 70(3), 5–40.

Harris, R. (1984). Applied general equilibrium analysis of small open economies with scale economies and imperfect competition'. *American Economic Review* 74(5), 1016–1032.

Hosoe, N., Gasawa, K., and Hashimoto, H. (2010). *Textbook of Computable General Equilibrium Modeling: Programming and Simulations.* Basingstoke: Palgrave Macmillan.

Hudson, E. A. and Jorgenson, D. W. (1974). U.S. energy policy and economic growth, 1975–2000. *Bell Journal of Economics and Management Science* 5, (2), 461–514.

Industries Assistance Commission (1989). Travel and Tourism Report. 423, September. Canberra: Australian Government Publishing Service.

Ivanova, O., Vold, A., and Jean-Hansen, V. (2002). Pingo – a model for prediction of regional and interregional freight transport. TØI report, 578/2002, Oslo.

Ivanova, O. (2003). The role of transport infrastructure in regional economic development. *The Institute of Transport Economics (TØI). TØI Report, 671,* 2003.

Johansen, L. (1960). *A Multisectoral Study of Economic Growth.* Amsterdam: North-Holland.

Joint Study on Aviation Capacity in the Sydney Region (2012). Report to Australian Government and N.S.W. Government. Canberra and Sydney.

Kamble, S.D. (2005). Relations Among En-route Air Traffic, Controller Staffing and System Performance, Master's Thesis, Department of Civil and Environmental Engineering, University of Maryland, College Park. Available at https://drum.lib.umd.edu/bit-stream/handle/1903/3006/umi-umd-2806.pdf?sequence=1&isAllowed=y.

Kim, E., Hewings, G. J.D., and Hong, C. (2004). Application of integrated transport network multiregional CGE model: a framework for economic analysis of highway projects. *Economic System Research* 16, 235–258.

Knowles, R. D. and Ferbrache, F. (2016). Evaluation of wider economic impacts of light rail investment on cities. *Journal of Transport Geography* 54, 430–439.

Konan, D. E. and Maskus, K. E. (2006). Quantifying the impact of services liberalization in a developing country. *Journal of Development Economics* 81(1), 142–162.

Konan, D. E. and Van Assche, A. (2007). Regulation, market structure and service trade liberalization. *Economic Modelling* 24(6), 895–923.

Kulmer, V., Koland, O., Steininger, K. W., Fürst, B., and Käfer, A. (2014). The interaction of spatial planning and transport policy: a regional perspective on sprawl. *Journal of Transport and Land Use* 7(1), 57–77.

Lofgren, H. and Robinson, S. (2002), Spatial-network, general-equilibrium model with a stylized application. *Regional Science and Urban Economics* 32, 651–671.

Mackie, P., Worsley, T., and Eliasson, J. (2014). Transport appraisal revisited. *Research in Transportation Economics* 47, 3–18.

Marin, P. L. (1995). Competition in European aviation: pricing policy and market structure. *The Journal of Industrial Economics* 43(2), 141–159.

Melbourne Airport (2003). *Melbourne Airport Economic Impact Study*. Melbourne: Sinclair Knight Merz.

Miyagi, T. (2006). Evaluation of Economic Impacts from the Accessibility-change by Transportation Investment: A SCGE Modeling approach (Working Paper). Gifu: Regional Studies, Gifu University.

MMRF: Monash Multi-Regional Forecasting Model: A Dynamic Multi-Regional Model of the Australian Economy. Available at www.copsmodels.com/ftp/workpapr/g-223.pdf).

Nitzsche, E. and Tscharaktschiew, S. (2013). Efficiency of speed limits in cities: a spatial computable general equilibrium assessment. *Transportation Research Part A: Policy and Practice* 56, 23–48.

Njoya, E. T. (2019). An analysis of the tourism and wider economic impacts of price-reducing reforms in air transport services in Egypt. *Research in Transportation Economics* 100795.

Pereira, R. H. (2018). Transport legacy of mega-events and the redistribution of accessibility to urban destinations. *Cities 81*, 45–60.

PWC (2013). The economic impact of air passenger duty. http://airlinesuk.org/wp-content/uploads/2013/09/APD-study-Abridged.pdf.

PWC (2017). The economic impact of air taxes in Europe, Germany. https://a4e.eu/wp-content/uploads/2017/10/The-economic-impact-of-air-taxes-in-Europe-Germany-004.pdf.

Robson, E. N., Wijayaratna, K. P., and Dixit, V.V. (2018). A review of computable general equilibrium models for transport and their applications in appraisal. *Transportation Research Part A: Policy and Practice* 116, 31–53.

Roson, R. (2006). Introducing imperfect competition in CGE models: technical aspects and implications. *Computational Economics* 28(1), 29–49.

Rutherford T. and Paltsev, S. (1999), From an Input-Output Table to a General Equilibrium Model: Assessing the Excess Burden of Indirect Taxes in Russia. Department of Economics, University of Colorado, mimeo.

Samuelson, P. A. (1954). The transfer problem and transport costs, II: analysis of effects of trade impediments. *Economic Journal* 64, 264–289.

Scarf, H. E. (1967). On the computation of equilibrium prices. In W. J. Fellner (ed.), *Ten Economics Studies in the Tradition of Irving Fisher*. New York: Wiley.

Scarf, H E., with the collaboration of T. Hansen (1973). *The Computation of Economic Equilibria*. New Haven, CT: Yale University Press.

Sebestyén, T. (2017). Moving beyond the iceberg model: the role of trade relations in endogenizing transportation costs in computable general equilibrium models. *Economic Modelling* 67, 159–174.

Shahrokhi Shahraki, H. and Bachmann, C. (2018). Designing computable general equilibrium models for transportation applications. *Transport Reviews* 38(6), 737–764.

Shoven, J. B. and Whalley, J. (1972). A general equilibrium calculation of the effects of differential taxation of income from capital in the U.S. *Journal of Public Economics* 1, 281–321.

Shoven, J. B. and Whalley, J. (1973). General equilibrium with taxes: a computational procedure and an existence proof. *Review of Economic Studies* 40, 475–489.

Tavasszy, L. A., Thissen, M. J. P. M., and Oosterhaven, J. (2011). Challenges in the application of spatial computable general equilibrium models for transport appraisal. *Research in Transportation Economics* 31(1), 12–18.

Taylor, L. (2016). CGE applications in development economics. *Journal of Policy Modeling* 38(3), 495–514.

Thissen, M. (1998). A Classification of Empirical CGE Modeling. SOM Research Report 99C01.

Truong, T. P. and Hensher, D. A. (2012). Linking discrete choice to continuous demand within the framework of a computable general equilibrium model. *Transportation Research Part B: Methodological* 46(9), 1177–1201.

Tscharaktschiew, S. and Hirte, G. (2012). Should subsidies to urban passenger transport be increased? A spatial CGE analysis for a German metropolitan area. *Transportation Research Part A: Policy and Practice* 46(2), 285–309.

Ueda, T., Koike, A., Yamaguchi, K., and Tsuchiya, K. (2005). Spatial benefit incidence analysis of airport capacity expansion: Application of SCGE model to the Haneda Project. *Research in Transportation Economics* 13, 165–196.

Venables, A. (2007). Evaluating urban transport investments. *Journal of Transport Economics and Policy* 41(2), 173–188.

Vickerman, R. (2007). Recent evolution of research into the wider economic benefits of transport infrastructure investments. OECD, 29–49.

Walras L. (1874). Eléments d'économie politique pure. In L. Walras, *Oeuvres économiques complètes*, VIII, Paris: Economica. English translation 1977. *Elements of Pure Economics*, Fairfield: Augustus M. Kelley.

Yamaguchi, K., Ueda, T., Ohashi, T., Takuma, F., Tsuchiya, K., and Hikada, T. (2001). Economic impact analysis of deregulation and airport capacity expansion in Japanese domestic aviation market. Available at www.mlit.go.jp/pri/shiryou/pdf/ronbun.pdf

Zhang, P., and Peeta, S. (2011). A generalized modeling framework to analyze interdependencies among infrastructure systems. *Transportation Research Part B: Methodological* 45(3), 553–579.

8 Economic impact analysis, cost benefit analysis, and computable general equilibrium modelling

Outline of techniques and where to use them

Peter Forsyth and Hans-Martin Niemeier

Introduction

Economic evaluation is essential for good governance, especially in the air transport industry, where there are many government interventions. There is a wide range of policy questions which need to be answered, such as those concerning investments in infrastructure, negotiating with foreign countries about air rights, and choosing whether to tax or subsidise flights. To making these decisions, governments need accurate and rigorous evaluations of the significance, impacts, and net benefits from these policies.

This chapter focuses on ex ante evaluation. There is a need for an ex post evaluation. It is important to know how well the existing investments have worked, and how large the costs and benefits from liberalisation are. However, the starting point for rational policymaking is good ex ante evaluation.

We concentrate on three techniques of evaluation – economic impact analysis (EIA), Cost benefit analysis (CBA), and computable general equilibrium (CGE) modelling. The first two of these have been used extensively in air transport evaluation in the past, though there are still new developments. The third is relatively new. There are individual chapters on each of these in this Handbook. These are the best documented and frequently used techniques, though there are others, such as described by Quinet (2000) and Partidário and Miguel (2011).

The objective of this chapter is to fit the three techniques into an overall perspective. This involves doing several things:

- Outlining the techniques, and explaining what their contribution might be;
- Summarising the uses to which they have been put in air transport evaluation;
- Explaining what the differences between them are and what they can, and cannot do;

- Explaining the problem areas and how these can be overcome; and
- How they can be used together to achieve the best possible evaluation.

We look at these aspects in turn.

The tasks and techniques for evaluation

At the risk of simplification, there are three distinct evaluation questions which are commonly asked, and there are three main techniques which have been employed to answer them. These questions are:

- What is the *economic significance* of the project or policy?
- What is the *impact* of the project or policy, and
- What are the *net benefits* of undertaking the project or policy?

To clarify matters, some definitions are of help. Significance is a broad term, which refers to how large the economic size or output of the project or policy is. An airport may be a large one, associated with a large amount of output, generated directly and indirectly. The positive or negative impact is the difference it makes to variables of interest, such as GDP, employment in a region or the whole economy, and the net change in consumption in the region and economy. A large new airport may have a relatively large or small impact on the overall economy; the latter could happen if it mainly serves traffic which was served adequately by existing airports. The net benefit, or welfare gain or loss, measures how much better or worse off the region or economy is as a result of the project or policy. A new airport many be large, but if it is poorly sited or not used much, it may create negative net benefit if its costs are greater than its benefits (see Waters, 1976, for a discussion of the difference between impacts and benefits).

In evaluation, it is important to be clear what the evaluation seeks to show. Sometimes, the significance is what is needed, however this not the same thing as the project or policy having a large impact, or positive for the economy. Many large projects do not have a large net impact on the economy (they merely shift economic activity around) or are beneficial for it. Many evaluations of significance go further and claim that they measure impacts or benefits – however, the calculations do not go beyond measuring significance – something which is very confusing for readers and users of the studies.

We distinguish three types of evaluation; all of these are commonly employed.

- Economic Impact Analysis (EIA);
- Cost Benefit Analysis (CBA); and
- Computable General Equilibrium (CGE) Modelling.

EIA is something of a misnomer, since it cannot measure the 'impact' of a project or policy, in the sense of making an estimate of all aspects of the impact,

Table 8.1 Techniques and results

	EIA	CBA	CGE
Measuring significance	Yes	No	Yes
Measuring impact	No	No	Yes
Measuring net benefit	No	Yes	Yes (possibly)

including direct and indirect effects. It is based on input-output models. It can be used to study the significance of a project in terms of its gross impact. CBA has been used for 60 years as a means of measuring the net benefits of a project, and it is based on welfare economics (Boardman, 2011; De Rus, 2010). It only provides results in terms of net benefits. It cannot measure the impact on variables such as GDP or employment. CGE modelling is the newest of the three techniques (see Burfisher, 2011). It starts with an input-output framework, but goes a lot further – it takes into account all markets in the economy, and models consumer behaviour, firm behaviour, possibly the government sector, and takes into account resource constraints. Because of this, it is able to evaluate the net impact of a project or policy; for example, it can estimate the negative as well as the positive impacts of a project, and potentially come up with a negative impact on GDP or employment. A complication with CGE concerns its ability to estimate net benefit or the impact on welfare. Models can be either simple or comprehensive, and may or may not be able to estimate net benefits. In some regions (especially in much of Europe) CGE models tend to include a welfare measure while in others (including the UK) they tend not to. Table 8.1 summarises the abilities of the three evaluation techniques.

The types of evaluation problems

In the air transport industry, there is a very wide range of evaluation problems which can come about. The three techniques outlined above are being continually used to assess significance, impacts, and net benefits. It is handy to group the types of evaluation problems into three:

- Airport issues;
- Airline policy issues, and
- Broader aviation policy issues.

Airports

There are many issues concerning airports which are subject to either formal evaluation (e.g. a CBA) or informal evaluation. The most obvious of these is assessing a new airport, gauging its significance, its impacts on the regional and national economy, and whether its net benefits warrant investment in it. Investment in a new terminal, aprons and airside facilities, and investment in surface access all pose evaluation issues. It is possible that the airport might be subsidised – this can be evaluated. In principle, government decisions such as whether to privatise can be subject to formal evaluation (in practice, most privatisation decisions are subjected to informal evaluation). Decisions to close an airport can be evaluated.

Airline policy options

Airline policy options have not been evaluated formally until recently. They have been the province of hardnosed negotiators in smoke-filled rooms. However, this is not the best way of doing things, and airline policies can be submitted to rigorous economic analysis. In several countries, such as the UK, Australia, and Canada, governments have been moving towards a more 'economic' evaluation of liberalisation. The costs and benefits to a country of permitting a new foreign airline to access its gateways, or schedule extra capacity are now sometimes evaluated by using CBA. Proposals to subsidise flights, for example to remote destinations, can be evaluated. The economic impacts of developing an open skies environment for a region is also something which can be evaluated.

Broader aviation policies

There is a very wide range of issues coming under the term of broader aviation policies which call out for evaluation. One of these, which is becoming very topical, is that of assessing the impacts, benefits, or costs of aviation taxes. Airport curfews and other noise related measures have been evaluated. Investments in the infrastructure of air traffic management are also being evaluated. There have been several suggestions for the limitation of aviation's greenhouse gas emissions, which can be evaluated. There are subsidies being granted to aircraft manufacturers – do countries gain from these?

It is easy to develop a long list of investments and policies which are currently subjected to formal economic evaluation in the aviation industry. There is also a long list of evaluation issues which are not analysed rigorously as yet, but which cry for more systematic evaluation than at present. We discuss some examples of evaluation problems in turn.

Airport evaluation

Economic impact analysis

Airports have been evaluated using EIA increasingly since the 1990s. The first extensive use of EIA was when the United States liberalised aviation in the early 1990s, when the US Department of Transportation recommended that EIA studies be done of airport investments to determine their regional significance (Federal Aviation Administration, 1992). A second wave of EIA studies came in Europe. Significantly, the proponents of EIA were industry and lobby groups, such as the Airports Council International-Europe (ACI-Europe, 1998). These industry groups claimed much more for airports than before – for example, labelling them as 'job machines'. Both the United States and Europe have become fertile ground for EIA studies. There have been very many studies done to highlight the role and benefits of airports in communities in the US, especially when extensions or new airports are being planned. In Europe, EIA has been used as a decision-making tool, to advise on the costs and benefits of investments. Thus EIA studies were used to measure the pros and cons of a new runway at Frankfurt airport (Bulwien et al, 1999). By the early 2000s, EIA studies were being used in studying regional airports, and whether sub-sidies were warranted to attract low-cost carriers. Perhaps the most significant use of EIA was that for the evaluation of the troubled new Berlin airport. Here the study was claimed to measure the costs and benefits of the airport (no cost benefit study was done of the investment in the airport).[1] Here it is easy to appreciate the finding of the World Bank that poorly evaluated investments also tend to be poorly performing investments (Jenkins, 1997).

It is worth noting that the claims being made on behalf of EIA have become much more questionable. EIA can be used as a way of evaluating the economic significance of airport investments – this was what it was used for in earlier studies. However, practitioners have gone much further than this, and EIA is claimed to be a way of measuring the impacts of the investment, and also the benefits and costs which creates (e.g. York Aviation, 2009; Oxford Economics, 2011a, 2011b). For an early critical view, see Niemeier, 2001, for a more recent one see Thießen, 2009). These claims are quite incorrect. The only way of measuring the impacts is to use a CGE (or equivalent model), and the only ways to assess the costs and benefits is to use a CBA, or a CGE model with a welfare measure.

Cost benefit analysis

CBA has been used very extensively in evaluating airport investments from the 1960s onwards. A milestone was the Roskill study, which used it to evaluate options for a new airport for London in the late 1960s and early 1970s (Commission on the Third London Airport, 1969). This study developed a number of new techniques and provided a template for valuation of large airports (Commission on the Third London Airport, 1969; Mishan, 1970). The Second Sydney Airport in the 1970s used this template (Mills, 1982), and the Netherlands used similar approaches in evaluating investments at airports (Central Planning Bureau, 1974). There have been many CBAs of both large and small airport investments around the world. In 2003 the UK revisited the London airport question, again using a CBA approach (Department for Transport, 2003). The recent London Airport Commission undertook a CBA to determine which of the options for a new runway would be most effi-cient (Airports Commission, 2015a, 2015b) (the Commission also used a CGE approach to analyse specific questions – see Airports Commission, 2014), and there was a CBA study of siting options for a new airport in Sydney which reported in 2012 (Joint Study, 2012).There have been many examples of the use of CBA to evaluate airport investments – recent studies have included those by CE Delft (2013) and Jorge-Calderón (2014).

Computable general equilibrium modelling

CGE modelling has been used to analyse particular tasks, notably the timing of a new airport for Sydney (2012), and it was used to analyse the wider economic impacts of a new runway for London (Airports Commission, 2014). Other examples include a study of the second airport for Sydney (Deloittes Access Economics, 2013), a new runway for Brisbane Airport (2007), and a study of Haneda Airport in Tokyo (Ueda et al, 2005). One of the earliest applications of CGE was the study of the lack of a noise curfew at Melbourne Airport (Melbourne Airport, 2003; Madden, (2004).

Air transport policy

Economic impact analysis

EIA studies of the consequences of governments allowing foreign airlines to access routes have become popular of late. In years gone by, bilateral regulation between countries to determine which airline was permitted to serve which cities was done in closed meetings of bureaucrats. More recently, route alloca-tion has become much more open and politicised. Countries and airlines have been putting forward cases as to why they should be granted extra routes or gateways. In some cases they have been emphasising the economic significance of the proposed route or route expansion, or the impact of granting them extra rights, or the benefits for the home economy.

There is no better example than Emirates. Emirates has been very active in promoting liberalisation, both in general and in particular country contexts. It has several commissioned studies using an EIA approach to measuring the benefits of liberalisation in countries in which it is seeking additional rights, such as Australia (Oxford Economics, 2011b), Canada (InterVISTAS, 2010), the United States, and Europe in general. It has commissioned a study of Germany from DLR (Alers et al., 2012). It has also commissioned a study by Oxford Economics of its impacts on the Dubai economy (Oxford Economics, 2011b). These studies highlight estimated GDP and employment effects. Other airlines have, from time to time, commissioned similar studies. There have also been studies done for governmental bodies – an example of this is the study of liber-alisation in Africa undertaken for the World Bank (Schlumberger, 2010).

As with all EIAs, one must be careful as to what they are really saying. If they are to be read simply as studies of *significance*, they can be regarded as acceptable. However, if they are claiming to measure the *impact* (for example, of Emirates being permitted to fly to Berlin), or the *benefits* from those flights, they must be regarded as questionable. EIA does not, and cannot, estimate the impact of these flights nor their benefits, if only because it is a technique which measures the positive effects of the change but not the negative effects. It is clear however that many readers would assume that the studies are measuring the *impacts* or the *benefits*.

Cost benefit analysis

CBA is an evaluation technique which has been used in a number of studies of liberalisation of domestic and international liberalisation, though it has not been used very widely. The theory of how it can be applied to evaluate whether a country gains or not from allowing access to the routes it controls to foreign airlines has been developed thoroughly, however. Several times studies have measured the costs and benefits of allowing access even though they have not used the term 'CBA' – nevertheless, these studies are indeed CBAs.

Perhaps the earliest use of CBA to examine liberalisation questions came in an Australian Government report, the International Civil Aviation Policy Report of 1978 (International Civil Aviation Policy, 1978) – this report measured the costs and benefits to airlines and passengers and the net surplus, of liberalisation options being considered. Morrison and Winston used an explicit cost and benefit framework to analyse the benefits of US domestic airline deregulation (Morrison and Winston, 1986). The Australian framework was further developed in a 1988 Report (Department of Transport and Communications, 1988). The most rigorous CBA studies were those used by the Australian Productivity Commission in 1998 (Productivity Commission, 1998) and the accompanying study by Gregan and Johnson (Gregan and Johnson, 1999), and in Canada by Gillen et al. (2002). Further developments of the CBA approach have been Gillen et al. (2001), and Forsyth (2014), where the importance of foreign ownership of airlines is emphasised.

Computable general equilibrium modelling

CGE has been used sporadically in the analysis of air transport liberalisation. An early study was that done by the Centre for International Economics in 1988 (Centre for International Economics, 1988), concentrating on liberalisation and tourism. This work was a submission to the Industries Assistance Commission (Industries Assistance Commission, 1989) (now the Productivity Commission) which further analysed the subject. One of the benefits or costs of liberalisation comes about from its effect on inbound and outbound tourism to a country. This aspect is studies in a number of papers reported on by Forsyth (2006). A more recent study is that by Njoya in liberalisation and tourism to Kenya (Njoya, 2016). This study paid particular attention to the distributional impacts of tourism made possible by liberalisation.

While there are only a few studies using a CGE approach, it is an approach well worth exploring and developing further. It is an approach which could capture general equilibrium aspects of liberalisation, something which CBA cannot do.

Broader aviation policy questions

There are several other evaluation issues which have been, or could be, analysed using the evaluation techniques discussed here. Some of them are:

- Assessing aviation taxes;
- Evaluating the impacts of greenhouse gas emissions reduction policies; and
- Evaluating the benefits and costs of investments in traffic control.

These are briefly discussed here. There have been several studies of aviation taxes, such as the UK Air Passenger Duty (APD) (Oxford Economics, 2011a). Others are the (repealed) Netherlands tax and the German tax (Berster et al, 2010). Most of these have been commissioned by interested parties, such as airlines. Furthermore, most of the studies have used EIA techniques. These studies emphasise the negative effect on passenger traffic, but they do not include the positive effects on government revenue – not surprisingly, they all claim that the nation imposing the tax is worse off as a result of imposing it (a study which does take account of both sides of the revenue issue is one under-taken for the European Commission, 2019).

There have been two groups of CGE studies. One was a study of the Australian Passenger Movement Charge (PMC) (Tourism Research Australia, 2011) which was revised in Forsyth et al, (2014). This concluded that the country gained from imposing the tax. The other was a study of the UK APD – this concluded that the UK lost from imposing the tax (PwC, 2013). More recently, there has been a study of other aviation taxes in Europe by the same consultant – this presumably used the same approach as the earlier study (and was similarly critical of the taxes). One reason for the difference in results is that the UK studies have assumed significant wider economic benefits (see section 5 below) of aviation.

A CGE approach is very well suited to exploring the impacts of measures to reduce greenhouse gas emissions from aviation and tourism. In spite of this, we are not aware of much research in this area.

Air traffic control systems require substantial investments. Not surprisingly, CBAs have been used to evaluate whether they provide net benefits. The EU is undertaking major investments to upgrade their systems – the SESAR program. These investments have been evaluated using CBA (Eurocontrol, 2014).

There are many other policy options which could be subjected to economic evaluation. Some are:

- Evaluating the privatisation of airports and similar assets;
- Assessing the costs and benefits of subsidy schemes for air transport, including services to remote regional locations – (see Forsyth, 2007);

- Evaluating changes to economic regulation (the Irish Aviation Commission has explored the costs and benefits of light handed regulation of airports);
- Evaluating alternative allocative arrangements for airport slots; and
- The evaluation of airline alliance and merger proposals from a public policy perspective.

Analysing the three techniques

Economic impact analysis

It is best to look at EIA first because it is rather different from the other two. It can be used to measure significance, but nothing more. Indeed, the very title is quite misleading – in spite of the use of the term 'impact', it cannot be used to measure impact (only a CGE approach can do this). It can estimate only part of the impacts on the economy. In spite of this, it is often misused.

A typical EIA, for example of an airport investment or the impact of airline liberalisation will first measure the initial direct effect, such as the effect coming about from the funds being spent on the airport or the expenditure on tourism enabled by the liberalisation. It will then use an input-output model to estimate additional multiplier effects. The ultimate impact will be a multiple of the initial effect – typically, the total impact as measured will be around twice the initial effect. If the policy change being considered is a negative one, such as the imposition of a tax, the final negative impact will be around twice as large as the initial effect.

There are many problems with using EIA in an attempt to measure impacts of a policy change or an investment. Some of the more important ones are:[2]

- It is a partial equilibrium approach, which only measures some of the impacts of a change, but ignores many others which are equally important as those included. Because of this, the impacts of an investment or policy change, on GDP or employment, will typically be very large (something which should provoke some questioning).
- It effectively assumes that resources are costless – labour and capital to build an airport are free, the tourism benefits which come about from an airline liberalisation can be produced at zero cost, and the effects of a tax on air passengers give rise to freeing up of resources which cannot be used in any other way in the economy.
- It measures the positive effects of an investment but not the (equally important) negative effects.
- It confuses benefits and costs to such an extent that all effects of an investment are benefits. EIA usually argues that investment creates a certain number of additional jobs, and that these are the benefits of a project, declares the inputs of project as outputs, or to put it differently, it redefines costs as benefits.

In effect, the result is that EIA is of no value in evaluating the impacts of a policy change or an investment. According to it, all investments are positive for the economy, and give rise to net benefits. The whole point of an evaluation is to determine a balance between the positive and negative effects – a technique which only measures the positive (or all of the negative effects) effects is of no value.

EIA is often used by proponents of schemes or by their consultants to claim that the impacts on employment or GDP or benefits will be large and positive (or the impacts of a tax will be large and negative). Claims are superficially convincing to those who are not aware of the flaws in the analysis. In many countries, Finance Departments (who often provide the funds for the investments) and, increasingly, Transport Departments (who determine whether air services can be operated), are extremely suspicious of EIA studies, and require CBA or CGE studies to be done.

CBA and CGE

CBA and CGE are both rigorously based evaluation techniques which are well established in the transport and in general economic literature. In the past, they have tended to be used for different tasks – CBA was developed to evaluate net benefits, while CGE was developed as a means of evaluating impacts, such as the effect on GDP of an economy or on employment. More recently, CGE studies have been used as a means of evaluating net benefits, initially in ground transport (see Broecker and Mercenier, 2011) and then in air transport – in this respect the results of a CGE study will be comparable to those of a CBA. For this to be the case, the CGE model needs to include a net benefits or welfare measure, and many CGE models do not have this. Some key characteristics of the two techniques are as follows:

CBA

- CBA has a rigorous theoretical basis in welfare economics;
- It is highly practical;
- It can be used for a very wide range of evaluation problems, and it can handle a very wide range of benefits and costs;
- It is easy to understand and straightforward, and relatively cheap to use;
- It is a partial equilibrium tool, which focuses on the markets directly affected and thus does not capture general equilibrium aspects of an evaluation problem;
- It does not capture macro effects, for example, it does not estimate the employment aspects of a project;
- It can handle localised externalities, such as noise emissions of an airport, but cannot measure well economy (or global) externalities, such as greenhouse gas emissions;
- It can measure the initial or direct distributional effects of a project or policy change, but not the ultimate distributional effects of a change.

CGE

- CGE models are model based evaluation techniques – in order to conduct an evaluation, one needs to have access to a model;
- They are complete models of economies, and embody all relevant markets and relationships (unlike EIA, which is a model based approach with only parts of an economy);
- The model is closed (if a project needs resources, they need to come from somewhere in the model, not like EIA);
- Models can be large (two sectors) or large (500 industries);
- Can be used to evaluate impacts on the economy (such as change in GDP or employment), or on net benefits from a change, but only if the model has a welfare measure;
- CGE models are a general equilibrium technique, and can handle everything if the model is detailed enough;
- They can evaluate impacts and benefits/costs of economy-wide or global externalities such as greenhouse gas emissions;
- They can evaluate detailed direct and indirect impacts on distribution.

There are several issues which arise from these points.

Coverage of effects

As noted, the CGE approach is, in principle, a more widely encompassing approach than CBA. It can measure everything, while CBA can only measure a range of (partial equilibrium) effects. However, it is limited by the model being used. If the model has very few industries, it will be too aggregate for accurate evaluation. To get more accuracy, it is possible to disaggregate the model. One way of doing this is to create sub models for the industries that are being explored. Thus, for example, a model might have a 'transport' industry; this will be too aggregative to measure precise effects in air transport. However it is possible to subdivide the transport sector into air transport and surface transport industries.

As mentioned above, CBA was often regarded as the appropriate means of evaluating net benefits for which it was designed, and CGE was regarded as appropriate for assessing impacts, normally, but not exclusively at a macro level. More recent research has emphasised the value of CGE in measuring net benefits (see Broecker and Mercenier, 2011); indeed, some would suggest that CGE models might render CBA redundant. To do this, the model needs to have a welfare measure. This can be done explicitly (the model produces effects on GDP, employment, and net benefits), or alternatively, the model can be adjusted to produce approximations to welfare using variables already documented in the model. However, there is a word of caution. Some users of CGE models which do not have a welfare measure claim that they can use approximations such as overall consumption or GDP as a welfare measure; in general, this is incorrect, and can lead to very inaccurate estimates.

In Table 8.2 the ability of the two techniques to measure these various effects is summarised.

Table 8.2 Ability to measure variables of interest: comparison of techniques

Ability to measure	CGE	CBA
Economic impacts (e.g. GDP, Employment)	Yes	No. Very difficult to handle
Welfare	Perhaps. Needs to be specified in model-often not done	Yes
Benefits and costs from inbound/outbound tourism	Yes	No. Very difficult to handle
Local externalities (e.g. noise)	Perhaps. Externalities normally addressed outside the model but environmental measures can be added easily	Yes
National/global (e.g. greenhouse gas emissions)	Yes – if specified in the model	No. Estimates from CGE modelling can be added in in some cases
General equilibrium effects	Yes	No. Shadow pricing can measure some of these
Distributional impacts	Yes	No. Can measure only direct, not indirect incidence
Detail and disaggregation	Perhaps if disaggregated sub models are used	Yes
Benefits of jobs created	Perhaps. Can measure quantitative effects, but needs additional valuation	Perhaps. Can value the effects but needs quantitative data on employment numbers

This table compares the ability of each technique to provide a measure of interest to event evaluation. Can the technique be adjusted so that it can provide a measure? In some cases a qualification is made.

One aspect which emerges from this table is that CGE can, with suitable adaptations, handle all of these key aspects of the aviation evaluation task, while CBA is not able to do this. This might be expected given that CGE is a more general technique. Thus, a CGE evaluation can be adjusted to account for local externalities and to value jobs, essentially using approaches from cost benefit analysis.

Difficult and practical issues

Partial and general equilibrium evaluations

A technique such as CGE is a general equilibrium technique, and it can be used to assess impacts on a wide range of variables, such as GDP, National Income, Consumption and Employment, and it can be used to evaluate the net benefit from a project or policy, as long as it embodies a net benefits or welfare measure (many CGE models do not, though with a little further information, most models can be adjusted to at least produce a simplified welfare measure). In other words, a CGE model can be used in much the same way as a CBA. The measures they produce will not be identical, since the two approaches involve different approximations (for example, a CGE model may be more aggregate than a CBA). However, they can, in principle, do the same job (Broecker and Mercenier, 2011 – see also Farrow and Rose, 2018).

CBA is a partial equilibrium approach, which means that it focuses only on directly affected markets. Thus, if a new airport is built, a CBA will measure the direct benefits which passengers gain – typically, it will not go beyond this, such as measuring implications for substitute modes like rail, and the benefits and costs which come about. A CGE approach can measure these costs and benefits. In fact, this problem is recognised in the CBA literature, and there has been the development of 'shadow pricing' – this is a means of correcting for market prices to better reflect important aspects which are not captured in a partial equilibrium evaluation (Dinwiddy and Teal, 1996). Typically an evaluation will shadow price a few key prices, such as the shadow price of fuel (which is often highly taxed) or government revenues. If everything is shadow priced, the result is a general equilibrium evaluation. This is recognised in the theory of CBA; an ideal CBA would be a general equilibrium evaluation (Dreze and Stern, 1987).

In principle, a CGE evaluation will be a more comprehensive evaluation. There are several distortions in typical economies which will mean that a general equilibrium evaluation is a more accurate evaluation. These include taxes and subsidies, monopoly pricing and externalities. In some cases, a CGE approach is helpful in quantifying impacts and benefits such as those coming about from wider economic benefits of aviation and tourism benefits – both of these are discussed below.

The value of a general equilibrium perspective when evaluating investments and policy actions is evident when taxation aspects are considered. A typical policy intervention will have an impact on a wide range of different taxes which may be affected, directly and indirectly. If the CGE model has a comprehensive fiscal structure, all of these effects will be measured in an evaluation automatically. A partial approach may not capture these effects at all, or, if shadow prices are used, some of the tax effects, may be measured approximately, at best. The tax impacts of the investment or policy change could be quite significant, especially if some taxes are high and heavily distorting – which they are in many economies.

Employment and evaluation

If there is full employment in the economy, evaluation is made a lot easier. There is no particular reason to estimate the employment consequences of a project or policy to estimate what an additional job is worth (it is zero). However, in many countries, there is less than full employment, and even if a country has nearly full employment, there may be an unemployment problem in a region. With much public discussion, there is a presumption that additional employment is desirable, and phrases such as 'airports are job machines' and passenger taxes 'kill jobs' are common. In this environment, there is a need for estimation of the significance, the impacts, and the net benefits of changes in employment.

Of the three types of evaluation, one is of little use, while the other two are of clear use, though the most useful approach is to combine the two. The EIA approach can be used to assess the significance of a project or policy on employment – whether they have direct effects on employment and on how big this effect will be. However this does not give us an estimate of the net impact on employment, after taking into account the inevitable negative as well as positive effects. Just because an investment employs 1000 people does not mean that it has a net impact of 1000 on total employment; the net impact could be much less.

The CGE approach is ideal for estimating the net impact on employment, and wages. This is what it is designed to do. If there is unemployment in the country or region, it is likely that an investment will lead to a net gain in employment, though, depending on the region and the industries affected, along with the fiscal policies of the government, this cannot be guaranteed and a negative impact is possible. While CGE models can provide an estimate of the impact on employment, most CGE models would not be able to answer the question of how much a job is worth, and what the net benefit of the change in employment is however.

This type of question is best analysed using the techniques of CBA. A CBA will not be able to estimate the net change in employment. However, once an estimate of the change in employment is provided, it may be possible to estimate its value to the economy. CBA is about estimating benefits and costs. With information about labour markets, and the estimate which workers themselves put on having a job, the benefit from increased employment can be assessed. The shadow pricing literature, and in particular, the shadow wage literature, provides a way of evaluating the net benefit of a jobs change (Ray, 1984; Dinwiddy and Teal, 1996). The theory is difficult to operationalise since it depends on magnitudes which are not often reported, such as the value which workers put on having a job, or their willingness to work if offered a job. Empirical studies have suggested that the benefit from getting a job is significantly greater than the income gain from having the job (Winkelmann and Winkelmann, 1998; Di Tella et al., 2003). Sometimes CBAs are done which make assumptions, such as the shadow wage is x% of the market wage, and work out what this does to the estimated net benefit of the investment. At the very least, the CBA shadow pricing approach tells us what should be done if we have access to the required information.

In short, the CGE approach provides a means of estimating the impact of a project or policy on employment, and the techniques used by the CBA approach provide a means of evaluating what this impact would be worth; together they can provide a complete evaluation.

Externalities

The evaluation of externalities can form a significant part of the overall evaluation exercise. Externalities can be negative, such as noise from an airport or greenhouse gas emissions from a flight, or positive such as greater connectivity (discussed below). CBA has long recognised them and attempted to value them. Over the years, techniques to value externalities have become more reliable and robust, though there are still many problems. Thus, there have been many studies which put a cost on noise around airports. The main problem with CBA is that it is a partial equilibrium technique. Local externalities such as airport noise are straightforward to value, but nationwide or global externalities, such as greenhouse gas emissions cannot be valued by partial equilibrium approaches. Some externalities, such the cost of airport noise, are essentially local in nature, and a CBA approach to valuing them is adequate.

However other externalities go far beyond the local, and if they are likely to be large, their impacts and often value can be measured using a CGE model (the impacts on greenhouse gas emissions can be estimated using suitable CGE models (e.g. Adams et al, 2000) and the cost of the emissions can be estimated using CBA techniques).

Distribution

The distribution of income and wealth has become much more of an issue in the years since the global financial crisis. Before this, economies were growing relatively fast, and wages were growing with them. Investments and policy changes were not often evaluated in terms of their impacts on the distribution. It was assumed that, if the project or policies were good ones, most parts of society would gain – even if the initial beneficiaries were to the well off, the less well off would gain through 'trickle down effects'. Since the crisis, there has been much more concern about distribution of income, and indeed, the rise of poverty. It is no longer enough to simply assume that everyone gains from a good project or policy. A complete analysis will provide some assessment of the impacts on distribution.

At different stages in the development of CBA, there has been interest in distributional aspects of projects and policies. In the 1970s and early 1980s there was considerable interest in distribution and how to measure impacts (e.g., see Nwaneri, 1970; Ray, 1984). The main problem was that partial equilibrium approaches could only measure the direct incidence, and were not able to assess the ultimate incidence, which could be quite different. This may be one of the reasons why analysts did not assess distributional aspects; it was regarded as too difficult.

What is difficult in a partial equilibrium approach can be handled quite straightforwardly in a general equilibrium approach. A CGE model, which has a range of different income groups built in (or wealth groups, or employment groups, or land tenure groups) can be used to study the distributional impacts of projects and policies. Of course, many CGE models do not have different income groups identified, and thus they cannot be used to study income distribution. However, the model can be expanded to incorporate different income groups, and thus it can be used to study distributional questions.

Consider an airport development, perhaps oriented to tourism markets. An expanded airport will enable more tourists from other countries. There may be several gainers (e.g. passengers) and losers (e.g. local communities) from this type of aviation investment. The home country can gain from tax receipts, from airport profits, from accommodation revenues, from farmers selling land for hotels, and much more. Nearby residents may lose through more noise nuisance. The foreign tourists are likely to gain from better services. Exchange rates will change, and this will have an effect on food prices. It is very difficult to sort out who ultimately gains and who loses, and the initial incidence of effects can be quite different from the ultimate incidence. However it is possible to explore these questions using a CGE model. One such model is that of Njoya, who developed a model to study the distributional impacts of expanded tourism to Kenya (Njoya, 2016).

The drawback of using a CGE model to study distribution comes from the effort to build income groups (or other groups) into the model. Many models, especially smaller ones, do not have much detail about income groups – often there is only one. Most countries, especially European ones, have adequate data on income groups, and estimates of income elasticities are available. A CGE model which identifies income groups can then be developed, and distributional impacts of projects and policies can be estimated.

Wider economic benefits

If you were to look for the term 'wider economic benefits' of aviation ten years ago, you would be unable to find any references, since the concept had not been developed. However, this is becoming an important idea, and it has particular relevance to economic evaluation. It is an idea which has as its origin in the wider economic benefit of surface transport, which is in turn, dates back around 20 years. The basic idea is that conventional evaluation, such as that embodied in a CBA, may be missing out on some benefits (or costs) which are potentially important. There have been estimates made of the WEBs of surface transport – in the early days, there were estimates that WEBs were around 40% of total other benefits, though lately, the estimates have centred around 10% (see Vickerman, 2013).

The study of the wider economic benefits or WEBs of aviation is only in its infancy, and there is no agreement as to what constitutes a WEB, nor how they should be measured. There have been several suggestions of potential benefits (and sometimes costs) and there have been some suggested ways of measuring them (Pearce, 2014; Forsyth, 2020). There are several very different possible benefits discussed in the literature, and their relationship with one another is not clear. This contrasts with the discussion of the WEBs of surface transport where the theory is fairly straightforward. Part of the genesis of the surface transport WEBs lies in the new economic geography literature, which puts emphasis on the benefits from agglomeration – the main problem has been to measure these (Krugman, 1991; Graham, 2007; Venables, 2007). Another strand has been benefits which arise from the existence of market imperfections, such as taxes and monopoly – these can be measured using a CGE approach (Venables, 2007). There may be benefits from agglomeration with air transport, though the theory has yet to be set out, and there can be benefits which arise because of market imperfections, but the theory for this has not been spelt out.

The WEBs from air transport which have been suggested are much broader, but unspecific. It is sometimes argued that additional air transport will increase productivity or GDP, though the ways in which it does so are not specified. There has been a lot of interest measuring connectivity, which is straightforward, but the benefits from increased connectivity are not easy to measure. Measuring the wider benefits of aviation is something which is very much related to CBA and CGE approaches. There is something of an equivalent for the EIA approach in the attempt to measure catalytic benefits or impacts. These are not the same as WEBs, though they have some elements in common. Catalytic impacts (as defined in the studies of Infras (2005), Baum et al. (2005 and 2007) and Klophaus (2013)) are even more vaguely defined than WEBs. Catalytic effects mix effects of input and output models (direct, indirect, and induced effects) with measures from cost benefit and welfare analysis. This leads to double counting and has the problem of adding up apples and pears (see Forsyth et al, 2020).

There have been several techniques suggested to measure WEBs. One approach is to use microsimulation to measure the benefits of additional links in a network, and thus the benefits from connectivity. The gains from additional frequency and connectivity can be estimated. As with surface transport WEBs, CGE models can be useful in measuring tax and market imperfection aspects. Finally, econometric approaches, at the micro level of specific markets, or the macro level, looking at the effects of additional air transport on national productivity or GDP can be used.

Of these techniques, the most common is the last. The approach is quite simple. A regression is run of productivity or GDP on total air transport or a measure of connectivity (for example, Gillen et al., 2015). There are econometric problems which need to be addressed, in particular, identifying causation – is it GDP which is stimulating air transport, or air transport which is boosting GDP? Some of the better studies recognise the problem and carry out a Granger causality test (for example, the InterVISTAS study for IATA, see Smyth and Pearce, 2007), though most do not. Typically, these studies report very large impacts of additional air transport or connectivity – sufficiently large to swamp other benefits and costs of airport investments or additional airline services. The typical connectivity study measures the impact of connectivity on GDP or industry productivity. It does not measure the net benefits from this increased connectivity. It this respect, it cannot be used directly as a measure of net benefits to be used in a CBA or CGE model.

Estimates of WEBs have occasionally needed to be used in evaluation. One of these is a CGE study of the economic effects of the UK Air Passenger Duty (PwC, 2013). This study addressed various benefits and costs of the duty, and concluded that imposing it would lower the UK's GDP. It relied heavily on a study claiming that the reduction alone in air travel would lower GDP significantly. Another use of WEBs was a (CGE) study of wider economic impacts done for the London Airports Commission (Airports Commission, 2014, and see the discussion in Airports Commission, 2015a).

The current state of knowledge surrounding WEBs is far from satisfactory. There is much dispute about whether they exist, how they can be measured, and how significant they might be. It is possible that they could be quite large and that leaving them out will lead to biased evaluations. Until research has come up with results which are clearly defined and rigorously based, one should be sceptical of assessments which rely on large WEBs to get their results.

The availability of CGE models

For a well trained economist it is easy to do a CBA with little equipment – these days, a laptop with appropriate programs (as long as one has the data). EIA studies are more complex, and they require an input-output model, along with appropriate data. The infrastructure of CGE is distinctly more demanding. A CGE model is complex and models a whole range of markets, and in addition, the data requirements are much larger. As a result, many believe that the requirements of CGE models are so great as for them to be feasible only for very large projects. However, one does not have to develop and own a CGE model to use it.

These days, there are very many CGE models which can be accessed, from most medium to large countries. Even small countries have several models. Models are owned by research institutes, individual researchers, international agencies, and government departments. In many countries, general consultancies such as PwC and Deloittes have models, and specialist economic research consultancies have their own models. If the government needed to have a study done of the economic impact of a new runway, or the benefits and costs of imposing an air passenger tax, the chances are that it would be done by an economic consultancy or a research centre. Certainly there would be no need to build a new model from the beginning (though it may be worthwhile to further develop the existing model to enable it to better handle key markets which would be affected by the proposal). General equilibrium aspects could be important for many evaluation problems no matter how large or small they are; thus in principle, a CGE evaluation would be worthwhile. In practice, it might be expensive to have a CGE evaluation of very small projects. For most evaluation exercises, whichever technique is used, assembling the data about the project of policy change is a more substantial and expensive exercise than processing them into results.

Measuring sensitivities

With all approaches, a good analysis reports on sensitivities. This is well recognised, though not always followed, with CBA which uses risk analysis with Monte Carlo simulations (see De Rus, 2010). With model based evaluation techniques, such as EIA and CGE, there are many more ways in which variables can change, and thus many more results. This means that there is a problem of how to summarise. Often analysts provide a most likely scenario and report on lower and higher cases. The art of summarising is to identify what variables the results are most sensitive to, and highlight these. Fortunately, in these days of enormous computing power, there is little problem in calculating a wide range of results for all of these techniques.

Very often, the analyst provides a report and it is discussed at a higher level, and no further analysis is done. However, with all of the techniques discussed there, it is highly worthwhile if possible to iterate the results to improve them. There will be many questions of the form 'what is the effect of changing this'? It will be relatively easy to answer these. If this is done, the evaluation will be improved.

Setting up the evaluation exercise and disaggregation

However, these days, it is becoming much easier to disaggregate models, and develop sub models which drill down into specific markets. Thus, if an investment in a Dublin airport is being evaluated, it will be possible to create a Dublin airport sub model. This will involve some modelling work and data gathering, but it will enable a much more accurate evaluation. It is often the case that the development of a sub model, along with the data gathering, is the most time intensive aspect of the CGE modelling exercise.

The interpretation of results

Users of evaluations are quite familiar with how to interpret CBA studies in the main, though they can be confusing (for example, when different evaluations are produced of the same project by different agencies). The model based evaluation techniques require more interpretation. This is particularly true when there are different CGE models to choose from. CGE models are more demanding for the user, but more rewarding in that they can show light on a wide range of questions.

One question concerns how the investment or policy change is modelled. Suppose there is an investment in an airport. A CGE approach would be for the analyst to answer the question of how the airport was being paid for. It could be paid for from taxes, or passenger tax, or an increase in airport charges. Each of these can have a quite different impact and net benefit. The investment could also be financed by borrowing, and perhaps from abroad – if this is the case, how will the borrowings be paid back in the longer term? It is important to determine which option has been used.

Another set of questions comes about from the structure of the model being used. For example, how is the labour market modelled? Different models use very different labour market assumptions – some assume that employment is fixed but labour hours are not, while others assume that both employment and hours are fixed. Some models assume variable employment, using a fixed wage rate while others use other assumptions. Evaluations assuming a variable labour force will be quite different from those assuming a fixed labour force (the impacts and benefits of a project evaluated using the latter will be considerably smaller – and potentially more similar to those using a CBA – than those assuming the former).

Ideally, if a modelling approach is being used to evaluate, it is desirable that the results be interpreted by someone who 'knows their way around' the model. This person need not be a modeller, but is someone who is familiar with this sort of model, and who knows what to expect from the results, and can work out why particular results come about. Quite often, modelling evaluations produce seemingly plausible results which have been obtained by using questionable assumptions or even by using faulty models.

It needs to be recognised that a CGE model involves a very large number of assumptions to be made, and relationships between variables to be specified. In most cases, it is unnecessary to develop a new model – an investment assessment will be done using an existing model. This is not a problem as long as the model being used is a good one which reflects the economy accurately. If this is not the case, the modelling of air transport may be good, but the modelling of other sectors, such as the finance sector or the trade sector, may be inaccurate, resulting in inaccurate results of evaluations of investments or policies in air transport. More can go wrong with a CGE approach than with an EIA or CBA approach. It is sometimes difficult to determine how good a model being used is. To this end, it makes sense to use well tested models which are transparently documented and whose properties are known.

Optimising the evaluation: using CBA and CGE techniques to increase the comprehensiveness of the evaluation

As has been shown, neither a CBA nor a highly aggregative CGE model will result in a completely comprehensive evaluation. There will be several aspects which are left out. However the analyst need to have an either/or choice of technique to conduct the evaluation. If the evaluation is to be done using a CBA, it may be possible to use CGE model results to handle the aspects which CBA is not capable of measuring. If the evaluation is to be done using a CGE model, it may be feasible to use CBA techniques to value aspects which are not captured by the model. An example of this has already been mentioned, evaluating the benefits from a project which come about from increased labour force participation. There are many other ways of making the evaluation more comprehensive. We outline three of these:

- Handling local noise in a CGE model;
- Using results from CGE simulations to evaluate the benefits and costs of inbound and outbound tourism; and
- Measuring the shadow price of government revenue.

Localised noise

A CGE model would not normally measure and value noise costs, such as those at an airport. However, CBAs have often been used to assess noise costs. The same techniques can be used to make an outside-the-model evaluation of the noise cost, which can then be added in to the overall evaluation. This would be a simpler and more practical approach to including noise costs than putting airport noise into the model. It is likely to be as accurate, since the general equilibrium effects of local noise are likely to be minimal. This can be used for a whole host of aspects which need not be included in the model, including externalities, and other aspects (such as travel time savings from adding airport capacity).

Measuring tourism benefits

Aviation evaluation tasks often involve measuring the benefits and costs of inbound and outbound tourism. Some evaluations take account of all consumers, while others may distinguish between home and foreign consumers, see Johansson and De Rus, 2015. One of the benefits of an airport expansion is likely to be an increase in tourism from abroad (there will be a cost of outbound tourism as well). In the past, the tourism benefits have simply been assumed – for example, the recent Second Sydney study assumed that tourism benefits were 25% of tourism expenditure (Joint Study, 2012). There will also be a need to measure tourism benefits if there is an aviation policy change, such as liberalisation of a route.

Measuring tourism benefits is difficult since it involves measuring a wide range of small effects, on taxes and profits. However, with a CGE model, tourism benefits can be easily measured, and this has been done for a number of countries (Dwyer et al. 2005; Forsyth, 2006; Blake, 2009). These measures can be used in evaluating the benefits of airports and policy changes. Tourism benefit measures have not been done for many countries; for these countries, estimates can be made by assuming the parameters for other, similar, countries. Thus, we are not aware of any CGE model estimates of tourism benefits for Germany, but there have been estimates for the UK, which has a similar fiscal system. This would be much more accurate than making an arbitrary assumption.

The shadow price of government revenue

Many projects, such as airports, involve government expenditure. Taxes are not raised without costs; increasing taxes to fund projects has a cost in terms of efficiency. This means that a euro to be spent on a project costs more than one euro. This should be taken into account when the airport is being evaluated. There have been many estimates of the shadow price of government funds, or the social opportunity cost of taxation, and they exist for most countries (for an air transport example, see Keen et al, 2013).

If a project is being evaluated using a CGE model, it is possible that the shadow price is evaluated in the model. However, many models do not model taxation and the fiscal system in sufficient detail to produce reliable shadow prices of funds. If this is the case, this effect needs to be incorporated using an outside-the-model estimate, using another estimate. Where CGE models do have a detailed fiscal structure, the shadow price can be estimated, and the results suggest higher shadow price than those obtained by partial equilibrium approaches (Stuart, 1984).

Conclusions and unresolved questions

The techniques of economic evaluation in air transport are nowadays quite well developed. The basics of the three main evaluation approaches are well set out. It is not clear that they are always well understood however. In particular, there is confusion as to what the results of EIA studies are; many consider that EIA is a means of measuring impacts, which is not correct. Of the three techniques, only CGE is capable of measuring overall impacts. There are confusions about the relationship between the techniques. For example, many believe that CGE cannot measure net benefits or welfare, in the way CBA does. If fact it can, as long as the model has a welfare measure amongst its outputs. One objective of this chapter has been to try to sort out confusions.

Another objective has been to analyse problem areas. The theory of evaluation is being advanced, especially in the case of CGE, but also in the case of the older technique, CBA. Suggestions of how problems can be resolved have been made here. Some issues are more intractable than others however. We can suggest many, but three stand out.

The relationship between partial and general equilibrium evaluations. Are the two likely to be very different? The answer to this depends on the evaluation problem at hand. If it is one of assessing an investment with few externalities, and where there is no need to measure distributional impacts, the partial and general equilibrium evaluations may be fairly similar – they will be different to the extent that the latter would capture tax and market power effects while the former would not. However, if economy-wide externalities are likely to be significant and if distribution is a concern, then the partial approach would not suffice. Further research on this would be valuable.

Valuing employment changes in an economy with unemployment. Over the past decade, many countries have experienced significant unemployment, and few OECD countries could be described as having full employment. As a result, policymakers keep asking 'what will be the impact on jobs?'. Many CGE models can answer this question, though only approximately, since their labour markets are not modelled accurately. It is also of value to be able to estimate the benefits from additional employment. This is a difficult problem to analyse, but further work on it would be very helpful.

What are the wider economic benefits (WEBs) from air transport? The WEB question is a new one, but it has the potential to have an impact on the evaluation of just about all investment and policy questions in air transport. If research indicates that they are large, then most evaluations in the past have been inaccurate. This is also a priority for research.

Notes

1 For a detailed critical appraisal of impact studies see Forsyth et al. (2020).
2 For a comprehensive criticism see Forsyth et al. (2020).

References

Adams, P., Horridge, J. M., and Parmenter, B. (2000) MMRF – Green: a dynamic, multi-sectoral multi-regional model of Australia, Melbourne: Centre of Policy Studies, Monash University.

Airports Commission (2014) *2 Economy: Wider Impacts Assessment*, London, PwC/ Airports Commission November.

Airports Commission (2015a) Airport Commission expert advisor note. A note from expert advisors, Professor Peter Mackie and Mr Brian Pearce, on key issues considering the Airports Commission Economic Case, London, Airport Commission, May.

Airports Commission (2015b) *Airport Commission Final Report*, London: Airport Commission, July.

Airports Council International-European Region [ACI-Eurpeo] (1998) *Creating Employment and Prosperity in Europe*, Brussels.

Alers, T., Berster, P., Ehmer, H., Fuhrmann, M., Gelhausen, M., Grimme, W., Horn, S., Keimel, H., Maertens, S., and Nieße, H. (2012) *The Impact of Emirates Airline on the German Economy*, Cologne: DLR Institute of Air Transport and Airport Research.

Australian and NSW Governments (2012) *Joint Study on Aviation Capacity in the Sydney Region, report to Australian Government and N.S.W. Government*, Canberra and Sydney.

Baum, H., Schneider, J., Esser, K., and Kurte, J. (2005) *Wirtschaftliche Effekte des Airport Berlin Brandenburg International BBI*, Cologne: IfV/KE-Consult.

Baum, H., Kurte, J., and Esser, K. (2007) *Regionalwirtschaftliche Effekte einer Betriebsgenehmigung mit Kernruhezeit für den Airport Berlin Brandenburg International BBI*, Cologne: IfV/KE-Consult.

Berster, P., Gellhausen, P., Grimme, W., Kiemel, H., Maertens, S., and Pabst, S. et al. (2010) 'The impacts of the planned air passenger duty in Germany', DLR.

Blake, A. (2009) 'The dynamics of tourism's economic impact', *Tourism Economics*, 15 (3): 615–628.

Boardman, A., Greenberg, D., A Vining, A., and Weimer, D. (2011) *Cost-Benefit Analysis: Concepts and Practice*, 4th ed., Upper Saddle River, NJ: Prentice Hall.

Brisbane Airport (2007) Volume A: Background and Need, Chapter 2, Need for the Project, the Environmental Impact Statement (EIS) and Major Development Plan (MDP), by Sinclair Knight Merz, www.bne.com.au/corporate/upgrading-your-airport/new-parallel-runway/eismdp.

Broecker, J. and Mercenier, J. (2011) 'General equilibrium models for transportation economics', in A. de Palma, R. Lindsey, E. Quinet and R. Vickerman (eds), *A Handbook of Transport Economics*, Cheltenham: Edward Elgar, pp. 21–45.

Bulwien, H., Hujer, R., Kokot, S., Mehlinger, C., Rürup, B., and Voßkamp, T. (1999) *Einkommens- und Beschäftigungseffekte des Flughafens Frankfurt/Main*, Frankfurt.

Burfisher, M. (2011) *Introduction to Computable General Equilibrium Models*, Cambridge: Cambridge University Press.

CE Delft (2013) *The Economics of Airport Expansion*, Delft, March 2013.

Central Planning Bureau (1974) 'Cost-benefit analysis second national airport', General Report, December 1974.

Centre for International Economics (1988) *Economic Effects of International Tourism*, Canberra: CIE.

Commission for the Third London Airport (1969) *Report*, London: HMSO.

Deloitte Access Economics (2013) 'Economic impact of a western Sydney airport', Report prepared by Deloitte Access Economics for the NSW Business Chamber Australian Department of Infrastructure and Transport and Ernst & Young, Joint Study on Aviation Capacity in the Sydney region, Ernst & Young, February 2012.

Department for Transport (2003) 'The future of air transport', London. www.dft.gov.uk/aviation/whitepaper.

Department of Transport and Communications Australia (1988) *Negotiating International Aviation Rights*, Consultants' Report, June, Canberra: .

De Rus, G. (2010) *Introduction to Cost-Benefit Analysis*, Cheltenham: Edward Elgar.

Di Tella, R., MacCulloch, R., and Oswald, A. (2003) 'The macroeconomics of happiness', *Review of Economics and Statistics*, 85 (4): 809–827.

Dinwiddy, C. and Teal, F. (1996) *Principles of Cost-Benefit Analysis for Developing Countries*, Cambridge: Cambridge University Press.

Dreze, J. and Stern, N. (1987) 'The theory of cost benefit analysis', in A Auerbach and M Feldstein, *Handbook of Public Economics II*, Amsterdam: North Holland, pp. 909–989.

Dwyer, L., Forsyth, P., Spurr, R., and T. Ho, (2005) *The Economic Impacts and Benefits of Tourism in Australia, A General Equilibrium Approach*, Technical Report, CRC for Sustainable Tourism, Gold Coast, Australia.

Eurocontrol (2014) EMOSIA make the right decisions on ATM investments, www.eurocontrol.int/sites/default/files/publication/files/emosia-brochure-2016.pdf.

European Commission (2019) *Taxes in the Field of Aviation and their Impact, Final Report*, June, Brussels.

Farrow S. and Rose, A. (2018) Welfare analysis: bridging the partial and general equilibrium divide for policy analysis, *Journal of Cost Benefit Analysis*, 9 (1): 67–83.

Federal Aviation Administration [USDOT] (1992) *Estimating the Regional Significance of Airports*, Washington, DC, DOT/FAA/PP-92–6.

Forsyth, P. (2006) 'Tourism benefits and aviation policy', *Journal of Air Transport Management*, 12 (1): 3–13.

Forsyth, P (2007) 'Estimating the costs and benefits of regional airport subsidies: a computable general equilibrium approach', Paper delivered at the Australian Conference of Economists, Hobart.

Forsyth, P. (2014) 'Is it in Germany's economic interest to allow Emirates to fly to Berlin? A framework for analysis', *Journal of Air Transport Management*, 41: 38–44.

Forsyth, P. (2019) 'Assessing the wider economic benefits of air transport', mimeo Monash University, November.

Forsyth, P. (2020) 'Assessing the wider economic benefits of air transport', Transport Policy, forthcoming.

Forsyth, P., Dwyer, L., Pham, T., and Spurr, R. (2014) 'The impacts of Australia's passenger movement charge on tourism and the economy', *Tourism Management*, 40: 126–136.

Forsyth, P., Njoya, E., and Niemeier, H-M. (2020) 'Economic evaluation of investments in airports: old and new approaches, *Journal of Benefit Cost Analysis*, forthcoming.

Gillen, D., Harris, R., and Oum, T., (2002) 'Measuring the economic effects of bilateral liberalization air transport', *Transportation Research E*, 38(3): 155–174.

Gillen, D., Hinsch, H., Mandel, B., and Wolf, H. (2001) *The Impact of Liberalizing International Aviation Bilaterals on the Northern German Region*, Aldershot: Ashgate.

Gillen, D., Landau, S., and Gosling, G. (2015) 'Measuring the relationship airline network connectivity and productivity', *Transportation Research Record*, 2501: 66–75.

Graham, D. (2007) 'Agglomeration, productivity and transport investment', *Journal of Transport Economics and Policy*, 41(3): 317–343.

Gregan, T. and Johnson, M. (1999) 'Impacts of competition enhancing air services agreements: a network modelling approach, productivity commission', Staff Research Paper, AusInfo, Canberra.

Industries Assistance Commission (1989) *Travel and Tourism Report* No. 423, Canberra: Australian Government Printing Service.

Infras (2005) *Volkswirtschaftliche Bedeutung des Flughafens Zürich*. Auswirkungen verschiedener Entwicklungszenarien, Zürich. www.infras.ch.

International Civil Aviation Policy (1978) *Review of Australia's International Civil Aviation Policy, Report of Review Committee*, Canberra: Australian Government Publishing Service.

InterVISTAS (2010) *Economic Impact Study for Emirates Airline, Executive Summary*, Additional Flights between Dubai and Canada, February.

InterVISTAS (2006) *Measuring the Economic Rate of Return on Investment in Aviation*. Report prepared for IATA, Vancouver: InterVISTAS.

Jenkins, G (1997) 'Project analysis and the world bank', *American Economic Review*, 8(2): 38–42.

Johansson, P-O. and de Rus, G. (2015) 'On the treatment of foreigners and foreign-owned firms in cost-benefit analysis', Documento de Trabajo 2015/13, Fedea, December.

Jorge-Calderón, D (2014) *Aviation Investment, Economic Appraisal for Airports, Air Traffic Management, and Airlines and Aeronautics*, Ashgate: Aldershot.

Keen, M., Parry, I., and Strand, J. (2013) 'Planes, ships and taxes: charging for international aviation and marine emissions', *Economic Policy*, 28: 710–749.

Klophaus, R. (2013) *Regionalökonomische Bedeutung und Perspektiven des Flughafens Kassel-Calden. Wissenschaftliche Forschungsstudie für den Betrachtungszeitraum 2012–2023*, Mannheim: Zentrum für Recht und Wirtschaft des Luftverkehrs.

Krugmann, P. (1991) *Geography and Trade*, Cambridge, MA: MIT Press.

Madden, J.R. (2004) 'Assessing the regional economic impact of an airport: a dynamic multiregional CGE study of Melbourne Airport'. Draft Paper presented to Fourth Biennial Regional CGE Modelling Workshop, Melbourne, 16 and 17 September2004, viewed September 2013, available at www.monash.edu.au/policy/regional/maddpap.pdf.

Melbourne Airport (2003) *Melbourne Airport Economic Impact Study*, Melbourne: Sinclair Knight Merz.

Mills, G. (1982) 'Investment in airport capacity – a critical review of the MANS, (major airport needs of Sydney) study', Working Papers 55, University of Sydney, School of Economics.

Mishan, E.J. (1970) 'What is wrong with Roskill?', *Journal of Transport Economics and Policy*, 4(4): 221–234.

Morrison, S. and Winston, C. (1986) *The Economic Effects of Airline Deregulation*, Washington, DC: Brookings Institution.

Njoya, E. (2016) 'Aviation, tourism and poverty relief in Kenya: a dynamic computable general equilibrium model analysis', Dissertation, Karlsruhe.

Niemeier, H.-M. (2001) 'On the use and abuse of impact analysis for airports: a critical view from the perspective of regional policy', in W. Pfähler (ed.), *Regional Input-Output Analysis*, Baden-Baden: Nomos, pp. 201–220.

Nwaneri, V. (1970) 'Equity in cost-benefit analysis: a case study of the third London airport', *Journal of Transport Economics and Policy*, 4(3): 235–245.

Oxford Economics (2011a) *An Alternative APD Regime*, Oxford: Oxford Economics.

Oxford Economics (2011b) Economic Benefits from Air Transport in Australia Australia Country Report, Oxford: Oxford Economics.

Partidário, M.R. and Miguel, C. (2011), 'The Lisbon new international airport: the story of a decision-making process and the role of strategic environmental assessment', *Environmental Impact Assessment Review*, 31(3): 360–367.

Pearce, B. (2014) *Economic Benefits of Air Transport: What Have we Learnt so Far?* GARS Workshop Bremen 10 July.

Pearce, B. and Smyth, D. (2007) *Aviation Economic Benefits*, IATA Economics Briefing 8.

PwC (UK), (2013) 'The economic impact of air passenger duty', A study by PwC, Main Report February.

Productivity Commission (1998) *International Air Services*: Report No. 2, Canberra: AusInfo.

Quinet, E. (2000) 'Evaluation methodologies of transportation projects in France', *Transport Policy*, 7(1): 27–34.

Ray, A (1984) *Cost-Benefit Analysis Issues and Methodologies*, Baltimore, MD: Johns Hopkins University Press.

Schlumberger, C.E. (2010) *Open Skies for Africa Implementing the Yamoussoukro Decision*. Washington, DC: The World Bank.

Stuart, C. (1984) 'Welfare costs per dollar of additional tax revenue in the United States', *American Economic Review*, 74(3): 352–362.

Thießen, F (2009) Die Bedeutung von Flughäfen für die regionale Wirtschaft, in: Heinrich-Böll-Stiftung, Kommunalpolitische Infothek Thema: Regionale Flughäfen, www.kommunale-info.de/, 2009, URL des Beitrages: www.kommunale-info.de/asp/search.asp?ID=3661.

Tourism Research Australia (2011) Factors affecting the inbound tourism sector: The impact and implications of the Australian dollar, Canberra, Department of Resources Energy and Tourism.

Ueda, Takayuki, Koike, A., Tsuchiya, K., and Yamaguchi, K. (2005), 'Spatial benefit incidence analysis of airport capacity expansion: application of SCGE model to the Haneda Project in global competition in transportation markets: analysis and policy making', *Research in Transportation Economics*, 13: 165–196.

Venables, A. (2007) 'Evaluating urban transport investments', *Journal of Transport Economics and Policy*, 41(2): 173–188

Vickerman, R. (2013) 'The wider economic impacts of mega projects in transport', in H Priemus and B van Wee (eds), *International Handbook on Mega-Projects*, Cheltenham: Edward Elgar, pp. 381–398.

Waters, W. (1976) 'Impact studies and the evaluation of public projects', *Annals of Regional Science*, 10(1): 98–103.

Winkelmann, L. and Winkelmann, R. (1998) 'Why are the unemployed so unhappy? Evidence form panel data', *Economica*, 65(257): 1–15.

York Aviation (2009) 'The economic impact of Edinburgh Airport', *Scottish Enterprise and BAA Edinburgh Final Report*.

9 How to estimate the social costs of airport negative externalities

A case study of Milan Bergamo airport

Gianmaria Martini, Mattia Grampella, and Davide Scotti

Introduction

In the last 30 years the increase of aircraft operations in the majority of European and world airports generated a growth in the environmental impacts of aviation on both a local and a global scale. Among these, the most important ones are environmental noise, aircraft pollutants, and greenhouse gas (GHG) emissions. The latter are mainly referred to as carbon dioxide (CO_2) production at global level contributing to climate change.

When dealing with negative externalities, the usual approach in economics is to proceed in three steps (Harris & Roach, 2018; Phaneuf & Requate, 2017): first, analysing the different types of negative externalities, i.e., in the case of aviation mainly emissions, GHG, and noise annoyance; second, identifying and estimating the impact of the negative externalities on human beings, animals, and the environment; third, expressing these impacts in monetary terms in order to have an estimate of the social costs of negative externalities. The latter is the benchmark for incentive regulation, through taxation, compensation and incentives towards more environmentally friendly equipment and business strategies.

Regarding the first step, in case of air transportation, emissions have both local and global effects. The former is concerned with emissions generated in the area surrounding an airport. The latter is related to emissions produced during the flight, mainly to GHG which have a long-distance effect (CO_2 generated during a flight in Europe can produce an effect in Oceania). Noise has instead only a local effect. The principal substances generated locally by air transportation are nitrogen oxides (NO_x), particulate matters (PM), sulphur oxides (SO_x), unburnt hydrocarbons (HC), carbon monoxide (CO), and soot. There are other important negative impacts produced by civil aviation at airports such as water and soil pollution, biodiversity problems, electromagnetic and luminous pollution, but these externalities are hard to quantify (HEATCO, 2006). Noise annoyance is due to a variation of the air pressure that generates harm for the human beings.

The impact of noise and emissions on human beings' health at the local level , according to the World Health Organization (WHO, 2018), leads to respiratory and brain diseases, cancers (emissions), and hearing impairment, hypertension, ischaemic heart disease, annoyance, stress, and sleep disturbance (Grampella et al. 2017).

The next step consists in quantifying the amount of emissions produced and the level of noise generated by airport operations, and then in estimating the social costs, i.e., a measure in monetary terms of the damages created to the population. These social costs can be per substance, per noise level, and can then be aggregated for total emissions, total noise harm, and aggregate social costs of air transportation externalities. There are few studies in the literature providing measures of the amount of emissions generated by aircraft, and their noise. Dings et al. (2003) and Lu & Morrell (2006) are the two benchmark studies adopted by many contributions on air transportation negative externalities. Eurocontrol (2018) has recently provided a further benchmark with a complete presentation of reference values that can be applied for implementing a cost-benefit analysis. Grampella et al. (2017) show a method to estimate local air transportation externalities using aircraft certification data that can be applied to all airports without requiring survey data. This is the approach we will follow in this chapter.

A further source of information regarding the impact of emissions and noise is provided by both technical and economic regulation. Regulatory models present standards that represent different categories of impacts generated by aircraft, while economic regulation is normally expressed in airport charges.

This chapter presents a review of the different approaches available in the literature to measure airport externalities at the local level, starting from the settings established by regulation and then presents the Grampella et al. (2017) method, based on aircraft certification standards. This method is then applied to a case study: the estimate of the social costs of airport externalities at Milan Bergamo airport. The chapter is structured as follows. First we present the main regulation settings, then review the methods to estimate airport emissions and noise, and finally present an application to the Milan Bergamo case.

The regulation of airport emissions, GHG, and noise

The regulation of airport negative externalities is important because it presents some standards and settings that can help identify parameters for the evaluation of airport social costs. Moreover, it is a framework that has to be taken into account when estimating the social costs of airport negative externalities. Hence, the aim of this section is to present a short review of the main dimensions of regulation in this subject. It involves global and local dimensions, and consists of both technical and economic regulation.

Concerning technical regulation, ICAO is the civil aviation authority for environmental aspects. Annex 16 to the Convention[1] contains the standards to limit emissions per movement and per kilogram of fuel burnt, respectively. The first volume of the Annex 16 is about noise and contains the different certification standards for each aircraft type (respectively, Chapter 3, Chapter 4, and the recent Chapter 14). The second concerns emissions. A new third volume regarding CO_2 was published in 2017 (ICAO, 2017).

Regarding noise, ICAO identifies four key aspects: (i) reduction of noise at source, (ii) land use planning and management, (iii) noise abatement operational procedures, and (iv) operating restrictions. By 'reduction of noise at source' regulation refers to technological progress. In this sense, the introduction of more new environmentally friendly aircraft (e.g., Airbus A320neo, Airbus A350 and Boeing 787) contributes to mitigate the impact of noise. Despite that, population exposure to high noise levels in the proximity of airports is not reduced yet in many circumstances it is mainly due to the general increase in air traffic volumes (EASA, 2019). As a result, the European Environment Agency (EEA) estimates that more than 4.1 million people are exposed to Lden[2] levels above 55 dB (i.e., the threshold value above where there are adverse health effects of noise) generated by aircraft at 85 major airports (EEA, 2014). At the European level, the Environmental Noise Directive (END) and the Balanced Approach Regulation (EEA, 2014; EC, 1996; EC, 2002; EEA, 2010; EU,2014) are the legislative instruments to manage environmental noise. Noise from airports should be measured and monitored in order to define strategic noise maps every five years. The results should be published together with the definition of specific noise action plans to mitigate the effects. A main goal of this procedure is to provide common criteria for noise mapping and action plans and to decrease the number of citizens exposed to Lden levels above 55 dB. Table 9.1 shows, for the same airport, the population living nearby and exposed to different levels of airport noise.

Another noise regulatory instrument – in this case through economic incentives and not technical limits – is given by airport charges. These charges are usually based on noise certification data. For instance, ICAO aircraft certification classification according to Chapter 3, Chapter 4, and the new Chapter 14 standards is the base for many noise surcharges adopted in European countries. The noise surcharge is then increased for night flights. Such charges have been

Table 9.1 Population exposure to aircraft noise at Milan Bergamo airport

Index	Noise level (dB)	Population affected
Lden	55–59	36,500
	60–64	11,000
	65–69	1,600
	70–75	200
	> 75	0
Lnight	55–59	14,600
	60–64	1,900
	65–69	900
	70 –75	0
	> 75	0

Source: SACBO, 2018.

adopted in most of the main European airports (EC, 2017). They are very heterogeneous across European countries, even if their overall proportion relative to total airport charges is increasing, they still remain approximately negligible in terms of airline operating costs.

In addition to the above, the regulation of noise refers basically to (i) flight curfews at nights, and (ii) constrained flight paths for take-off and landing. These actions need to be integrated in the air traffic management (ATM) procedures. An example is the continuous descent approach[3] which is implemented in Europe by Eurocontrol (Eurocontrol, 2011).

Regarding emissions, regulation discriminates between greenhouse gases (GHG) and local pollutants. Concerning GHG, the contribution of civil aviation is minor in proportion to total emissions. According to the most recent evaluation of UNFCCC,[4] GHG is around 3.6% (UNFCCC, 2018). The main issue is that such contribution is growing faster, while emissions from other sources are decreasing (EEA, 2017). Regarding climate change, on the European level, in November 2018 the European Commission presented its vision for long-term European Union (EU) GHG reductions in accordance with the Paris Agreement, showing that zero-emission target can be achieved by 2050. The EU aims to fulfil this target through the definition of different projects related to optimising air traffic management (e.g. Clean Sky, SESAR), and the introduction for civil aviation of the Emission Trading Scheme (ETS), and the Carbon Offsetting and Reduction Scheme for International Aviation (CORSIA).[5]

Concerning local pollution, civil aviation has also an important role in the emission of pollutants, especially nitrogen oxides (NO_X). According to EASA (2019), in 2015, the air transport sector accounted for 14% of all EU transport NO_X emissions, and for 7% of the total EU NO_X emissions. EASA (2019) states that civil aviation since 1990 has doubled NO_X emissions and has quadrupled its share while other economic sectors have achieved reductions in the same period. Emission of pollutants concerns not only aircraft but also other sources such as ground operations, surface access road transport, and airport on-site energy generation and heating. EU air pollution legislation follows an approach quite similar to noise implementing (i) local air quality standards (EEA, 2017), (ii) the reduction of emissions at source and (iii) the introduction of emission charges at airports.

While previous standards have been updated over time, the latest global environmental standards were adopted by ICAO in 2017 and are contained in the new third volume of the Annex 16 (ICAO, 2017). These standards regard CO_2 emissions and aircraft engine non-volatile Particulate Matter (nvPM) mass concentration. These standards have been integrated into European legislation (EU, 2016; 2018) and they will be implemented from 1 January 2020 (EASA, 2019). These new CO_2 standards provide an additional requirement for the design process in order to increase the fuel efficiency in the aircraft design (EASA, 2019). This will contribute to assessing and to mitigating the impact of growing CO_2 emissions from the aviation sector (UNFCC, 2015).

It is important to underline that all emissions are related to the fuel burnt and, therefore, airlines have an incentive to reduce them indirectly, since their main concern is to save fuel costs.

Concerning the reduction of emissions at source, regulation is focused on both engine emissions and fuel quality standards. As far as emission charges are concerned, as in the case of noise, they are dependent on several factors including the aircraft and engine type. Emission surcharges are adopted by a small number of European airports.

Methods to estimate the social costs of airport emissions and noise

The first step in estimating the social costs of civil aviation consists in the quantification of the amount of negative externalities produced. This can be implemented through different methodologies. A first approach is risk assessment analysis (Torija et al., 2018; ACI & CANSO, 2015). It combines, at the single airport level, a monitoring system based on the direct measure of the specific externalities with the use of simulation models. It quantifies with a good approximation the real quantity of pollution emitted and noise annoyance. Besides the quantification of airport environmental impact, this approach allows the social costs borne by the local population thanks to the definition of noise/air pollution contours to be measured.

The noise contours provide the number of people exposed to a specific threshold value (Lden 55 dB) for the onset of adverse health effects from noise exposure. Such a threshold is correlated with health problems (WHO, 2018). This is the standard procedure to assess noise in Europe and it is the core of the actions contained in the END 2002 EU Directive. Bernardo et al. (2016) show that this procedure is not always practical for decision-making processes and strategic planning.[6] To address this issue Torija et al. (2017) provide an overview of the state of the art for simplified aircraft noise models for a strategic and multidisciplinary environmental impact assessment of civil aviation.

The detailed procedure for noise can be adapted also for the emissions. Emission inventory and dispersion analysis could be done with mathematical models alongside airport pollutants measures. There are three aspects that prevent to the emission and dispersion analysis to be as robust as the regulation standard of noise assessment. The first is that European airport operators are not required to produce emission concentrations maps (EU, 2016). The second is that, due to the different emitted substances, measure campaigns are more complex and expensive to manage and generally limited to the detection of few substances. In the literature there are several examples of measure campaigns. Schurmann et al. (2006) evaluate through emission measures the impact of NO_x, CO and VOC on air quality at Zurich Airport, Herndon et al. (2009) measure hydrocarbon emissions at Oakland Airport and Lobo et al. (2012) describes a PM real time measurement analysis of an active runway at Oakland airport as well. All these studies focus on a single airport and on a specific category of substance, through a case study analysis. The third aspect is the different nature of dispersion models due to the different mathematical approach. An overview of this issue is provided by Holmes & Morawska (2006).

The second approach is based on hedonic prices (Navrud, 2002), i.e., the definition of the social costs of aviation negative externalities is the connection between the amount of pollutant emitted and the assignment of a specific monetary indicator given by house prices. Schipper & Rietveld (2001) analyse the environmental externalities in air transport markets providing a description of the hedonic prices method. The idea is that the price of real estate is a sign of the market value of these assets and if they suffer from noise and pollution generated by airports, these externalities should be reflected in lower house prices. The difference in these prices as function of different noise and pollution contours represents the unit costs of adding more exposure at the externalities, and are therefore taken as a base for computing the social costs.[7] Hedonic price methods are usually applied to estimate the social costs of noise annoyance.

Generally, hedonic prices analysis results are presented in the form of a specific indicator called the Noise Depreciation Index (NDI) or the Noise Sensitivity Depreciation Index (NSDI). NSDI describes the average decrease in house values caused by a 1 dB increase in aircraft noise. According to Navrud (2002), the main advantage of this method is that it relies on the real behaviour of the housing market where there is a clear measure of individual willingness to pay (WTP) for noise characteristics. According to Schipper et al. (1998), the main weakness of this method is that it is not a reliable comparison between different scenarios due to the influence of model settings and local house market conditions that could produce a sensible variation of NSDI. An historical overview of the hedonic price method studies, mostly in the US, for air traffic noise is provided by Bateman et al. (2001). At the European level, few studies focus on the effect of transport noise on house values. Among these, Dekkers & Van der Straatens (2008) perform a hedonic analysis for the impact of Amsterdam airport. Puschel & Evangelinos (2012) utilise the hedonic method and NSDI index to analyse noise annoyance at Düsseldorf airport focusing on the depreciation of rent price. Lavandier et al. (2016) use hedonic price model and develop a new indicator (called real estate tolerance level, RETL) to evaluate airport noise impact at Paris CDG. The literature on hedonic price methods applied to air quality is much more limited. The reference study is Smith & Huang (1993) but, to the best of our knowledge, no contributions apply this method to air transport.

As this method is based on providing monetary values representing unit social costs for the amount of chemical substances emitted by aircraft and for the noise levels (Lu & Morrel (2001); Dings et al. (2003); Schipper (2004); Lu & Morrel (2006), HEATCO Project (2006); Givoni & Rietveld (2010); Korzhenevych et al. (2014); Eurocontrol (2018)). These monetary values are the result of a process of comparison of the possible direct health effects generated by noise and pollution.

Looking specifically at integrated studies (i.e., at papers on both airport noise and air pollutants) that do not focus on single airport case studies, only a few contributions are available. Among these, Schipper (2004) analyses the impact of airports' operations (i) on local and global air pollution, (ii) on noise nuisance, and (iii) on accident risk focusing on a small sample of routes linking some of the main European airports. Lu & Morrell (2006) estimate the local environmental costs of noise and air pollution in a limited sample of European airports (Heathrow, Gatwick, Stansted, Schiphol, and Maastricht). Morrell & Lu (2007), focusing on a small sample of eight airports, compare the environmental costs of two different models of organising the aviation activities: hub–hub versus hub by-pass networks. Lu (2009) studies the impact on airlines' demand of introducing emission charges by adopting a methodology similar to the one applied by Lu & Morrell (2006). Givoni & Rietveld (2010) analyse the environmental costs of linking some cities (e.g., London and Amsterdam, Tokyo, and Sapporo) using two aircraft types of different sizes (B747 and A320). A limitation of the abovementioned studies is that they are limited to a small sample of airports.

A different and indirect method for evaluating the social costs of airport negative externalities is the stated preference approach (SPA) (Kroes & Sheldon, 1988; Baranzini & Ramírez, 2005). The basic idea of SPA is to measure through surveys and interviews the people's willingness to pay for limiting the amount of pollution and noise. The main limits of SPA are (i) how reliable are the answers provided in the survey (people respond to hypothetical and not real situation), (ii) the small sample bias (the number of interviewed people is rather small in comparison to the universe, and (iii) the strong influence of local conditions.

A recent approach based on a specific estimate of the amount of pollution and noise generated by airport operation using aircraft certification standards is in Grampella et al. (2017). It describes a methodology to estimate the emissions and noise levels produced during a period of time by the aircraft operations at a specific airport. The advantage of this approach is that it is applicable to any aircraft fleet operating at any airport because it is based on certification values; hence, without resorting to survey or field analysis. It has to be noted that, however, certification values are measured under standardised conditions, whereas in reality, an aircraft's certification values might be high or low – with a significant influence on noise emissions especially during take-off. Despite these limitations and taking into account that the computed aggregated environmental effect cannot be considered as a social cost,[8] the method provides a good proxy of the amount of pollution and noise generated by airport operations.

The first step of the Grampella et al. (2017) procedure is the definition of two indices measuring respectively the amount of pollution and noise produced by a specific aircraft model. Local air pollution is given by the amount of gases produced by aircraft during their landing-and-take-off-cycle (LTO) cycle (ICAO, 2017). The latter, following ICAO standards, is split into four phases: take-off (lasting 0.7 min), climb (up to 3,000 ft above ground, lasting 2.2 min), approach (from 3,000 ft to landing, lasting 4 min), and idle (when the aircraft is taxiing or standing on the ground with the engines on).[9] The aviation operations by aircraft model at a specific airport are obtained from the Official Airline Guide database (OAG). Then, information at the aircraft engine level is collected from the ICAO Engine Emissions Databank (EED), which provides the certification information for each engine type. More specifically, EED provides, for each phase of the LTO cycle, the CO, HC, and NO_X emission factors and the fuel consumption. By multiplying emission factors by their duration and fuel consumption, the per-phase amounts of CO, HC, and NO_X produced are obtained at the engine level. These are then aggregated to obtain the amount of CO, HC, and NO_X produced by each engine type during each departure or arrival operation. A different procedure is followed to compute the amounts of SO_2 and PM_{10} produced: the fuel burnt by each engine type during the LTO cycle is multiplied by a stoichiometric coefficient (Dings et al., 2003; Givoni & Rietveld, 2010; Eurocontrol 2018).[10] The matching between the aircraft model operating a flight coming from OAG and the engine type coming from the EED data is made on the basis of maximum take off weight (MTOW). The amount of different pollutants emitted during the LTO are then obtained as the weighted average of the different engine types associated to each aircraft model, using the International Register of Civil Aircraft (IRCA) frequency as a weight. The final outcome of the above procedure is an engine-weighted average value for each of the four pollutants emitted during the LTO cycle by each aircraft model. In order to compute the total quantity of pollutant p produced by aircraft i during the LTO cycle (Q_p^i), the following equation is used:

$$Q_p^i = n_j^i \times \left(\sum_{f=1}^{4} E_{pif} \times d_f \times F c_{if} \right)$$

where n_j^i is the number of type-j engines installed on aircraft i, E_{pif} is the type-j engine emission factor (kilograms) during phase f of the LTO cycle, d_f is the time-duration of the phase f, and $F c_{if}$ is the type-j engine fuel consumption. Then the amount (kilograms) of pollutant produced by an airport h during a specific period of time P_{ph} is computed as follows:

$$P_{ph} = \sum_i m_h^i \times Q_p^i \tag{9.1}$$

where m_h^i is the number of flights operated by aircraft i in airport h.

The level of noise generated yearly by airports is computed using a procedure similar to the one adopted for emissions. The level of noise of each engine/aircraft combination is obtained from the European Aviation Safety Agency (EASA) and the Federal Aviation Administration (FAA) databases. These sources provide data (e.g., the manufacturer, model, maximum take-off weight, engine type and number, and noise certification data) on the majority of aircraft models. OAG records reporting the airport's movements operated by a specific aircraft model are therefore linked to EASA and FAA databases. This process is carried out in two steps. In the first one, the aircraft are matched according to their model name. In the second one, among the associations resulting from the first step, those having similar take-off weights are considered. Given that the amount of noise produced (in Effective Perceived Noise Level, EPNL) by an aircraft during an LTO cycle is certified at three different points (i.e., Lateral, Approach, and Flyover), the average noise level for aircraft i is computed as follows:

$$AN^i = 10 \times log \times \left(\frac{1}{3} \times \sum_{q=1}^{3} 10^{\frac{EPNLi}{10}} \right)$$

where AN^i is the energetic mean of the three noise levels at the three certification points. A level of noise describing the noise emitted from an airport in a specific period of time is then computed as follows:[11]

$$LVA_t = 10LOG\left[\frac{1}{N} \sum 10^{\frac{AN^i}{10}} \right] \tag{9.2}$$

where N is the number of days in the period of time under investigation. This method, as an example, will be applied in the next section to Milan Bergamo airport.

The last step in Grampella et al's. (2017) method is passing from quantities to money, in order to obtain estimates of the social costs. The latter is done by resorting to estimates of unit social costs of emissions and noise available in the literature. Hence, social costs are assigned to noise, HC, NOx, PM_{10}, and SO_2. Regarding emissions there are three main available sources of unit social costs. According to Dings et al. (2003) emissions have the unit social costs presented in Table 9.2.

Lu & Morrel (2001) provide the values shown in Table 9.3 for the same pollutants. They are calculated as average values from data coming from four different studies.[12] The main weakness is that the values of Table 9.3 are not industry specific. Moreover, the method adopted to measure the unit social costs of the different substances in Lu & Morrell (2006) is different from that in Dings et al. (2003). The two methods assign different weights to the damages generated on human beings and the environment. Moreover, in Dings et al. (2003) the estimate of the unit social costs takes into account the density of the population, separating the local areas into rural, medium, and urban zones. Nevertheless, the estimates reported by Lu & Morrell are quite similar to those of Dings et al., even if figures for PM_{10} and SO_2 are not available.

A third set of estimates is provided by Eurocontrol (2018). These costs (see Table 9.4) integrate other studies regarding the cost-benefit analysis (CBA) of air transport projects and the definition of external costs of transport sector (HEATCO, 2006; Korzhenevych & Dehnen, 2014).[13]

CO is not included in the evaluation of the emission costs by Eurocontrol.[14] The reasons are different for the two substances: regarding CO, it has been proved recently that the damages for human beings of CO are due to an acute and high exposition, while they are negligible for very low but quite permanent ones (Korzhenevych & Dehnen, 2014).[15]

The total social costs per pollutant is obtained by multiplying the amount of pollutant by these unit costs, as shown in Equation (1). By adding up the total costs of all pollutants we have the aggregate amount of pollution generated by an airport in a given period. If we divide this amount by the total number of seats/passengers in the same period we have an intensity indicator, i.e., the amount of pollution per seat/passenger, which does not depend upon the size of the airport/aircraft.

Concerning the noise social costs, Grampella et al. (2017) provide an extension of Schipper (2004) average noise cost per aircraft movement. More specifically, the authors take as reference of the noise social costs the value of a representative aircraft provided by Schipper (2004), equal to €324[16] and, given that a decrease/increase of 3 dB corresponds to a half/double level of noise exposure, and that the average noise level (AN) in the current commercial fleet corresponds to about 95.3 dB, each AN^i (i.e., the average noise generated by aircraft i) is converted into euros through the following expression:

Table 9.2 Social costs of emissions, Dings et al. (2003)

Unit social cost of emission (in €2010 per kilogram)

CO	HC	NO_x	PM_{10}	SO_2
€0.001	€5.02	€11.30	€188.43	€7.54

Note: The original costs in Dings et al. (2003) are in €1999 and have been updated to €2010 to make comparison between costs methodologies.

Table 9.3 Social costs of emissions, Lu & Morrell (2006)

Unit social cost of emission (in €2010 per kilogram)

CO	HC	NO_x	PM_{10}	SO_2
€0.008	€4.16	€11.56	N.A.	N.A.

Table 9.4 Social costs of emissions, Eurocontrol (2018)

Unit social cost of emission (in €2010 per kilogram)

CO	HC	NO_x	PM_{10}	SO_2
N.A.	€1.70	€11.50	€132.90	€11.08

Note: Particulate matters value is the average costs between the three estimates (rural, suburban and urban) that take into account population density around airports.

$$MAN^i = 2^{\frac{AN^i - 95.3}{3}} \times €324 \qquad\qquad (9.3)$$

where MAN^i is the monetary value of the noise exposure of a flight operated by aircraft i in a given airport. A daily (or monthly/yearly) estimate of the amount of noise produced by airport h is obtained by summing the MAN^i values over the number of movements operated in the airport. Noise costs per seat are obtained by dividing the noise cost by the number of seats.

The Grampella et al. (2017) approach gives estimates of the airport social externalities costs. However, these social costs are based on measures of unit social costs per kilogram of substance emitted or per dB level as in a typical cost-benefit analysis (CBA). The method does not consider the actual population affected by pollution and noise (e.g., the number of people reported in Table 9.1 for Milan Bergamo airport). Despite this limit, the unit social costs are based on estimates of the harm generated by large airports in urban areas with high population density. This means that it overestimates the social costs of airports located in areas with low population density.

An application of the method based on standards: the social costs of negative externalities at Milan Bergamo airport

This section applies the Grampella et al. (2017) method to a case study, i.e., the estimate of the social costs of pollution and noise generated by Milan Bergamo airport in a specific day. The starting point are the data regarding the daily departure and arrival flights operated at the Milan Bergamo airport on a specific day, i.e., 29 January 29 2018. As previously mentioned, the source is OAG for scheduled flights. Figure 9.1 shows the total number of flights operated at Milan Bergamo airport on that day by aircraft model and airline. It is evident that operations are dominated by Ryanair, using the Boeing 737–800, while the second most used aircraft is the Airbus A320 operated by Wizz Air. There are also some regional jets, such as the Embraer R145 and R135.

Table 9.5 shows the quantities (in kilograms) of each pollutant generated by the flights shown in Figure 9.1.

Figure 9.2 shows instead the noise levels by aircraft model computed according to the methodology presented in the previous section, i.e., Equation (9.2). The application of the noise metric LVA_{j} provides a noise exposure in the proximity of the certification points of 67.4 dB (A). Notice that this value is given by the energetic sum of the levels of dB presented in Figure 9.2 weighted for the frequency according to Equation (9.3). This simple example shows that the procedure can be easily applied to any airport in the world once the required information is available. This means that environmental performance of airports might be compared one to each other. Despite being the most operated aircraft, the B737-800 of Ryanair is not the noisiest one. The latter is the B737 aircraft operated by Blue Panorama. Moreover, the two regional jet aircraft are the least noisy.

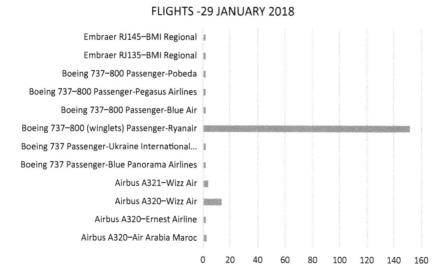

FLIGHTS -29 JANUARY 2018

Figure 9.1 Aircraft operations at Milan Bergamo airport on 29 January 2018.

Table 9.5 Total emissions generated at Milan Bergamo airport on 29 January 2018

Substance emitted in a day	kilograms
CO	649
HC	59
NO_x	1,218
PM_{10}	17
SO_2	68

Table 9.6 shows the results of the estimates of the pollution social costs in Milan Bergamo using the three metrics presented in Dings et al. (2003, Lu & Morrell (2006, and Eurocontrol (2018). Total costs, per-seat costs and costs per available seat kilometre (ASK) are compared. In order to compare the three metrics, we include in the estimates of the emissions social costs only those substances that are present in all three metrics. The estimates are rather similar, especially for Dings et al. (2003) and Eurocontrol (2018). Lu & Morrel (2006) have slightly higher estimates because they also consider some non-aviation specific emissions generated at the airport, such as car pollution. Hence, the estimate of emissions social costs on a specific day at Milan Bergamo airport are about €19,000.

Concerning the noise social costs, the results obtained by applying the Grampella et al. (2017) method, i.e., Equation (9.3), for Milan Bergamo airport on 29 January 2018 are shown in Figure 9.3. It shows the social noise costs per

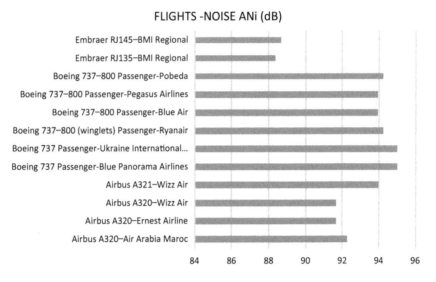

FLIGHTS -NOISE ANi (dB)

Figure 9.2 Noise levels (dB) generated by operations at Milan Bergamo airport on 29 January 2018.

Table 9.6 Social costs of emissions at Milan Bergamo airport on 29 January 2018

Type of social costs	Unit social costs metrics		
	Dings et al. (2003)	*Lu & Morrell (2006)*	*Eurocontrol (2018)*
Total costs (€2018)	19.522	20.366	18.807
Costs per seat (€2018)	0.50	0.52	0.48
Costs per ASK (€2018)	0.0002	0.0003	0.0002

seat taking into account all the flights operated that day. By inspection, Airbus models exhibit lower values per seat compared to Boeing ones due to the fact that the Boeing models of our sample are, on average, noisier (+1/1.5 dB) and with less capacity (160 vs 212 seats) than the Airbus ones. Embraer models are the least noisy in terms of entire aircraft, but are also the ones with the smallest capacity. As a result, their cost per seat is the highest in our case.

The aggregate total social costs of noise generated by Milan Bergamo airport on 29t January 2018 are shown in Table 9.7. The total social noise costs produced by the daily airport operations are about €61,000, with a per-seat cost equal to €1.72.

Table 9.8 presents the total aggregated emissions social costs, noise costs, and all environmental costs, and the corresponding values per seat and per ASK.

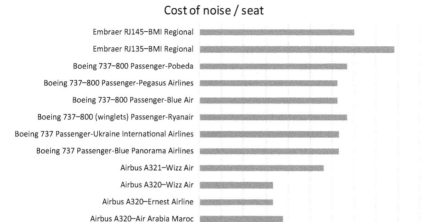

Cost of noise / seat

Figure 9.3 Noise social costs per seat (€2010) by aircraft at Milan Bergamo airport (29 January 2018).

Table 9.7 Social noise costs at Milan Bergamo airport, 29 January 2018

Total noise social costs	Social costs per seat	Social costs per ASK
€61,286	€1.72	€0.0009

Table 9.8 Aggregate and per externality category social costs at Milan Bergamo airport, 29 January 2018

Externality	Total	Per seat	Per ASK
Emissions	€18.807	€0.48	€0.0002
Noise	€61.286	€1.72	€0.0009
Aggregate (emissions + noise)	€80.093	€2.20	€0.0011

In a specific day the total social costs at Milan Bergamo airport are equal to about €80,000, with a per-seat costs of €2,20. The latter figure could be the benchmark for a total externalities charge imposed on airlines; alternatively, the airport could generate an airline specific externality charge, that should give to the carrier the incentive to replace older more polluting and noisy aircraft with newer ones, that are more environmentally friendly. Another important issue is to identify who has to pay the charge, the passengers, the airlines, or the airport. It is possible to devise a form of cost-sharing, in order to distribute the burden among several subjects.

Conclusions

This chapter provides an overview of the methodologies adopted to quantify the impact of environmental externalities produced by civil aviation. The focus is on environmental noise and substance emissions contributing to pollute the airport and its surrounding area. The adopted method is taken from Grampella et al. (2017) and is based on aircraft certification standards. It is then applied to a case study: the social costs of emissions and noise generated in a single day of operation at Milan Bergamo airport. The method can be easily replicated to all airports, with the only requirement of having data on scheduled flights and their model, so that matching with certification standards is possible.

The application of this method to several airports could allow us to make a comparison among them and to identify an *optimal* level of negative externalities that each airport should reach. This application may be done using frontier analysis, including both good and bad items (in this case emissions and noise), or only bad items. Moreover, it can be the base for airport incentive regulation, providing the necessary incentives for fleet replacement.

This method of estimating social costs of airport negative externalities identifies a hypothetical level of social costs based on social unit costs as in CBA and considering that airports are in urban areas, i.e., without taking into account the actual population living in the surroundings of each airport. This step could be done by tracking the territory and looking at the density of dwellings, and it is left for future research.

Notes

1 The ICAO Convention established rules for civil aviation. It is divided into articles and is supported by 19 annexes containing standards and recommended practice.
2 Lden (day-evening-night level) is an acoustic metric based on energy equivalent noise level (Leq) over a whole day with a penalty of 10 dB(A) for night time noise (22.00–7.00) and an additional penalty of 5 dB(A) for evening noise (19.00–23.00) (EEA glossary).
3 An operation, enabled by airspace design, procedure design, and ATC facilitation, in which an arriving aircraft descends continuously, to the greatest possible extent, by employing minimum engine thrust, ideally in a low-drag situation, prior to the final approach point (ICAO, 2010).
4 United Nations Framework Convention on Climate Change (UNFCCC).
5 For a discussion of EU ETS and ICAO CORSIA see Scheelhaase et al. (2018), and Lam Lo et al. (2019).
6 Some factors are the complexity of simulation due to input data and the integration with other models.
7 Concerning noise, the logarithmic nature of decibels complicates the monetary conversion of this externalities using hedonic prices.
8 Measuring the social cost would require taking into account the population living in the vicinity of the airports. However, notice that this methodology could be upgraded in the future by using some simplified models capturing the population.

9   The 3,000 ft (approximately 915 m) boundary is the standard set by ICAO for the average height of the mixing zone, the layer of the earth's atmosphere where chemical reactions of pollutants can ultimately affect ground level pollutant concentrations.

10 This procedure can be used also to compute CO_2 produced (see the following example related to Bergamo airport). However, we notice that CO_2 contributes to climate change and not to local air pollution.

11 Equation (11.1) describes a metric called LVAt similar to the Italian regulation metric (DM 31/10/1997) that indicates the total environmental noise produced by an airport.

12 Mayeres et al. (1996), Eyre et al. (1997), Perl et al. (1997), and Levinson et al. (1998).

13 It is very important to underline that the HEATCO study focus primary on the monetary quantification of the effects of environmental impact (i.e. on health, land use). They also provide damage costs of main pollutants from generic transport so we can make a comparison between the three methodologies.

14 For un-combusted hydrocarbons (HC) they specified the cost only for nmVOC that are a category of substances that influence the determination of secondary pollutants generated by chemical reactions in the atmosphere.

15 In terms of CO_2, it has been demonstrated that the effects on human health of local amounts are very difficult to estimate.

16 Schipper (2004) provides different values of noise costs per aircraft movement. Such values are the result of an estimation of the relation between noise annoyance and aircraft movements. Schipper's estimates are based on noise and aircraft movements data referring to a small sample of European airports for the period 1974–1997. Notice that such values vary according to (1) the reference studies used (i.e., absolute noise cost values vs. costs relative to property values), (2) the (if applicable) high/low property value used, and (3) the period considered. The value of €324 is Schipper's euro €281 value that has been inflated into the €2010 base according to Grampella et al. (2017). The authors also perform some robustness analysis.

References

ACI and CANSO (2015) Managing the impacts of aviation noise: a guide for airport operators and air navigation service providers.

Baranzini, A. Ramírez, J.V. (2005) Paying for quietness: the impact of noise on Geneva rents, *Urban Studies*, 42(4), 633–646.

Bateman, I.J., Day, B., Lake, I, Lovett, A. (2001) The effect of road traffic on residential property values: a literature review and hedonic prices study. Report for the Scottish executive, University of East Anglia, Economic and social research council. London; University College London.

Bernardo, J.E., Kirby, M.R., Mavris, D. (2016) Probabilistic assessment of fleet-level noise impacts of projected technology improvements, *Journal of Air Transport Management*, 57, 26–42.

Dekkers, J.E.C, Van der Straaten, J.W. (2009) Monetary evaluation of aircraft noise; a hedonic analysis around Amsterdam airport, *Ecological Economics*, 68(11), 2850–2858.

Dings, J.M.V, Wit, R.C.N., Leurs, B.A, Davidson, M.D, Fransen, W. (2003) External costs of Aviation. Federal Environmental Agency, Umweltbundesamt, Berlin.

DM 31/10/1997 Metodologia di misura del rumore aeroportuale.

EASA (2019), European Aviation Environmental Report.

EC (1996) Future noise policy, European Commission Green paper, COM 96 (540).

EC (2002), Directive 2002/49/EC of the European Parliament and of the Council of 25 June 2002 relating to the assessment and management of environmental noise.

EC (2008) Directive 2008/50/EC of the European Parliament and of the Council of 21 May 2008 on ambient air quality and cleaner air for Europe.

EC (2017) Support study to the ex-post evaluation of Directive 2009/12/EC on Airport Charges.

EEA (2010) Good practice guide on noise exposure and potential health effects, EEA Technical report No. 11/2010.

EEA (2014) Noise in Europe, EEA Report No. 10/2014.

EEA (2017) Air quality in Europe – 2017 report, EEA Report No. 13/2017.

EEA (2017) Transport and Environment Reporting Mechanism (TERM) 2017.

EEA (2017) Trends and projections in Europe 2017, EEA Report No. 17/2017.

EU (2014) Regulation (EU) 598/2014 of the European Parliament and the Council of 16 April 2014 on the establishment of rules and procedures with regard to the introduction of noise related operating restrictions at Union airports within a Balanced Approach and repealing Directive 2002/30/EC.

EU (2016) Directive (EU) 2016/2284 of the European Parliament and of the Council of 14 December 2016 on the reduction of national emissions of certain atmospheric pollutants, amending Directive 2003/35/EC and repealing Directive 2001/81/EC new National Emission Ceilings Directive 206/2284.

EU (2018) Regulation (EU) No. 2018/1139 of the European Parliament and of the Council of 4 July 2018 on common rules in the field of civil aviation and establishing a European Union Aviation Safety Agency.

Eurocontrol (2011) Continuous descent: a guide to implement continuous descent.

Eurocontrol (2018) Standard inputs for Eurocontrol Cost-Benefit analysis, Brussels.

Eyre, N. J., Ozdemiroglu, E., Pearce, D. W. Steele, P. (1997) Fuel and location effects on the damage costs of transport emissions, Journal of Transport Economics and Policy, 31, 5–24.

Givoni, M., Rietveld, P. (2010) The environmental implications of airline's choice of aircraft size, *Journal of Air Transport Management*, 16, 159–167.

Grampella, M., Martini, G., Scotti, D., Tassan, F., Zambon, G. (2017) Determinants of airports' environmental effects, *Transportation Research Part D*, 50, 327–344.

Harris, J.M., Roach, B. (2018) *Environmental and Natural Resource Economics. A Contemporary Approach*, Abingdon: Routledge.

HEATCO Project (2006) Developing Harmonised European Approaches for Transport Costing and project assessment Deliverable 5, Proposal for Harmonised guidelines.

Herndon, S.C., Wood, E.C., Northway, M.J., Myake-Lye, R., Thornhill, L., Beyersdorf, A., Anderson, B.E., Dowlin, R., Dodds, W., Knighton, W.B. (2009) Aircraft hydrocarbon emissions at Oakland international airport, *Environmental Science & Technology*, 43, 6, 1730–1736.

Holmes, N.S, Morawska, L. (2006) An overview of dispersion modelling and their application to the dispersion of particles: an overview of different dispersion models available, Atmospheric Environment, Elsevier.

ICAO (2017) Annex 16 to the Convention on International Civil Aviation – Environmental Protection, Volume I, 8th Edition – Aircraft Noise.

ICAO (2017) Annex 16 to the Convention on International Civil Aviation – Environmental Protection, Volume II, 4th Edition – Aircraft Engine Emissions.

ICAO (2017) Annex 16 to the Convention on International Civil Aviation – Environmental Protection, Volume III, 1st Edition – Aeroplane CO_2 Emissions.

ICAO (2010) Doc. 9931, Continuous Descent Operations (CDO) Manual.

Korzhenevych, A., Dehnen, N. (2014) Update of the Handbook on External costs of Transport Final Report to European Commission DG Move, Ricardo-AEA/R/ED57769,1.

Kroes, E.P., Sheldon, R.J., (1988) Stated preference methods: an introduction, Journal of Transport Economics and Policy, 22(1), 11–25.

Levinson, D. M., Gillen D., Kanafani, A. (1998) The social costs of intercity transportation: a review and comparison of air and highway, Transport Reviews, 18, 215–240.

Lavandier, C., Sedoarisoa, N., Desponds, D., Dalmas, L. (2016) A new indicator to measure the noise impact around airports: the real estate tolerance level (RETL) – case study around Charles De Gaulle airport, *Applied Acoustics*, 110, 207–217.

Lo, L.P., Martini, G., Porta, F. and Scotti, D. (2019) The determinants of CO_2 emissions of air transport passenger traffic: an analysis of Lombardy, *Transport Policy*, forthcoming.

Lobo, P., Hagen, D.E., Whitefield, P.D. (2012) Measurement and analysis of aircraft downwind of an active runway at the Oakland international airport, *Atmospheric Environment*.

Lu, C. (2009) The implications of environmental costs on air passenger demand for different airline business models, *Journal of Air Transport management*, 15, 158–165.

Lu, C. (2012) The economic benefits and environmental costs of airport operations; Taiwan Taoyuan International Airport, *Journal of Air Transport Management*, 17, 360–363.

Lu, C., Morrel, P. (2001) Evaluation and implications of environmental charges on commercial flights, *Transportation* 33, 45–61.

Lu, C, Morrel, P. (2006) Determinants and application of environmental costs at different sized airports aircraft noise and engine emissions, *Transportation*, 33, 45–61.

Mayeres, I., Ochelen, S., Proost, S. (1996) The marginal external costs of urban transport, Transportation Research, 1D, 111–130.

Morrel, P., Lu, C. (2007) The environmental cost implication of hub to hub versus hub by pass flight networks, *Transportation Research Part D*, 12, 143–157.

Navrud, S. (2002) The state of the art on economic valuation of noise, Final Report to European Commission DG Environment 14.

Perl, A., Patterson, J., Perez, M. (1997) Pricing aircraft emissions at Lyon-Satolas Airport, *Transportation Research*, 2D, 89–105.

Phaneuf, D.J., Requate, T. (2017) *A Course in Environmental Economics. Theory, Policy, and Practice*, Cambridge: Cambridge University Press.

Püschel, R., Evangelinos, C. (2012) Evaluating noise annoyance cost recovery at Dusseldorf International airport, Transportation Research Part D: Transport and Environment, 17(8), 598–604.

Region Lombardy Environmental Agency (ARPA). Available at www.arpalombardia.it

SACBO s.p.a. (2018) Bergamo Airport Noise Action Plan 2018 Report.

Scheelhaase, J., Maertens, S., Grimme, W. and Jung, M. (2018) EU ETS versus CORSIA – a critical assessment of two approaches to limit air transport's CO_2 emissions by market-based measures, *Journal of Air Transport Management*, 67, 55–62.

Schipper, Y. (2004) Environmental costs in European aviation, *Transportation Policy*, 11, 141–154.

Schipper, Y., Rietveld, P., Nijkamp, P. (1998) Why do aircraft noise value estimates differ? A meta-analysis, *Journal of Air Transport Management*, 42(2), 117–120

Schipper, Y., Rietveld, P., Nijkamp, P. (2001) Environmental externalities in air transport markets, *Journal of Air Transport Management*, 7(3).

Schürmann, G., Schäfer, K., Jahn, C., Hoffmann, E., Bauerfind, M., Fleuti, E., Rappenglück, E. (2007) The impact of NOx, CO and VOC emissions on the air quality of Zurich Airport, *Atmospheric Environment*, 41(1), 103–118.

Smith, V.K., Huang, J.C. (1995) Can markets value air quality? A meta-analysis of hedonic property value models, *Journal of Political Economy*, 103, 1.

Torja, A.J., Self, R.H., Flindell, I.H. (2017) A model for the rapid assessment of the impact of aviation near airports, *The Journal of Acoustical Society of America*, 141(2), 981–995.

Torija, A.J, Self, R.H., Flindell, I.H. (2018) Airport noise modelling for strategic environmental impact assessment of aviation, *Applied Acoustics*, 132, 49–57.

UNFCCC (2015) COP 21 Paris Agreement.

UNFCCC (2013) Reporting guidelines on inventories for Parties included in Annex I to the conventions.

WHO World Health Organization Europe (2018) Environmental Noise Guidelines for the European Region.

10 Econometric approaches to the study of air transport impacts on regional development

Main methods and results

António Pais Antunes and Gianmaria Martini

Introduction

The study of the impacts of transport infrastructure and services on regional (and urban or metropolitan) development has a long history, within which both *ex-ante* impacts (i.e., effects expected before the implementation of the infrastructure or services) and *ex-post* impacts have been of interest. In this chapter, we specifically focus on *ex-post* impacts of air transport, and on a particular type of approach to evaluate impacts. In this context, two types of approaches can, in principle, be used. The first one is impact analysis. It aims to estimate, in monetary terms, the direct, indirect, induced, and catalytic economic effects generated globally or in some particular territory (e.g., a country or a region) by the air transport industry. The application of this approach typically involves the use of an input-output model or, desirably, a computable general equilibrium model to evaluate how the effects of the industry under analysis spread across the economy (see Chapters 6 and 7 of this Handbook). Models of this type, and especially those of the second type, are not easy to build (notably because of their substantial data requirements), and are rarely available or are outdated. Even when they are available and are not outdated, they are generally built at the country level, which makes them inadequate for applications at more disaggregate levels of analysis. The alternative is then to resort to econometric approaches, to investigate statistically the extent to which an economy is influenced by air transport. This approach can be used to study the relationship between air transport and regional development using a model capturing the main determinants of regional development, and, among them, to identify the impact of air transport. The econometric approaches more often adopted in the literature usually rely on a reduced form model, where all potentially endogenous variables that may affect the possible determinants of regional development have been replaced by other structural equations. Hence, the reduced form model is an attempt to consider, as explanatory factors of regional development, only exogenous variables. The possible endogeneity between regional development and air transport (i.e., is it air transport that causes regional development or is it the contrary?) is a possible exception, as we will show later. Econometric approaches are the focus of this chapter.

The first (journal) article where an econometric approach was used to investigate the (*ex-post*) impacts of air transport on regional development is Goetz (1992). According to a search performed in the Web of Science with the keywords (air transport★ OR aviation OR airport) AND (econom★ OR region★ OR metropolitan OR urban OR city OR cities) AND (development OR growth) AND (econometr★ OR regression), a total of 128 articles has been published and registered in that bibliographic database during the 27 years which have elapsed since 1992, 70 (55%) of which have been published in the last five years (see Figure 10.1). Authors affiliated with universities and research institutions of European Union countries are involved in 58 (45%) of those 128 articles and 49 (39%) articles have authors affiliated to universities and research institutions from North America countries. China and Australia are other countries well represented in the database, with 18 and 12 articles, respectively. The main transport journals where these articles appear are the *Journal of Air Transport Management* (13), the *Journal of Transport Geography* (10), *Transportation Research Part A* (8), *Transportation Research Record* (7), and Transport Policy (4). The rising interest in this subject is also reflected by the steady growth of the number of citations to this literature (over 200 in recent years as shown in Figure 10.1).

Our aim in this chapter is not to provide a detailed review of the increasingly vast econometric literature on the impacts of air transport on regional development, but only to present and discuss its main results and the methods used to obtain them. For this, we will concentrate on a relatively limited number of articles – articles that, in our opinion, are essential to comprehend the progress achieved by the scientific community with respect to the research subject

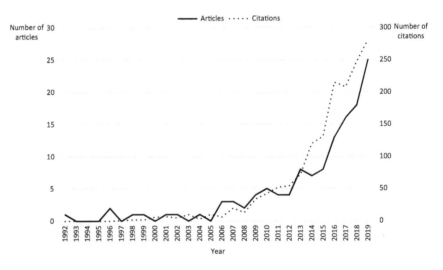

Figure 10.1 Evolution of the number of articles on air transport and regional development published until the end of 2019 in journals listed in the Web of Science, and of the number of citations to those articles.

under analysis. These articles are examined in three sections, corresponding to three periods. The earlier works, dating back to the period 1992–2002, essentially set the research objectives, and the dependent and explanatory variables considered in the literature. The following period, 2003–2008, encompasses two key contributions, Brueckner (2003) and Green (2007). These authors were the first who carefully looked into endogeneity (causality) issues. Up to this point, practically all articles had focused on North America. The subsequent articles, published in the period 2009–2019, present recent advances. In many cases, they apply methods developed in earlier periods, or improvements of those methods, to geographic contexts other than North America. In the final part of the chapter, we summarise the previous sections and identify some research gaps that, in our opinion, are yet to be overcome.

Early works

The late 1980s and early 1990s were a time when a great deal of attention was devoted to the development effects of infrastructure provision. Prominent articles like Aschauer (1989) and Gramlich (1994), where the economic impacts of public spending (particularly on transport infrastructure) were examined, date back to this period.

The first article to have addressed air transport impacts on regional development, Goetz (1992), is from the same period, but of a rather different nature. Specifically, it focused on the 'relationship between air passenger transportation and the growth of U.S. urban places from 1950 to 1987', because, in the view of its author, 'this form of transportation would bear some relationship to patterns of differential urban growth and economic development'. This article used data from the 50 largest air passenger cities of the United States and relied on ordinary least-squares (OLS) regression analysis (and on a subsequent outlier analysis). Both previous and subsequent population and employment growth were (alternatively) linked with air transport activity 'in order to account for the bidirectionality of the relationship'. The dependent and explanatory variables of the four regression equations considered are described in Table 10.1.

Based on the results of this analysis, it was concluded that air transport activity has significant positive impacts on subsequent population growth. However, as shown in Table 10.1, both the magnitude and the significance of the impact had been decreasing over time. For example, the regression coefficient for the air transport activity variable was 20.7 in 1960–1970 and the respective *t*-ratio was 9.3, whereas the figures for 1980–1987 were 2.5 and 3.5 respectively. In addition, the level of explanation of the impacts provided by the regression equations (as measured by the coefficient of determination, R^2) went down from 0.64 to 0.20. It was also concluded that population growth impacts on subsequent air transport activity were significant and positive, and that their significance was decreasing, but their magnitude was increasing, as the regression coefficient changed from 0.017 (*t*-ratio = 7.1) in 1960 to 0.089 in 1987 (*t*-ratio = 3.4). The results obtained replacing population growth by employment growth were, in general, of a similar nature.

Table 10.1 Variables and results in Goetz (1992)

	1950		1960		1970		1980	
	Mean	SD	Mean	SD	Mean	SD	Mean	SD
PAXCAP[1]	0.403	0.230	0.891	0.671	1.353	0.985	2.281	1.925
PAXEMP[2]	1.062	0.574	2.449	1.682	3.928	2.616	5.145	3.912

	1950–60	1960–70	1970–80	1980–87
	National Avg.	National Avg.	National Avg.	National Avg.
PCPX[3]	26.4%	16.6%	10.2%	12.3%
PCEX[4]	23.4%	22.1%	27.4%	–

A. PAXCAP = f (Previous PCPX)

PAXCAP	PCPX	b	t	R²	F	Sig
1960	1950–60	0.017	7.088	0.5114	50.23	.0000
1970	1960–70	0.045	7.335	0.5285	53.81	.0000
1980	1970–80	0.046	3.977	0.2478	15.82	.0002
1987	1980–87	0.089	3.402	0.1943	11.57	.0014

B. Subsequent PCPX = f (PAXCAP)

PAXCAP	PCPX	b	t	R²	F	Sig
1960	1950–60	41.966	3.565	0.2094	12.71	.0008
1970	1960–70	20.686	9.333	0.6447	87.11	.0000
1980	1970–80	9.576	4.518	0.2984	20.42	.0000
1987	1980–87	2.494	3.471	0.2006	12.05	.0011

1 PAXCAP: Air Passengers per Capita Index
2 PAXEMP: Air Passengers per Total Employed Index
3 PCPX: Percent Population Change
4 PCEX: Percent Employment Change

Practically from the same time is a study developed by Benell & Prentice (1993) with the aim of predicting the economic impacts of Canadian airports by including emplaned and deplaned passengers and a number of other variables concerning the airports or the wealth of respective regions. Information on those impacts was taken from the economic impact studies performed in the late 1980s for 44 airports in the country (such studies were also performed then for many airports of the United States). The study was also in this case carried out using OLS regression analysis. The motivation of the authors was to provide a 'low-cost method of updating the economic impact studies', thus avoiding the *ad hoc* techniques (or simple inflation-adjustment procedures) that were being used for these updates. The variables considered in the study are presented in Table 10.2.

The conclusions of Benell & Prentice (1993) were based on the results reproduced in Table 10.2. Since the dependent and explanatory variables were logged, the regression coefficients can be interpreted as response elasticities. In

Table 10.2 Variables and results in Benell & Prentice (1993)

Dependent variables		
E	=	Person–years of employment that is directly attributable to the airport
R	=	Revenue, or economic output, that is the result of airport activity in one year

Explanatory variables		
b0	=	A constant
P	=	Enplaned and deplaned passengers at the airport in 1988
W	=	The relative wealth of the community, as measures by the average price of all the houses sold that year
L	=	The number of movements of large aircraft (> 35,000 kg)
B	=	1 if there is an air carrier's maintenance base at the airport, 0 otherwise

Independent variable	Dependent variable/ employment (ln E)	Estimated coefficients revenue (ln R)
Constant	$a0 = -10.337$ (-5.29)	$b0 = -0.821$ (-0.29)
Passenger traffic (ln P)	$a1 = 0.754$ (19.02)	$b1 = 0.493$ (4.47)
Wealth (ln W)	$a2 = 0.593$ (3.05)	$b2 = 0.937$ (2.93)
Large aircraft (ln L)	N/A	$b3 = 0.178$ (2.43)
Maintenance base (ln B)	$a3 = 0.332$ (2.31)	$b4 = 0.482$ (3.22)
Adjusted R2	0.989	0.948
F-Statistic	387.7	169.6

particular, the regression coefficient of 0.754 for the emplaned and deplaned passengers (P) in the employment (E) regression equation means that a 10% increase in P led to a 7.54% increase in E. This effect was very significant statistically (t-ratio $= 19.02$). However, it is important to underline that this was employment 'directly attributable to the airport', since there was no information on total employment impacts (obviously, this circumstance seriously affects the relevance of the results of this study).

Another important early contribution to the subject is a study by Button & Taylor (2000), who examined the impacts of air transport on regional development for 41 'metropolitan standard areas' of the United States served by airports of different sizes (from large to medium size) using data from the period 1994–1996. The focus was on new economic activity (high-technology companies) and its relation with air transport service to/from Europe. OLS was the method used to estimate the regression equation(s). The dependent variable was new economy employment. The number of enplanements (total and of European passengers) and the number of European flight destinations were amongst the explanatory variables. Several possible equations were tested, and, as stated by the authors, the best results were obtained for the following equation:

$$HT = -23257.8 + 0.021POP + 3965.35\ln(ENP)$$
$$+ 6122.41\ln(DEST) + 0.559MIL$$
$$- 1235.91TZ + 0.0015TENP \quad (R^2 = 0.82)$$

where *HT*: new economy employment in 1996, *POP*: population of the surrounding Metropolitan Area in 1996; *ENP*: number of European on-plane passengers in 1994; *DEST*: number of European airports served in 1994; *MIL*: military expenditure in 1996; *TZ*: time zone (East Coast Standard Time = 0); *TENP*: total enplanements in 1994.

The results obtained in this study suggest that international air services to Europe have contributed to the growth of new economy employment, with both the number of destinations and the quality of service being relevant for the final effect. This effect was much more important in airports serving a small number of such destinations than in those that already served many: an increase of destinations from three to four would lead to the creation of an expected 2,900 jobs, while only 440 jobs would be created if the destinations increased from 20 to 21. The overall conclusion was that 'within limits, more international air transportation is likely to stimulate further growth in the new economy'.

The last study from this initial period is due to Kulendran & Wilson (2000). These authors investigated the relationship between international trade (total, exports and imports) and international travel (total, business and holiday) for Australia and its most important trading partners – Japan, New Zealand, the United Kingdom and the United States – with data from the period 1982–1997. Even though this study did not deal with regional development, we include it here because it addresses the relationship of our interest through an approach different from OLS regression analysis and, especially, because a number of recent studies concerned with regional development impacts have employed the same type of approach. This study involved the application of cointegration and Granger-causality analyses. Cointegration analysis is relevant when data are non-stationary (i.e., means and variances vary over time), which is often the case. Granger-causality analysis is used to test whether a set of explanatory lagged variables $X_{-1}, \ldots, X_{-T}$ can explain a dependent variable Y even when a set of explanatory variables $Y_{-1} \ldots, Y_{-T}$, is also considered in the regression equation (if this is the case, then Y is said to be Granger-caused by X).

We summarise in Table 10.3 the results described in Kulendran & Wilson (2000) focusing on the relationship between total travel and total trade. These results are different depending on Australia's trading partner. For the United States, a clear relationship, characterised by a significance level of 1%, was found to exist in both directions; i.e., total travel Granger-caused total trade and vice versa. However, for Japan, only the first direction (travel to trade) was significant (at the 5% level), and, for the United Kingdom, only the second direction

Table 10.3 Main results of Kulendran & Wilson (2000)

Country	Identified Granger causation relationships		Significance level
USA	Business travel	→ Real total trade	1%
	Total travel	→ Real exports	1%
	Total travel	→ Real total trade	1%
	Total travel	← Real total trade	1%
	Holiday travel	→ Real total trade	10%
	Holiday travel	← Real exports	10%
Japan	Total travel	→ Real exports	5%
	Total travel	→ Real total trade	5%
	Holiday travel	→ Real exports	5%
	Holiday travel	→ Real total trade	5%
UK	Business travel	→ Real imports	5%
	Total travel	← Real total trade	1%
	Business travel	← Real total trade	5%

Note: Arrows indicate direction of causation.

(trade to travel) was significant (at the 1% level). Finally, for New Zealand, there was no evidence of the relationship in any one of the two directions (in this regard, the authors note that 'their respective economies are now increasingly integrated and perhaps they should no longer be seen as trading partners in the traditional sense'). The lack of consistency in these results was explained by the diversity of trading relationships between Australia and the four countries under study.

Two key contributions

We will now focus our attention on two similar studies that are central to research about the impacts of air transport on regional development: Brueckner (2003) and Green (2007). Despite the difference of four years between the publication dates of the articles, they were written contemporaneously (Green *dixit*). Both studies used OLS regression analysis as well as two-stage least-squares (2SLS) regression analysis to deal with possible endogeneity problems. The main differences between the two studies are mentioned below. The reason we classify these articles as key contributions is because they have been used as a reference and quoted by a large number of subsequent articles addressing the impacts of air transport on regional development.

The specific topic addressed by Brueckner (2003) was the link between airline traffic and employment in the 91 metropolitan areas of the United States. The dependent and explanatory variables of the regression equations he analysed are described in Table 10.4. The dependent variable was (non-farm) employment (total, goods-related, or service-related) and the explanatory variables were the (potentially) endogenous variable airline traffic (passenger enplanements) and a vector of variables that could 'reasonably be viewed as exogenous determinants of employment'. Instrumental variables have also been included in the table below. These variables are necessary to identify the regression equations, enabling the effect of *TRAFFIC* on *EMP* (or *GDSEMP*, or *SVCEMP*) to be properly estimated. For this to happen, the number of instrumental variables should be at least equal to the number of endogenous variables, and each instrumental variable should be highly correlated to an endogenous variable but uncorrelated or weakly correlated to the error term. The four instrumental variables chosen by Brueckner (2003) were *HUB*, *PROXIMITY*, *SLOT*, and *LEISURE*. The arguments for their choice are explained in detail in the article, but the validity of these instrumental variables has not been statistically tested (at least, no information is provided on this issue). Data for all variables were in general from 1996.

The regression results reported in Brueckner (2003) are summarised in Table 10.4. It can be seen there that airline traffic has contributed significantly to total employment (*t*-ratio = 3.15). The response elasticity was 0.08, i.e., an increase in airline traffic of 10% led to an increase of 0.8% in total employment. This effect was more intense and significant in relation to service-related employment, for which the response elasticity was 0.11 (*t*-ratio = 3.52). In contrast, it was not significant in relation to goods-related employment (*t*-ratio = 0.29). The level of explanation of the regression equations was very high ($R^2 > 0.94$) for the three equations estimated. The general conclusion was that 'good airline service is an important factor in urban economic development' and that 'airline traffic has no effect on manufacturing and other goods-related employment'.

The work described in Green (2007) pursued the same general objectives of Brueckner (2003), but involved a number of differences that deserve to be highlighted. The first one relates to the dependent variables. In this case, population and employment growth variables (for the period 1990–2000) were considered, instead of employment (stock) variables. A second difference was that four air transport activity variables were alternatively considered (in the year 1990): passenger boardings per capita (measuring the total airport activity); passenger originations per capita (measuring the airport activity more directly related to the regional economy); hub status (dummy allowing to examine 'whether bringing people to an airport to change planes spills over into economic activity'); and cargo activity per capita. A total of 83 metropolitan areas of the United States was considered in the analysis.

The results obtained by Green (2007), displayed in Table 10.5, point very much in the same directions as those presented by Brueckner (2003). With the exception of cargo per capita, the air transport activity variables were all clearly significant (*t*-ratios clearly greater than 2.0). A 10% increase in airport boardings per capita was shown to have led to a 3.9% increase in the population growth rate and a 2.8% increase in the employment growth rate over the period 1990–2000, and these effects due to an increase in airport originations was 3.3% and 2.8% respectively. The second set of estimates was obtained through OLS regression, as the Wu-Hausman test indicated that no endogeneity issues affected the

Table 10.4 Variables and results in Brueckner (2003)

Variable	Definition
TRAFFIC	Total 1996 passenger enplanements at metro-area airport(s)
EMP	Total metro-area non-farm employment for 1996 (in 1000s)
GDSEMP	Total metro-area goods-related employment for 1996 (in 1000s)
SVCEMP	Total metro-area service-related employment for 1996 (in 1000s)
POP	Metro-area population for 1990
YOUNG	Percentage of 1996 metro-area population of age 14 or younger
OLD	Percentage of 1996 metro-area population of age 65 or older
RTW	Dummy variable equal to one if metro area's state has right-to-work law
HEATING	Average heating degree days for metro area
COLGGRAD	Percentage of metro area's 1990 population over 25 with a college degree
CORPTAX	Maximum 1996 marginal corporate income tax rate for metro area's state
PERSTAX	Maximum 1996 marginal personal income tax rate for metro area's state
HUB	Enplanement share of any hub airports in metro area
LEISURE	Dummy variable equal to one for Las Vegas and Orlando
PROXIMITY	Dummy variable equal to one for smaller metro areas within 150 miles of large airport
SLOT	Enplanement share of any slot-controlled airports in metro area

Independent variables	TRAFFIC (OLS)	EMP (2SLS)	EMP (OLS)	GDSEMP (2SLS)	GDSEMP (OLS)	SVCEMP (2SLS)	SVCEMP (OLS)
				Dependent variables			
INTERCEPT	−0.887	−6.246	−6.304	−7.532	−7.668	−6.509	−6.552
	(0.41)	(16.60)	(16.79)	(8.58)	(8.56)	(16.95)	(17.86)
POP	0.979	0.889	0.903	0.992	1.023	0.858	0.868
	(11.63)	(24.24)	(35.39)	(11.82)	(14.54)	(21.56)	(35.60)
TRAFFIC	0.0437	0.0886	0.0782	0.0168	−0.00768	0.110	0.102
		(3.15)	(4.34)	(0.29)	(0.16)	(3.52)	(5.60)
		−0.0469	−0.0460	−0.0639	−0.0619	−0.0429	−0.0423

(continued)

Table 10.4 Cont.

Independent variables	TRAFFIC (OLS)	EMP (2SLS)	EMP (OLS)	Dependent variables GDSEMP (2SLS)	GDSEMP (OLS)	SVCEMP (2SLS)	SVCEMP (OLS)
YOUNG	(0.86)	(5.72)	(5.53)	(3.07)	(2.84)	(4.92)	(4.87)
OLD	0.0223 (0.74)	−0.0235 (4.82)	−0.0233 (4.28)	−0.0400 (−3.39)	−0.0396 (3.06)	−0.0204 (4.43)	−0.0202 (3.99)
RTW	0.0176 (0.11)	0.114 (4.36)	0.118 (4.25)	0.157 (1.95)	0.164 (1.96)	0.0968 (3.16)	0.0991 (3.07)
HEATING	−0.0000128 (0.32)	0.0000328 (5.51)	0.0000332 (5.30)	0.0000732 (4.25)	0.0000741 (4.14)	0.0000221 (3.44)	0.0000224 (3.28)
COLGGRAD	0.0540 (3.63)	0.00157 (0.48)	0.00202 (0.62)	−0.0145 (1.69)	−0.0135 (1.50)	0.00549 (1.54)	0.00583 (1.60)
CORPTAX	−0.0637 (1.78)	−0.00141 (0.21)	−0.00214 (0.31)	−0.0174 (1.13)	−0.0192 (1.21)	0.00390 (0.59)	0.00336 (0.47)
PERSTAX	−0.00908 (0.42)	0.00135 (0.34)	0.00107 (0.26)	0.0178 (1.66)	0.0172 (1.53)	−0.00356 (0.81)	−0.00377 (0.83)
HUB	0.922 (5.76)						
LEISURE	1.653 (3.92)						
PROXIMITY	−0.315 (1.96)						
SLOT	−0.338 (0.82)						
R2	0.872		0.992		0.947		0.991

Notes: TRAFFIC, POP, EMP, GDSEMP, SVCEMP in logs; absolute t-statistics in parenthesis, based on robust standard errors; observations = 91.

Table 10.5 Main results of Green (2007) with boardings per capita as dependent variable

	Population growth 1990–2000		Employment growth 1990–2000	
	OLS	2SLS	OLS	25L5
Intercept	−0.265	−0.157	−0.363	−0 313
	0.179	(0.)80)	(0.223)	(0.205)
Boardings per capita	0.025	0.039	0.021	0.028
	(0.004)	(0.005)	(0.004)	(0.006)
Per cent of workforce in	0.293	0.508	0.329	0.424
manufacturing	(0.206)	(0.210)	(0.257)	(0.242)
Per cent of workforce in	−0.787	−0.902	−1.04	−1.090
FIRE jobs	(0.594)	(0.586)	(0.740)	(0.671)
State capital located within	0.091	0099	0.095	0.099
CMSA/MSA	(0.026)	(0.026)	(0.032)	(0.029)
Per cent of population with	0.796	0.753	1.12	1.11
high school degree and	(0.205)	(0.201)	(0.255)	(0.231)
above				
Per cent of population with	−0.473	−0.514	−0.426	−0.449
collage degree	(0.242)	(0.238)	(0.302)	(0.273)
Cooling degree days	−0.000003	−0.00002	0.00002	0.000008
	(0.000024)	(0.00003)	(0.00013)	(0.00003)
Top corp. income tax rate	−0.580	−0.276	−0.587	−0.453
state level	(0.479)	(0.479)	(0.597)	(0.549)
Top personal income tax	−0.529	−0.628	−0.846	−0.9
rate state level	(0.534)	(0.524)	(0.664)	(0.602)
Top corp. income tax rate −	0.026	0.035	0.023	0.027
city level	(0.012)	(0.016)	(0.020)	(0.018)
Top personal income tax	−0.025	−0.027	−0.012	−0.012
rate − city level	(0.022)	(0.021)	(0.027)	(0.025)
MSA/PMSA property tax	0.00004	0.0003	−0.0009	−0.0008
rates per $1,000	(0.00213)	(0.0021)	(0.0027)	(0.0024)
Right-to-work state	0.024	0.018	0.036	0.032
	(0.026)	(0.026)	(0.033)	(0.030)
Failures versus	0.010	0.015	0.013	0.016
business starts	(0.014)	(0.014)	(0.017)	(0.016)
starts				
Heating degree days	−0.00002	−0.00003	−0.00001	−0.00002
	(0.00001)	(0.00001)	(0.00001)	(0.00001)
Average commute time	−0.00003	−0.0039	−0.004	−0.006
	(0.00381)	(0.0039)	(0.005)	(O.OM)
N	83	83	83	83
R2	0.72		0.69	

Note: Heteroskedacticity corrected standard errors in parenthesis.

variables (this was not regarded as a surprise by the author because air transport activity variables were lagged in relation to population and employment growth variables). With respect to hub status effects, the regression results revealed that ('astonishingly') the population of hub cities grew between 9% and 16% faster than that of non-hub cities, and employment grew between 8.4% and 13.2% faster. Since the dependent variables were flow and not stock variables in this case, the level of explanation provided by the regression equations was lower, but still very reasonable ($R^2 > 0.60$ for all regression equations estimated in this study).

Recent advances

In the last ten years, the efforts devoted by the scientific community to ana-lyse the impacts of air transport on regional development have increased sub-stantially, including those relying on econometric approaches. These efforts involved applications of more sophisticated regression and Granger-causality analyses to geographic contexts in many cases different from North America or Australia – e.g., Italy (Percoco, 2010); China (Yao & Yang, 2012); (parts of the) European Union (Mukkala & Tervo, 2013; Van de Vijver, Derudder, & Witlox, 2016); Germany (Allroggen & Malina, 2014); Turkey (Baltaci, Sekmen, & Akbulut, 2015); and Norway (Tveter, 2017). We review in this section the recent articles that, in our opinion, gave a more significant contribution to the advancement of the state-of-the-art, distinguishing those that used regression analysis from those based on Granger-causality analysis.

Regression analysis

The first article we will mention in this subsection is Percoco (2010). It reports what we believe to be the first study on the impact of air transport on regional development focusing on a European country, namely Italy. The framework of analysis adopted in this study is based on the one proposed by Brueckner (2003), which was extended to take account of possible selection bias and spa-tial spillover effects. Selection bias effects could arise because the majority of the 103 Italian provinces analysed do not have an airport (in total, 35 airports were considered in the study). Because of this, since the same airport could and, in most cases, would serve several provinces, spatial spillover effects were likely to occur. To handle this, the econometric approach adopted in the study, explained in the article in detail, combined a tobit model with a regression model and a spatial regression model to analyse spatial spillover effects. As shown in Table 10.6, the variables included in the regression model were quite similar (or equivalent) to those considered in Bruckner (2003).

Table 10.7 describes the regression results presented in Percoco (2010), which are similar to the ones obtained by Brueckner (2003) in the sense that, also in Italy, the number of air passengers had a significant impact on total employment (t-ratio = 3.027) and even more so on service employment (t-ratio = 3.332), but not on industry employment (t-ratio = 1.546). However, the magnitude of the impact was clearly lower, with the response elasticity being 0.024 for total employment (i.e., on average, an increase of airline traffic of 10% caused a 0.24% increase of total employment) and 0.052 for service employment. The reason

Table 10.6 Variables considered in Percoco (2010)

Variable	Definition	Source
EMP	Total province employment for 2002 (in 000s)	ISTAT, *Conti territoriali*
INDEMP	Total province industrial employment for 2002 (in 000s)	1STAT, *Conti territoriali*
SEREMP	Total province service employment for 2002 (in 000s); Tourism-related activities are excluded	ISTAT, *Conti territoriali*
PASS	Total 2002 passengers	Assaereo
MOV	Total 2002 flights (arrivals + departures)	Assaereo
POP	Province population in 1991	ISTAT, *Conti territoriali*
OLD	Percentage of 2002 population age 65 or over	ISTAT, *Conti territoriali*
COLLEGE	Percentage of 1991 population with a college degree	ISTAT, *Conti territoriali*
ROAD	Total km of paved roads in the province in 1996	ISTAT, *Conti territoriali*
NORTH	Dummy variable equal to one for northern region provinces	Own elaborations
SOUTH	Dummy variable equal to one for southern region provinces	Own elaborations
CENTRALITY	Distance between the provincial capital and the national centroids	Own elaborations
TOURIST	Number of presences in province hotels	ISTAT, *Conti territoriali*
HUB	Dummy variable for Malpensa and Fiumicino airports	Own elaborations

suggested in the article for this difference was the stickiness of Italy's labour market, which, compared to the United States, limited the 'possibility of down-sizing during periods of firms' demand instability or for production flexibility'. Table 10.8 displays the results of the analysis on the spatial spillover effects. The effect of airline traffic on the total employment of airport provinces (i.e., provinces with at least one airport) was less significant (t-ratio = 1.865) and the response elasticity of 0.019 was slightly smaller than when spatial spillovers were not explicitly taken into account. In neighbouring provinces (as shown by the results for variable W_PASS), the effect was more significant (t-ratio = 3.384) and the response elasticity was 0.012. In the case of service employment, the response elasticity was 0.045 in airport provinces and 0.017 in neighbouring provinces.

Along the same lines of Percoco (2010), Allroggen & Malina (2014) studied the impact of air transport on regional development in Germany including in their analysis several innovative features. In the regression equation that they estimated, regional output was represented by a Cobb-Douglas production function coupled with a second-order specification of multifactor productivity. In addition to regional capital stock and total labour force, the arguments of the

Table 10.7 Main results of Percoco (2010) without considering spatial effects

Independent variables	PASS (tobit)	EMP (2SLS)	INDEMP (2SLS)	SEREMP (2SLS)
Intercept	−25.370(1.126)	−3.747(1.228)	−5.721 (2.318)**	5.927 (9.830)***
POP	0.578 (2.133)**	0.054 (8.480)***	0.010 (0.240)	0.019(1.802)**
PASS		0.024 (3.027)***	0.010 (1.546)	0.052(3.332)***
OLD	−0.014(1.895)*	−0.002 (1.760)*	−0.001 (−1.279)	0.001 (4.507)***
COLLEGE	0.041 (4.115)***	0.115(1.882)*	0.015 (0.421)	0.018(0.235)
ROAD	1.142(2.334)**	0.004 (0.067)	−0.049 (0.905)	0.029 (2.259)**
WORTH	1.365(1.282)	0.007 (0.053)	0.050 (3.466)***	−0.032 (1.216)
SOUTH	−0.876(0.531)	−0.415 (2.287)**	−0.426 (2.905)***	−0.038(1.079)
CENTRALITY	0.254 (2.114)**			
TOURISM	0.24 (3.254)***			
HUB	7.475 (3.408)***			
R2	0.422	0.678	0.586	0.726

Notes: t-statistics in parentheses. *** p<0.001; **p<0.05; * p<0.1.

function included the average travel time to 'economic centres' (to reflect the connectivity provided by the road network and rail scheduled services), the airport capital stock, the number of aircraft movements, and the product of the last two variables to account for possible interdependencies between them (Table 10.9). The Limited Information Maximum Likelihood (LIML) method was used to estimate the function using panel data for 19 airports grouped into 11 airport clusters and respective 'affected areas' (formed by all municipalities within 50 km of each airport) for the period 1997–2006. The instrumental variables were population, the lagged relative importance of each airport for German air transport, and the lagged values of potentially endogenous variables. This estimation method was preferred to 2SLS because it is more robust to weak instruments.

Based on the results presented in Table 10.10, it can be concluded that aircraft movements had a significant positive impact on GDP, but this impact decreased as airport size increased (as shown by the negative sign of the term where the logs of *A.CAP* and *MOVE* are multiplied). In contrast, the accessibility of airports (at least as it was measured), did not have a significant impact on GDP. The tests performed (Kleibergen-Paap *F*-Statistic and Hansen *J*-test) indicate that the instruments considered were sufficiently relevant and should not be considered endogenous.

Table 10.8 Main results of Percoco (2010) considering spatial effects

Independent variables	EMP	INDEMP	SEREMP	EMP	INDEMP	SEREMP
Intercept	−3.214 (2.028)*	−9.151 (2.335)**	5.201 (9.985)***	−3.805 (1.250)	−5.676 (2.J74)**	5.904 (9.776)
POP	0.454 (8.480)***	0.010 (0.240)	0.025 (2.254)**	0.452 (8.413)***	0.018 (1.720)*	0.019(1.789)*
OLD	−0.002 (1.660)*	−0.001 (1.789)*	−0.001 (3.957)***	−0.002 (1.766)*	−0.001 (1.267)	−0.001 (4.481)***
COLLEGE	0.115(1782)*	0.015 (0.782)	0.017 (0332)	0.017(1.877)*	0.014 (0.221)	0.022(2.101)*
ROAD	0.007 (0.058)	−0.051 (0.984)	0.032 (2.548)**	0.008 (0.131)	−0.051 (0.943)	0.030 (2.332)**
NORD	0.004 (0.089)	0.056 (3.002)***	0.032 (1.206)	0.010 (0.074)	0.051 (0.474)	0.032 (1.233)
SOUTH	−0.805 (3.171)** —	−0.354 (2.984)***	−0.038 (1.009)	−0.410 (2.259)**	−0.429 (2.915)***	−0.039(1.109)
PASS	0.019(1.865)*	0.018 (0.420)	0.045 (8.457)***			
W_PASS	0.012 (3.384)*** —	−0.012 (0.254)	0.017 (4.088)***			
MOVS				0.015(1.144)	0.022 (1.002)	0.028 (2.011)**
W MOVS				0.015 (3.114)***	0.002 (2.121)*	0.005 (3.854)***
R2	0.701	0.665	0.796	0.644	0.599	0.776

Notes: t-statistics in parentheses. *** p<0.001;**p<0.05: * p<0.1.

Table 10.9 Variables considered in Allroggen & Malina (2014)

Variable	Parameterisation	Data processing
Y	GDP [€, *year 2000 price level*]	Price adjusted
L	Labour force	Adjusted by hours worked
K	Capital stock [€. *year 2000 price level*]	
A.CAP	Fixed assets valued through acquisition and production costs [€, *year 2000 price level*]	Price adjusted
MOVE	Aircraft movements (count of arriving and departing aircraft: non-commercial traffic and training flights excluded)	
INFRA	Average road and rail travel time to the nearest three economic centres in Germany and abroad	Index [2006 average = 1]
POPULATION	Population	
WLU_SHARE	WLU Share of the Airport: Relative importance of airport/airport cluster for German air transport	

Table 10.10 Main results of Allroggen & Malina (2014)

ln(Yi)	(1)
Period fixed ef&tts	Yes
ln(Li)	0.697**
	(0.339)
ln(Ki)	0.357*
	(0.216)
0.5 ln(MOVEi)²	0.115**
	(0.036)
ln(MOVEi)	
0.5 ln(INFRAi)2	−0.518
	(0.448)
ln(INFRAi)	
0.5 ln(A.CAPi)²	0.036**
	(0.011)
ln(A.CAPi)	
ln(A.CAPi) ln(MOVEi)	−0.066**
	(0.020)
F	6.26
R2	0.443
Serial autocorrelation *p*-value[a]	0.800
CD-Test (*p*-value)[b]	0.105
Kleibergen–Paap *F*-statistic[c]	5,151
Hansen *J*-statistic ($J \sim \chi_2^2$)	3.412

Note:*$p < 0.1$.
**$p < 0.05$.
a Null hypothesis of the serial autocorrelation-test is autocorrelation.
b Null hypothesis of the CD-test is cross-sectional independence.
c Critical values are 4.72 (LIML) or 16.87 (TSLS).

To conclude this subsection, we will focus on the work performed by Bilotkach (2015) with respect to all metropolitan areas of the United States (with airports handling over 10,000 passengers via scheduled commercial services) for the period 1993–2009. Three (alternative) dependent variables were considered in the regression equation: total employment, number of business establishments; and average wage (Table 10.11). The air traffic volume and the number of destinations served with non-stop flights by the airports in the metropolitan areas, both lagged one year, were the endogenous air transport variables. Population, unemployment rate, airport level HH Index (a well-known market concentration metric), and mean airfare (also lagged one year) were included as exogenous variables. To estimate the model, the author applied the fixed-effects panel data method as well as the system generalised method of moments (GMM) for dynamic panel data as proposed in Arellano & Bover (1995). This method is specifically designed to address endogeneity issues.

We only present here the results obtained by Bilotkach (2015) through the GMM method, which are summarised in Table 10.11. They show that a 10% increase in the number of destinations served by non-stop flights had a positive impact in the three measures of economic development considered in this chapter: a 0.10% increase in employment; a 0.13% increase in the number of business establishments; and a 0.15% increase in average wages. In comparison, the effect of the total number of passengers is stronger with respect to average wages (0.16%), but weaker with respect to employment (0.06%) and not significant with respect to the number of business establishments. The author suggests that 'attracting services to new destinations will have a larger impact on [the] local economy than expanding services from a local airport to existing destinations'.

Table 10.11 Variables and Results in Bilotkach (2015)

	Mean	*Standard deviation*	*Median*
Dependent variables			
Total employment	565,551	1,328,718	120,366
Total number of establishments	33,885.5	85,889.1	6,693.12
Real weekly wage	496.22	104.86	474.83
Airport level variables			
Total passengers	1,782,273	4,302,731	180,930
Number of non-stop destinations	33.02	39.12	16.00
Airport level HHI	0.5120	0.3039	0.4311
Mean airfare, constant dollars	307.07	110.31	310.75
MSA level controls			
Population	1,189,265	2,854,425	254,401
Unemployment rate	5.44	2.48	4.90

Note: Sample includes all metropolitan areas with airports handling over 10,000 passengers via scheduled commercial services.

Table 10.11 Cont.

	Dependent variable					
	Log(employment)		*Log(establishments)*		*Log(wage)*	
Lagged dependent	0.4257**	0.3799**	0.6458**	0.5987**	0.6090**	0.6360**
	(0.0727)	(0.0797)	(0.0511)	(0.0536)	(0.1001)	(0.0970)
Log(total passengers)	0.0087**	0.0058*	-0.0015	-0.0055	0.0238**	0.0162**
	(0.0031)	(0.0032)	(0.0032)	(0.0036)	(0.0094)	(0.0081)
Log(number of destinations)	–	0.0101**	–	0.0133**	–	0.0148**
Log(population)	0.3425**	(0.0039)	0.3298**	(0.0045)	0.2072*	(0.0063)
	0.3742**		0.3730**		0.2206*	
	(0.0584)	(0.0627)	(0.0835)	(0.0856)	(0.1159)	(0.1212)
Log(unemployment rate)	-0.0558**	-0.0617**	-0.1359**	-0.1315**	-0.0579**	-0.0493**
	(0.0083)	(0.0093)	(0.0050)	(0.0238)	(0.0210)	(0.0208)
Log(average airfare)	0.0013	-0.0012	-0.0500**	-0.0513**	-0.0203	-0.0187
	(0.0058)	(0.0062)	(0.0127)	(0.0128)	(0.0126)	(0.0130)
Log(airport HHI)	0.0124**	0.0160**	0.0116**	0.0238**	-0.0103	-0.0039
	(0.0033)	(0.0036)	(0.0050)	(0.0054)	(0.0062)	(0.0058)
Jansen's J-statistic	49.33	43.77	32.82	30.76	22.72	30.87
(p-value)	(0.7235)	(0.9009)	(0.8697)	(0.9346)	(0.9999)	(0.9955)

Notes: Number of observations = 4057
Estimation methodology = dynamic panel data GMM with MSA fixed effects
All independent variables are lagged one period. Second lags of total flights, number of destinations, airfare and HHI are used as instruments
Year indicator variables are included into all regressions
Airline market shares at the airport, lagged one period, are included into all specifications, but not reported
Conventional significance notations are used: * < 10%; ** < 5%.

Granger-causality analysis

Mukkala & Tervo (2013) is another key article that analyses the impact of air transport on regional development for 86 NUTS 2 or 3 regions of 13 Western European countries using annual data from the period 1991–2010. This article is, to the best of our knowledge, the first where Granger-causality analysis has been applied to the study of this kind of impact. The regions considered, which represent almost 40% of Europe's population and GDP, were classified into three groups: core, intermediate, and peripheral. Two regional development variables were, alternatively, considered: employment and (corrected real GDP) purchasing power (Table 10.12). The variables characterising air transport activity were, alternatively, the number of air passengers and the quantity of air cargo (freight and mail). In addition, an accessibility variable was included in the analysis. Specifically, this variable was an index expressing the weighted multimodal (air-rail-road) average travel time to 291 European regions. All variables were logged and differenced 'to eliminate possible

Table 10.12 Variables considered in Mukkala & Tervo (2013)

Region type	Accessibility index	Air passengers (thousands)	Employment (thousands)	Real GDP (€ million ppp)[a]
Peripheral	88.7	1981.8	376.4	19992.3
Intermediate	102.4	4794.8	703.2	44819.7
Core	113.3	16539.6	1154.0	77196.3
Across all regions	101.5	7806.7	745.0	47365.3

a PPP – purchasing power parity

unit roots and to reach time stationarity'. This means that the analysis was conducted in terms of growth rates. The explanatory variables were lagged one or two years.

The results presented by Mukkala & Tervo (2013) were obtained by the three-stage procedure proposed in Hurlin & Venet (2001) and Hurlin (2005): the authors first tested the existence of a (Granger-causal) relationship between the variables under analysis in both directions for the whole set of regions (test 1); they then tested the nature of the relationship (test 2); and finally, they tested the existence of a relationship for subsets of the regions (test 3). All tests performed were based on Wald F-statistics. Based on these results which are described in Table 10.13, it was concluded that regional development had a clear impact on air transport activity, but the converse was not true at least in core and intermediate regions. However, in peripheral regions, air transport activity seems to have given a significant contribution to regional development. This finding led the authors to affirm that 'there are good reasons to defend local airlines because they are important to the development of remote regions' as well as for subsidising local airports 'although subsidies often distort competition and waste money'.

The results obtained by Van de Vijver, Derudder, & Witlox (2016) using the same procedure as that employed by Mukkala and Tervo (2013) are summarised in three maps where the NUTS 2 regions are discriminated according to whether there has been no significant (Granger-) causality between employment and air transport passengers, or whether there has been causality in both directions (mutual), or in only one of the directions (Figure 10.2). The observation of the maps for total employment reveals rare cases of mutual causality and relatively common cases of no causality. With respect to one-way causality, it occurs more frequently in the direction from air transport to employment than in the opposite direction. Even though there is no clear pattern in the manner how these causality relations are geographically distributed, it is nonetheless possible to discern that air transport has impacted on total employment especially in Sweden, Scotland, Ireland, Spain, Southern France, and Austria (i.e., in relatively peripheral European regions), and that the converse happened almost exclusively in Central European regions. In the case of service employment, the contribution of air transport to development is felt not only in the periphery

Table 10.13 Main results of Mukkala & Tervo (2013)

Test 1

Direction of causality and lags	*F-statistic and its significance*			
	air passengers and GDP	*air passengers and employment*	*accessibility and GDP*	*accessibility and employment*
Causality from air traffic to regional growth				
Lag 1	1.602★★★	1.591★★★	1.947★★★	1.947★★★
Lag 2	0.576	0.716	0.991	1.391★★★
Causality from regional growth to air traffic				
Lag 1	0.956	1.206★	0.694	1.016
Lag 2	0.420	0.604	0.470	0.586

Rejection of H0 at ★★★ 1%, ★★ 5%, ★ 10% level of significance.

Test 2

Direction of causality and lags	*F-statistic and its significance*			
	air passengers and GDP	*air passengers and employment*	*accessibility and GDP*	*accessibility and employment*
Causality from air traffic to regional growth				
Lag 1	1.646★★★	1.521★★★	2.018★★★	1.950★★★
Causality from regional growth to air traffic				
Lag 1		0.925★		

★★★Rejection of H0 at 1% level of significance.

Test 3

Direction of causality and lags	*F-statistic and its significance*			
	air passengers and GDP	*air passengers and employment*	*accessibility and GDP*	*accessibility and employment*
Causality from air traffic to regional growth				
Peripheral regions	2.527★★★	3.533★★★	2.952★★★	4.685★★★
Intermediate regions	1.374★	0.760	1.152	0.618
Core regions	0.873	0.393	1.607★	0.385

Rejection of H0 at ★★★1%, ★10% level of significance

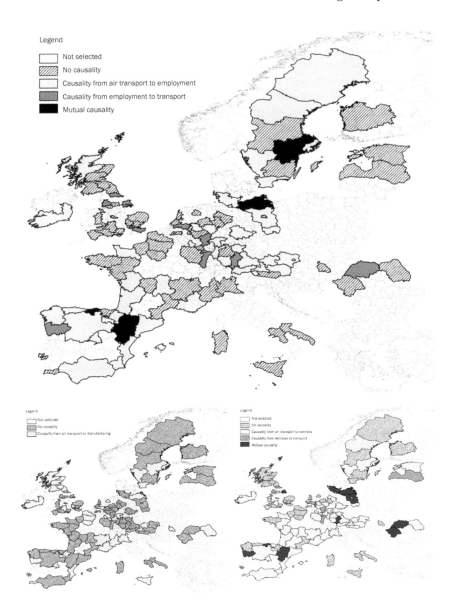

Figure 10.2 Main results of Van de Vijver, Derudder & Witlox (2016) for total employ-
      ment (top), manufacturing employment (bottom left) and service employ-
      ment (bottom right)

but also in central regions, notably in Germany, and the cases of no causality are much more infrequent. This is in sharp contrast with what happens for manufacturing employment, for which no causality is the most common situation. It should also be noted that there is not a single region where manufacturing employment has significantly contributed to air transport activity.

We finalise this subsection by mentioning a study developed by Baker, Merkert, & Mamruzzaman (2015) for Australia. The work described in this study differs from the two previous ones in this subsection not only because it addresses a distinct geographical reality, but also because it focuses solely on the country's less developed regions (officially classified as 'Regional Australia' and 'Remote Australia'). In total, 88 airports were considered in the study, 51 regional and 37 remote. The variables analysed were revenue passenger movement growth and aggregate real taxable income growth, using data from the period 1985–2011. This study also differs from the two previous ones because of its greater depth with respect to cointegration and Granger-causality testing.

The results obtained by Baker, Merkert, & Mamruzzaman (2015) clearly indicate that, as shown in Table 10.14, the long-term causality between air transport and regional development was strong in both directions (this causality was also observed in the short term, but this is not shown in the table). The authors emphasise the higher magnitude and significance of the one-year lagged impact of air transport (growth) on economic growth in regional airport areas in comparison to remote airport areas. This trend changes in the following year and then changes again. The degree of explanation of the impacts is greater in regional areas. However, in the authors' view, 'what is more important is that the positive impact of regional aviation growth on economic growth remains significant even with the four-year lag, which demonstrates how vital aviation is particularly to remote regions'. The overall conclusion was that funding should be provided directly to airports to promote regional development.

Conclusion

Since 1992, and especially in the last 15 years, a rich body of literature has accumulated on the impact of air transport on regional development using econometric approaches. We have reviewed in this chapter what we consider to be the most relevant articles of this literature, but others could have been included e.g., Blonigen & Cristea (2015), Florida, Mellander, & Holgersson (2015), and the very recent Brugnoli et al. (2018), Campante (2018) and Sheard (2019). The econometric approaches, the regional development and air transport variables, and the geographic context of the case studies we have analysed are summarised in Table 10.15. With respect to results, the main takeaway from the literature we reviewed is that air transport impacts on regional development with a high degree of probability and, at least in some cases, the impact is strong. Possibly, it is not as strong as suggested by the first articles where the subject was dealt with – the response elasticity (of regional development to air transport) of 10% estimated by Brueckner (2003) for the United States may overestimate

Table 10.14 Main results of Baker, Merkert, & Mamruzzaman (2015)

Explanory factors	Regional airports				Remote airports			
	Model 3: ΔARTI		Model 4: ΔPAX		Model 5: ΔARTI		Model 6: ΔPAX	
	coefficient	t-value	coefficient	t-value	Coefficient	t-value	coefficient	t-value
Constant	8176738.0	3.46	4934.66	3.06	2185689.00	326	2531.17	3.73
1-year lag of ΔARTI	028	8.52	−0.0001	−1 78	0.30	7.04	0.0002	4.04
2-year lag of ΔARTI	0.17	4.84	0.0001	2.25	0.08	1^6	−0.0001	−224
3-year lag of ΔARTI	−0.04	−0.97	0.0001	141	−0.06	−1.48	−0.0001	−266
4-year lag of ΔARTI	0.42	9.76	0.0001	1.29	0.08	1.46	0.0000	−0.27
1-year lag of ΔPAX	138.38	343	0J3248	1155	73.33	222	0.1498	4.15
2-year lag of ΔPAX	4130	1 00	0.1457	5.04	12124	3.65	0.2499	7.01
3-year lag of ΔPAX	162.37	3.89	0.1842	6.32	97.16	342	0.2259	6.67
4 year lag of ΔPAX	240,80	−521	0.1106	3.75	424	0.13	0.1378	4.20
Long run causality	−0.01	−1.03	−0.1651	−12.38	−0.04	−1.59	−02813	−9.96
R-squared	0.43		0.45		0.18		0.19	
Adjusted R-squared	0.43		0.44		0.17		0.18	
Log likelihood	−19145.27		−12093.92		−13081.70		−8142.56	
F-statistic	81.90		87.80		17.93		1927	
Prob (F-statistic)	0.00		0.00		0.00		0.00	

Note: Bold coefficients are significant at the 0.05 level.

what happens in reality – but, still, is quite important. Another sound conclusion is that air transport is clearly more relevant for the service sector than for the manufacturing sector. These conclusions are valid irrespective of the geographic context, but, in some regards, the context matters: for instance, the response elasticity is clearly higher in the United States than in the European countries analysed up to now (Germany and Italy, as discussed in this chapter, and also Norway and Turkey).

Another point that deserves to be mentioned here relates to the econometric methods employed to analyse the impact of air transport on regional development. These methods are essentially of two types: regression analysis (OLS and 2SLS) and Granger-causality analysis. The way they are applied has improved considerably throughout the years, and there is now plenty of

Table 10.15 Summary of papers reviewed

Author	Econometric approach	Dependent variables regional development	Air transport explanatory variables	Case study (geographic context)
Goetz (1992)	Regression analysis (OLS)	• Population change • Employment change	• Air passengers per capita • Air passengers per employment	United States
Benell & Prentice (1993)	Regression analysis (OLS)	• Direct employment (log) • Airport revenue (log)	• Air passengers (log)	Canada
Button & Taylor (2000)	Regression analysis (OLS)	• New economy employment	Air passengers & European air passengers (log)	United States
Kulendran & Wilson (2000)	Granger-causality analysis	International trade: total, exports and imports	• Air passengers: total, business and holiday	Australia
Brueckner (2003)	Regression analysis (2SLS)	Employment: total, goods-related and services-related(log)	• Air passengers (log) • Air cargo (log)	United States
Green (2007)	Regression analysis (2SLS)	• Population change (log) • Employment change (log)	Air passengers per capita: boarding and originations (log) • Air cargo per capita (log) • Airport hub status	United States
Percoco (2010)	Regression analysis (2SLS)	• Employment: total, industrial and services (log)	Air passengers (log) & flight movements (log)	Italy
Mukkala & Tervo (2013)	Granger-causality analysis	• GDP • Employment	• Air passengers • Average travel time (road, rail and air) to other regions weighted by GDP	Western Europe

Study	Method			Country
Allroggen & Malina (2014)	Regression analysis (LIML)	• GDP (log)	• Flight movements (log) & average travel time between an airport and the three closest economic centres	Germany
Baker, Merkert, & Mamruizaman (2015)	Granger-causality analysis	• Taxable income growth	• Air passengers growth	Australia
Bilotkach (2015)	Regression analysis (GMM and 2S LS))	• Employment (log) • Number of business establishments (log) • Average weekly wage (log)	• Air passengers (log) or • Flight movements (log) & destinations (log) & No. of destinations (tog) & average airfare (log) & Airport HHI (log)	United States
Van De Vijver Derudder & Witlox (2016)	Granger-causality analysis	• Employment: total, manufacturing and services	• Air passengers	Europe (mostly Western)

information – notably in the articles we have reviewed – on why and how a particular method should be applied instead of another.

Given the progress achieved in these 25 years, major research gaps do not exist anymore. However, there are a few issues that, in our opinion, require some attention. One of these issues has to do with the multidimensional nature of regional development. Up to now, regional development has been assessed through a single measure, typically the (volume of) employment or GDP; i.e., the economic dimension of sustainable development is the only one that has been at stake, and the social and environmental dimensions have been neglected. Data envelopment analysis and stochastic frontier analysis may be useful in this respect. Two other issues to investigate are the impact of airport accessibility (i.e., how difficult it is to travel by land from/to airports) and airport connectivity (i.e., which destinations can be reached directly and indirectly from airports) on regional development. These issues have been dealt with before by a few authors, but probably not with the depth that we believe they deserve. Finally, it should be underlined that a regression analysis study on the impact of air transport on regional development in the European Union is still missing. It would certainly be interesting to compare the results obtained for such a complex multinational context with the ones available for the United States.

References

Allroggen, F., & Malina, R. (2014). Do the regional growth effects of air transport differ among airports? *Journal of Air Transport Management* 37, 1–4.

Arellano, M., & Bover, O. (1995). Another look at the instrumental-variable estimation of error component models. *Journal of Econometrics* 68, 29–52.

Aschauer, D. A. (1989). Is public expenditure productive? *Journal of Monetary Economics*, 23(1), 177–200.

Baker, D., Merkert, R., & Mamruzzaman, M. (2015). Regional aviation and economic growth: cointegration and causality analysis in Australia. *Journal of Transport Geography* 43, 140–150.

Baltaci, N., Sekmen, O., & Akbulut, G. (2015). The relationship between air transport and economic growth in Turkey: cross-regional panel data analysis approach. *Journal of Economics and Behavioral Studies* 7(1), 89–100.

Benell, D. W., & Prentice, B. E. (1993). A regression model for predicting the economic impacts of Canadian airports. *Logistics and Transportation Review* 29(2), 139–158.

Bilotkach, V. (2015). Are airports engines of economic development? A dynamic panel data approach. *Urban Studies* 52(9), 1577–1593.

Blonigen, B. A., & Cristea, A. D. (2015). Air service and urban growth: evidence from a quasi-natural policy experiment. *Journal of Urban Economics*, 86, 128–146.

Brueckner, J. K. (2003). Airline traffic and urban economic development. *Urban Studies* 40(8), 1455–1469.

Brugnoli, A., Dal Bianco, C., Martini, G., & Scotti, D. (2018), The impact of air transportation on trade flows: a natural experiment on causality applied to Italy, *Transportation Research Part A*, 112, 95–107.

Button, K., & Taylor, S. (2000). International air transportation and economic development. *Journal of Air Transport Management* 6(4), 209–222.

Campante, F., & Yanagizawa-Drott, D. (2018). Long-range growth: economic development in the global network of air links. *The Quarterly Journal of Economics* 133(3), 1395–1458.

Florida, R., Mellander, C., & Holgersson, T. (2015). Up in the air: the role of airports for regional economic development. *Annals of Regional Science* 54(1), 197–214.

Goetz, A. R. (1992), Air passenger transportation and growth in the U.S. urban system 1950–1987. *Growth and Change* 23(2), 217–238.

Gramlich, E. M. (1994). Infrastructure investment: a review essay. *Journal of Economic Literature* 32(3), 1176–1196.

Green, R. K. (2007). Airports and economic development. *Real Estate Economics* 35(1), 91–112.

Hurlin, C., & Venet, B. (2001). Granger causality tests in panel data models with fixed coefficients', mimeo, University of Paris IX.

Hurlin, C. (2005). Testing for Granger causality in heterogeneous panel data models. *Revue Économique* 56(3), 799–809.

Kulendran, N., & Wilson, K. (2000). Is there a relationship between international trade and international travel? *Applied Economics* 32(8), 1001–1009.

Mukkala, K., & Tervo, H. (2013), Air transportation and regional growth: which way does the causality run? *Environment and Planning A: Economy and Space* 45(6), 1508–1520.

Percoco, M. (2010). Airport activity and local development: evidence from Italy. *Urban Studies* 47(11), 2427–2443.

Sheard, N. (2019). Airport size and urban growth. *Economica* 86, 300–335.

Tveter, E. (2017). The effect of airports on regional development: evidence from the construction of regional airports in Norway. *Research in Transportation Economics* 63, 50–58.

Van De Vijver, E., Derudder, B., & Witlox, F. (2016). Air passenger transport and regional development: cause and effect in Europe. *Promet – Traffic & Transportation* 28(2), 143–154.

Yao, S., & Yang, X. (2012). Air transport and regional economic growth in China. *Asia-Pacific Journal of Accounting & Economics* 19(3), 318–329.

11 Stated preference and travel behaviour modelling

An application to airport accessibility analysis at regional level

Angela Stefania Bergantino and Mario Catalano

Introduction

In recent years, there has been a growing interest in eliciting consumer preferences in order to obtain accurate forecasts of consumer behaviour. The increasing relevance of consumer's tailored production, of competitive stance in service markets and of pressures for efficient spending of public funding is, in fact, requiring an increasingly detailed analysis of demand in many sectors where public investments are relevant. Transport and infrastructures have a significant impact on the socio-economic and cultural development of society and one of the main issues receiving growing attention at worldwide level from transport experts and policy makers is, in fact, the mobility patterns and choice of individuals. The growing need for mobility of people and goods motivated mainly by the spatial differences of the origin-destination movements makes transport modelling a matter of utmost importance for any government, at local, national, and international level and, given the relevance of private funds in this sector, also for private investors. This issue is fundamental to the proper planning of any transport system, including infrastructures and services. An efficient transport system must serve the mobility needs of individuals (commuters vs. occasional travellers), at various times, for various reasons, depending on a number of exogenous factors or attributes (cost, quality of services, congestion, etc.) and their levels. A fundamental role is played by the availability of alternatives. In order to determine the variables that affect travel behaviour and the choice probability for every available option, disaggregated demand models are used (McFadden, 1981). The main objective is to determine the consumer behaviour in the decision-making process, since supply is neither storable nor cumulative (Domencich and McFadden, 1975; de Dios Ortúzar and Willumsen, 2011; McFadden, 2001) and often requires relevant investment in a specific infrastructure. So, there is the need to understand people's preferences in order to define cost-benefit analysis parameters, tariffs, or access pricing.

Consumer preferences can be elicited using either revealed preference (RP) or stated preference (SP) data. RP data are drawn from the past behaviour of consumers, as observed in market situations, where consumers make real choices. SP data are obtained through surveys, namely SP choice games, through which consumers declare their preferences when faced with choices which may or may not mimic real case scenarios. They may be used to elicit consumer preferences in situations where analysts are interested in hypothetical scenarios or there are just no relevant real market situations to construct revealed preference data.[1]

SP discrete choice models may be combined with econometric methods to deliver the willingness-to-pay measures for products or services attributes which may be interpreted in light of the microeconomic utility theory. In fact, economists use a number of SP discrete choice models in order to estimate the willingness-to-pay measures in a variety of situations.[2] Hence, SP data have been applied in a vast and growing number of fields and they have long been popular in transport economics, where there is a widespread interest in eliciting consumer preferences for hypothetical transport services or infrastructures.[3] In this chapter we focus on the opportunities represented by the SP analysis and its technicalities to analyse passengers' accessibility through a set of examples.

We start with a brief comparative assessment of choice models and common probabilistic models to be used according to the underlying hypothesis and to the characteristics of the data. Details of how to structure a SP survey are given. Starting from the selection of alternatives and determination of attribute levels, various alternatives are presented for the questionnaire design methodology. We also take into consideration a number of practical issues particularly relevant in structuring SP experiments correctly, such as sampling and pre-testing of the choice contexts. All these are steps which allow users to obtain credible data and analysis, dealing with all potential bias. Finally, in the last part of the chapter we summarise the main elements of a published study (Bergantino, Capurso, and Hess, 2020) on the system of Apulian airports in Italy in order to show how the techniques can be employed to support decision-makers in planning regional air transport infrastructures and related accessibility levels.

Methodological framework to model consumer choice behaviour

From an economic perspective, consumer theory provides the framework to model the behaviour of an economic agent that consumes goods and services. This theory bases the consumer demand function on preferences, indifference curves, and budget constraints. The fundamentals of the neoclassical individual choice theory assume that individuals choose an amount of goods in order to maximise their level of satisfaction or utility, subject to income constraints. Therefore, under the assumption of rational consumer behaviour, namely perfect rationality *à la* Simon (1957), a deterministic utility function can be conceived to order individual preferences and represent consumer behaviour as the choice of the alternative giving him the greatest satisfaction. Some extensions to this simple model have been proposed in the relevant literature. The most relevant to our scope is the seminal work of Lancaster (1966) who considers three novel assumptions: (1) goods *per se* do not contribute to usefulness, which is, instead, influenced by the characteristics they possess; (2) a good has multiple characteristics, and many of these can be shared by more than one good; (3) if different goods are combined, different characteristics can be obtained from those of the separate goods. These assumptions, as it is well known, underpin the definition of utility in terms of the attributes of goods. Another crucial advance in the economic theory of consumer choice behaviour occurred with the inclusion of goods characterised by a discrete nature (McFadden, 1981) that led to the development of Discrete Choice Modelling. In discrete choice or Random Utility Models (RUM) the dependent variable indicates in which one of several mutually exclusive categories the outcome of interest falls: e.g., whether or not a consumer makes a purchase (binary case) or which one of m (>2) services or modes of transport an individual chooses to reach his destination (multinomial case).

In the RUM formulation, a decision-maker (individual or household) with certain socio-economic characteristics (e.g. age, gender, education, income, etc.), dealing with a choice set of multiple alternatives with certain attributes (e.g. price, quality, etc.), opts for the alternative yielding the highest satisfaction, which is represented by a random variable called 'perceived utility function'. For a generic alternative and a certain choice situation, the utility function can be expressed in formal terms as follows (Ben-Akiva and Lerman, 1985):

$$U_j^i = V_j^i + \varepsilon_j^i \qquad i = 1,2,\ldots,n; j = 1,2,\ldots,m \qquad (11.1)$$

where:

   i is a generic decision-maker;
   j is a generic alternative;
   V_j^i is the systematic or deterministic part of the utility function;
   ε_j^i is the utility function random component capturing the effect of unobserved variables and measurement errors;
   V_j^i can be function of a series of alternative and individual-specific explanatory variables:

$$V_j^i = \beta_1 \cdot x_{1j}^i + \beta_2 \cdot x_{2j}^i + \ldots + ASC_j \qquad (11.2)$$

where:

   x_{kj}^i is the value of attribute k perceived by individual i for alternative j;
   β_k is the coefficient for attribute k, representing its marginal utility, that is
       the variation of the utility function from a unit variation of attribute k;
   ASC_j is the alternative j-specific constant (for all alternatives but one).

Hence, it is possible to determine the probability of choosing a generic alternative j as the likelihood for j to provide the highest utility function value within the given choice set (for notational simplicity, the individual superscript i is suppressed; P stands for probability):

$$
\begin{aligned}
P(j) &= P\left(U_j \geq U_k\right), & \text{all } k \neq j \\
&= P\left(U_k - U_j \leq 0\right), & \text{all } k \neq j \\
&= P\left(\varepsilon_k - \varepsilon_j \leq V_j - V_k\right), & \text{all } k \neq j
\end{aligned}
\tag{11.3}
$$

Alternative-specific probabilities sum to one and the whole model framework is consistent with the standard economic theory of decision-making. Different hypotheses on the joint distribution of the error terms lead to different mathematical forms of the random utility multinomial model. A sensible assumption is that each error is the sum of many random variables capturing unobserved attributes (e.g. mood, experience, …) and measurement errors. On the basis of the *Central-Limit Theorem*, this leads to the choice of the normal random variable for error distribution, which generates the Probit model (Cameron and Trivedi, 2005). This model presents a very flexible mathematical structure, at the expense of the need to use numerical or simulation methods for determining the choice probability of a generic alternative (there is not a closed-form solution).

Another sensible conjecture is that each error term represents the maximum of many random variables capturing unobserved attributes (e.g. comfort, privacy, …) and measurement errors, which implies, on the basis of the *Gumbel Theorem*, that they are *Extreme Value* distributed, with the following probability density and cumulative distribution functions (Cameron and Trivedi, 2005):

Probability density function

$$
f(t) = \mu \cdot exp\left[-\mu \cdot (t - \rho)\right] \cdot exp\left\{-exp\left[-\mu \cdot (t - \rho)\right]\right\}
\tag{11.4}
$$

Cumulative distribution function

$$
F(t) = exp\left\{-exp\left[-\mu \cdot (t - \rho)\right]\right\}
$$

where ρ and μ are the parameters determining the mean and variance of the distribution.

In more detail, if the errors are assumed to be statistically independent (no correlation) and extreme value distributed with mean equal to 0.5772 and variance equal to $\pi^2/6$ ($\rho=0$ and $\mu=1$), the Multinomial Logit model arises and the probability for a generic alternative to be chosen amongst m available options has a closed form:

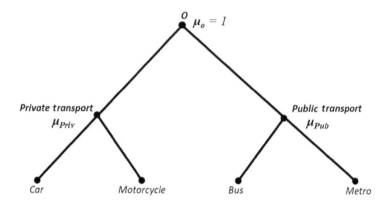

Figure 11.1 Example from travel behaviour analysis of a nesting structure to capture with a Nested Logit model.

$$P(j) = exp(V_j) / \sum_{i=1}^{m} exp(V_i) \tag{11.5}$$

The assumption that the errors are independent across alternatives is violated if any two options are perceived as similar (e.g. bus and tram, two forms of surface public transport). The *Nested Logit* model relaxes this assumption grouping errors so as to obtain independence across groups but correlation within them. In particular, it models decision-making as a multi-step process where, at the upper levels, the decision-maker chooses among groups of similar alternatives and, at the lowest level, he opts for a specific alternative. So, in a transport mode choice case based on a one level nesting structure, the first step could be, for example, choosing between private modes (e.g. car and motorcycle) and public transport (e.g. bus and metro) and the final step could be selecting one specific option of the chosen group (Figure 11.1).

In Fig. 11.1, μ_o, μ_{Priv} and μ_{Pub} represent the parameters determining the error term variance, respectively, at the upper level (choice between private and public transport) and within the two given groups of similar alternatives. Usually, the variance parameter for the first decision-step is normalised to 1 and the other μ-parameters are estimated along with the model predictors coefficients.

In the Nested logit framework, if only one level of nesting is present, the probability for a generic alternative j to be chosen is formulated as the probability of a composite event, that is selecting the considered alternative provided that the relative set S_k has been chosen:

$$P(j) = P(j \mid S_k) \cdot P(S_k) = \left[exp(\mu_k V_j) / \sum_{s \in S_k} exp(\mu_k V_s) \right] \cdot \left[exp(\delta_k \cdot I_k) / \sum_h exp(\delta_h \cdot I_h) \right] \tag{11.6}$$

where:

V_j (V_s) is the detemistic part of utility for alternative j (s).

μ_o (usually normalised to 1) and μ_k determine the error term variance, respectively, at the upper level (choice among the available groups of similar alternatives) and within set k.

$\delta_k = \mu_o/\mu_k$ is a scale parameter to be estimated from data and is function of the correlation of alternatives within nest S_k; it is normalised to lie between 0 and 1, with 0 meaning full correlation and 1 implying no correlation (the model collapses to the basic multinomial logit form).

I_k is given by $ln \sum_{j \in S_k} exp\left[\mu_k V_j\right]$

The coefficients (marginal utilities and scale parameters) of discrete choice models employing the logit formulation can be estimated with the maximum likelihood technique (Ben-Akiva and Lerman, 1985; Cameron and Trivedi, 2005), which is based on the *likelihood principle* (Fisher, 1922): choose as estimator of a vector of unknown parameters that vector value maximising the model-based likelihood of observing the actual sample of data. In the case of independent observations, the above likelihood function is a joint probability obtained multiplying all observation-specific likelihoods. In applications, for analytical convenience reasons, the log-likelihood function is maximised.

To account for the presence of unobserved taste heterogeneity (e.g. random variation of travel time marginal utility across decision-makers), the Mixed Logit model can be adopted (McFadden and Train, 2000). This is a flexible model with random parameters to capture unobserved taste heterogeneity, as well as correlation among alternatives, alternative-specific variances, and correlation across choice scenarios. The basic assumption is that the vector of model coefficients varies in the population with density $f(\boldsymbol{\beta})$, and $\boldsymbol{\beta}_n$ is the vector of coefficients associated with individual n. For a certain $\boldsymbol{\beta}_n$, the conditional probability that a respondent chooses alternative j in choice situation s can be expressed by the logit formula:

$$P^n\left(j \mid x_{njs}, \boldsymbol{\beta}_n\right) = exp\left(\boldsymbol{\beta}'_n \cdot x_{njs}\right) / \sum_{i=1}^{J} exp\left(\boldsymbol{\beta}'_n \cdot x_{nis}\right) \qquad (11.7)$$

where:

x_{njs} is the vector of explanatory variables for individual n, alternative j, and choice scenario s.

Since $\boldsymbol{\beta}_n$ is unknown, the unconditional choice probability is the integral of the conditional probability (P^n) over all the possible values of $\boldsymbol{\beta}_n$:

$$P^n\left(j \mid \boldsymbol{x}_{njs}\right) = \int P^n\left(j \mid \boldsymbol{x}_{njs}, \boldsymbol{\beta}_n\right) \cdot f\left(\boldsymbol{\beta}\right) \cdot d\boldsymbol{\beta} \tag{11.8}$$

which is referred to as the random parameter logit model. In other words, this is a weighted average of the logit formula evaluated at different values of the vector of coefficients; the weights are given by the density function.

As the above probability does not have a closed form, it can be approximated by drawing from $f(\boldsymbol{\beta})$, in order to obtain the simulated log–likelihood, and hence the simulated maximum likelihood estimator of the parameters that characterise the distribution of $\boldsymbol{\beta}_n$. In general, the coefficients of RUM can be estimated employing observed actual choices (RP) or preferences expressed in hypothetical choice scenarios or experiments (SP).

On the one hand, SP are necessary when the researcher intends to investigate the impact on individual choice behaviour of introducing new alternatives, new attributes for existing alternatives or when there is an interest is analysing the effect of attributes variations beyond the range of RP data. It is also worth mentioning that RP data frequently may present limited variability and collinearity, which hopefully might be overcome by increasing the sample size. Furthermore, when collecting RP data, it is particularly difficult to get from respondents the attribute levels of the alternatives that have not been chosen (very often the respondent is not even fully aware of his choice set). On the other hand, unlike SP, the choices observed in RP data, under the random sampling assumption, will reflect the actual market shares of alternatives. For this reason, it is not uncommon to combine RP and SP observations to estimate discrete choice models so as to exploit their respective merits while avoiding their weaknesses. In more detail, as variance of random utility error terms may differ between SP and RP observations, a scale correction is needed that is normalising the scale factor for RP data to 1 and multiplying the SP utility functions by an additional scale parameter to be estimated from the data (Ben-Akiva and Morikawa, 1990).

Discrete choice analysis and stated preference survey

SP surveys have been widely applied in the areas of marketing and travel demand modelling to analyse consumers' evaluation of products and services based on multiple attributes, when there are hypothetical choice alternatives and/or new attributes of established or innovative infrastructures and services.

The SP survey design process can be broken down into the following main steps:

1. identifying socio–economic, attitudinal and alternative-specific potentially important attributes;
2. development of the questionnaire to collect data on the aforementioned attributes;

3. design of a SP experiment (experimental design) to elicit individual preferences towards actual and hypothetical choice alternatives;
4. pilot study;
5. implementation of Internet and/or in presence surveys.

Selection of alternatives and determination of attribute levels

The methodological foundation of a SP study is the experimental design. An experiment is designed to analyse in quantitative terms the effect on a dependent (response) variable of interest produced by the manipulation of the levels of one or more explanatory (independent) attributes or factors (Hensher, Rose and Green, 2007; Lewicki and Hill, 2005). Such manipulations have to meet specific statistical requirements.

The basis stage of an experimental design process is the identification and refinement of stimuli, which involves primary decisions on the list of alternatives, attributes and relative levels of variation. In the case of stated choice analysis, the response variable may assume three forms:

1. *choice*, that is selecting the preferred alternative;
2. *ranking* the alternatives in order of preference;
3. *rating*, that is assigning to each option a measure of preference.

The last two methods can yield more detailed data on choice behaviour but at the expense of a higher cognitive effort for the respondent.[4]

If the *choice* response approach is adopted, the individual behaviour (the selection of an option) can be interpreted as a decision-making process based on an underlying unobserved continuous random variable (latent variable), called utility function, which represents, for a generic alternative, the utility perceived by a single user depending upon a series of alternative-specific characteristics.

The number of alternatives, attributes, and levels of variation per each attribute determines the complexity of the SP experiment.

Full factorial design

The most general class of experimental designs is the full factorial design, which employs all possible combinations of attribute levels, i.e. a set of possibilities given by the number of levels raised to the number of varying attributes (Lewicki and Hill, 2005). So, the higher the number of alternatives and related attributes, the more complex is the design for any given constant number of attribute levels.

In order to ensure the quality of data deriving from a SP survey, it is crucial for the analyst to restrain the design size with particular regard to the number of alternatives and related factors. A survey requiring the respondent to consider more than ten choice scenarios and/or more than four to five alternatives and/or more than four to five attributes per each alternative could be too demanding for the decision-maker, with the result of a dramatic decrease in response rates and/or reliability (Hensher, Rose and Green, 2007; Cascetta, 2001). For this reason, an effective strategy often applied is selecting a set of alternatives and related attributes in line with the study aims and likely to be the most important to respondents, as well as presenting the attribute levels at the extremes only (Hensher, Rose and Green, 2007). The designs using only the two extremes of each attribute-level range, known as end-point designs, can be very effective in limiting the design size and making the attribute-level variation significant to the decision-maker (provided that the assumption of linear part-worth utilities is plausible).

Experimental design methodology: orthogonal, efficient, and Bayesian designs

As stated previously, experimental methods are widely used in research to investigate the statistical significance of the effect of a specific factor on the dependent variable of interest. The most general class of experimental designs is the full factorial design, which employs all possible combinations of factor levels. In the case of SP studies, this could result in a too demanding task for the respondent who might face too many choice situations with the consequence of low response rates and/or biased output data (Hensher, Rose and Green, 2007; Lewicki and Hill, 2005).

Two common methods to reduce the number of choice scenarios to a manageable value (no more than ten according to many previous studies; see Cascetta, 2001) while ensuring factors orthogonality (all explanatory variables are linearly independent) are the *fractional factorial design* and the *blocking strategy* (Lewicki and Hill, 2005; Louvière, Hensher and Swait, 2000).

Linear independence of the factors is important to make reliable the choice models based on SP data. In fact, if any pair of attributes is characterised by linear correlation to some extent, at the model estimation stage, the analyst won't be able to separate the effect of one factor from that of the other, since they covary.

Recently, the relevant literature has introduced a novel class of designs known as optimal or efficient designs, which are aimed at maximising the amount of information gained about the attribute parameters (estimator statistical efficiency) rather than their statistical independence (Hensher, Rose and Green, 2007).

Fractional factorial designs based on two-level attributes

The fractional factorial design is based on two fundamental concepts:

1) *main effect*, which is essentially the overall effect of a factor, that is the effect of an independent variable on a dependent one averaged across the levels of any other independent variable;

2) *interaction effect*, which arises when the effect of one factor on the response variable depends on the state of one (*two-way interaction*) or more (*n-way or n-order interaction* with $n > 2$) other factors; therefore, it measures the effect of two or more factors which, when acting together, produce an influence different from the mere sum of their individual impacts.

A fractional factorial design is basically a subset of the full factorial one and, in the case of two-level attributes, can be defined in formal terms as follows:

$$2^{(k-p)} \text{ design} \tag{11.9}$$

where:

2 is the number of levels per each factor;

k is the total number of factors;

p is the number of factors whose levels are generated by the levels of selected high order interactions of the remaining $(k-p)$ attributes.

Fractional factorial designs give up the effect of high order interactions whilst maintaining main effects and lower order interactions still estimable. Different criteria can be employed in identifying the high order interactions to use as generators. One very effective criterion is known as *maximum unconfounding design* (Lewicki and Hill, 2005).

A design of resolution R is one where no j-way interactions are confounded (linearly correlated) with any other interaction of order less than $(R - j)$. So, for example, a design of resolution IV is one where main effects are unconfounded with each other and with two-way interactions. On the contrary, these might be confounded with each other to some extent; hence, they represent the so-called 'crucial order', that is the interaction order for which confounding of effects first appears.

The *maximum unconfounding design* criterion searches for the maximum design resolution and, given the resolution and the related crucial order c, requires generators to be chosen such that the maximum number of interactions of order $j \leq c$ are unconfounded with all other interactions of order c.

Since the state of practice suggests that it is more likely that two-way interactions are statistically significant than three-way or higher order interactions, a design of resolution IV (main effects uncorrelated with each other and with all two-way interactions) with a minimised level of correlation within the group of two-way interactions can be considered a minimum standard when developing micro-econometric choice models.

Such a design, in fact, for model specifications including the factor main effects and omitting interactions, would prevent the problem of multicollinearity (linear correlation for one or more pairs of main effect predictors) and the omitted variable bias (correlation between one or more main effects and one or more omitted interactions), both leading to unreliable model estimations.

Table 11.1 Summary of the different experimental design strategies

Method	Pros	Cons
Orthogonal designs	No correlations among attribute levels, which permits an independent estimation of the impact of each attribute on choice behaviour.	They may not be optimal in terms of statistical efficiency of the choice model coefficient estimates and may lead to useless or unreasonable combinations of the attribute levels.
D-optimal designs	Smallest possible errors in estimating the choice model coefficients.	They are not aimed at minimising the correlation of the choice factors for estimation purposes.
Bayesian efficient designs	Besides yielding statistical efficiency, they can allow for the uncertainty about the parameter priors needed to generate efficient designs.	As above.

Concerning the blocking strategy, it is important to emphasise that, differently from the fractional factorial approach, this method splits the full design (all the possible combinations of attribute levels) into sub-sets (blocks) that are submitted to different groups of respondents, with the consequence of fewer observations per each choice scenario. Specifically, the method uses one or more blocking variables corresponding to interaction effects as additional factors, in order to divide the full factorial design into as many blocks as the levels or level combinations of the blocking variables (one blocking factor for a two-block split, two blocking factors for a four-block split, and so on).

The above experimental design strategies are summarised in Table 11.1.

Optimal or statistically efficient designs

As we have already recalled, efficient designs aim at optimising the statistical efficiency of attribute parameters' estimators. In particular, this amounts to maximising the determinant of the variance-covariance matrix of the model maximum likelihood estimators (Fisher information matrix), thus leading to the D-optimal designs (Hensher, Rose and Green, 2007). It is common practice to obtain the same final result by minimising the determinant of the inverse of the above variance-covariance matrix, which is known as D-error.

It can be demonstrated that, in the multinomial logit case, the distribution of the vector of model coefficients is asymptotically normal with mean equal to its true value and variance-covariance matrix:

$$\Delta = \sum_{r=1}^{R} \sum_{j=1}^{J} x_{ijs}' \cdot P_{ijs} \cdot x_{ijs} \tag{11.10}$$

where:

x_{ijs} is the vector of model explanatory variables for individual i, alternative j and choice situation s;

P_{ijs} is the model-based probability for individual i to choose alternative j in choice scenario s;

R is given by the number of decision-makers multiplied by the number of choice situations.

A widely used measure of design efficiency is based on the D-error parameter, which is to be minimised, and can be expressed as follows:

$$D - error = \left(Det \Delta^{-1} \right)^{1/k} \tag{11.11}$$

where k is the total number of parameters to estimate.

Minimising (11.11) means identifying an optimal design in terms of estimator statistical efficiency and, hence, information that can be elicited from the experiment.

Prior knowledge of the model parameters is required to develop an optimal design. However, in general, this knowledge is not available when designing an experiment, hence *a priori* assumptions need to be taken. In order to allow for the uncertainty about the parameter priors, Bayesian efficient designs can be adopted which employ non-fixed priors, described by random distributions (Sándor and Wedel, 2001).

Given the above, the Bayesian D-error is determined over different random draws from the selected prior distributions, and the optimisation process can be based on the error mean or other indices (median, minimum, maximum). It is also possible, given a single design, to evaluate at the same time different models that may have different mathematical forms, utility functions, and priors. Different parameter priors and model types will result in diverse variance-covariance matrices. Hence, a single combined variance-covariance matrix (from which efficiency measures will be calculated) can be derived by assigning different weights to the various model forms assumed (Rose, Scarpa and Bliemer, 2009).

For designs assuming a mixed multinomial logit form, Bayesian draws from prior distributions may affect also random coefficients. In this case, different distributions may be required for each random coefficient population moment (e.g., mean and standard deviation).

In the relevant literature a number of algorithms have been proposed in order to change the attribute levels when searching for efficient choice designs. Basically, they can be grouped in two classes: row-based methods and column-based ones. In a row-based algorithm, in each iteration, choice situations are selected from a predefined set that can be either a full factorial or a fractional factorial design. With this approach, it is possible to remove specific cases (e.g. dominated choice situations) at the beginning, but it is more difficult to meet attribute-level balance. For this reason, this method is very suitable for the special case of constrained designs. Each iteration of a column-based algorithm, instead, creates different columns for every attribute. This means determining, for every attribute, the related levels over all choice situations. The columns are not created randomly, but systematically. In this case, attribute-level balance can be more easily satisfied, but it is less likely to obtain useful combinations of attribute levels in each choice scenario.

Sampling approach: guidelines from the scientific literature and the state of practice

Several guidelines are provided by the relevant literature about the sample size required for a useful SP survey outcome, based on theoretical and practical considerations (budgetary limitations and common practice). In general, if random sampling is adopted and the objective of the study is reproducing the true market shares of alternatives, the minimum sample size can be calculated so as to guarantee a given allowable per cent deviation between the estimated and true choice proportion of the least popular alternative (that with the smallest population proportion; Hensher, Rose and Green, 2007).

In formal terms, this can be expressed as follows:

$$n \geq \left(q / pa^2 \right) \cdot \left[\phi^{-1} \left(1 - \alpha / 2 \right) \right]^2 \tag{11.12}$$

where:

   p is the true population proportion;
   q is defined as $1 - p$;
   a is the level of allowable per cent deviation between the estimated and true choice proportion;
   φ^{-1} is the inverse cumulative distribution function of a standard normal random variable;
   $1-\alpha$ is the estimation confidence level.

However, this approach may result in very large minimum sample sizes, even though, to be precise, formula (11.12) refers to the minimum number of respondents required to replicate the actual population proportions, if each decision-maker is shown just one choice set. Thus, for SP studies, where decision-makers have usually to evaluate more than one choice scenario, the minimum sample size gets lower all else remaining the same. Conversely, if the main objective of a SP analysis is estimating robust choice models and eliciting marginal utilities and willingness-to-pay parameters, the literature suggests a series of rules of thumbs based both on theoretical and practical considerations.

In particular, following the guidelines provided by Orme (2010) and Hensher, Rose and Green, (2007), if the research focuses in particular on the econometric estimation of marginal utilities and willingness-to-pay parameters, a two-stage sampling process can be performed:

1. start drawing at least 300–400 respondents;
2. if necessary, increase the sample size until the less popular alternative (the option that is chosen less) is selected by about 50 different respondents.

This is important to assure a sufficient degree of variability (especially in the socio-economic covariates) to obtain robust estimations of model coefficients.

Choice contexts description and warm-up tasks

Explaining the decision context and using warm-up or practice tasks are common in SP surveys (Hensher, Rose and Green, 2007). When explicating alternatives and relative attributes to introduce the respondents to the SP experiment, it is essential to give them some information about the specific decision context. The description of the decision situation is important because preferences are often context-dependent. For example, in a transport mode choice case, preferences may differ significantly depending upon the journey purpose (business or holiday, study or leisure, etc.). Context description usually takes the form of a narration explaining to the decision-maker the setup in which he has to consider a given set of alternatives and related characteristics: e.g., 'imagine a situation where you are taking a journey for business purposes to ... Four different modes of transport are available, namely ... Each mode is characterised by the travel time in hours (in and out-of-vehicle), the travel cost in euros, ...'. Attribute and level descriptions can be provided using text, pictures, videos, and respondents could even be asked to experience attribute levels through, for example, virtual reality (Steiner and Meißner, 2018). In some cases, laboratory experiments are starting to take place (Bergantino, De Carlo and Morone, 2015).

In the past, choice modellers used to include extra choice scenarios within the SP experiment to make respondents get familiar with the trade-off task and aware of the bandwidth of levels at the early stage of the survey; these 'practise and learn' exercises were then discarded from the analysis. However, since this approach made the survey more time consuming and demanding for the respondent and was supported by little evidence in terms of bias-mitigating effects, the current trend is providing an example showing as clearly as possible what the decision-maker is required to do: e.g., 'After comparing the four alternative transport modes on the basis of their characteristics (time, cost, ...), tick the most appealing option to you as the following example displays ...'.

Strategies to deal with potential biases

The relevant scientific literature warns against the possibility for the respondent to compare the hypothetical scenarios shown, so that the decision made for each scenario is not independent. This is likely to occur when the respondent can observe all or some of the choice sets simultaneously: a typical situation for paper and pencil surveys, even though computer/internet surveys may be affected by the same problem. The respondent might even return to already completed choice scenarios and change his response. Such behaviours are likely to affect the model estimations.

To overcome this problem, several strategies can be adopted:

1) in an on-line survey case, the presentation of only one choice scenario at a time and the prevention of the return to previous choice scenarios could be carried out;
2) in the door-to-door survey, the option of face-to-face interviews should be considered, so that the way decision-makers accomplish their choice tasks could be monitored and supported. The choice scenarios could even be left out of the questionnaire and administered to the respondents as choice cards, one at a time.

During a SP experiment, it is likely that the respondent uses the first few choice sets to gain an understanding of the decision-making process required by the analyst. Likewise, respondents might get tired by the end of the survey, especially if a great deal of choice scenarios are to be evaluated. These 'learning and fatigue' effects may represent a source of bias. For this reason, the current practice amongst choice modellers is changing on a random basis the order of presenting choice scenarios. So, for example, the decision-makers facing the same block of choice sets could have to evaluate them in different orders to one another, which can minimise learning and fatigue-related biases.

In principle, the full randomisation of choice scenario presentation is the optimal approach, in practice, a common strategy is creating several versions of the same block of scenarios, which differ in the sequence of choice sets and are shown to different subgroups of the sample assigned to the considered block.

Using discrete choice models to support regional policy-making in favour of airport accessibility

In this section we summarise, with the objective of giving some insights on potential real-world applications in the air transport sector, a very recent application of combined SP and RP analysis. It is a very brief overview of an application to the airport accessibility issue and its implications in terms of policy choices. The review is carried out with the objective of accompanying the reader through the steps of the work, highlighting the various aspects described in the previous sections. The original analysis has been carried out by Bergantino, Capurso, and Hess (2020) and to this the readers are referred to for greater details.[5]

The context

The study was motivated by the considerations that increasing the accessibility towards main airports might constitute a valid instrument to increase the air connectivity of a territory, without having to invest on opening or maintaining in operation 'local' airports the scale of which makes them very unprofitable to run. The case study analysed by Bergantino, Capurso and Hess (2020) refers to Apulia, where there are two airports, Bari and Brindisi (see Figure 11.2), which are managed by a regional government company, in concession by the Civil Aviation Authority (ENAC). The flow of passengers using Bari and Brindisi airports is continuously growing (ENAC, 2018). The two airports partly share the same catchment area. The Apulian airport network also includes the regional airports of Foggia and Grottaglie (see Figure 11.2), which are not being used for commercial purposes.

While Bari and Brindisi are effectively connected to the respective airports through a sufficiently frequent schedule of bus and train services (the latter only for Bari), many other areas in Apulia and in neighbouring regions, which are important from a demographic and tourist perspective, suffer from insufficient supply of public transport services and poor accessibility to the major regional airports (Bergantino and Madio, 2020). For instance, Matera, one of the most appealing cultural destinations in Italy (the second largest city of Basilicata and the European Capital of Culture for the year 2019, see Figure 11.2), does not have an airport and it is not even served by the national railway network.[6] A number of measures have been discussed and designed in the past few years

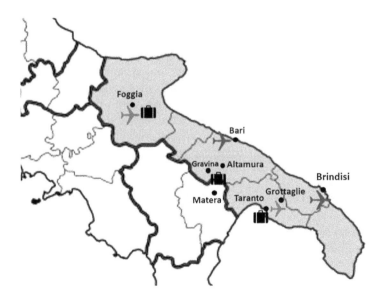

Figure 11.2 The Apulian airport system.

in order to improve the accessibility of the city: from the opening of small local airport (Pisticci and Grottaglie), to improved connections to existing Apulian airports. In particular in order to improve its connection to Bari, the capital city of Apulia, €50 million are being invested to enhance the Matera-Bari railway line, while €1.2 million are devoted to the improvement of the Bari airport shuttle services.

Staring from this evidence, the research of Bergantino, Capurso, and Hess (2020), which is summarised in the following subsections, focuses on the effectiveness of several policy measures designed to improve the Apulian airport system's accessibility for public transport services, some of which have been implemented in 2019. Improvements in the accessibility to major airports might be a more economically sustainable alternative to creating or maintaining inefficient 'local' airports, as well as a source of economies of scale for the main airports that could thus enlarge their catchment area. The study of Bergantino, Capurso and Hess (2020), thus, aims at obtaining the value of travel time and elasticities (key input for cost-benefit analysis of investments) and at assessing the effectiveness of policy measures designed to improve airport accessibility. It contains also a simulation on demand of the impact of the introduction of the subsidised shuttle service. In the study, both RP and SP data are used to estimate probabilistic demand models for the analysis of travel behaviour to reach an airport. The results are employed to calculate the relevant elasticities, separately for airport users and non-users, with respect to dedicated existing and planned/potential public transport services. The effectiveness of specific policies and measures to foster a mode choice switch from private modes (car and taxi) towards public transport is assessed.

Although the research regarding the Apulian context, its methodology and findings might be generalised to similar areas and, since the explanatory factors of access mode choice behaviour were deeply investigated, it might provide interesting insights for airport managers and transport authorities in other contexts for the analysis of future investments on airport accessibility. Similar local contexts exist, in fact, in many other areas of Italy and of the European Union. Airports tend to compete with peers localised in the same catchment area (Bergantino, Intini, and Volta, 2020). The *Airport Regions Conference and Airportwatch* reveals that, in a number of cases, airports are located less than 100 km apart (more than half of the European airports), with the consequence of a low efficiency in the use of such infrastructures.

Data collection

Data for this research was gathered with paper-based surveys involving a sample of residents (1,229) in five important cities in the catchment area of Bari and Brindisi airports (Altamura, Foggia, Gravina in Puglia, Matera, and Taranto) and were collected over three instalments in the 2015–2018 period. A first sub-sample included airport users, defined as individuals who had flown from Bari and Brindisi airports in the previous three months. For these respondents, the survey consisted of two parts. The first part was a SP experiment in which they were first required to choose their preferred access mode amongst those available from their city to the airports (five choice tasks): mixed transit (Train + Train, Train + Bus), direct bus, car driver/passenger and taxi. Then, the respondents were asked to consider a richer choice set due to the introduction of a new hypothetical alternative, a direct train serving the airport of Bari (which led to five additional tasks). In the second part, information on the last access trip (RP data), and the last air journey were collected.

A second sub-sample of non-users of both airports was also involved, but only in the first section of the SP experiment. Asking individuals, who had not recently flown from Bari airport, to consider a future hypothetical scenario proposing a totally novel mode to reach the airport could have increased the hypothetical bias of the SP experiment. For all respondents (travellers and non-users), socio-economic data were also gathered.

The SP experiment was created using city/airport-specific Bayesian efficient designs. As for the attributes of alternatives, time and cost variables were employed, namely in- and out-of-vehicle travel time (i.e., the waiting time between two interconnected services), travel cost (i.e., the ticket price for public transport, the taxi fare, as well as fuel costs, highway tolls, and parking fees for car journeys), headway time (i.e., the time between two consecutive public transport services). Attributes levels were based on the current state of transport supply. Moreover, the order of presenting alternatives within the choice scenarios was randomised across respondents in order to avoid possible biases.

Methodology

The observations from the above mixed SP-RP survey are used to estimate mode choice random utility models. In particular, to capture the data correlation pattern, the Nested logit framework is adopted exploring and comparing three possible nesting structures of the individual decision-making process, reported in Figure 11.3.

In the first one, direct access modes and non-direct ones are grouped in two separate nests, while the car driver alternative stays alone in a third nest. In the second formulation, access modes are grouped into four separate nests: mixed-transit modes are included in one group, direct bus and taxi are two stand-alone nests, and private modes (car driver and car passenger) are together in a fourth set. The third nesting hypothesis assumes three separate nests: one comprises the mixed-transit modes, another group includes direct bus and taxi, while the third one contains the private transport modes (car driver and car passenger).

Random taste heterogeneity across individuals is taken into account through the estimation of mixed multinomial and mixed nested logit models,[7] separately for airport users and non-users. Utility was represented as a function of the alternatives' core characteristics (travel time, travel cost, headway), and individuals' socio-demographics (age, sex, education). For airport users only, utility

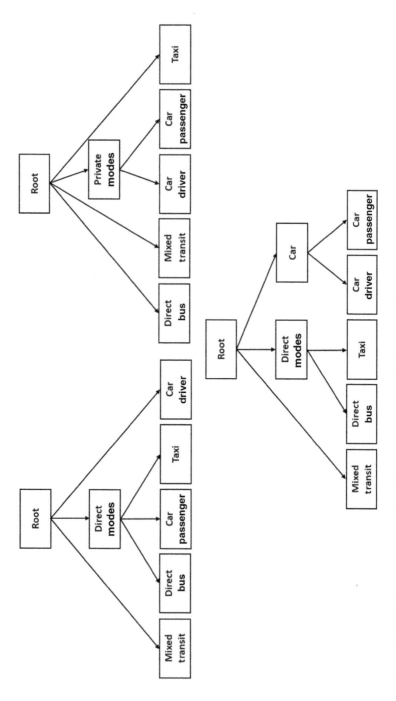

Figure 11.3 Nesting structures explored for the transport mode choice model.

was also dependent upon some characteristics of their last trip to the airport (departing airport, luggage, air party size, trip destination).

Synthesis of results

The analysis carried out allows the authors to calculate values of times for different categories of respondents (business and non-business) and for different types of travelling. In particular, they are able to identify the value of time for five different categories of connecting services: mixed transit (public services which require also a change of vehicle), direct bus, car as driver, car as passenger, taxi. Furthermore, the analysis differentiates also between in-vehicle time (IVT) and out-of-vehicle time (OVT) for the mixed-transit alternative. The calculations are carried out using the estimates of the two best performing models (MNL and NL2). Using the coefficients estimated through the models, Bergantino, Capurso, and Hess (2020) show that the value of time varies between €99.58 per hour for OVT for business travellers using the most 'uncomfortable' alternative, i.e. mixed transit, and €15.05 for IVT of non-business travellers for the same alternative. For car-owner drivers and non-business travel, the value of time is €13.20 while it is €37.35 for non-business travellers using taxis. Values are comparable for the two models.

Using the estimated values the authors were able to construct a detailed analysis of the policy programmed by the Regional Government of Basilicata aimed at reducing headway time for the existing service to 60 minutes (from the actual 220 minutes, a 70% reduction) with a subsidy of €1.2 million (€126 for additional service).

The simulation shows that at no additional costs for the users (i.e. leaving the fare at the current level) the market share for the direct bus alternative is expected to increase by 62%. If costs for users increase, the market share reduces. For instance, the authors show that with a +70% increase in fares, the market share increases by 35%.

The authors show also that it would be possible to carry out a what if scenario analysis, analysing the impact of specific service characteristics and fares on the reallocation of demand.

Implications for the regional policy in favour of airport accessibility

Model estimation results reveal that policies aimed at increasing the frequency of direct bus services have a positive impact, especially for airport users. Non-users are far more sensitive to travel costs. Bergantino, Capurso, and Hess (2020)'s study, thus, demonstrates that improvements in the bus service frequency can be successful in terms of market share only if travel costs do not increase as well.

In more detail, as for the actual airport users, results indicate that reductions in the bus headway time, and in the mixed-transit travel time, would yield significant increases in the relative market shares, even if such reductions are traded-off against increases in travel costs.

Estimation and analysis of direct and cross elasticities show that non-users are more sensitive to travel cost than to headway time for the direct bus alternative; hence, only policies designed to reduce headway time – while restraining the service price increase – would be effective. Conversely, in the mixed-transit case, non-users would also be willing to pay more for improved services.

Importantly, in all the proposed scenarios, the car passenger remains the alternative with the largest predicted market share. The results are interpreted arguing that many users prefer to travel by car, because they may wish to spend additional time accompanying relatives or friends or because, as passengers, they do not fully allow for the cost of using the car alternative.

The outcome of this study allows policy makers to quantify the benefits of any investments in term of travelling and headway-time reduction. It also shows the trade-off between various characteristics of the service and of the introduction of a new alternative. The analysis shows how airport accessibility policies impact on current demand and how investments can be assessed and compared in relation to different alternatives.

The above results and interpretations are only an example of the insights which can be retrieved through the use of SP experiments carried out with the objective of yielding policy advice and strategic information on consumer behaviour. The power of the instrument is self-evident. Many different applications can be found in the related literature.

Concluding comments

In this chapter, we have reviewed the SP methodologies and tools, in order to give an insight of its uses and possibilities in analysing transport demand and guiding policies, pricing, operational and strategic choices with respect to services and infrastructures. The aim is to show how these techniques can be used to improve the analysis of traveller behaviour and to inform the choices of decision-makers and agents dealing with transport.

After a brief introduction, an introductory explanation of the SP and RP analysis methodology within the framework of Discrete Choice Modelling is provided in order to detail its uses in consumer choice behaviour. In this section, the most common probabilistic models used in estimating the relevant parameters are briefly presented so that potential users can identify, on the basis of the hypothesis of the model and of the characteristics of the data, the one or the ones which is/are closer to his/her needs. Space is assigned also to detail SP survey and tools. Starting from the selection of alternatives and determination of attribute levels, various alternatives are presented for the questionnaire design methodology. We also take into consideration the issue of sampling, particularly relevant in structuring correctly SP experiments, and represent the relevance of testing the choice contexts defined, before proceeding with the full sample survey. All these are steps which allow users to obtain credible data and analysis, dealing with all potential bias. Finally, in the last part of the chapter, we have presented a synthesis of an application to the Apulian region (Italy), carried out by Bergantino, Capurso, and Hess (2020). This study is illustrated in some detail, in order to show how the above techniques can be practically employed to support decision-makers in planning regional air transport infrastructures and related accessibility levels.

Although SP is a very powerful instrument, its applications should be carefully planned and checked. Evaluations in terms of the preference information they produce and the assumptions they require in order to yield credible measures of willingness-to-pay distributions and policy scenario analysis should always be carried out. As Schläpfer (2017) points out in his survey of SP applications in various sectors, progress in this field could greatly benefit from a routine implementation of powerful experimental validity tests in applied work. This is one of the challenges ahead.

Notes

1 Louvière, Hensher and Swait (2000) provide a seminal survey of the methodological aspects and applications of stated choice methods. Verhoef and Franses (2003) and references therein demonstrate that stated preferences discrete choice models deliver accurate forecasts of consumer behaviour.
2 See McFadden and Train (2000) for an authoritative study on the econometrics of such models.
3 See, for instance, Hensher (1994) for a detailed account of the evolution of the applications of stated preferences methods in transport economics while Schläpfer (2017) contains a detailed review of the method applied in relation to the analysis of demand for public services in general.
4 Ranking and rating are mentioned to underlie that, though the choice approach can yield less detailed data on choice behaviour compared to other methods, it is less demanding and, hence, more reliable in the case of surveys requiring a high cognitive effort to the respondent.
5 The data gathered in this study were also used to analyse the decision-making process when a respondent is faced with more alternatives. In particular in the Bergantino, Capurso, Dekker and Hess (2019) study, we allow for heterogeneity in the consideration of airport access modes. We used the wide set of indicators collected with the interviews for the 2020 study of Bergantino, Capurso and Hess which either directly or indirectly measured respondents' consideration of the public transport alternatives. These entered the utility function as a latent variable, through a 'discounting' factor. The proposed integrated choice and latent variable approach allows the analyst not only to overcome potential endogeneity and measurement error issues associated with the indicators, but also makes the model suitable for forecasting. For more details the reader is referred to the original article.
6 Its attractiveness is mainly due to the impressive cave-dwellings, called 'Sassi', where many inhabitants lived in the past (UNESCO World Heritage Site).
7 The expression 'nested mixed logit model' refers to an error component logit model with random terms to capture correlations amongst the alternatives of the choice set.

References

Ben-Akiva, M. and Lerman, S. (1985). *Discrete Choice Analysis: Theory and Application to Travel Demand*, Cambridge, MA: MIT Press.

Ben-Akiva, M. and Morikawa, T., 1990. 'Estimation of switching models from revealed preferences and stated intentions', *Transportation Research Part A*, 24 (6), 485–495.

Bergantino, A.S., Capurso, M., and Hess, S. (2020). 'Modelling regional accessibility to airports using discrete choice models: an application to a system of regional airports', *Transportation Research Part A*, 132, 855–871.

Bergantino, A.S., Capurso, M., and Hess, S. (2019). 'Allowing for heterogeneity in the consideration of airport access modes: the case of Bari airport', *Transportation Research Record*, 2673 (8), 50–61, https://doi.org/10.1177/0361198118825126.

Bergantino, A.S., De Carlo, A., and Morone, A. (2015). 'Individuals' behaviour with respect to parking alternatives: a laboratory experiment', *MPRA Paper 63815*, University Library of Munich, Germany.

Bergantino, A.S., Intinia, M., and Volta, N. (2020). 'Competition among airports at worldwide level: a spatial analysis', *Transportation Research Procedia*, 45, 621–626, https://doi.org/10.1016/j.trpro.2020.03.049.

Bergantino, A.S. and Madio L. (2020). 'Intermodal competition and substitution. HSR versus air transport: understanding the socio-economic determinants of modal choice', Research in Transportation Economics, https://doi.org/10.1016/j.retrec.2020.100823.

Cameron, A.C. and Trivedi, P.K. (2005). *Microeconometrics: Methods and Applications*, New York: Cambridge University Press.

Cascetta E. (2001). *Transportation Systems Engineering: Theory and Methods*, Dordrecht: Kluwer Academic Publishers.

Connected Places Catapult (2019a). *Demand Modelling and Assessment Through a Network Demonstrator (DeMAND) Project – Measuring Attitudes Towards Shared and Emerging Mobility Services – Design of a Stated Preference Experiment for Modelling Traveller Choice Behaviour towards Shared Transport.*

Connected Places Catapult (2019b). *Demand Modelling and Assessment through a Network Demonstrator (DeMAND) Project – Utility Function Development for Shared Mobility Services through Discrete Choice Modelling.*

de Dios Ortúzar J. and Willumsen L. (2011). *Modelling Transport*, Hoboken, NJ: Wiley.

Domencich, T. and McFadden, D. (1975). *Urban Travel Demand: A Behavioral Analysis*, Amsterdam: North-Holland Publishing Co.

ENAC – National Civil Aviation Authority. Studio sullo sviluppo degli aeroporti italiani (in Italian). www.enac.gov.it/pubblicazioni/studio-sugli-aeroporti-nazionali/studio-sullo-sviluppo-degli-aeroporti-italiani. Accessed November 14, 2018.

Fisher, R.A. (1922). 'On the mathematical foundations of theoretical statistics', *Philosophical Transactions of the Royal Society of London A*, 222, 309–368.

Hensher, D.A. (1994). 'Stated preference analysis of travel choices: the state of practice', *Transportation*, 21 (2), 107–133.

Hensher, D.A., Rose, J.M., and Green, W.H. (2007). *Applied Choice Analysis – A Primer*, New York: Cambridge University Press.

Lancaster K.J. (1966). 'A new approach to consumer theory', *Journal of Political Economy*, 74, 132–157.

Lewicki, P. and Hill, T. (2005). *Statistics: Methods and Applications*, Tulsa, OK: StatSoft.

Louvière J., Hensher D. A. and Swait J. (2000). *Stated Choice Methods: Analysis and Application*, Cambridge: Cambridge University Press.

McFadden, D. (1981). 'Econometric models of probabilistic choice', in *Structural Analysis of Discrete Choice Data with Econometric Applications*, edited by C. Manski and D. McFadden, Cambridge, MA: MIT Press, 198–272.

McFadden, D. (2001). 'Disaggregate behavioral travel demand's RUM side – a 30-year retrospective', In *Travel Behavior Research*, edited by D.A. Hensher, Amsterdam: Elsevier, 17–63.

McFadden, D. and Train, K. (2000). 'Mixed MNL models for discrete response', *Journal of Applied Econometrics*, 15 (5), 447–470.

Orme, B. (2010). *Getting Started with Conjoint Analysis: Strategies for Product Design and Pricing Research*, 2nd ed., Madison, WA: Research Publishers LLC.

Rose, J.M., Scarpa, R., and Bliemer, M.C.J (2009). 'Incorporating model uncertainty into the generation of efficient stated choice experiments: a model averaging approach', International Choice Modelling Conference, March 30–April 1, Yorkshire, UK.

Sándor, Z. and Wedel, M. (2001). 'Designing conjoint choice experiments using managers' prior beliefs', *Journal of Marketing Research*, 38, 430–444.

Schläpfer, F. (2017). 'Stated preferences for public services: a classification and survey of approaches', *Journal of Economic Surveys*, 31 (1), 258–280.

Simon H.A. (1957). *Models of Man: Social and Rational.* New York: Wiley, 1–287.

Steiner, M. and Meißner, M. (2018). 'A user's guide to the galaxy of conjoint analysis and compositional preference measurement', *MARKETING ZFP*, 40 (2), 3–25.

Verhoef, P.C. and Franses P.H. (2003). 'Combining revealed and stated preferences to forecast customer behaviour: three case studies', *International Journal of Market Research*, 45 (4). 1–8.

12 Entry games for the airline industry[1]

Christian Bontemps and Raquel M. B. Sampaio

Introduction

Being able to evaluate the nature of competition between firms in a given sector and how it has changed over time or with a new economic environment is an important feature of the empirical IO literature. The use of the Herfindhal index has been proved to be a poor proxy of the degree of competition (see Sutton, 1991). Ideally, one would like to get data where both supply and demand could be estimated. However, such data are often difficult to get, to the exception of the data provided by the US Department of Transportation for the US interior market. Entry games are therefore very popular in the empirical Industrial Organisation (IO) literature because they allow to study the nature of competition between firms from data that are generally easy to collect. Observing how firms operate in different markets with different characteristics allows the empirical economist to estimate how these characteristics affect the profitability of each potential player and how the entry of an additional competitor harms everyone's profit.

In this chapter, we seek to explain how static entry games can be used to estimate the decision of a firm to operate or not in a market by endogeneising everyone's decision. These models have been estimated in the empirical IO literature in many sectors including the airline industry (Bresnahan and Reiss, 1991a; 1991b; Berry, 1992; Mazzeo, 2002; Seim, 2006; Cleeren et al. 2010; Grieco, 2014, among plenty other contributions).[2] Although the estimation of an entry model raises some econometrics issues, which are exposed in this chapter, the alternative option of estimating standard ordered choice models is a bad idea because it implicitly considers that the firms' decisions to operate or not are independent, an assumption ruled out by the data.

Additionally, most of the entry games are games with multiple equilibria unless some order of entry is assumed.[3] Multiple equilibria creates potential identification issues and requires adapted econometric techniques to handle it. In this review, we present some of the solutions used in the literature and introduce briefly the recent advances on moment inequality models that permits us to consider more general entry games.[4] We also we focus on static games with simultaneous moves. Contrary to dynamic games, one should view an entry as a decision of being active in a market rather than entering/exiting a market in which there are incumbents and potential entrants. Estimating a dynamic game poses other econometric challenges which are out of the scope of this chapter.[5]

First, we present the literature on static entry games with complete information where all firms observe the profitability of all other competitors. We introduce in particular the specification of Berry (1992) for heterogeneous firms, which encompasses Bresnahan and Reiss's (1991a) homogeneous version. Understanding this seminal paper is sufficient for grasping the key developments of this literature. Some of them are introduced at the end of the section. Then, we extend our presentation to the case of models with incomplete information where firms decide to enter before observing everybody's profit shocks. Subsequently, we briefly review applied papers which have estimated entry games for the airline industry. Finally, we offer a short illustration of the potentialities of an entry game on European data collected for 2015 from the Official Airline Guide.

Entry games of complete information

In this section, we present the standard entry game with complete information and simultaneous moves widely used in empirical Industrial Organisation. In these types of models, firms decide to be active in a given market if the profits collected after the entry decision are positive. Here, all the firms observe their profitability shocks as well as the ones of their competitors. However, the applied economist does not observe them and, usually, postulates a parametric distribution for these shocks. We focus on Berry (1992), which encompasses as a special case the homogeneous version of Bresnahan and Reiss (1991a). These two models are the basis of more complex models introduced later in the section. As in any structural or semi-structural economic model, the question of the identification of the profit function is at stake. A discussion about the identification of entry games can be found in Tamer (2003) and Berry and Tamer (2007).

The standard entry game with heterogeneous firms

Let N_p be the number of firms potentially active in market m. In the standard game, we assume that the profit of an active firm, labelled i, in a market with N^* active firms, is equal to

$$\pi_{i,m}(N^*) = \pi(X_m, Z_{i,m}; \theta) - h(N^*; \delta) + \varepsilon_{i,m}. \tag{12.1}$$

The usual normalisation is to assume that a non-entrant firm gets a profit of 0. In Equation (12.1), X_m is a vector of market characteristics, $Z_{i,m}$ is a vector of firm i specific characteristics for market m, $\pi(X, Z; \theta)$, a parametric profit function known up to a vector of parameters and θ and $h(N; \delta)$ is a strictly increasing in N, positive, parametric function that drives the degree of competition. It captures the property that more competitors harm profits.[6] First, note that there are many possibilities to introduce heterogeneity among the firms. Here, we only assume that the profit function depends on the firm's characteristics whereas the impact of competitors only matters through their number and not their identity. As we shall see shortly, this specification poses practical problems for empirical researchers, the most important one being the possibility of having multiple equilibria.[7] Note that we can easily extend the model by allowing both $\pi(X, Z; \theta)$ and $h(N; \delta)$ to be firm specific, i.e. $\pi_i(X, Z; \theta)$ and $h_i(\delta, N)$ without changing any of the derivations made in this section.[8] Finally, $\varepsilon_{i,m}$ represents a profit shock for firm i in market m, unobserved by the econometrician. It allows markets with similar observed characteristics to have different equilibrium outcomes. Profit shocks are correlated within each market. These shocks are observed by all firms who could potentially enter (complete information) and who decide, simultaneously, to enter or not.

In Berry (1992), the profit $\pi(X_m, Z_{i,m}; \theta)$ is linear in the explanatory variables, i.e. $\pi(X_m, Z_{i,m}; \theta) = X_m^\top \beta + Z_{i,m}^\top \gamma$, where $\top$ denotes the transpose operator. The market characteristics, X_m, are the product of the population at the two end-points served by the airline, the distance between the two end-points, its square, and a dummy variable for tourist markets. The firm characteristics, $Z_{i,m}$ are some measures of airport presence, i.e. a dummy that indicates if the airline was operating from the two end-point cities during the previous period and a measure of market share at these two end-points.

In this model of complete information, firm i decides to enter in a market m with N^* active firms if $\pi_{i,m}(N^*) \geq 0$, otherwise it does not enter. The action $y_{i,m}$ taken by firm i in market m is therefore $y_{i,m} = 1\{\pi_{i,m}(N^*) \geq 0\}$ and, obviously $N^* = \sum_{i=1}^{N_p} y_{i,m}$. Consequently, for each market m, the actions $y_{i,m}, i = 1, \ldots, N_p$ are the solutions of the simultaneous equation system:

$$y_{i,m} = 1\left\{\pi\left(X_m, Z_{i,m}; \theta\right) - h\left(y_{1,m} + y_{2,m} + \ldots + y_{N_p,m}; \delta\right) + \varepsilon_{i,m} \geq 0\right\},$$
$$i = 1, 2, \ldots, N_p. \tag{12.2}$$

Therefore, the entry game makes the market structure endogenous. First, the simultaneous equations in (12.2) prevent us from estimating the parameters of the model with the econometric procedures designed for standard binary models because of the endogenous variables on the right hand side of Equation (12.2).[9] Additionally, estimating a probit or a logit while omitting the actions $y_{i,m}$ on the right hand side implicitly makes the assumption that more competitors do not change each firm's profit. This assumption is rejected in most empirical applications, leading to inconsistent estimators. One way to treat this simultaneity correctly is to characterize the solutions of this system of equations. This is the objective of the next part.

The problem of multiple equilibria

Assume for the sake of simplicity that there are only two potential entrants, 1 and 2, and that the equilibrium concept is the Nash equilibria in pure strategies. Adapting Equation (12.1), our entry game can be summarised as follows:

$$y_{1,m} = 1\{\beta_{1,m} - \delta y_{2,m} + \varepsilon_{1,m} \geq 0\}, \tag{12.3}$$

$$y_{2,m} = 1\{\beta_{2,m} - \delta y_{1,m} + \varepsilon_{2,m} \geq 0\}. \tag{12.4}$$

Here, with the notations above, $\beta_{i,m} = \pi(X_m, Z_{i,m}; \theta)$ for $i = 1, 2$ and they are generally different because of the firms' heterogenity assumption. Figure 12.1 plots the different regions of interest.

In region I, the profit shocks are too negative and no firm is profitable even in monopoly. Nobody enters, i.e., $y_{1,m} = y_{2,m} = 0$. In region IV, the shocks are very high and both firms can be profitable even with one competitor. Both enter, i.e., $y_{1,m} = y_{2,m} = 1$. In region II, we have two subcases (separated by the vertical line). In region II-A, firm 1 is not profitable even in monopoly and firm 2 is profitable. Consequently, $y_{2,m} = 1$ and $y_{1,m} = 0$. In region II-B, firm 1 is profitable only in monopoly, whereas firm 2 can sustain a competitor. Then,

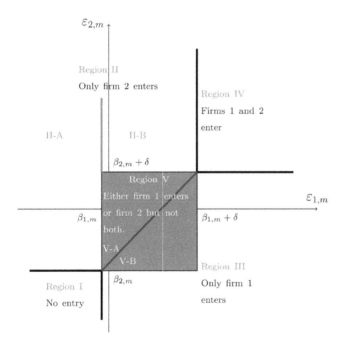

Figure 12.1 The multiple equilibria problem with 2 potential entrants.

firm 2 undoubtedly decides to enter and firm 1, knowing that, does not, so that $y_{2,m} = 1$ and $y_{1,m} = 0$. Analogously, in region III, $y_{1,m} = 1$ and $y_{2,m} = 0$. Finally, in region V, each firm is profitable in monopoly but is not in duopoly. Without further information or another equilibrium concept, the model cannot predict the outcome. Either $y_{1,m} = 1$ and $y_{2,m} = 0$ or $y_{2,m} = 1$ and $y_{1,m} = 0$. This entry game with heterogeneous agents is a game with multiple equilibria.

The multiple equilibria problem prevents the econometrician from estimating the model with the usual techniques because there is no one-to-one mapping between the regions and the four possible outcomes. Region V predicts either (1,0) (i.e. $y_{1,m} = 1$ and $y_{2,m} = 0$) or (0,1). The model is said to be incomplete because we do not know what the mechanism of outcome selection in region V is.[10] There are different solutions to tackle this problem.

Solutions to the problem of multiple equilibria

In order to solve the problem raised by the multiple equilibria, the econometrician has a few solutions. First, one can add some assumptions to complete the model, like in standard problems of missing information in economic models. Bajari et al. (2010) assume large support for the profit shocks, leading to point identification and the possibility of estimating the equilibrium selection mechanism of this model.[11] One can also make assumptions about the order of entry of the different firms. Bjorn and Vuong (1985) assume that the order is purely random whereas Berry (1992) proposes one estimator where the most profitable firm enters first. For the latter, Region V-A now predicts the outcome (0,1) whereas Region V-B predicts (1,0). Consequently, the probability to observe the outcome (1,0) is the sum of the areas of the Regions III and V-B with respect to the true distribution of $(\varepsilon_{1,m}, \varepsilon_{2,m})$ and, we can calculate similarly the probability of observing the outcome (0,1). This solution is ad-hoc, of course, and suffers from the risk of misspecification, i.e., adding a wrong assumption that may bias the estimators.

Another solution consists in using the recent literature on moment inequalities and set identification (see Tamer, 2010 or Bontemps and Magnac, 2017, for a survey). It is out of the scope of this chapter to formally introduce this econometric solution but the general idea is to bind the probability of each outcome.[12] Ciliberto and Tamer (2009) are the first to apply this literature on entry games. For example, in Figure 12.1, the probability of observing the outcome (1,0) is bounded by the probability that the shocks belong to region III and the probability that they belong to region III or V. Similarly, the probability of observing the outcome (0,1) is bounded by the probability that the shocks belong to region II and the probability that they belong to region II or V. Using such bounds allows to exploit all the information provided by the structure of the model and leads to more precise estimates of the parameters of interest. However, generalising this to more players is cumbersome and requires more sophisticated inference techniques.

Bresnahan and Reiss (1991b) observe that, in the case with two players considered above, despite the presence of a multiple equilibria region, the number of firms entering is always the same. The inference can therefore be conducted from the number of firms rather than the set of actions. Here, the probability of observing 0 firm entering is the area of region I, 2 firms entering is the area of region IV, and 1 is the sum of the areas of regions II, III, and V. Nevertheless, this simplification is at the cost of having less precise estimators because of some informational loss; for example, the probability to observe the outcome (1,0) is at least greater than the area of region III, a fact no longer taken into account in the new strategy. However, it allows us to estimate the model by standard techniques, here maximum likelihood, as the one-to-one mapping between regions of shocks and number of firms is restored.

A simulated estimator

In his seminal paper, Berry (1992) generalises the last example to the entry games with more than two potential entrants. The number of multiple equilibria regions is much higher than with two potential entrants. It increases exponentially (8 regions with 3 entrants, 81 regions with 4, 2008 regions for 5 entrants, etc. Bontemps and Kumar (2020) provide, in particular, an exact estimate). Nevertheless, Berry (1992) proves that the number of active firms is constant in these regions. The key assumption is that the impact of the competitors on each firm's profit does not depend on their identity (the function $h(N; \delta)$ depends only on N in Equation (12.1) and does not vary when we switch one active firm and one non-entrant).[13]

Therefore, like the case with two entrants, one can estimate the entry game from the number of entrants in each market. We consider that we observe M independent markets, $m = 1, \ldots, M$ in which the N_p firms compete. The characteristics $X_m, Z_{1,m}, \ldots, Z_{N_p,m}$ and the profit shocks $\varepsilon_{1,m}, \ldots, \varepsilon_{N_p,m}$ are assumed to be identically distributed and independent across markets.[14]

Our goal is to estimate the parameters θ of the profit function, δ of the function $h(N; \delta)$ and, the correlation matrix of the within market profit shocks, $\varepsilon_{1,m}, \ldots, \varepsilon_{N_p,m}$ (in its simplest form, one can assume, like in Berry, that $\varepsilon_{i,m} = \rho u_{0,m} + \sqrt{1-\rho^2} u_{i,m}$, where all the shocks $u_{j,m}$ are independent and standard normally distributed; $u_{0,m}$ is the market shock common to all firms). Let us denote α the vector gathering all parameters in θ, δ, and ρ and $P(N_m^*; \alpha)$, the probability of observing N_m^* active firms at the equilibrium. One can estimate α by maximum likelihood:

$$\hat{\alpha}_{MLE} = \arg\max_{\alpha} \left(L(\alpha) = \sum_{m=1}^{M} \log P(N_m^*; \alpha) \right).$$

If one estimates a probit model without a common market shock (assuming $\delta = 0$ and $\rho = 0$), we have a closed form for $P(N_m^*; \alpha)$. However, such restrictions are generally empirically rejected. The homogeneous version of Bresnahan and Reiss (1991a) is also a particular example of the model for $\rho = 1$ and homogeneous firms (i.e., no $Z_{i,m}$) in which we obtain a closed form for the likelihood (it is an ordered model, see Bresnahan and Reiss (1991a) for further details). Generally, due to the huge number of regions involved and their difficulty in being characterised explicitly, it is not possible to get such an explicit form. However, one can use simulated methods to estimate (across simulations) $P(N^*;\alpha)$ for each α using the following six-step algorithm proposed by Berry (1992).

Algorithm for simulating $P(N_m^*;\alpha)$ for any α

Step 1: Choose the number of simulations S (at least 500).

Step 2: For each s in $1,\ldots,S$, and for each m, draw iid sequences $u_{0,m}^{(s)},u_{1,m}^{(s)},\ldots,u_{N_p,m}^{(s)}$ from the standard normal distribution.

Step 3: Choose a value for the vector of parameters α. The next three steps estimate $P(N_m^*;\alpha)$.

Step 4: For each market m and each s, compute $\Phi_{i,m}^{(s)} = \pi(X_m, Z_{i,m}; \theta) + \rho u_{0,m}^{(s)} + \sqrt{1-\rho^2}\, u_{i,m}^{(s)}$, for $i = 1,\ldots,N_p$.

Step 5: For each market m and each s, calculate from these $\Phi_{i,m}^{(s)}$s, the number of active firms at the equilibrium in market m for simulation s, $N_m^{*,(s)}$, by counting how much firms are profitable in a market with $1, 2, 3, \ldots$ active firms.

Step 6: For each market m, calculate the empirical frequency, $\widehat{P(N_m^*;\alpha)}$, of observing the outcome $N = N_m^*$ across simulations:

$$\widehat{P(N_m^*;\alpha)} = \frac{1}{S}\sum_{s=1}^{S} 1\{N_m^* = N_m^{*,(s)}\}.$$

One can now estimate α from observing market characteristics and decisions of firms to enter or not by maximising the Simulated Maximum Likelihood (SML):

$$L_{sim}(\alpha) = \sum_{m=1}^{M}\log \widehat{P(N_m^*;\alpha)},$$

where, for each step in the optimisation procedure, $\widehat{P(N_m^*;\alpha)}$ is estimated using the algorithm above with a unique and fixed sequence of random terms.

The SML estimator is consistent but asymptotically biased. When S is sufficiently large, this bias can be neglected. The standard errors can be computed using the classical variance formula, assuming S is large enough to neglect the simulation bias.[15]

The results of Berry (1992)

Berry estimates the decision to enter for airlines in markets whose end-points are two of the 50 largest cities of the United States.[16] The simulation method proposed above is slightly modified by adding an order of entry in Step 4. It is therefore possible to estimate on top of the number of active firms, the probability of entering for each firm in each market.

One particular empirical finding is the importance of airport presence at both end-points to explain the decision to operate a market and a numerical evaluation of this impact. This result can be put in perspective, for example, with the empirical findings of Goolsbee and Syverson (2008), where it is shown that the threat to entry (i.e. being present at both end-points) would put pressure on the active firms even if the airline does not serve the corresponding market. Also, the larger the market size, the higher the probability to enter. This effect is quantified and one can estimate which markets are under-exploited. Besides, based on estimated parameters of the model, it is also possible to simulate the number of entrants in different market configurations. Furthermore, Berry's model encompasses the homogeneous model of Bresnahan and Reiss (1991a) as well as the probit model where the competitor's presence does not harm each firm profit ($\delta = 0$), allowing these restrictions to be tested empirically. Usually, they are rejected by the data.

Extensions

The assumption that the profitability of one airline does not depend on the identity of its competitors may seem extreme in the case of the airline sector where at least two types of firms are present, full-service carriers and low-cost carriers (even three with the regional version of the full-service carriers). However, relaxing this assumption is difficult because of the problem of multiple equilibria. This problem is recurrent in this literature.

Cleeren et al. (2010) assume that there are two types of firms which decide whether to enter or not in a version of the game where firms within each type are exchangeable. Their model is applied to competition between supermarket chains with traditional supermarket chains and discounters. Multiplicity of equilibria is dealt with by adding assumptions about the nature of competition between types and by selecting the equilibria with the highest number of traditional supermarket chains, which are argued to have entered the market first. Mazzeo (2002) proposes an equivalent version in which the format (or the quality) is also endogeneised. He considers two or three quality levels. Again, the multiple equilibria problem is solved by assuming a sequence of quality choice. Both models can therefore be estimated by maximum likelihood.

Bajari et al. (2010) goes one step further into the estimation of complete information games with equilibrium selection. Instead of picking one selection rule, they explicitly model and estimate the probability that each one of several equilibrium selection possibilities will be played in a game.

A number of studies (Mazzeo, 2002; Jia, 2008; Cleeren et al., 2010; Sampaio, 2011) that specified a sequential order of movement to solve the multiple equilibria also investigated the robustness of their results to an alternative order of movements, and found fairly similar coefficients to profit functions under the alternative specifications.

Finally, Ciliberto and Tamer (2009) introduce much more heterogeneity on firms' profit functions. They also apply their model to the US domestic airline industry and allow each variable (market and firm observed characteristics) and competition effect to potentially differ among airlines. Not surprisingly, such flexibility comes at a cost of more general multiple equilibria structure. They estimate their model using moment inequalities. They find that the competitive effect of full-service-carriers on other FSCs is smaller than the competitive effect of FSC on low- cost carriers (excluding Southwest). Furthermore, these effects are not symmetric, in the sense that the effect of American Airlines (AA) on a LCC's profit is greater than the effect of a LCC entry on AA's profit. Finally, the competitive effects of Southwest and full-service carriers are symmetric.

Entry games of incomplete information

The previous sections have analysed entry models under the assumption that part of airlines' profits are unobserved by the econometrician, but are common knowledge held by all airlines that could potentially enter the market. We now investigate how to recover airlines' profits assuming that information about a specific airline profitability is privately held by that airline, thus not being shared by their competitors as well as the econometrician.

With incomplete information, the equilibrium concept used is the Bayes-Nash equilibrium, in which airlines base their entry decisions on expected profits. The models presented here were developed in the context of static entry models by Seim (2006) and Bajari et al. (2010). Also, we recommend Bajari et al. (2013) for a survey of the econometrics with game interactions. In this section, we first look into an entry game with only two players. Then, we extend this entry game to multiple competitors.

The case of two firms

Let $y_{i,m}$ denote a dummy variable representing the entry decision of airline i in market m. Profits of not entering a market are also normalised to zero. The profit function of an active firm is the same as in the complete case, i.e., in Equation (12.3) or (12.4). Firm i gets the following profit if it enters:

$$\pi_{i,m} = \pi_i(X_m, Z_{i,m}; \theta) - \delta y_{-i,m} + \varepsilon_{i,m}, \tag{12.5}$$

where $-i$ denotes the rival's index ($-i = 1$ if $i = 2$ and vice-versa). In the usual linear setting, like the one considered above, $\pi_i(X_m, Z_{i,m}; \theta) = X_m^\top \beta + Z_{i,m}^\top \gamma$ but, again, any parametric specification is possible. Like above, δ represents the decrease in airline i's profits caused by the actual entry of airline $-i$. Now, $\varepsilon_{i,m}$, the profit shock, is unknown to both airline $-i$ and the econometrician. It is assumed that $\varepsilon_{i,m}$ has an extreme value distribution to guarantee some analytical tractability of the computation of the equilibrium of the game. This distribution is common knowledge of the players and the econometrician.[17]

Then, since airline 1 does not observe airline 2's profit shock, but knows its distribution, airline 1's entry strategy is based on its own expected profits on market m:

$$y_{1,m} = 1 \Leftrightarrow \mathbb{E}\left[\pi_1\left(X_m, Z_{1,m}; \theta\right) - \delta y_{2,m} + \varepsilon_{1,m} \mid \text{Information of firm 1}\right] \geq 0$$

$$\Leftrightarrow \varepsilon_{1,m} \geq -\pi_1\left(X_m, Z_{i,m}; \theta\right) + \delta \mathbb{E}\left[y_{2,m}\right].$$

In the derivation above, the only uncertainty comes from the non-observation of $\varepsilon_{2,m}$ and its impact on the expected value of $y_{2,m}$. Since $y_{2,m}$ is a dummy variable, $\mathbb{E}\left[y_{2,m}\right]$ corresponds to the probability that airline 2 actually enters the market, $Prob(y_{2,m} = 1)$. Let $\sigma_{2,m}$ represent this probability.

The probability that airline 1 enters market m, also known as airline 1 best response function, depends on the probability that airline 2 also enters market m. With the extreme value distribution for $\varepsilon_{1,m}$:

$$\sigma_{1,m} = Prob\left(y_{1,m} = 1\right) = Prob\left(\varepsilon_{1,m} \geq -\left(\pi_1\left(X_m, Z_{1,m}; \theta\right) - \delta\sigma_{2,m}\right)\right)$$

$$= \frac{\exp\left(\pi_1\left(X_m, Z_{1,m}; \theta\right) - \delta\sigma_{2,m}\right)}{1 + \exp\left(\pi_1\left(X_m, Z_{1,m}; \theta\right) - \delta\sigma_{2,m}\right)}. \tag{12.6}$$

Similarly, airline 2's best response function is given by:

$$\sigma_{2,m} = Prob\left(y_{2,m} = 1\right) = \frac{\exp\left(\pi_2\left(X_m, Z_{2,m}; \theta\right) - \delta\sigma_{1,m}\right)}{1 + \exp\left(\pi_2\left(X_m, Z_{2,m}; \theta\right) - \delta\sigma_{1,m}\right)}. \tag{12.7}$$

The equilibrium of the game, $(\sigma_{1,m}^*, \sigma_{2,m}^*)$, corresponds to the solution of equations (12.6) and (12.7) for each market m. The problem of multiple equilibria present in the entry games with complete information still arises here. To solve this problem, we have to assume some form of uniqueness of equilibrium across markets or over time. As discussed in Pesendorfer and Schmidt-Dengler (2008), if we have data on the same market in multiple periods of time, it is easier to support the assumption of uniqueness of equilibria. However, in airline entry models, we typically gather information about multiple origin-destination markets. In this case, we need the same equilibria $\left(\sigma_{1,m}^*, \sigma_{2,m}^*\right)$ to emerge in markets having the same market share and the same airline characteristics, $(X_m, Z_{1,m}, Z_{2,m})$.

Following the uniqueness assumption, Seim (2006) and Bajari et al. (2010), propose a two-step method of estimation of the parameters of the model, which is easy to implement using standard commands of statistical software. In the first step, the entry probability of each airline, σ_1 and σ_2, is estimated as depending on all available information on market and airline characteristics, $(X_m, Z_{1,m}, Z_{2,m})$, but ignoring the interactions between players' decisions.[18] Estimation can be performed using a parametric model, such as a logit model, or a nonparametric model, such as a local linear model.

In the second step, interactions between airlines' decisions are brought back, by plugging the estimates of $\hat{\sigma}_1(X_m, Z_{1,m}, Z_{2,m})$ and $\hat{\sigma}_2(X_m, Z_{1,m}, Z_{2,m})$ obtained from the first step in equations (12.6) and (12.7), so that:

$$\sigma_1 = \frac{\exp\left(\pi_1\left(X_m, Z_{1,m}; \theta\right) - \delta\hat{\sigma}_2(X_m, Z_{1,m}, Z_{2,m})\right)}{1 + \exp\left(\pi_1\left(X_m, Z_{1,m}; \theta\right) - \delta\hat{\sigma}_2(X_m, Z_{1,m}, Z_{2,m})\right)}$$

and

$$\sigma_2 = \frac{\exp\left(\pi_2\left(X_m, Z_{2,m}; \theta\right) - \delta\hat{\sigma}_1(X_m, Z_{1,m}, Z_{2,m})\right)}{1 + \exp\left(\pi_2\left(X_m, Z_{2,m}; \theta\right) - \delta\hat{\sigma}_1(X_m, Z_{1,m}, Z_{2,m})\right)}.$$

Finally, the parameters of interest (θ, δ) can be recovered with the estimation of the following pseudo log-likelihood:

$$L(\theta, \delta) = \sum_{m=1}^{M} \sum_{i=1}^{2} y_{i,m} \log\left(\frac{\exp\left(\pi_i\left(X_m, Z_{i,m}; \theta\right) - \delta\hat{\sigma}_{-i}(X_m, Z_{1,m}, Z_{2,m})\right)}{1 + \exp\left(\pi_i\left(X_m, Z_{i,m}; \theta\right) - \delta\hat{\sigma}_{-i}(X_m, Z_{1,m}, Z_{2,m})\right)}\right),$$

which is actually just a conditional logit likelihood estimation.

The case of multiple firms

The last entry model can be very easily extended to multiple players. Suppose now that there are N_p potential players in each market. In a simple model with symmetric competition effects of different rival airlines, if airline i decides to enter market m, it collects profits given by:

$$\pi_i\left(X_m, Z_{i,m}; \theta\right) - \delta\sum_{j \neq i} y_{j,m} + \varepsilon_{i,m},$$

where, once again, $\varepsilon_{i,m}$ is private information to airline i and is assumed to have an extreme value distribution. Profits of not entering a market are also normalised to zero. The decision to enter a market is based on expected profits, which alongside the extreme value distribution, yields the following best response function for airline i:

$$\sigma_{i,m} = \frac{\exp\left(\pi_i\left(X_m, Z_{1,m}; \theta\right) - \delta \sum_{j \neq i} \sigma_{j,m}\right)}{1 + \exp\left(\pi_i\left(X_m, Z_{1,m}; \theta\right) - \delta \sum_{j \neq i} \sigma_{j,m}\right)}, \forall i = 1, \ldots, N_p.$$

The Bayes-Nash equilibrium is now implicitly defined by a system with N_p unknowns $(\sigma_{i,m}^*, i = 1, \ldots, N_p)$ and N_p equations.

The multiple equilibria problem still arises and is once again solved by assuming that there exists a unique equilibrium in the same market over time or in a cross-section of markets. The estimation of the model is undertaken likewise in two steps.

In a first step, $\sigma_{i,m}$ is estimated based on all market and airline characteristics $(X_m, Z_{1,m}, \ldots, Z_{Nm})$. Given this first step estimates, $\hat{\sigma}_{i,m} = \hat{\sigma}_{i,m}(X_m, Z_{1,m}, \ldots, Z_{N_p,m})$, the parameters of interest can once again be estimated by maximum likelihood on the log-likelihood:

$$L(\theta, \delta) = \sum_{m=1}^{M} \sum_{i=1}^{N_p} y_{i,m} \log\left(\frac{\exp\left(\pi_i\left(X_m, Z_{i,m}; \theta\right) - \delta \sum_{j \neq i} \hat{\sigma}_{j,m}\right)}{1 + \exp\left(\pi_i\left(X_m, Z_{i,m}; \theta\right) - \delta \sum_{j \neq i} \hat{\sigma}_{j,m}\right)}\right). \quad (12.8)$$

Note that the model above can easily accommodate the case where an airline might decide between K options. The unobserved profit shocks now are action specific, that it, each possible action is associated to a different error term, and it is unknown to their competitors. As before, competitors know the distribution of these error terms, but not the specific realisation that occurred in a market. The solution to this problem follows the same two steps of the simple entry game.

Discussion and extensions

This section has presented a simple version of an entry game with incomplete information, with the main goal of illustrating the traditional assumptions made in the literature. As discussed, the biggest advantage of the private information framework is that the estimation of game parameters are much simpler than in complete information set-up, since it can be easily performed on available software commands at low time cost, without any simulations being necessary. This simplification is also driven by the fact that it is assumed explicitly that the same strategy is played across observations when there may be multiple equilibria. This is a strong assumption and deriving bounds like in the complete case would be a solution that could be investigated more systematically though it is not the case yet.

One argument that has been put forward in the literature in favour of the complete information assumption is the following: since static entry models are supposed to represent firm's long run decisions, there should be no ex-post regret, which is a property of Nash equilibria. In games with incomplete information, since decisions are made ex-ante, before knowing the real realisation of their competitors' unobserved profits, airlines may be surprised by the entry (or lack of entry) of their competitors and end up with ex-post realised profits that do not correspond to their most profitable action.

Einav (2010) incorporates sequential moves into entry games with incomplete information to study competition in movie release dates. This model derives a unique perfect Bayesian equilibrium, even for quite heterogeneous profit functions. Conditional on a fixed order of moves, estimation can be easily done with maximum likelihood. The author argues that, with sequential choices, there is less ex-post regret, since firms that move later on have more information on which to base their decisions.

There is no consensus in the literature on what is the most appropriate assumption about the degree of information on the unobserved profitability shared by competitors on entry models of airlines. To the best of our knowledge, no unifying framework has been developed.

The set-up of games with private information also provided a nice framework to dynamic considerations on entry models. In the dynamic setting, ex-post regret is no longer an issue, since airlines are allowed to freely enter and exit markets as long as they pay some sunk costs. Aguirregabiria and Mira (2010) and Bajari et al. (2013) offer excellent surveys of dynamic structural econometric models with more in-depth details about estimation, inference and efficiency.

Entry games applied to the airline sector

In this section, we present some of the *structural* empirical entry games papers applied to the airline industry in the recent years. Some are static models, and some are dynamic models. There is also a huge and vast literature of reduced form estimations (see, for example, Bogulaski et al., 2004, or de Oliveira, 2008) which is not cited here.

Complete information

Sampaio (2011) uses Cleeren et al. (2010)'s model to study competition between low-cost and full-service airlines. The model is estimated with the assumption that full-service carriers enter the market first and then low-cost carriers make their decisions. Results suggest the existence of strong competition effects on this industry. Entry of same type rivals has a large significant effect on profits. Besides, entry of low-cost carriers seems to affect profits of full-service airlines more than vice-versa.

Dunn (2008) also introduces product quality to entry models. He studies competition between airlines offering non-stop and one-stop routes to investigate cannibalisation and business stealing competition effects. One-stop routes passing through hubs are taken as fixed, and entry with non-stop services is modelled with a game theoretical model à la Berry (1992). However, the inclusion of a cannibalisation effect in the model implies multiple equilibria in the total number of firms with non-stop operations in a market, and, to deal with this problem, the author selects the equilibria with the highest number of entrants. Their results suggest both the presence of strong competition effects as well as relevant cannibalisation effects.

On the same direction of Mazzeo (2002) and Cleeren et al. (2010), Blevins (2015) investigates entry models with complete information and sequential movement in the US domestic industry. Now, the order of moves is not observed (or assumed) by the econometrician. Instead it is estimated alongside the coefficients of the profit function. In contrast to Mazzeo (2002) and Cleeren et al. (2010), and similar to Berry (1992), the model focuses on pure entry, without product differentiation, but it allows firm observed heterogeneity.

Ciliberto and Tamer (2009) introduce much more heterogeneity on firms' profit functions. They also apply their model to the US domestic airline industry and allow each variable (market and firm observed characteristics) and competition effect to potentially differ among airlines. The complicated multiple equilibria problem (there is no obvious outcome invariant in the multiple equilibria regions) is tackled by using moment inequalities. They found evidence of a greater impact of an entry of Southwest on the three major airlines' profits compared to the impact of the entry of another major airline.

Incomplete information

An important contribution of dynamic entry models to the airline industry is the ability to analyse network effects of entry decisions and to rationalise hub-and-spokes networks. Static models usually incorporate network effects via a hub dummy variable or market presence. In contrast, Aguirregabiria and Ho (2010, 2012) create the concept of local managers that maximise profits of several interconnected routes inside an airline's network, so that the airlines recognise that entering in one route affects profits on other routes. This also creates scope for entry deterrence effects, since airlines might enter a route with negative profits, as long as they are compensated by positive profits on the rest of the network. The entry threat is credible to potential most efficient competitors in one specific route, since no profit loss is actually incurred by the network airline at each period of time. In the papers mentioned before, they document relevant network effects on the sunk entry cost as well as large entry deterrence effects.

Benkard et al. (2018) advocate the need for introducing dynamic considerations on merger analysis to understand medium and long run effects of a proposed merger, since potential negative short run effects of a merger implied by an increase in concentration might be offset by the entry of other potential competitors. They use a simplified version of Bajari et al's. (2007) estimation method to investigate the effects of three proposed mergers in the

airline industry between 2000 and 2010. Interestingly, their long run analysis would motivate a competition authority conduct at odds with what was
actually adopted in practice. However their model is much less flexible than
Aguirregabria and Ho (2012) and does not allow for entry deterrence effects.
Thus the question of how entry deterrence effects might affect medium and
long run competition after mergers remains.

Finally, Gillen et al. (2015) analyse the relationship between network and
regional airlines in a game with three stages. In the first stage, network airlines
decide the number of regional airlines they are going to sign contracts with. In
the second stage, they choose if they are also going to operate the market with
their own fleet. In the last stage, each of the regional airlines determines how
many passengers to serve, independently, given their knowledge of the traffic
provided and served by the network airlines. Their model is an extension of the
classical incomplete information entry game where, instead of modelling a 0/1
decision, one models the choice of an integer $n_{i,m}$, here, the number of regional
airlines airline i is contracting with.

Except for the inclusion of terms related to the number of contracts signed
by all network airlines with regional airlines, the best response function of network airlines can be estimated following the procedure described in the previous section. Their results for both stages corroborate the existence of negative
network airlines competition effects on each other in both stages ($\delta > 0$). They
also indicate a positive correlation between its own number of contracts with
regional airlines and its decision to also operate in a market.

Example on European data

We now illustrate the approach by estimating a static entry game with complete information on Western European data for the year 2015. The data were
collected from the Official Airline Guide database (OAG) which contains all
posted flights for the year 2015, their schedules and eventually, their code share
agreements.

A market is defined as an origin/destination flight (non-directional)
between two European cities. Therefore, we group the different airports of
a given city (London, Paris).[19] We restrict our investigations to the decision
to operate between the 50 most populated cities of Western Europe.[20] The
distance between these cities and socioeconomic variables such as GDP and
population of the metropolitan areas are collected from additional statistical
sources.[21] We eliminate markets for which the distance between the cities is less
than 150 kilometres; 1,204 potential markets remain.

Contrary to the US market, the Western European market has more players.
Each country has its own flag carrier which usually plays a significant role in
the industry.[22] We group the different airlines as follows. The first 15 airlines in
number of routes (see Table 12.1) are kept as they are. All the other airlines are
gathered according to their alliance membership (if any), otherwise according
to their type.[23]

Descriptive statistics

In 2015, 900 million passengers were transported. The most frequented routes were Paris-Toulouse and Barcelona-Madrid with respectively 3.5 and 2.5 millions of passengers. Out of the possible 1,204 markets, we observe 670 existing connections. Tables 12.1 and 12.2 present some descriptive statistics of the final dataset.

Most of the growth in markets served from 2014 to 2015 is due to an increased activity of low-cost carriers who opened 95 markets out of 148 new markets. They serve around 41% of the routes with a share in seats offered of approximately 29.4%. On average, there are 2 airlines per market served. Less than 6% of the markets have more than 4 competitors.

Following Berry (1992), we consider the following explanatory variables for the profit function:

- *Pop* is the geometric mean of the population of market end-point metropolitan areas in millions. It is a proxy for the market size.
- *Gdppercap* is the mean GDP per capita of market end-point metropolitan areas in thousands of euros per capita.

Table 12.1 Airline characteristics in markets served between the top 50 cities of Western Europe.

Airline	Type	# Routes Served		Total seats offered	Share
		2015	2014		
Ryanair	LCC	195	173	36,036	11.5%
Easyjet	LCC	158	139	31,245	9.9%
Vueling	LCC	88	76	15,875	5.1%
Norwegian	LCC	73	68	11,164	3.6%
Lufthansa	FSC	71	71	39,219	12.5%
Germanwings	LCC	69	58	9,592	3.1%
SAS	FSC	64	61	16,156	5.1%
Air Berlin	FSC	47	46	12,325	3.9%
British Airways	FSC	39	38	22,270	7.1%
Air France	FSC	38	38	22,087	7.0%
TAP	FSC	38	38	8,253	2.6%
Alitalia	FSC	36	29	10,334	3.3%
Aer Lingus	FSC	36	32	7,595	2.4%
KLM	FSC	34	34	13,496	4.3%
Iberia	FSC	34	30	11,890	3.8%
StarAlliance	FSC	76	71	16,017	5.1%
SkyTeam	FSC	70	61	10,841	3.5%
OneWorld	FSC	33	30	7,462	2.4%
Main_Others	FSC	87	71	7,876	2.5%
Other LCCs	LCC	58	32	4,382	1.4%

Notes: Total seats in millions.
Type= FSC for full service carriers and LCC for Low-cost carriers.

Table 12.2 Market frequency by the number of competitors per market

N_{2015}	Frequency	Percent	Cumulative
0	534	44.35	44.35
1	268	22.26	66.61
2	223	18.52	85.13
3	108	8.970	94.10
4	55	4.570	98.67
5	11	0.910	99.58
6	4	0.330	99.92
7	1	0.080	100.00
Total	1,204	100	

- *Dist* is the distance in thousand of kilometres, *Dist2* is its square.
- *Sun* is a dummy equal to 1 if one of the end-points is on the Mediterranean Sea.
- *LCC* is a dummy for low-cost airlines.
- *City2* is a dummy variable equal to 1 if the airline serves both cities in the city pair.
- *Nbroutes* is the mean number of cities served by the airline out of the two end-points.

Table 12.3 displays some descriptive statistics of these variables. Table 12.4 presents the results of the OLS regression of the number of firms on the exogenous market characteristics (distance, population, gdppercapita, dummy for Sun cities). It allows us to measure how these characteristics impact the number of active firms, but does not permit us to estimate the competitive effect N_{2015}. All variables but the dummy *Sun* are significant.

Results of the estimation and comments

We use a Simulated Maximum Likelihood method to estimate the static entry game with complete information. The profit function has the form of Equation (12.1), more specifically,

$$\pi_{i,m}(N) = \beta^\top X_m + \gamma^\top Z_{i,m} - \delta\log N + \underbrace{\rho u_{0,m} + \sqrt{1-\rho^2}\, u_{i,m}}_{=\varepsilon_{i,m}},$$

where the market variables X^m are *Pop, Gdppercap, Dist, Dist2* and *Sun* whereas the firm specific variables are *LCC, City2* and *Nbroutes*. The results are displayed in Table 12.5. We also put the results of a probit estimation without the inter-action term (i.e. assuming $\delta = 0$) and assuming $\rho = 0$. The results are totally different as expected. δ, the interaction parameter is significantly positive.

Table 12.3 Descriptive statistics the econometric variables

Variables	N	Mean	Sd	Min	Max
N_{2015}	1,204	1.116	1.283	0	7
Pop (in millions)	1,204	2.4	1.2	1.1	12.8
Gdppercap (in '000 euros per cap)	1,204	38.8	10.5	14.4	72.7
Dist (in kms)	1,204	1,167	617	156	3,362
Sun	1,204	0.370	0.483	0	1
City2	1,204	0.212	0.409	0	1
Nbroutes	1,204	4.66	8.48	0	75.5

Table 12.4 Results of the regression of N_{2015} on the market characteristics

	Estimate	Std. Error	T stat	P-value
(Intercept)	-1.3590	0.1782	-7.63	0.0000
Pop	0.5782	0.0244	23.65	0.0000
Gdppercap	0.0203	0.0031	6.50	0.0000
Dist	0.3987	0.1753	2.27	0.0231
Dist^2	0.1052	0.0621	-1.69	0.0903
Sun	0.0597	0.1654	0.36	0.7181

Table 12.5 Simulated maximum likelihood estimates

	Estimate (Std. error)	Probit est. (Std. error)
(Intercept)	-2.616 (0.044)	-3.163 (0.123)
Pop	0.090 (0.009)	0.060 (0.013)
Gdppercap	-0.0003 (0.0001)	-0.004 (0.002)
Dist	0.342 (0.033)	0.560 (0.119)
Dist^2	-0.126 (0.012)	-0.178 (0.042)
Sun	0.0002 (0.002)	-0.068 (0.101)
LCC	-0.121 (0.058)	-0.001 (0.040)
City2	1.518 (0.056)	0.783 (0.040)
Nbroutes	0.047 (0.002)	0.076 (0.002)
δ	0.274 (0.030)	
ρ	0.306 (0.025)	

Assuming (wrongly) that the value is equal to zero leads to biased estimates. The percentage of good predictions[24] is equal to 78.1%. Like in Berry (1992), we obtain the expected signs. When the size of the cities grows, it is more likely to serve the corresponding market. The effect of distance is first increasing then decreasing from 1,357 kilometres onwards. It captures the fact that people fly more to distant cities but less when it starts to be too far. Moreover, the coefficient of City2 is positive and economically significant. Airport presence is a good predictor of the decision to enter in a market. The more important the presence, the more likely that the airline will enter. The interaction coefficient δ is positive as expected. Finally ρ is positive and captures the fact that profits shocks within markets are correlated across firms.

We can now use these estimates to evaluate in which markets, not served in 2015, airlines are more likely to enter by checking markets where the discrepancy between our model prediction and the actual number of firms is the highest. We report in Table 12.6 the top ten markets distant from at least 500 kilometres. Among these 10 markets, 7 are actually served in 2019. Alternatively, we report in Table 12.7 the top ten markets for which the model predicts too many entries. We report the number of competitors for the year 2019. Seven out of these 10 markets have experienced a decrease in the number of competitors.

The model could obviously be better adapted to the European context by taking into account the fragmentation of countries and their relation to their flag carriers. More specific characteristics could be tested but this is left for additional research. The goal of this section is to show what kind of results we can expect and how they can be used to predict some market structure change in markets between top European cities.

Table 12.6 Characteristics of markets where entry is predicted

N_{2015}	Predicted	Diff	Market	Distance	2019 (airline)
0	1.58	1.58	Brussels–Glasgow	808	√ (Ryanair)
0	1.7	1.7	Bordeaux–Manchester	955	√ (Ryanair& Easyjet)
0	1.86	1.86	Berlin–Marseille	1,177	√ (Easyjet)
0	1.74	1.74	Lille–Rome	1,200	No airline
0	1.68	1.68	Birmingham–Stockholm	1,360	√ (SAS)
0	1.68	1.68	Glasgow–Milan	1,504	No airline
0	1.9	1.9	Birmingham–Lisbon	1,623	No airline
0	1.54	1.54	Athens–Toulouse	1,996	√ (Aegean Airlines)
0	2.48	2.48	Athens–Valencia	2,119	√ (Aegean Airlines)
0	2.12	2.12	Athens–Malaga/Seville	2,615	√ (Aegean Airlines)

Note: √ indicates an entry by, at least, one airline between 2015 and 2019.

Table 12.7 Characteristics of markets where there is too many entries

N_{2015}	N_{model}	Diff	Market	Distance	N_{2019}
5	1.24	-3.76	Rome–Vienna	777	3
5	1.68	-3.32	Paris–Palermo	1,471	2
6	2.74	-3.26	Porto–Paris	1,224	6
4	0.96	-3.04	Copenhagen–Dublin	1,239	3
7	4.04	-2.96	Lisbon–Paris	1,454	5
5	2.3	-2.7	Copenhagen–Rome	1,535	3
4	1.48	-2.52	Barcelona–Birmingham	1,273	2
4	1.5	-2.5	Glasgow–Seville	1,966	4
4	1.5	-2.5	Marseille–Rome	608	3
4	1.54	-2.46	Madrid–Porto	436	4

Conclusion

In this review, we presented static entry games with complete or incomplete information. These models are useful to estimate market structure from data that are relatively easy to obtain. However, the problem of multiple equilibria complicates the estimation procedure. Despite the fact that it occurs in both information cases, complete or incomplete, it has been treated more seriously in the games with complete information.

The recent literature on moment inequality models could propose a unified treatment of the two cases. Based on a revealed preference argument, one can derive inequalities by setting that the choice of a firm to enter (resp. to not enter) a market is made because the choice of not entering (resp. entering) would have been less profitable. These inequalities are however difficult to handle in a game with a medium number of players. Nevertheless this is an interesting way to work on.

Most of the empirical work on entry games, applied to airlines, have considered the US market. The data are easy to collect, available online and the market has only a few large players. We hope that the online access to flights proposed in other continents would allow researchers to study more systematically the market structure of the airline sector in Europe and Asia.

Notes

1 We thank Alex Pedurand for his research assistance. We also thank two external reviewers for their comments. We also thank Mariane Bontemps for help in the editing process. The usual disclaimer applies.

2 See Berry and Reiss (2007) for a survey.

3 Assumptions often combined with additional minor assumptions.

4 See de Paula (2013) for a full survey.

5 Aguirregabiria and Mira (2010) and Bajari et al. (2013) propose a survey including dynamic games.

6 With the normalisation $h(1; \delta) = 0$ when there is the constant term in X_m. Berry (1992) uses $h(N; \delta) = \delta \log N$ whereas Bresnahan and Reiss (1991a) estimate each value $h(2; \delta), h(3; \delta)$, *etc.* separately.

7 The extensions consider specifications which relax some of these constraints, still finding solutions to treat the multiple equilibria problem.

8 See Bontemps and Kumar (2020) for the problem of multiple equilibria for this augmented specification.

9 One could estimate this system using instrumental variables, but estimating binary models with endogenous explanatory variables is notoriously more complicated than for the linear case. See Blundell and Powell (2003), for example.

10 See also Heckman (1978).

11 See also Tamer (2003).

12 Moment inequality procedures are now well developed in the partial identification literature, which includes contributions by, among others, Chernozhukov et al. (2007), Andrews and Soares (2010) and Beresteanu et al. (2011). It becomes complicated and numerically challenging for entry games with more than 5 players. Bontemps and Kumar (2020) propose a computational solution for games with more players.

13 Bontemps and Kumar (2020) show that this result remains valid when the function $h(\cdot)$ depends on the firm identity as long as this is the number of competitors which matters in the profitability, i.e., for the specification $\pi_{i,m}(N^\star) = \pi(X_m, Z_{i,m}; \theta) - h_i(N^\star; \delta) + \varepsilon_{i,m}$.

14 There may be correlation within markets for the profit shocks like in Berry (1992). Jia (2008) is the first one to depart from the iid assumptions. She analyses competition between K-Mart and Wal-Mart with network effects. Her model is applicable for games with two players only.

15 See Gourieroux and Monfort (1996) for a review of simulated methods.

16 There is no clear consensus about what is the right market definition, i.e. city pairs or airport pairs and whether the markets are directional or not. For example, Berry (1992), Berry and Jia (2010) consider cities whereas Ciliberto and Tamer (2009) and Ciliberto, Murry, and Tamer (2018) consider airports. Any assumption can be handled within this framework.

17 Up to some parameters for the econometrician, eventually.

18 Tamer (2003) also proposes it for the complete model with two players.

19 We also grouped Alicante and Valencia, Malaga, and Seville.

20 These cities are Amsterdam, Antwerp, Athens, Barcelona, Berlin, Birmingham, Bilbao, Bordeaux, Bristol, Brussels, Copenhagen, Cardiff, Dresden, Dublin, Düsseldorf, Frankfurt, Glasgow, Gothenburg, Hanover, Hamburg, Helsinki, Leeds-Bradford, Lille, Lisbon, London, Liverpool, Lyon, Madrid, Manchester, Milan, Marseille, Munich, Naples, Newcastle, Nottingham, Nantes, Porto, Oslo, Paris, Palermo, Rome, Rotterdam, Thessaloniki, Stockholm, Stuttgart, Seville, Turin, Toulouse, Valencia, Vienna.

21 Eurostat.

22 British Airways, Lufthansa, Air France, KLM, and Alitalia are among the top 15 airlines counting for 85% of the traffic.

23 The first fifteen airlines are: Ryanair, Easyjet, Vueling, Lufthansa, Germanwings, Norwegian, SAS, Air Berlin, British Airways, Air France, TAP, Alitalia, Aer Lingus, Iberia and KLM. The five fictive airlines are defined as: StarAlliance which gathers Brussels Airlines, Aegean Airlines, Austrian airlines mainly; Skyteam which gathers Transavia, Garuda, Air Europa, Hop and Czech Airlines; Oneworld which gathers Finnair, Niki; Main_others which gathers all classic airlines; and LCC which gathers all the other low-cost airlines.

24 We assume that the prediction is right when the true number of competitors is either equal to the integer part of our mean predicted number or to the next integer.

References

Aguirregabiria, V., and Mira, P. (2010), 'Dynamic discrete choice structural models: A survey', *Journal of Econometrics*, 156(1), 38–67.

Aguirregabiria, V., and Ho, C. Y. (2010), 'A dynamic game of airline network competition: Hub-and-spoke networks and entry deterrence', *International Journal of Industrial Organization*, 28(4), 377–382.

Aguirregabiria, V., and Ho, C. Y. (2012), 'A dynamic oligopoly game of the US airline industry: Estimation and policy experiments', *Journal of Econometrics*, 168, 156–173.

Andrews, D. W. K., and Soares, G. (2010), 'Inference for parameters defined by moment inequalities using generalized moment selection', *Econometrica*, 78, 119–157.

Andrews, D.W.K., and Shi, X. (2013), 'Inference based on conditional moment inequalities', *Econometrica*, 81, 609–666.

Bajari, P., Benkard, C. L., and Levin, J. (2007), 'Estimating dynamic models of imperfect competition', *Econometrica*, 75, 1331–1370.

Bajari, P., Hong, H., and Ryan, S. (2010), 'Identification and estimation of discrete games of complete information', *Econometrica*, 78, 1529–1568.

Bajari, P, Hong, H. and Nekipelov, D. (2013), 'Game Theory and econometrics: A survey of some recent research', In D. Acemoglu, M. Arellano, & E. Dekel (Eds.), *Advances in Economics and Econometrics: Tenth World Congress (Econometric Society Monographs)*, 3–52.

Benkard, C. L., Bodoh-Creed, A., and Lazarev, J. (2018), 'Simulating the dynamic effects of horizontal mergers: Us airlines', Working Paper, Stanford University.

Beresteanu, A., Molchanov, I., and Molinari, F. (2011), 'Sharp identification regions in models with convex moment predictions', *Econometrica*, 79, 1785–1821.

Berry, S. (1992), 'Estimation of a model of entry in the airline industry', *Econometrica*, 60, 889–917.

Berry, S. and P. Jia (2010). 'Tracing the woes: An empirical analysis of the airline industry', *American Economic Journal: Microeconomics*, **2**(3): 1–43.

Berry, S.,and Reiss, P. (2007), 'Empirical Models of entry and market structure'. In M. Armstrong and R. Porter (Eds.), *Handbook of Industrial Organization*, Amsterdam: Elsevier, Volume 3.

Berry, S., and Tamer, E. (2007), 'Identification in models of oligopoly entry' In R. Blundell, W.K. Newey, and T. Persson (Eds.), *Advances in Economics and Econometrics: Theory and Applications, Ninth World Congress*. Cambridge: Cambridge University Press, Volume 2.

Bjorn, P., and Vuong, Q. (1984), 'Simultaneous equations models for dummy endogenous variables: A game theoretic formulation with an application to labor force participation', Working Paper, California Institute of Technology.

Blevins, J. R. (2015), 'Structural estimation of sequential games of complete information', Economic Inquiry, 53, 791–811.

Blundell, R., and Powell, J.L. (2003), 'Endogeneity in nonparametric and semiparametric regression models'. In M. Dewatripont, L. P. Hansen, and S. J. Turnovsky (Eds.), *Advances in Economics and Econometrics*, Eighth World Congress, Cambridge: Cambridge University Press, Volume 2.

Boguslaski, C., Ito, H., and Lee, D. (2004), 'Entry patterns in the Southwest Airlines route system', *Review of Industrial Organisation*, 25, 317–350.

Bontemps, C., and Magnac, T. (2017), 'Set identification, moment restrictions and inference', *Annual Review of Economics*, 9(103), 1–79.

Bontemps, C., and Kumar, R. (2020), 'A geometric approach to inference in set-identified entry games', *Journal of Econometrics*, 218, 373–389.

Bresnahan, T. and P. Reiss (1991a), 'Entry and competition in concentrated markets', *Journal of Political Economy*, 99, 977–1009.

Bresnahan, T.F., and Reiss, P. (1991b), 'Empirical models of discrete games', *J. Econometrics*, 48, 57–81.

Ciliberto, F., and Tamer, E. (2009), 'Market structure and multiple equilibria in airline markets', *Econometrica*, **77**, 1791–1828.

Ciliberto, F., Murry, C., and Tamer, E. (2018) "Market Structure and Competition in Airline Markets", working paper.

Chernozhukov, V., Hong, H. and Tamer, E. (2007), 'Inference on parameter sets in econometric models', *Econometrica*, 75, 1243–1284.

Cleeren, K., Verboven, F., Dekimpe, M.G., and Gielens, K. (2010), 'Intra-and interformat competition among discounters and supermarkets', *Marketing science*, 29, 456–473.

de Oliveira, A.V.M. (2008), 'An empirical model of low-cost carrier entry', *Transportation Research Part A Policy and Practice*, 42, 673–695.

de Paula, A. (2013), 'Econometric analysis of games with multiple equilibria', *Annual Review of Economics*, 5, 107–131.

Dunn, A. (2008), 'Do low-quality products affect high-quality entry? Multiproduct firms and nonstop entry in airline markets', *International Journal of Industrial Organization*, 26(5), 1074–1089.

Einav, L. (2010), 'Not all rivals look alike: Estimating an equilibrium model of the release date timing game', *Economic Inquiry*, 48(2), 369–390.

Gillen, D., Hasheminia, H., and Jiang, C. (2015), 'Strategic considerations behind the network– regional airline tie ups – a theoretical and empirical study', *Transportation Research B: Methodological*, 72, 93–111.

Goolsbee, A., and Syverson, C. (2008) "How Do Incumbents Respond to the Threat of Entry? Evidence from the Major Airlines", *The Quarterly Journal of Economics*, 123, (4), 1611–1633.

Gourieroux, C., and Monfort, A. (1996), *Simulation Based Econometric Methods*, Louvain, CORE Lectures Series, Oxford: Oxford University Press.

Grieco, P.L.E. (2014), 'Discrete games with flexible information structures: An application to local grocery markets', *RAND Journal of Economics*, 45, 303–340.

Heckman, J. J. (1978), 'Dummy endogenous variables in a simultaneous equation system', *Econometrica*, 46, 931–959.

Jia, P. (2008), 'What happens when Wal-Mart comes to town: An empirical analysis of the discount retailing industry', *Econometrica*, 76(6), 1263–1316.

Manski, C. (1995), *Identification Problems in the Social Sciences*, Cambridge, MA: Harvard University Press.

Mazzeo, M.J. (2002), 'Product choice and oligopoly market structure', *Rand Journal of Economics*, 33(2), 221–242.

Pesendorfer, M., and Schmidt-Dengler, P. (2008), 'Asymptotic least squares estimators for dynamic games', *The Review of Economic Studies*, 75(3), 901–928.

Reiss, P. (1996), 'Empirical models of discrete strategic choices', *American Economic Review*, 86, 421–426.

Sampaio, R.M.B. (2011), 'Competition between low-cost carriers and traditional airlines: an empirical entry model', Working Paper, Toulouse School of Economics.

Seim, K. (2006), 'An empirical model of firm entry with endogenous product-type choices', *Rand Journal of Economics*, 37, 619–640.

Sutton, J. (1991), *Sunk Costs and Market Structure: Price Competition, Advertising, and the Evolution of Concentration*, Cambridge, MA: MIT Press.

Tamer, E. (2003), 'Incomplete simultaneous discrete response model with multiple equilibria', *Review of Economic Studies*, 70(1), 147–165.

Tamer, E. (2010), 'Partial identification in econometrics', *Annual Review of Economics*, 2, 167–195.

13 Applying game theory to analyse aviation markets and their impact on regional development with a case study of the EU-Israel aviation agreement

Nicole Adler

Introduction

This chapter presents a game-theoretic framework that models airline behaviour in regulated and liberalised markets. The methodology is first tested under an existing regulatory framework, known as the baseline scenario, which attempts to estimate current transport equilibria outcomes. After this form of validation of the modelling approach, comparative statics are undertaken in order to understand the likely response to changes in a market and in a second-stage analysis, the potential impact of changes on the local economy. Such a framework could analyse the market from either the producer or regulatory perspectives. For airlines, this methodology could help determine preferable routes, levels of frequency, and design airfares whilst accounting for competitors' potential responses. For regulators, this methodology could help determine appropriate subsidies for public service obligation routes and the impact of airport slot allocation systems on downstream competition. In other words, this style of analysis is relevant to setting decisions a-priori, which provides advantages over the classic econometric approach.

Much research has been undertaken in understanding aviation markets since the early 1990s. In the beginning, the aim of the research was to understand airline networks and their impact on competition within the aviation markets. Subsequently, the modelling approaches were extended to consider competition with alternative modes, for the most part, high-speed rail. In order to consider competition, it was necessary to also shed light on passenger behaviour. Subsequently, market design has been considered in relation to both public service obligations and slot allocations. The literature search refers to each of these topics in turn.

Modelling producer decisions

In the beginning, airline competition and network strategies were generally treated as separate subjects in the literature. Ghobrial and Kanafani (1985) sought to identify equilibrium in an airline network, however they restricted the case to single hub networks. Subsequently, Hansen (1990) developed a non-cooperative game in which the airline's sole strategy set is frequency of service, assuming fixed airfares, adequate capacity, and inelastic demand. Using regression analysis, Hansen could not prove the existence of an equilibrium, and his application to the US air-transportation industry showed quasi-equilibrium. These ideas were extended in Dobson and Lederer (1993) to study the competitive choice of flight schedules and route prices by airlines operating in a single hub system. Utilising a sub-game perfect Nash equilibrium for a two-stage game, they found equilibria in a five-node network. Assumptions in their model include a single aircraft size, one class of customers, and that duopolists serve the identical set of spoke cities using the same hub.

Adler (2001) evaluates airline profits based on profit maximisation under deregulation and its connection to hub-and-spoke networks. Through a two-stage Nash best-response game, equilibria in the air-transportation industry are identified. The game is applied to an illustrative example, where profitable hubs are clearly recognisable and monopolistic and duopolistic equilibria are found, the latter requiring sufficient demand. Subsequently, Adler (2005) analyses Western European markets by developing a model framework to identify the most profitable hub-spoke networks, with the aim of classifying airports most likely to remain major hubs following liberalisation. This model differentiates between consumer types and includes multiple transport operator types, which demonstrates the applicability of game theory to applied research. Schipper et al. (2007) model airline competition following a spatial, Salop, oligopolistic approach in which airlines first set frequencies and then airfares, in line with the timing of such decisions. The model is applied to the Amsterdam-Maastricht corridor. The authors find asymmetric sub-game perfect equilibria outcomes due to either a differing cost structure between the two airlines and/or varying consumer loyalties towards a specific airline. The equilibrium outcome suggests that both low-cost carriers and network incumbent airlines could serve the corridor, which is in the interest of consumer welfare too.

Wei and Hansen (2007) investigate aircraft size and frequency decisions within a competitive environment. The game-theoretic models are solved numerically using empirically derived cost and market share functions, which are calibrated based on airline data. Vaze and Barnhart (2012) model airline frequency competition in order to shed light on congestion issues and slot constraints at major hubs. Airlines maximise profits by setting frequencies assuming average fares and deterministic demand. The authors show that the model predictions match frequencies reasonably well after analysing LaGuardia airport in New York. In an extension of the game to a two-stage frequency and price analysis considering 11 airports and four airlines covering the Western United States, Vaze and Harder (2012) argue that such a behavioural model could be utilised as a planning, forecasting, and policy decision support tool.

Modelling demand

Marianov et al. (1999) discuss the re-location of hubs in a competitive environment given changes in the origin-destination demand matrix over time. The model includes one or two hubs and allows an airline to capture customers if providing a shorter distance or time from the origin to the destination. However, the model is entirely cost-based and does not consider pricing policies, thus an airline with a shorter flight distance from airport i to airport j could theoretically charge a substantially higher price and still capture the entire relevant market. Furthermore the issue of frequency and quality of service is not considered. In Adler (2001), the modelling approach was extended to include a market share model, which permits the game formulation to consider passenger choice indirectly. Passenger utility is defined as a function of frequency, willingness-to-pay for a direct flight, and airfare. The utility of a traveller flying via a hub is based on the minimum frequency along one of the legs of the route, since this will cause the most important restriction on choice (Hansen, 1990). The utility function also ensures that passengers required to travel via one or two hubs will pay less than those travelling directly. Whilst this clearly does not include all possible factors affecting a passenger's decision to travel, it does ensure tractability of the formulation. The maximum, potential, origin-destination, passenger demand is assumed to be known and the airline strategy therefore affects the number of passengers carried rather than the total volume of demand. It is therefore important to also include a no-fly option or alternative ground mode in order to calibrate the model. Sensitivity analysis ought to be applied in order to understand the effects of an increase or decrease in maximal demand. The game formulation utilises multinomial logit to describe passengers' utilities, permitting the computation of the market share of multiple airlines (Ben-Akiva and Lerman, 1985). Alamdari and Black (1992) argue that there is strong evidence to show the broad validity of the logit share model in analysing market share in the air-transportation market.

Adler and Smilowitz (2007) develop a two-stage location-allocation game with a multinomial logit market share function in order to analyse airline competition with the potential for the creation of alliances or mergers. In the first stage, airlines choose their partner(s) and hub locations and in the second stage, the remaining actors in the market participate in a Bertrand-Nash pricing game. The airline cost function is defined by the p-hub median problem (O'Kelly, 1987). Adler et al. (2010) develop a framework in order to assess imperfectly substitutable transport networks in the medium to long distance passenger market. A game-theoretic framework analyses competition between high-speed rail and airlines, with the latter including both low-cost and network carriers. A second-stage social welfare function generates an objective analysis of the equilibria outcomes across multiple potential scenarios (Small and Rosen, 1981). The passengers' choice among alternatives is based on the nested discrete choice theory of product differentiation (Anderson et al., 1992). Nested logit ensures that the independence of irrelevant alternatives assumption holds, which may cause issues for the standard multinomial logit analyses. The case study covers 27 European Union countries and models six transport operators whilst highlighting the potential impact of four Trans-European network projects costing in the region of 85 billion euros (in 2010 values). The main conclusion is that a policy with the intention of stimulating the modal shift of passengers from aviation to rail, for example for environmental reasons, would require on-track high-speed rail competition, price regulation and/or substantial carbon taxes.

In Doyme et al. (2019), the authors develop an *n*-player non-cooperative game in order to analyse the domestic, four-airline, Australian market. The authors include a gravity model in order to estimate potential demand and a multinomial logit function in order to estimate market shares. This formulation thus extends the previous work described here by allowing the potential demand to expand or contract as a function of airline choices. By comparing the transport equilibria in 2014 to that predicted by the model, the results suggest that the modelling approach is able to accurately predict frequencies, passenger flows, air fares, and market shares. This would suggest that the modelling approaches have developed substantially over time and could be used to understand and predict market equilibria.

Market design: airport slot resources

The modelling approaches discussed in this chapter could be utilised by regulators in order to understand the impact of their decisions on the resulting transport equilibria outcome. Hong and Harker (1992) were one of the first to develop a two-stage game for a slot allocation mechanism, which they solved for a three node example. Bhaumik (2002) used non-cooperative game-theoretic model to study how a regulator could ensure a reasonable equilibrium outcome by setting airfares, licence fees, or essential air service requirements.

Adler et al. (2014) develop a multi-modal, differentiated Bertrand, network game to analyse the impact of slot allocation and open skies policies on future transport equilibria in the Far East. The underlying analysis is based on a counter-factual approach in which the existing equilibria outcome is reproduced and potential changes are examined through what-if analysis. The framework involves a number of regulators that set the rules of the market thus creating scenarios and a set of transport operators maximising profit best-response functions in a single-stage game. Multiple passenger types are modelled indirectly via a market share model based on a nested logit function (Hensher et al., 2005). General conclusions including liberalisation policies benefit both consumers and producers albeit to varying degrees. Much of the welfare gains are derived from higher frequency after liberalisation which increases service quality hence consumer utility. Furthermore, the airport slot allocation system has significant spill-over effects.

In Sheng et al. (2015), potential airport slot auctions are assessed based on a two-stage model. The first stage involves an ascending-bid multi-unit auction and the second stage involves competition in frequencies, airfares and aircraft size over a congested network. Results suggest that the auction-based scheme is only preferable when substantial demand uncertainty exists; consequently auctioning grandfathered slots could improve social welfare but the marginal effect may diminish quickly.

In this chapter, we present a modelling approach to analyse competitive airline markets across a network based on the ideas developed in the papers just described. We describe the case of Israel, which was debating whether to sign a liberalised agreement with the European Union (EU) almost a decade ago. Under the Euro-Mediterranean aviation agreement ratified in the summer of 2013, all EU and Israeli airlines would be free to operate direct flights between any airport in the EU and Israel after a gradual five-year implementation policy. The analysis undertaken is based on data from 2010 and first re-creates the market equilibrium at that time. Subsequently, the rules are relaxed in order to determine the market outcome had liberalisation been in place in 2010, under multiple assumptions as to the number of local carriers serving the market. Today, we are in a position to compare the current market outcome to the predictions of the model hence show that such a framework indeed emulates the likely outcome. Finally, we discuss the second stage, social welfare estimation that is possible with this style of analysis, which enables us to approximate the likely impact of changes on regional development.

Modelling framework

We model a single-stage game in which airlines compete given their network choices. In a preliminary stage, the regulator sets rules with respect to bi-lateral or multi-lateral liberalisation policies and slot availability. Decisions at this level are considered exogenous to the game defined hence create multiple scenarios to be assessed. The airlines modelled are divided into two types: network carriers, some of which operate within the framework of alliances, and low-cost carriers, all of which compete through a market share model. Two types of passengers choose their preferred option from the schedules and airfares offered by all companies. The multinomial logit model includes the decision variables of the airlines within a utility function whose parameters are dependent on the passenger type. Each company chooses frequencies and prices given its competitors, in order to maximise profits in either the short- or long-term. The game is solved using best-response dynamics (Monderer and Shapley, 1996; Garcia et al., 2000). The algorithm solves the game iteratively such that the model is solved for a specific airline, assuming that all other airlines' decisions remain constant, and the search continues until no player deviates from their choice set over two successive rounds of the game. At this point, the equilibria outcome represents one potential scenario. After that, the game is repeated across multiple policies, and we discuss the results compared to the current market outcome named the baseline scenario. It should be noted that a Nash equilibrium cannot be guaranteed due to the non-linearity of the objective function but is likely based on spatial price equilibria of the sort analysed by Caplin and Nalebuff (1991) and Anderson et al. (1992).

Two types of transport operators are modelled, namely legacy airlines with the largest set of decisions variables and low-cost carriers. Legacy carriers set airfares for all origin-destination pairs, irrespective of whether the flights are direct or not, for both premium and economy class passengers. Passenger trips may be composed of up to three flights, if the origin-destination requires stopping at both hubs, since all legacy carriers are assumed to consist of two-hub networks. The legacy carriers determine frequencies on all legs flown and adjust aircraft seat size per leg, which amounts to $[(N+2)(N-1)]$ decision variables over N nodes. The low-cost carriers have fewer decision variables, $(2N-1)$, including airfares for a single passenger type, frequency per leg, and a single aircraft size based on a single hub, pure star network, but enjoy lower cost parameters. Most low-cost carriers utilise a single aircraft type strategy to reduce maintenance costs and personnel training and do not attempt to distinguish between business and leisure travellers directly. Low-cost carriers use yield management to maximise revenues by changing ticket prices over time, a strategy designed to capture as much of the consumer surplus as possible. Including this strategy in the model would substantially increase complexity, as the number of decision variables would increase greatly, as would the search for an equilibrium outcome in a repeated game. In order to simplify the modelling approach, we assume a single, average airfare but this could be adapted to better account for revenue management by developing a repeated game.

The majority of recent papers utilise discrete choice analysis to evaluate demand for routes, based on an aggregation of individual travellers' preferences. Ben-Akiva and Lerman (1985) define discrete choice analysis as 'the modelling of choice from a set of mutually exclusive and collectively exhaustible alternatives… Briefly, a decision-maker is modelled as selecting the alternative with the highest utility among those available at the time a choice is made.' Hansen (1990) used a market share model based on the logit function, including price, log of frequency and the travellers' preference for a direct service as variables. Hansen argues that the logarithmic form of service frequency is preferable because 'one would expect diminishing returns with respect to the gain in service attractiveness from adding additional flights'. Hong and Harker (1992) utilise a linear combination of flying time, connection delay, price, frequency, aircraft size, and the number of legs in their disutility function based on Morrison and Winston's (1986) study. Dobson and Lederer (1993) assume that a traveller's demand for each route is based on their cost function, which can be split into three elements that are subsequently aggregated linearly; the cost of departing at a time that differs from the customer's most preferred departure time (referred to today as schedule delay), the costs associated with the route duration and the airfare. Alamdari and Black (1992) discuss the use of the logit model in evaluating the influence of liberalisation on passenger demand. They argue that

> simple 'all or nothing' models that assume the cheapest airline is chosen by all the passengers are not suitable for determining airlines' market share. Passenger demand is influenced by a combination of fare and the many attributes that make up the quality of service provided...

In this research we utilise a nested logit model in order to avoid some of the problems encountered with standard logit, namely the problem of the independence of irrelevant alternatives (Hensher et al., 2005), as discussed in the introduction.

In this section, we present the airline carrier's best-response function, including the revenue and cost functions, market share model as well as the second-stage social welfare computation.

Notation

$a \in A$	index of airline a belonging to A set
$i,j,y,z \in N$	indices of n nodes belonging to N set
R_{ija}	set of legs connecting route (i,j) served by airline a
$k \in Arc(a)$	set of legs served by airline a
$s \in \{b,\ell\}$	type of passenger where b = business and l = leisure class
m	mode of transport, namely air or no-travel alternative
U_{ijsa}	deterministic utility of traveller type s taking path (i,j) with operator a
β_{us}	weights in logit model setting importance of parameters, $u = \{0,1,2,3\}$ per passenger type s
d_{ijs}	maximum potential demand from i to j for traveller type s
C_{ka}	cost function per leg k for airline a
c_{la}	cost parameters

Decision variables

f_{ka}	frequency of flights on leg k via operator a
p_{ijsa}	airfare to travel from i to j via operator a per traveller type s
S_{ka}	number of seats on aircraft/train per leg k for operator a

Auxiliary variables

M_{ijsa}	market share of demand between (i,j) for traveller type s with operator a
D_{ka}	sum of passengers carried on leg k for airline a
F_{ija}	passenger reduction factor for airline a on route (i,j) if there are insufficient seats to serve all demand

$$\underset{f_{ka},p_{ijsa},S_{ka}}{Max} \quad \pi_a = \sum_{\substack{i,j,s \\ i>j}} F_{ija}d_{ijs}M_{ijsa}p_{ijsa} - \sum_{k'\in R_{ija}} (\gamma_1 S_{k'a} + \gamma_2)f_{k'a}$$

$where\ \forall i,j \in N, i>j, \forall s, \forall a \in A, \forall k \in Arc(a)$

$$M_{ijsa} = \left(1 + \chi_{ijsa}\left(\sum_{a'\in l(m)} e^{U_{ijsa'}}\right)^{-\mu}\right)^{-1} [1 + \psi_{ijsa}e^{-U_{ijsa}}]^{-1}$$

$$U_{ijsa} = \beta_0 - \beta_1 TTT_{ija} - \beta_2 p_{ijsa} + \beta_3 \ln\left(\min_{k'\in R_{ija}} f_{k'a}\right)$$

$$\chi_{ijsa} = \sum_{\substack{m'\neq m \\ a\in l(m)}} \left(\sum_{a'\in l(m')} e^{U_{ijsa'}}\right)^{\mu}, \quad \psi_{ijsa} = \left(\sum_{a'\in l(m)\setminus\{a\}} e^{U_{ijsa'}}\right) \qquad (13.1)$$

$$D_{k'a} = \sum_{\substack{y,z,s\,|y>z \\ k'\in R_{yza}}} d_{yzs}M_{yzs'a}$$

$$F_{ija} = \left[1 + \sum_{k'\in R_{ija}} \left(\frac{f_{k'a}S_{k'a}}{D_{k'a}}\right)^{\tau}\right]^{\frac{1}{\tau}}$$

$C_k = c_{1a}(c_{2a} + GCD_k)(c_{3a} + S_{ka})f_{ka}$

$thus \quad \gamma_1 = c_{1a}GCD_k + c_{1a}c_{2a} \quad and \quad \gamma_2 = (c_{1a}c_{3a}GCD_k + c_{1a}c_{2a}c_{3a})$

$where\ C_{ka} = c_{1a}(c_{2a} + GCD_k)(c_{3a} + S_{ka})f_{ka}$

$hence\ \gamma_1 = c_{1a}GCD_k + c_{1a}c_{2a}\ and\ \gamma_2 = (c_{1a}c_{3a}GCD_k + c_{1a}c_{2a}c_{3a})$

The airlines maximise their contribution to fixed costs and profits using an objective function which consists of revenues less costs as shown in model (13.1). The revenues depend on market share, demand, fares, and a reduction factor. The market share model permits passengers to participate in the game by choosing between the available alternatives or not travelling at all. The passengers choose an alternative based on the total trip time (TTT), the total price (p_{ijsa}) and the log of frequency (f_{ka}), which acts as a proxy for level of service (Hansen, 1990; Pels et al., 2000). Specifically, passengers choose the alternative that yields the highest utility. U_{ijsa} defines the systematic utility of passenger type s travelling with operator a from origin i to destination j. The utility function includes a constant value (β_0), which represents the value of home bias or carrier preference, trip time, cost of travelling, and frequency. Since the trip may be indirect, only the leg with the lowest frequency is considered because this represents the bottleneck in the total trip time which is the Tel Aviv to hub leg in more than 75% of the itineraries analysed in the dataset described in the case study below. Utilising nested multinomial logit, the alternatives have been split into two nests, one air nest consisting of all hub-spokes and low-cost alternatives and the second nest including the no-travel/road alternatives. The revenue estimation in the best-response objective function multiplies potential demand with market share, airfare, and also a reduction factor (F_{ija}). The model could either include a set of constraints preventing airlines from selling more seats than produced or reduce demand in the objective function through a reduction factor should this occur. The advantage of the reduction factor is that the objective function is already non-linear due to the market share model whereas adding a set of non-linear constraints would complicate the solution algorithm further. An approximation of the minimisation function is applied in order to solve the continuous objective function (Adler, 2005).

The airline cost functions are dependent on great circle distance and the number of seats on an aircraft, which are the two main factors affecting aircraft trip costs (Swan and Adler, 2006). Two equations were used, one for the medium haul markets (i.e. less than 5,000 kilometres) using narrow-bodied aircraft and one for the long haul markets (more than 5,000 kilometres) using wide-bodied, two aisle aircraft. In addition, we calibrate the differing airline cost parameters as a function of their base location using ICAO data presented in Table 13.1.

Linear constraints are included in the mathematical program as follows. A passenger travelling on a low-cost carrier via their hub will need to purchase two tickets and it is assumed that this will simply be the sum of the two tariffs as specified in Equation (13.2).

$$p_{ijsa} = p_{ihsa} + p_{hjsa} \quad for \; \{i, j\} \notin Arc(a) \tag{13.2}$$

Additional constraints limit the aircraft size to lie between 150 and 401 seats because the cost parameters were calibrated based on Airbus and Boeing jets whereas regional jets may have very different values.

Table 13.1 Carriers analysed

Carrier	Hubs	Available seat-km	CASK
El Al	TLV	22,688,115	0.082
One World	LHR	139,346,722	0.090
	MAD		
Skyteam	CDG	152,267,757	0.108
	AMS		
Star Alliance	FRA	163,154,890	0.103
	GVA		
American Airlines	JFK	197,068,518	0.095
Royal Jordanian	AMM	31,426,776	0.056
Transaero	DME	11,169,590	0.084
easyJet	LTN	57,464,750	0.069
Air Berlin	TXL	54,920,588	0.089
Arkia	TLV		

The second-stage social welfare computation enables us to compare the results across the different scenarios and estimate the impact of aviation on regional development. Much of the literature on transportation systems concerns the maximisation of overall social welfare, which in a game-theoretic analysis covers the aggregate surplus of all players, covering consumers (passengers) and producers (airlines and airports) and potentially governments (taxes, subsidies, and environmental externalities) and additional industries (for example tourism). Consumer surplus is often a more complicated concept to estimate as it measures the difference in the value of the product or service to the individual and the generalised costs. In a linear demand function, consumer surplus is the area above the equilibrium price and below the demand curve. Small and Rosen (1981) provide a detailed methodology for estimating social welfare within a discrete choice demand model. De Jong et al. (2007) survey the logsum estimation, the log of the denominator of the multinomial logit function which we apply here. The welfare function in Equation (13.3) is thus defined as the total consumer surplus (maximum expected utility defined in monetary terms) and producer surplus (total profits from all operators). Additional variables that could be included would account for government surplus, which may also consider the environmental impacts of such changes.

$$W = \sum_i \sum_j \sum_s \left(d_{ij} \frac{1}{\mu_s} \ln \sum_m \frac{1}{\beta_{2a}} e^{\left(\mu_s \sum_{a' \in N_m} U_{ijsa'} \right)} \right) + \sum_a \pi_a \qquad (15.3)$$

Modelling the Israeli market

In order to understand the impact of open skies on airlines, passengers, and regional development, we develop a game in which ten carriers choose their schedules and prices to maximise profits given market demand and choice of network. We analyse a representative week in 2010 under the liberalisation levels that existed during this period. Accordingly, we limit the flight frequencies based on the bi-lateral agreements in place at the time and define this week as the base scenario. It should be noted that the analysis uses a conservative approach in the sense that we limit the maximum potential demand to those served in the baseline scenario, while it could be assumed that this number will increase as a result of population growth and per capita GDP growth. All scenarios, including the baseline scenario, are analysed with reference to overall demand across 29 geographical regions, of which 22 are located in Europe and the Middle East, and seven outside Europe. They were carefully selected to best represent most of the relevant demand. We model the largest airlines that carried over 80% of the demand, including ten of the 60 regular companies that operated during that period. The aim is to minimise the number of operators in order to solve the game in reasonable time but to capture the main actors in order to draw useful policy insights.

The operator types consist of two-hub legacy carriers with one regional and one international gateway and low-cost carriers with a pure star network. Of the seven legacy carriers modelled, one is based in Israel, three represent the major alliances with international gateways in Europe, and three serve direct links to the United States, Russia, and Jordan. It is assumed that only hub-spoke legacy carriers fly outside the continent and the international gateways connect Israel to seven zones representing the rest of the world (the Middle East (Amman), Africa (Johannesburg), the Far East (Bangkok), Asia (Mumbai), South America (São Paulo) and North America (New York)). The model distinguishes between the business models in terms of decision variables: legacy carriers determine airfares per origin-destination, separating premium from economy class passengers. Low-cost carriers set airfares per leg hence passengers choosing to fly indirectly will purchase two tickets, one for each flight segment. In addition, low costs do not distinguish between premium and economy class passengers. By studying a specific market, the Israeli carriers choose their frequencies on all destinations whereas the remaining carriers only set frequencies on the Tel Aviv-hub routes. Consequently, all other frequencies were pre-set according to the relevant airline schedule in 2010 because Israeli demand is very small relatively. The ten airlines in the model are described in Table 13.1.

The cost of the flight was calculated in the model depending on the great circle distance and the number of seats on the aircraft, which are the most influential factors in flight costs. EasyJet and TransAero achieve the lowest costs in the group and Skyteam the highest, which is a function of average stage length, service levels, and managerial ability.

The parameters of the passengers' utility function was estimated from MIDT data purchased from InterVISTAS. Table 13.2 presents raw data for three markets in order to show passenger preferences in 2010 (composed of the months of August and February). From the analysis of this table, travellers prefer to fly directly, which is particularly pronounced on business oriented routes such as London (~ 94%). New York has a relatively high percentage of direct passengers (~85%) since there are three carriers competing directly. Even for travellers to Bangkok, two-thirds of the passenger market choose to fly directly. The EU sets competition levels in short-distance city pairs only on the basis of direct frequencies, while in international routes it also considers indirect paths up to a certain level (Steer Davies Gleave (2007)).

In analysing the level of competition for destinations that do not have direct lines, we noticed greater competition. For example, in the analysis of the indirect market between Israel and Chicago, we see that 17 airlines flew passengers on a non-direct route. The largest market share was El Al (20%), although Continental (16%) and Delta (11%) are not far behind. El Al's advantage in its home market can also be seen in financial terms, as it charges the highest fares among all airlines. According to the raw data analysis, about 40% of the passengers preferred transit hubs in Europe, and the rest flew via a transit hub in North America, probably because of the higher frequencies to Chicago

Table 13.2 Summary data of three Israeli markets

	Hub	Frequency from TLV (month)	Frequency beyond (month)	Economy class (#)	Premium class (#)	Economy fare ($)	Business fare ($)	Market share
TLV–London								
El Al		72	–	38,392	2,913	294	1,096	61%
British Airways		59	–	20,249	2,094	290	1,131	33%
Alitalia	Rome	75	144	702	2	117	840	1%
Turkish Airlines	Istanbul	105	104	480	1	170	525	1%
Air Baltic	Riga	22	39	397	314	174	161	1%
Lufthansa	Frankfurt	59	330	333	16	275	1,028	1%
Swiss	Zurich	60	177	330	54	227	647	1%
TLV–New York								
El Al		79		42,563	3,655	743	3,482	57%
Continental		59		11,129	850	612	1,854	15%
Delta		30		10,096	41.5	594	2,903	13%
Turkish Airlines	Istanbul	105	37	2,983	10	333	1,557	4%
Swiss	Zurich	59	71	1,764	72	656	1,400	2%
Alitalia	Rome	75	70	1,594		306	–	2%
Aerosvit	Kiev	41	19	1,227	65	345		2%
Austrian	Vienna	59	28	989	90	425	1,244	1%
British Airways	Heathrow	59	247	982	25	448	2,233	1%
TLV–Bangkok								
El Al		30		11,805	147	719	2,116	63%
Uzbekistan Airlines	Tashkent	14	16	2,678	29	455		14%
Royal Jordanian	Amman	59	30	2,615	97	438	1,122	14%
Aerosvit	Kiev	41	19	843	223	335		6%
Turkish Airlines	Istanbul	105	30	452	18	517	2,430	2%

from within North America. We also note that Israeli passengers are more willing to pay for flights on El Al as a result of the company's security concept, the crew speaking the local language and the frequent flyer program. The logit regression results were used to calibrate the demand function in the model. For example, the analysis suggested that El Al could charge an additional $145 per direction for an average economy class ticket and maintain an equal market share to that of the foreign companies as presented in Table 13.3.

By applying these parameters to the frequencies and airfares in Table 13.2, we were able to reasonably accurately predict the airline market shares as shown in Table 13.4. Having calibrated the parameters of the underlying model, we next present the results of the analysis.

Table 13.3 Logistic regressions for peak and off-peak seasons in 2010

		August 2010		February 2010	
		Estimate	*Std. Dev.*	*Estimate*	*Std. Dev.*
Airfare one way ($)					
	Premium	−0.001		−0.0009	
	Economy	−0.0027		−0.0022	
Log (min freq)					
	Premium	0.5753	0.0293	0.6635	0.0158
	Economy	0.6118	0.0017	0.8477	0.003
Total trip time (hours)					
	Premium	−0.323	0.0012	−0.3385	0.0055
	Economy	−0.4725	0.0018	−0.4689	0.0024
Home Bias (El Al)		0.4429	0.0015	0.5305	0.0024
Constant		1.7959	0.0075	1.7495	0.0103
Adjusted R²		0.43		0.43	

Table 13.4 Predicting market shares in the Tel Aviv–London and New York routes

	Trip time (hours)	*Frequencies (week)*	*Airfares ($)*	*Market share estimates*	*Real market share (from Table 13.2)*
Tel Aviv–London					
El Al	5	17	294	63.9%	61%
British Airways	5	14	290	29.4%	33%
Alitalia	9	**12**	117	0.03%	1%
Lufthansa	9	**14**	275	0.02%	1%
Air Baltic	9	5	174	0.01%	1%
Tel Aviv–New York					
El Al	12	18	743	**57%**	57%
Continental	12	14	612	**18%**	15%
Delta	12	7	594	**12%**	13%
Turkish Airlines	15	9	333	**4%**	4%
Alitalia	16	**16**	**306**	**4%**	2%

Results of scenario analysis

In this section, we discuss the results of multiple scenarios. The first scenario analyses fifth freedoms between Israel and Europe and the second scenario simulates open skies globally. The agreement between the State of Israel and 31 European countries belonging to the EU Open Sky Initiative grants the freedoms gradually over five years by weakening restrictions on frequencies and harmonising the aviation laws of Israel with those of the EU. The results of the scenarios show that market share elasticities relative to frequency and price correspond to expectations according to the academic literature. For example, economy class price elasticities are over 1 and those of business class below 1, consistent with the literature. Business class frequency elasticity is higher (about 0.4) than that of economy class (about 0.3). Furthermore, for the base scenario, the decision variables in the model, including the frequencies, prices and market share for the Israeli carriers, approximately match the results in 2010. Perhaps interestingly, when using the average CASK, the model was not able to emulate the market equilibria outcome. After many discussions with airline management, we realised that the Schedule Department considered only variable CASK estimates and once the costs were adjusted accordingly, the results of the modelling approach indeed estimated the existing frequencies. As a result, we believe that airlines maximise short-term rather than long-term profits.

According to the EU open skies results presented in Table 13.5 column (i), alliances and low-cost carriers increase their frequencies significantly. The alliances raise premium airfares and lower economy class fares, which represent 95% of passengers according to the MIDT data. The overall result is a significant increase in market share from 10% to 20%. As a result, non-European foreign airlines that cannot increase their frequencies due to bi-lateral restrictions are forced to lower the price of premium and economy tickets in order to minimise the loss in market share. The profit of the Israeli airline is up 66% under the assumption that the company is making decisions based on long-term profit maximisation. Small increases in international leisure fares increase revenues, but ticket prices in the premium class need to be reduced in order to handle the indirect routes of European carriers that have improved their schedules by increasing frequencies, which is important for premium passengers. The Israeli airline's market share drops to approximately 10%, due to a decrease in the frequency of regional flights. Demand in the international markets remained almost constant because the frequencies were maintained. It is possible that increasing frequencies offered by the European carriers and the fall in airfares leads to an increase in demand such that Israeli airlines will not reduce the number of passengers carried overall.

In the two Israeli carrier scenario presented in Table 13.5 column (v), we include an Israeli low-cost carrier and find that the profits of the existing Israeli airline market declines slightly. Israel's low-cost carrier offers the lowest prices and attracts 2% of the market by stealing demand from all companies except Star Alliance. Of course, this is a very conservative analysis because it is likely

Table 13.5 Social welfare surplus compared to base scenario

Changes compared to 2010 equilibria in '000$	Without local carriers		Single local carrier		Two local carriers		One Israeli fixed carrier
	EU open skies (i)	global OS (ii)	EU open skies (iii)	global OS (iv)	EU open skies (v)	global OS (vi)	EU open skies (vii)
Consumer surplus:	359,893	378,677	332,806	347,760	366,098	382,256	207,581
Israeli premium	14,604	15,190	15,078	15,043	15,388	15,110	9,740
Israeli economy	235,685	247,999	216,881	226,904	239,214	250,658	136,680
Foreign premium	4,162	4,337	4,314	4,301	4,410	4,318	2,664
Foreign economy	105,443	111,150	96,533	101,512	107,085	112,169	58,498
Producer Surplus:							
Israeli network carrier	−108,669	−108,669	72,768	63,681	61,261	47,831	−249,269
Israeli low-cost					15,444	11,232	
Social Welfare	251,224	270,008	405,574	411,441	442,803	441,319	−41,688

that the market will grow due to the increased frequency and lower fares. The leisure airfares are lower in this scenario consequently the number of passengers increases with fewer choosing the no-fly alternative. Overall, two Israeli airlines achieve a higher level of profitability than one company.

In the scenario of global open skies (columns (ii), (iv), and (vi)), we see that consumer surplus increases by a further 5%. However, the increased competition imposes a toll on the Israeli carriers, leading to slightly lower profits. In the scenario with no Israeli carriers (columns (i) and (ii)), the European low-cost carriers increase their market share significantly from 5% to about 20%. The remaining airlines raise business airfares and lower the price of economy class tickets compared to 2010, but to a lesser extent than in the scenario in which there are two Israeli companies. From this we understand that both in terms of the industry and for consumers, it is preferable to have a local industry. However, even without an Israeli carrier, the consumer surplus grows by around 60% relative to the situation in 2010.

In conclusion, it is worth noting that the market share of the low-cost carriers rises to serve about 30% of the market, at the expense of the three alliances whose market share drops from 64% to 36%. Finally, we limit the Israeli carrier to continue setting frequencies at least at the same level as that of 2010 (column (vii)) by assuming that the carrier does not change its behaviour and continues to maximise short run profits. In this scenario, under open skies with Europe, the Israeli carrier serves most of the passengers and their market share is high. However, the Israeli legacy carrier is making large losses and will not survive in the medium term. Moreover, if more aggressive low-cost carriers were to enter the market, as occurred in Morocco, the losses could potentially be even higher.

Conclusions and social welfare analysis

In a second-stage analysis, we compare the scenarios with reference to consumer and producer surplus and total social welfare for the local market on an annual basis, after summing the peak and low seasons (Table 13.6). We assume that during the low season the supply drops by 20% based on the MIDT database. Welfare analysis shows that consumers are directly affected by deregulation and consumer surplus will double under open skies with Europe, with a small addition of a further 5% under global open skies. On the other hand, Israeli carriers will need to react substantively in order to make long-term profits in a more competitive market. Social welfare rises by up to 90% with two local carriers serving the market but only by 57% without local producers. The existence of an Israeli aviation industry contributes both to lower airfares and to increased supply. The low-cost carrier market share is predicted to grow to at least 25% after the opening of the sky and this will be the most important factor in lowering future ticket prices. It should be noted that the counterfactual approach is extremely prudent and therefore likely to underestimate the impact on consumer surplus as demand dependent on frequency may increase

Table 13.6 Estimating local social welfare from Euro-Mediterranean agreement with Israel

In $000's annually	Israeli legacy carrier	Two Israeli carriers
Local consumer surplus		
Premium	15,078	15,388
Leisure	216,881	239,214
Local producer surplus		
Israeli legacy carrier	72,768	61,261
Low-cost carrier		15,444
Local tourism industry		
Lower bound	113,000	113,000
Upper bound	189,000	189,000
Loss of employment in local aviation sector		
	−33,000	−33,000
Overall social welfare		
Lower bound	384,727	411,307
Upper bound	460,727	487,307

significantly. As a result, it is likely that the market share of the Israeli companies will decrease, but the total size of the market will increase.

So far, we have concluded that although Israeli airlines may benefit less from increasing competition, overall welfare reaches its peak when the sky is opened globally and there are two Israeli companies in the market. However, it should be borne in mind that this conclusion ignores the changes in employment, both in aviation and in tourism. In Table 13.6 we refer to changes in employment in Israel which may impact up to 7,000 airline employees locally but offset by any increases in the tourism industry. The streamlining process is never simple, as suggested by the fact that the local legacy carrier was privatised in 2004 yet significant changes in the financial and operational data have yet to be discerned. We estimate that the process will cost about $33 million a year over a ten-year period. An Israeli airline that maximises long-term profits, seeks new destinations and codeshares or allies with foreign carriers, may reduce the loss substantially.

The change in welfare attributed to the tourism industry is based on the following assumptions:

(i)   the decline in prices indicated by the results of the model reach an order of 20% on average despite the likelihood that the dispersion of prices as a result of price discrimination will increase;

(ii)   the price elasticity of European tourists is unitary (i.e. −1) and the weight of the average airfare in the tourism package is 33% hence we expect a 7% increase in the number of European tourists;

(iii) European tourists accounted for about 60% of all tourist arrivals in 2010, so the expected increase will be 4.2% of total arrivals; and

(iv)   the value added of the tourism industry in 2010 equalled \$4.5 billion (or 2.3% of GDP) hence we expect an increase of up to \$189 million in value added. However, if we consider only the employment share contribution, we need to consider 60% of this added value therefore the lower bound of \$113 million.

The bottom line is that the implementation of the Euro–Mediterranean agreement for the Israeli party was estimated to be worth around \$440 million annually based on a game-theoretic estimation and second-stage welfare computation that also considers impacts on local employment.

Writing this in 2019 allows us the luxury of looking at the data since this work was completed in 2013. The first comment would be that demand has grown from 12.4 million passengers in 2012 prior to deregulation to 22.3 million in 2018 after complete implementation, which represents an annual compound increase of 10%. The airfares have dropped on average by 18%[1] which was the expected outcome according to the results of the model. Furthermore, the market share of El Al has dropped from 33% in 2012 to 25% in 2018 despite carrying 1.6 million more passengers, as was also predicted. El Al has cancelled many destinations and plans to serve six new markets as advertised recently. This is a positive sign and the optimal way to respond to greater competition according to the results of the model although the failure to achieve profitability remains of concern. The low-cost carrier market has grown substantially with the entry of easyJet, Wizz Air, and Ryanair among others. Together with two small Israeli carriers, the low costs are currently serving approximately 20% of the market. The main error of the analysis described here was to ignore Turkish Airlines in the game because today it is the third largest carrier serving 5% of the market (after El Al (25%) and Lufthansa (6%)). Choosing a limited set of representative carriers is difficult and somewhat subjective which needs to consider both the political and the socio-economic processes that impact industries such as aviation. Overall, game theory has proven to be of use in the practical policy sphere, providing decision-makers with the ability to understand the impact of aviation on regional development considering both positive and negative effects simultaneously.

Note

1   https://blogs.timesofisrael.com/open-skies-brings-israel-and-europe-closer-together/ 18 August 2018 and www.economist.com/gulliver/2015/07/08/in-it-for-the-long-haul 8 July 2015.

References

Adler, N. 2001. Competition in a deregulated air transportation market. *European Journal of Operational Research*, 129/2, 337–345.

Adler, N. 2005. The effect of competition on the choice of an optimal network in a liberalized aviation market with an application to Western Europe. *Transportation Science*, 39/1, 58–72.

Adler, N., Fu, X., Oum, T.H., and Yu, C. 2014. Air transport liberalization and airport slot allocation: the case of the Northeast Asian transport market. *Transportation Research Part A: Policy and Practice*, 62, 3–19.

Adler, N., Pels, E., and Nash, C. 2010. High-speed rail and air transport competition: game engineering as tool for cost-benefit analysis. *Transportation Research Part B: Methodological*, 44/7, 812–833.

Adler, N. and Smilowitz, K. 2007. Hub-and-spoke network alliances and mergers: price-location competition in the airline industry. *Transportation Research Part B: Methodological*, 41/4, 394–409.

Alamdari, F.E. and Black, I.G. 1992. Passengers' choice of airline under competition: the use of the logit model. *Transport Reviews*, 12(2), 153–170.

Anderson, S.P., de Palma, A. and Thisse, J.F. 1992. *Discrete Choice Theory of Product Differentiation*, Cambridge, MA: MIT Press.

Bailey E., Graham D., and Kaplan D. 1985. *Deregulating the Airlines*, Cambridge, MA; MIT Press.

Ben-Akiva, M. and Lerman, S.R. 1985. *Discrete Choice Analysis: Theory and Application to Travel Demand*. Cambridge, MA: MIT Press.

Bhaumik, P.K. 2002. Regulating the domestic air travel in India: an umpire's game. Omega, 30(1), 33–44.

Brons, M., Pels, E., Nijkamp, P., and Rietveld, P. 2002. Price elasticities of demand for passenger air travel: a meta-analysis. *Journal of Air Transport Management*, 8/3, 165–175.

Button, K. 2002. Debunking some common myths about airport hubs. *Journal of Air Transport Management*, 8, 177–188.

Caplin, A. and Nalebuff, B. 1991. Aggregation and imperfect competition: on the existence of equilibrium. *Econometrica*, 51, 25–59.

De Jong, G., Daly, A., Pieters, M. and Van der Hoorn, T. 2007. The logsum as an evaluation measure: Review of the literature and new results. Transportation Research Part A: Policy and Practice, 41(9), 874–889.

Dobson, G. and Lederer, P.J. 1993. Airline scheduling and routing in a hub-and-spoke system. *Transportation Science*, 27/3, 281–297.

Doyme, K., Dray, L., O'Sullivan, A., and Schäfer, A., 2019. Simulating airline behaviour: application for the Australian domestic market. *Transportation Research Record*, 2673/2, 104–112.

Garcia, A., Reaume, D. and Smith, R.L. 2000. Fictitious play for finding system optimal routings in dynamic traffic networks. *Transportation Research Part B: Methodological*, 34/2, 147–156.

Ghobrial, A. and Kanafani, A. 1985. Airline hubbing: some implications for airline economics. *Transportation Research Part A: Policy and Practice*, 18/4, 15–27.

Gonzalez-Savignat, M. 2004. Competition in air transport: the case of the high speed train. *Journal of Transport Economics and Policy*, 38/1, 77–108.

Hansen, M. 1990. Airline competition in a hub-dominated environment: an application of non-cooperative game theory. *Transportation Research Part B: Methodological*, 24/1, 27–43.

Hansen, M. and Liu, Y. 2015. Airline competition and market frequency: a comparison of the S-curve and schedule delay models. *Transportation Research Part B: Methodological*, 78, 301–317.

Hendricks, K., Piccione, M., and Tan, G.F. 1999. Equilibria in networks. *Econometrica*, 67/6, 1407–1434.

Hensher, D.A., Rose, J.M. and Greene, W.H. 2005. *Applied Choice Analysis: A Primer*. Cambridge: Cambridge University Press.

Hong, S. and Harker, P.T. 1992. Air traffic network equilibrium: toward frequency, price and slot priority analysis. *Transportation Research Part B: Methodological*, 26/4, 307–323.

Ida, T. and Suda, M. 2004. The cost structure of the Japanese railway industry: the economies of scale and scope and the regional gap of the Japan railway after the privatization. *International Journal of Transport Economics*, 31/1, 23–37.

Li, Z.C., Lam, W.H., Wong, S.C., and Fu, X. 2010. Optimal route allocation in a liberalizing airline market. *Transportation Research Part B: Methodological*, 44/7, 886–902.

Mandel, B., Gaudry, M., and Rothengatter, W. 1997. A disaggregate Box-Cox logit mode choice model of intercity passenger travel in Germany and its implications for high-speed rail demand forecasts. *The Annals of Regional Science*, 31, 99–120.

Marianov, V., Serra, D., and ReVelle, C. 1999. Location of hubs in a competitive environment. *European Journal of Operational Research*, 114, 363–371.

Monderer, D. and Shapley, L.S. 1996. Potential games. *Games and Economic Behavior*, 14/1, 124–143.

Morrison, S. and Winston, C. 1986. *The Economic Effects of Airline Deregulation*. Washington, DC: Brookings Institution.

Nero, G. 1996. A structural model of intra European Union duopoly airline competition. *Journal of Transport Economics and Policy*, 30, 137–155.

O'Kelly, M.E. 1987. A quadratic integer program for the location of interacting hub facilities. European Journal of Operational Research, 32(3), 393–404.

Pels, E., Nijkamp, P., and Rietveld, P. 2000. Airport and airline competition for passengers departing from a large metropolitan area. Journal of Urban Economics, 48(1), 29–45.

Schipper, Y., Nijkamp, P., Rietveld, P. 2007. Deregulation and welfare in airline markets: An analysis of frequency equilibria. *European Journal of Operational Research*, 178, 194–206.

Sheng, D., Li, Z.C., Xiao, Y.B., and Fu, X. 2015. Slot auction in an airport network with demand uncertainty. *Transportation Research Part E: Logistics and Transportation Review*, 82, 79–100.

Small, K.A. and Rosen, H.S. 1981. Applied welfare economics with discrete choice models. Econometrica: Journal of the Econometric Society, 105–130.

Steer Davies, G. 2007. Competition impact of airline code-share agreements. *Report prepared for the European Commission*.

Swan, W. and Adler, N. 2006. Aircraft trip cost parameters: a function of stage length and seat capacity. *Transportation Research Part E: Logistics and Transportation Review*, 42/2, 105–115.

Vaze, V. and Barnhart, C. 2012. Modelling airline frequency competition for airport congestion mitigation. *Transportation Science*, 46/4, 512–535.

Wei, W. and Hansen, M. 2007. Airlines' competition in aircraft size and service frequency in duopoly markets. *Transportation Research Part E: Logistics and Transportation Review*, 43, 409–424.

14 Stochastic frontier analysis

Davide Scotti and Nicola Volta

Introduction

This chapter applies a Stochastic Frontier Analysis (SFA) approach to the European NUTS2 regions. As for Chapter 15, the aim is to measure the relationship between air transport service provision and regional development. The chapter is structured as follows. First, we present a short explanation of SFA methodology and its main assumptions. This is done with introductory and, at the same time, summary purposes and further details can be found in the cited literature. Second, the production process under investigation in this contribution is presented together with the dataset used in the analysis. Third, the specific SFA models adopted in the application and the main results obtained are presented and discussed. Finally, the main findings are summarised in the concluding section.

In Chapter 15 on DEA, we introduce a measure of efficiency consisting of the ability of the DMU to get the maximum amount of output from a given amount of inputs (measure also called output oriented technical efficiency). As explained extensively in Coelli et al. (2005), DEA is a nonparametric approach. Indeed, the technology and the relative frontier are obtained without assuming a specific functional form underlying the input-output relation. Furthermore, DEA is deterministic – i.e., all the deviations from the frontier are assumed to be the result of technical inefficiency. As a consequence, in DEA methodology measurement errors and other sources of statistical noise are basically ignored. A way to tackle this issue is to estimate the frontier parametrically introducing a random component capturing statistical noise. The resulting model is called stochastic production frontier and has been introduced by the seminal contributions of Aigner et al. (1977) and Meeusen and van den Broeck (1977). The model can be specified (with output orientation) as follows (Kumbhakar et al., 2015):

$$\ln y_i = f\left(x_i, \beta\right) + v_i - u_i \tag{14.1}$$

$$\ln y_i^\star = f\left(x_i, \beta\right) + v_i \tag{14.2}$$

where y_i and x_i are respectively the observed output and the input vector of firm i, β is the vector of input coefficients, v_i is a random error and $u_i \geq 0$ is the production inefficiency. $u_i \geq 0$ implies that the observed output y_i is bounded below y_i^* that is the stochastic production frontier function, i.e., the maximum possible level of output. u_i is the log difference between the actual output and the maximum feasible one and gives, when multiplied by 100%, the percentage by which actual output can be increased to achieve full efficiency (Kumbhakar et al., 2015). In other words, $\exp(-u_i)$ is the ratio of actual output to the maximum feasible one. Specific assumptions on the shape of the frontier (i.e., the functional form $f(.)$) and the distribution of the terms u and v are needed to be included prior the estimation.

Figure 14.1 shows the case of production process using a unique input (x) in order to produce the output y. Three observations (A, B, C) are considered in this example. The production function, whose shape has to be assumed a priori, is represented by the black solid curve ($f(x)$). As defined above, the vertical distance (i.e., output orientation) between the observations and the production frontier can be decomposed in random noise (v) and inefficiency (u). It is important to notice that differently from DEA, the observations are (i) not defining the frontier (i.e., no observation is fully efficient lying on the frontier) and (ii) may be positioned outside the feasible technology (i.e., above the frontier).

Concerning the functional form of $f(x_i, \beta)$, the most commonly used algebraic forms in the empirical analysis are the Cobb-Douglas (CD) and the translog. The CD is as follows:

$$y = A \prod_{j=1}^{J} x_j^{\beta_j} \Rightarrow \ln y = \beta_0 + \sum_j \beta_j \ln x_j$$

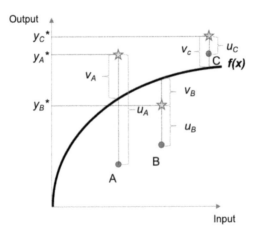

Figure 14.1 The stochastic production frontier model.

where J is the number of inputs. The translog is instead given by

$$\ln y = \beta_0 + \sum_j \beta_j \ln x_j + \frac{1}{2} \sum_j \sum_k \beta_{jk} \ln x_j \ln x_k$$

Among the two forms, translog is usually preferred due to its greater flexibility (it is second-order flexible) even if it has more parameters to estimate (i.e., the estimation process needs a greater number of observations to converge).[1]

Concerning parametric distributional assumptions, the random error component v_i is generally normally distributed with zero mean and σ_v^2 variance. Assumptions on the distribution of the inefficiency component u_i can instead vary between the most common half-normal and other forms such as truncated normal, exponential, and gamma. Both Coelli et al. (2005) and Bogetoft and Otto (2011) explain that the differences between the distributions tend to be not of great empirical relevance, with observations rankings being robust to distributional choices.

Standard SFA models have an important limitation – namely they only allow for the analysis of production processes with a single output. However, such limitation can be easily overcome by estimating a distance function, where the distance corresponds to the measure of performance. From the practical point of view this requires (in case of output distance function) (i) to divide all outputs by one output and use that output as the explanatory variable and (ii) to estimate the resulting equation exactly as a stochastic production frontier (see Bogetoft and Otto, 2011 for further details).

As for the Data Envelopment Analysis, the issue of outlier is worth discussing. Bogetoft and Otto (2011) highlight three major reasons on why a DMU may be an outlier: (i) errors in the data, (ii) high atypicality, and (iii) exceptionally low or high relative performance. The risk connected with outliers is that such firms either do not reflect a real production process or lead to a distortion caused by fitting such extreme observations. More specifically, in the case of SFA, outliers may distort the frontier curvature or affect the magnitude of the idiosyncratic error component and in turns average efficiency estimates.[2] It is therefore important to identify outliers and remove them from the sample before estimating the production frontier (in the following application we adopt the same methodology used in Chapter 15, i.e., data cloud method).

Advanced SFA models allow for the possibility of accounting for the so called 'production environment', i.e., exogenous variables that may exert an influence on the ability of a DMU to transform inputs into outputs. In the case of SFA, it is important to discriminate between non-stochastic observable factors (e.g., government interventions, ownership structure, market concentration, etc.) and unpredictable stochastic factors that are potentially sources of production risk (e.g., natural disasters, weather conditions, pandemics, etc.). In the case of non-stochastic environmental factors (z_i), there are two main adoptable approaches (Coelli et al., 2005): (i) to incorporate them into the deterministic component f of the production frontier as in Equation (14.3) or (ii) to allow them to directly affect the stochastic component u_i of the production frontier (i.e., Equation (14.4)).

$$\ln y_i = f\left(x_i, \beta; z_i, \gamma\right) + v_i - u_i \tag{14.3}$$

$$\begin{cases} \ln y_i = f\left(x_i, \beta\right) + v_i - u_i \\ \quad u_i \sim N(z_i \gamma, \sigma_u^2) \end{cases} \tag{14.4}$$

In the first case (Equation (14.3)), the vector of exogenous factors z_i acts as shifter of the level of production attained by the DMUs. In the second case (Equation (14.4)), the production inefficiencies have distributions that vary according to z_i.[3] In the case of production risk, a common approach is to adopt the conventional model of Equation (14.1), although recognising that the two error components now capture the effects of risk in addition to that of noise and inefficiency.

A further advantage of SFA is that it can easily deal with panel data. This requires the imposition of some structure on the inefficiency term u_{it} (Coelli et al., 2005). More specifically, it is possible to classify the SFA panel models into time-invariant models, where $u_{it} = u_i$, and time-varying models, where $u_{it} = f(t)u_i$. In the first group we mention Pitt and Lee (1981) and Battese and Coelli (1988). In the second one, Kumbhakar (1990), Battese and Coelli (1992), and Kumbhakar and Wang (2005) are among the most applied in the literature. Battese and Coelli (1995) combine the panel dimension with the incorporation of the exogenous factor determining efficiency previously discussed. Another popular approach to deal with panel data is the one developed by Greene (2005a) and (2005b), where firm fixed/random effects are separated from inefficiency.[4]

Finally, a recent branch of the literature claims the importance of separating short-run (transient) from long-run (persistent) efficiency (e.g., Tsionas and Kumbhakar, 2014; Colombi et al., 2014; Filippini and Greene, 2016). Such approach requires generally a four-components error term that can help in evaluating firms whose management has time-invariant and a time-varying component or in separating long-run inefficiency attributable to regulation from managerial inefficiency.

An SFA application to estimate the relationship between air transport and regional development

Production process, dataset, and research hypothesis

The idea of production process proposed in this chapter is in line with what is discussed in Chapter 15. The empirical question is still whether aviation service provision influences gross domestic product (GDP) generation for European NUTS2 regions. In Chapter 15 we discuss the connection between air transport and regional development. As a short summary, we recall that the literature suggests that the level and the quality of infrastructure is a significant determinant of regional economic growth. According to previous contributions, aviation is found to be a determinant of employment growth and population (Green, 2007; Bloningen and Cristea, 2012), agglomeration economies (Glaeser et al., 1992; Rosenthal and Strange, 2001), international trade (Button et al., 2015), and FDI flows (Fageda, 2017). Hence, our aim is to investigate this connection between aviation and regional economic development through a stochastic frontier approach. To the best of our knowledge, this is the first contribution that tries to address the issue applying an SFA analysis.

In order to do so, we make use of the same dataset of the DEA chapter. The analysis is therefore based on a panel of 270 NUTS 2 European regions observed for 11 years (2005–2015 period).

Our regional-level production process generates the single output *gdp* through the usage of (i) capital stock (k) and (ii) economically active population (l). Air transport services provision (AT) is initially the unique variable considered as a factor characterising the production environment. AT is computed as the total scheduled seats by NUTS 2 region. In a following step of the analysis, (i) a measure of human capital (HC) quality (i.e., the ratio of the population with tertiary education) and (ii) the unemployment ratio (UN) are incorporated into the analysis. Units of measures and sources of the data are provided in Table 14.1, while descriptive statistics at the sample level are shown in Table 14.2.

Table 14.1 Variables in the dataset

Variable	Description	Unit of measurement	Source
Input			
k	'Govern.'+'private'+'public– private' Capital stock	Billions of constant 2011 int. $ (PPP adjusted)	Our elaboration on IMF data
l	Economically active population 15–64 years	Thousand	Eurostat
Output			
gdp	GDP by NUTS 2 regions	Million euro PPS	Eurostat
Environmental factors			
AT	Total scheduled seats by NUTS 2	Number	Our elaboration on OAG data
UN	Unemployment rates by NUTS 2 regions	Percentage	Eurostat
HC	Population aged 25–64 with tertiary education	Percentage	Eurostat

Table 14.2 Descriptive statistics

Variable	Observations.	Mean	Standard deviation	Minimum	Maximum
k	2,970	149	143	2.7	1,142
l	2,970	885	716	14	5,802
gdp	2,970	51,978	57,055	1,047	619,466
AT	2,970	5,962,977	14,117,420	0	123,282,100
HC	2,970	0.26	0.09	0.07	0.70
UN	2,970	0.09	0.05	0.02	0.37

As discussed in Chapter 15, the choice of the main variable is in line with many studies at country level (Mastromarco and Ghosh, 2009; Arazmuradov et al., 2014). Our focus is initially on the air transport variable that, in an SFA model, can play the role of either production shifter or efficiency determinant. Then, we introduce the other efficiency determinants in the models to test whether the impact of air transport is robust in different specifications of the model.

Methodology

We consider a panel SFA with time-varying efficiency. Despite our context being slightly different from an industry setting with highly competitive firms, we believe it is unrealistic to assume that efficiency scores do not change over time, especially in a period of 11 years.

We start by estimating a simple production function (i.e., without considering the production environment). We compare, as a first step, a Cobb-Douglas specification (model M1) to a translog one (M2). The equations describing the production functions are as follows:

$$\ln gdp_{it} = f(x_{it}, \beta) = \beta_0 + \beta_k \ln k_{it} + \beta_l \ln l_{it} + v_{it} - u_{it}$$

$$\ln gdp_{it} = f(x_{it}, \beta) = \beta_0 + \beta_k \ln k_{it} + \beta_l \ln l_{it} + \frac{1}{2}\beta_{kk}(\ln k_{it})^2$$
$$+ \frac{1}{2}\beta_{ll}(\ln l_{it})^2 + \beta_{kl}\ln k_{it}\ln l_{it} + v_{it} - u_{it}$$

The two production functions of M1 and M2 are first estimated by applying a Battese and Coelli (1992) model. This implies that technical inefficiency has a truncated normal distribution and is assumed to vary over time according to an unknown parameter η as follows:[5]

$$u_{it} = \exp\left[\eta(t - T)\right] \tag{14.5}$$

As a second step, we estimate a model (M3) where the variable aviation ($\ln AT_i$) is incorporated into the deterministic component of the production frontier.

$$\ln gdp_{it} = f\left(x_{it},\beta\right) + z_{AT} \ln AT_{it} + v_{it} - u_{it}$$

Then we allow (M4) air transport to directly affect the stochastic component u_i of the production frontier as a determinant of efficiency according to the model proposed by Battese and Coelli (1995):

$$\ln gdp_{it} = f\left(x_{it},\beta\right) + v_{it} - u_{it}$$
$$\mu_{it} = z_0 + z_{AT} \ln AT_{it} + \epsilon_{it}$$

where μ is the mean of the Truncated Normal distribution that is expressed as a linear function of aviation.[6]

Finally, we expand the model M4 by including (M5) the other efficiency determinants (*HC* and *UN*) as follows:

$$\ln gdp_{it} = f\left(x_{it},\beta\right) + v_{it} - u_{it}$$
$$\mu_{it} = z_0 + z_{AT} \ln AT_{it} + z_{HC} HC_{it} + z_{UN} UN_{it} + \epsilon_{it}$$

For all the models, efficiency estimates are computed according to Battese and Coelli (1988).[7]

There is an issue here related to the highly discussed causality relation between aviation and economic growth and therefore to the potential endogeneity of aviation in the model. Some work has been done on the treatment of endogenous variables in SFA framework (Kumbhakar et al., 2015; Griffiths and Hajargasht, 2016; Karakaplan and Kutlu, 2017; Karakaplan 2018). However, developing such a framework may result a bit difficult for an introductory application of SFA like the one developed here. Indeed, it would require an entire chapter to discuss methodologies and correct instruments. Therefore, we rely, more simply, on the branch of previous literature that has found that air transportation can facilitate economic growth (Button et al., 2015).

Outliers are identified by applying the same methodology explained in Chapter 15 – i.e., the data cloud method (see Bogetoft and Otto, 2011 and Wilson, 1993 for further details). We recall that the idea of such a method is based on measuring the reduction of the volume of the so called 'data cloud' (i.e., of the determinant of the matrix *[X Y]* containing all the observations) caused by the eliminations of group of observations. Significant reductions are associated to the elimination of outliers. Hence, the application of the same criteria leads to the same outliers identified in the DEA chapter – namely ITC4-Lombardy, FR10-Île de France, UKI3-Inner London (West), ES61–Andalusia, ITF2-Molise, PL12- Mazowieckie, ITG1-Sicily, DE21-Oberbayern).[8]

SFA results

Results from models M1–M5 are presented in Table 14.3. All the estimates are obtained through the Stata command *sfpanel* (Belotti et al., 2013). We start by comparing M1 and M2 that are quite similar in terms of significances and signs. However, the elasticities of k and l exhibit some differences. Notice that variables have been divided by their sample mean before the estimation implying that first order translog coefficients represent the elasticities.

Looking at efficiency parameters, the negative η (see Eq. (14.5)) suggests a decreasing trend over time of efficiencies both in M1 and M2. The parameter $\gamma = \dfrac{\sigma^2_u}{\sigma^2_u + \sigma^2_v}$ equals 0.947 and 0.954 for M1 and M2, respectively. These values are quite similar and indicate a relevant role of inefficiency in explaining the distance from the frontier. The correlation of the efficiency scores is 0.97. The average efficiency scores are respectively 0.46 for M1 and 0.47 for M2.

For comparative purposes, we report (for the year 2015) the ten most efficient regions according to M1, M2, and the biased corrected efficiency scores of DEA chapter (Table 14.4).

Despite the different ranking orders, most of the top ten regions are confirmed in all the three models. More specifically, UKI4-Inner London-East, DE60-Hamburg, RO32-Bucharest-Ilfov, DE71-Darmstadt, BE10-Région de Bruxelles-Capitale, CZ01-Prague, and HU10-Közép-Magyarország figure constantly in the top ten of the efficient regions.

We proceed investigating the role of aviation in GDP generation by analysing the results of M3 and M4. In doing so, we choose, as a base model, the translog specification of M2 due to its greater flexibility (as discussed in the first part of the chapter). This choice is also validated by a likelihood-ratio test. The test suggests a statistically significant improvement in model fit when we add the interaction terms and the squared terms to the production function. We recall that the M3 and M4 differ for the role played by the variable relative to aviation. AT affects the deterministic part of the frontier in M3, while acts as a determinant of inefficiency in M4.[9]

The aviation variable is positive as expected, both when considered as a shifter of the production function (+0.189 in M3) and as a determinant of efficiency (-0.178 in M4). The higher the level of air transport services is, the higher the level of GDP (M3) or the level of efficiency in generating GDP (M4). The correlation between the efficiency scores of M3 and M4 is, however, lower (0.37) compared to M1 and M2 (0.97) in passing from the Battese and Coelli (1992) model to the Battese and Coelli (1995) one. Correlation between rakings is higher and equal to 0.51.

Finally, we estimate M5 to analyse whether the role played by air transport is robust to the introduction of further variables. This is done in M5, whose estimates are provided in the last columns of Table 14.3. The effect of aviation

Table 14.3 Models M1–M5 estimation results

Variable	M1		M2		M3		M4		M5	
	coefficient	Standard error	Coefficient	Standard error	Coefficient	Standard error	Coefficient	Standard error	Coefficient	Standard error
k	.518 ***	.0171	.475***	.0295	.448 ***	.0267	.562 ***	.0166	.548 ***	.0139
l	.356 ***	.0235	.441***	.0335	.412 ***	.0240	.418 ***	.0179	.436 ***	.0160
k2	—	—	-.112***	.0350	-.110 ***	.0316	.035 ***	.0368	.218 ***	.0313
l2	—	—	-.366***	.0472	-.345 ***	.0445	.211 ***	.0419	.284 ***	.0351
k x l	—	—	.288***	.036	.256 ***	.0313	-.130 ***	.0358	-.235 ***	.0302
AT	—		—		.189 ***	.0192	—		—	
cons	.737 ***	.0456	.706***	.0361	.566 ***	.0218	.369 ***	.0836	.325 ***	.0323
η	-.011***	.0006	-.012***	.0007	-.014 ***	.0007	—		—	
u	.858***	.0462	.840***	.0407	—		—		—	
HC	—		—		—		-.178***	.0112	-.220 ***	.0114
AT	—		—		—		—		-.170 ***	.0091
UN	—		—		—		—		.176 ***	.0064
cons	—		—		.785 ***	.0286	.489***	.0832	.513 ***	.0337
σ2	.0843	.0096	.0934	.0106	.0796	.0083	—		—	
γ	.9468	.0064	.9540	.0056	.9469	.0058	—		—	
σ2u	.0798	.0096	.0891	.0106	.0753	.0083	—		—	
σ2v	.0045	.0001	.0043	.0001	.0042	.0001	—		—	
λ	—		—		—		.9540 ***	.0056	.0619 ***	.0192
σu	—		—		—		.0891 ***	.0106	.1778 ***	.0069
σv	—		—		—		.0043 ***	.0001	.3481 ***	.0256

Note: Legend: * p<0.05; ** p<0.01; *** p<0.001

Table 14.4 Top 10 efficient regions of 2015 (M1, M2, and DEA)

Ranking	M1		M2		DEA	
	NUTS2	Score	NUTS2	Score	NUTS2	Score
1	BE10	0.973	SK01	0.973	UKI4	1.088
2	LU00	0.969	DE60	0.912	DE60	1.092
3	DE60	0.938	CZ01	0.908	DE11	1.118
4	CZ01	0.923	BE10	0.877	RO32	1.118
5	SK01	0.892	UKI4	0.837	DE71	1.129
6	UKI4	0.852	DE71	0.813	BE10	1.132
7	HU10	0.832	HU10	0.792	CZ01	1.136
8	RO32	0.813	RO32	0.778	ES30	1.153
9	DE71	0.774	DE11	0.755	ES51	1.153
10	UKJ1	0.746	SE11	0.737	HU10	1.157

Legend: □ common to the three models

□ common to DEA and M2 only

as a positive determinant of efficiency is confirmed also in M5. A comparison between M4 and M5 through a likelihood-ratio test suggests that a statistically significant improvement in model fit when *HC* and *UN* are added as factors affecting efficiency. Human capital quality is another factor exerting a positive effect on efficiency according to M5. On the other hand, unemployment is, as expected, a driver of inefficiency (the results support the findings presented in the DEA chapter despite some differences in the model specifications). Notice that efficiency scores of M5 have a high correlation with those of M4 (0.80).[10] However, when ranking the NUTS2 in terms of efficiency only four observations (DE60-Hamburg, DE71-Darmstadt, CZ01-Prague, and SE11-Stockholm) are shared in the top 10 between the two models. Inefficiencies, whose distributions vary according to the exogenous variables, affect the ranking produced by the models.

The differences between the models M1-5 are summarised in Table 14.6. The table also includes the descriptive statistics of the efficiency scores. The results suggest that, as the number of parameters to estimate increases (passing from M1 to M3 and from M4 to M5), the average efficiency tends to grow. This may suggest that the models without exogenous factors influencing the stochastic part of the frontier tend to underestimate efficiency.

Table 14.5 Top 10 efficient regions of 2015 (M5)

M5 NUTS2	Score
UKI7	0.990
UKJ2	0.984
DE71	0.983
NL32	0.982
SE11	0.978
DK01	0.977
IE02	0.972
CZ01	0.968
FI1B	0.965
DE60	0.960

Legend: in common with M2

Table 14.6 Efficiency scores descriptive statistics in the different models

Model	Mean	Standard deviation	Minimum	Maximum
M1	0.459	0.131	0.206	0.976
M2	0.470	0.137	0.191	0.976
M3	0.495	0.130	0.219	0.986
M4	0.665	0.080	0.522	0.944
M5	0.679	0.117	0.348	0.990

The different evolution of the average inefficiencies estimated by the models are presented in Figure 14.2, where the yearly average efficiency scores are presented for each model. M1, M2, and M3 exhibit an evident decreasing trend of the average efficiency over time. M4 and M5 show a different (but comparable) evolution. The main differences between the evolution sit in the inefficiency specifications.

Looking at efficiency distributions, Figures 14.3 and 14.4 show the histograms of the efficiency scores from the five models for the first and the last years of our sample.

Once again models M1–M3 score distributions are consistent with each other. It is also confirmed what is suggested by Table 14.6, i.e., M4 scores are more flattened compared to M5. Given the similar average value of the

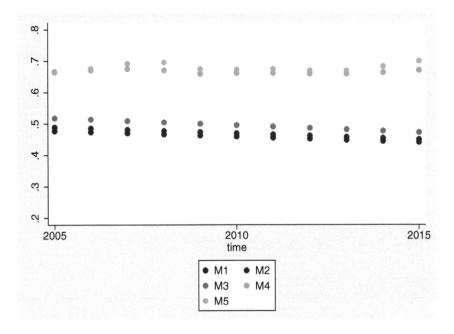

Figure 14.2 Evolution over time of average efficiency score by model.

two models (Table 14.6), this means that in M5 there are more observations with high efficiency scores and some observations are particularly inefficient compared to M4 (Figure 14.3 and 14.4).

Conclusions

This chapter provides an introduction to Stochastic Frontier Analysis applying the approach in order to analyse the connection between air transport and regional development. More specifically, in the first part of the chapter we show how SFA accounts for estimation noise and can consider a panel data structure. This comes at the cost of specifying (i) a functional form for the production function and (ii) a distributional form for the inefficiency term. SFA is then applied to study the effect of aviation on regional GDP generation on the wave of previous literature which suggests that air transport services provision helps regional economic growth. In this regard, we test through five different SFA models the role of aviation in fostering the generation of GDP for European NUTS2 regions. Our analysis is based on a panel of 270 NUTS 2 European regions observed for 11 years (2005–2015). Our results show that aviation positively affects the generation of GDP of European regions with such effect being robust to different model specifications.

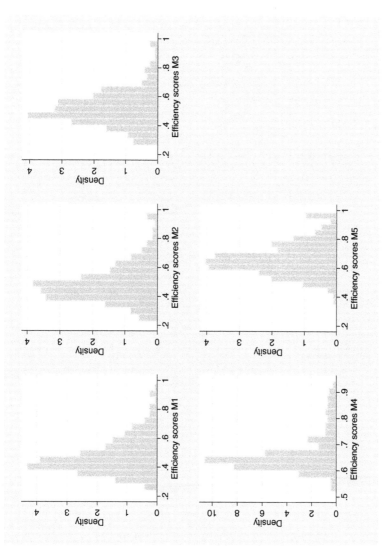

Figure 14.3 Histograms of efficiency scores models 1–5 (year 2005).

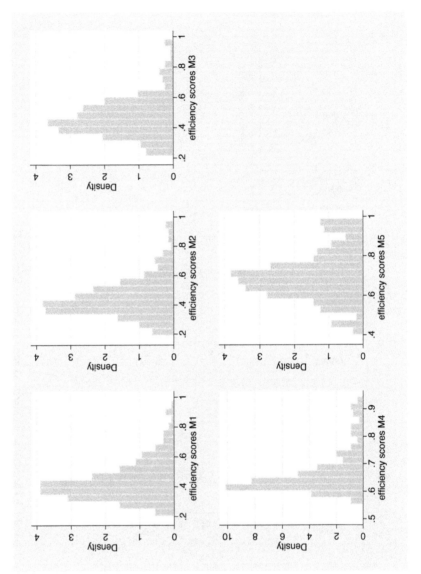

Figure 14.4 Histograms of efficiency scores models 1–5 (year 2015).

Notes

1 Differently from the Cobb-Douglas, the translog does not impose a constant coefficient of substitution between production factors.

2 In regulatory benchmarking, extreme difference in the relative performance lead to classify individual observation as an outlier as a sort of precaution (Bogetoft and Otto, 2011). Despite that, the authors underline that such observations could have a value for the analysis in case their performances reflect the introduction of some kind of innovation from which other DMUs might want to learn.

3 This requires a generalization of the likelihood function because u_i is no longer identically distributed (see Coelli et al., 2005).

4 There are many further SFA models in the literature. See for example Kumbhakar et al. (2015) for an updated overview.

5 The adoption of a truncated normal distribution implies the estimation of an additional parameter (the point of truncation) and may lead to more complexity in terms of computations. However, it brings the advantage of having an efficiency distribution mode not necessarily at 0. This in turn means that efficiency scores are not necessarily close to 1 (Coelli et al., 2005).

6 Belotti et al. (2013) highlight that some models exist that allow exogenous factors to affect the inefficiency variance. According to these models, technical inefficiency is heteroskedastic and its variance can be expressed as a function of z_i. We do not apply such models in this chapter. To deepen the issue, see for example Caudill and Ford (1993), Caudill et al. (1995), Hadri (1999), and Wang (2002).

7 This means that efficiency is given by $E\{e^{-u|\varepsilon}\}$, where ε represents the composed error term. An alternative specification $e^{-E\{u|\varepsilon\}}$ is provided by Jondrow et al. (1982).

8 Bogetoft and Otto (2011) underline that outliers may also be among the least efficient firms.

9 For the Battese and Coelli (1995) M4, the software provides the values of σ_u, σ_v and of $\lambda = \dfrac{\sigma_u}{\sigma_v}$.

10 The correlation between M5 and M2 efficiency scores is about 0.7 and 0.73 is the correlation between the rankings of the two models.

References

Aigner, D., Lovell, C. K., & Schmidt, P. (1977). Formulation and estimation of stochastic frontier production function models. *Journal of Econometrics*, 6(1), 21–37.

Arazmuradov, A., Martini, G., & Scotti, D. (2014). Determinants of total factor productivity in former Soviet Union economies: a stochastic frontier approach. *Economic Systems*, 38(1), 115–135.

Battese, G. E., & Coelli, T. J. (1988). Prediction of firm-level technical efficiencies with a generalized frontier production function and panel data. *Journal of Econometrics*, 38(3), 387–399.

Battese, G. E., & Coelli, T. J. (1992). Frontier production functions, technical efficiency and panel data: with application to paddy farmers in India. *Journal of Productivity Analysis*, 3(1–2), 153–169.

Battese, G. E., & Coelli, T. J. (1995). A model for technical inefficiency effects in a stochastic frontier production function for panel data. *Empirical Economics*, 20(2), 325–332.

Belotti, F., Daidone, S., Ilardi, G., & Atella, V. (2013). Stochastic frontier analysis using Stata. *The Stata Journal, 13*(4), 719–758.

Blonigen, B. A., & Cristea, A. C. 2012. Airports and urban growth: evidence from a quasi-natural policy experiment. National Bureau of Economic Research. Working paper 18278.

Bogetoft, P., & Otto, L. (2011). *Benchmarking with Dea, Sfa, and R* (Vol. 157). Springer Science & Business Media.

Button, K., Brugnoli, A., Martini, G., & Scotti, D. (2015). Connecting African urban areas: airline networks and intra-Sub-Saharan trade. *Journal of Transport Geography, 42*, 84–89.

Caudill, S. B., & Ford, J. M. (1993). Biases in frontier estimation due to heteroscedasticity. *Economics Letters, 41*(1), 17–20.

Caudill, S. B., Ford, J. M., & Gropper, D. M. (1995). Frontier estimation and firm-specific inefficiency measures in the presence of heteroscedasticity. *Journal of Business & Economic Statistics, 13*(1), 105–111.

Fageda, X. 2017. International air travel and fdi flows: evidence from Barcelona, *Journal of Regional Science, 57*(5), 858–883.

Coelli, T. J., Rao, D. S. P., O'Donnell, C. J., & Battese, G. E. (2005). An introduction to efficiency and productivity analysis. New York: Springer Science & Business Media.

Colombi, R., Kumbhakar, S. C., Martini, G., & Vittadini, G. (2014). Closed-skew normality in stochastic frontiers with individual effects and long/short-run efficiency. *Journal of Productivity Analysis, 42*(2), 123–136.

Filippini, M., & Greene, W. (2016). Persistent and transient productive inefficiency: a maximum simulated likelihood approach. *Journal of Productivity Analysis, 45*(2), 187–196.

Glaeser, E. L., Kallal, H. D., Scheinkman, J. A., & Shleifer, A. (1992). Growth in cities. *Journal of Political Economy, 100*(6), 1126–1152.

Green, R. K. (2007). Airports and economic development. *Real Estate Economics, 35*(1), 91–112.

Greene, W. (2005a). Fixed and random effects in stochastic frontier models. *Journal of Productivity Analysis, 23*(1), 7–32.

Greene, W. (2005b). Reconsidering heterogeneity in panel data estimators of the stochastic frontier model. *Journal of Econometrics, 126*(2), 269–303.

Griffiths, W. E., & Hajargasht, G. (2016). Some models for stochastic frontiers with endogeneity. *Journal of Econometrics, 190*(2), 341–348.

Hadri, K. (1999). Estimation of a doubly heteroscedastic stochastic frontier cost function. *Journal of Business & Economic Statistics, 17*(3), 359–363.

Jondrow, J., Lovell, C. K., Materov, I. S., & Schmidt, P. (1982). On the estimation of technical inefficiency in the stochastic frontier production function model. *Journal of Econometrics, 19*(2–3), 233–238.

Karakaplan, M. U., & Kutlu, L. (2017). Endogeneity in panel stochastic frontier models: an application to the Japanese cotton spinning industry. *Applied Economics, 49*(59), 5935–5939.

Karakaplan, M. U. (2018). Statistical Software Components S458445, Boston College Department of Economics.

Kumbhakar, S. C. (1990). Production frontiers, panel data, and time-varying technical inefficiency. *Journal of Econometrics, 46*(1–2), 201–211.

Kumbhakar, S. C., & Wang, H. J. (2005). Estimation of growth convergence using a stochastic production frontier approach. *Economics Letters, 88*(3), 300–305.

Kumbhakar, S. C., Wang, H. J., & Horncastle, A. P. (2015). *A practitioner's guide to stochastic frontier analysis using Stata*. Cambridge: Cambridge University Press.

Mastromarco, C., & Ghosh, S. (2009). Foreign capital, human capital, and efficiency: a stochastic frontier analysis for developing countries. *World Development, 37*(2), 489–502.

Meeusen, W., & van Den Broeck, J. (1977). Efficiency estimation from Cobb-Douglas production functions with composed error. *International Economic Review*, 18(2), 435–444.

Pitt, M. M., & Lee, L. F. (1981). The measurement and sources of technical inefficiency in the Indonesian weaving industry. *Journal of Development Economics*, 9(1), 43–64.

Rosenthal, S., & Strange, W. C. 2001. The determinants of agglomeration. *Journal of Urban Economics*, 50, 191–229.

Tsionas, E. G., & Kumbhakar, S. C. (2014). Firm heterogeneity, persistent and transient technical inefficiency: a generalized true random-effects model. *Journal of Applied Econometrics*, 29(1), 110–132.

Wang, H. J. (2002). Heteroscedasticity and non-monotonic efficiency effects of a stochastic frontier model. *Journal of Productivity Analysis*, 18(3), 241–253.

Wilson, P. W. (1993). Detecting outliers in deterministic nonparametric frontier models with multiple outputs. *Journal of Business & Economic Statistics*, 11(3), 319–323.

15 Data envelopment analysis

Davide Scotti and Nicola Volta

Introduction

This chapter presents an application of data envelopment analysis (DEA) on European NUTS2 regions. In this chapter, DEA is applied in order to investigate the possible relationship between air transport service provision and regional development. We start by introducing the basic notions of the DEA methodology and its main assumptions. Second, we describe the production process under investigation together with the dataset and the research hypothesis to test. Third, the methodology adopted and the main results obtained are presented and discussed. Finally, the main findings are summarised in the conclusions.

As discussed in Bogetoft and Otto (2011), firms' performances are reflected in their ability to choose the best alternatives to chase their preferences. According to standard microeconomics, it is possible to measure firms' *effectiveness* by comparing the attained utility to the maximally attainable one given the technological feasible alternatives (i.e., the isoquant) and the utility function (i.e., the indifference curve). This theoretical evaluation of performances (i.e., the measure of effectiveness) is ideal and requires clear priorities as well as clear information on the technology. Unfortunately, none of these elements (i.e., priorities/preference and technology) are known a priori. Here comes in the concept of *efficiency* which allows for the evaluation of a firm in the absence of a maximally attainable performance to be confronted with. The underlying idea is to replicate the actual firm behaviours through data by approximating the relations between inputs and outputs in a specific production process. In this context, it is possible to estimate the relative efficiency of the firms under examination (also called decision-making units or DMUs) in terms of converting inputs (resources) into outputs (products/services). Efficiency refers to the ability of using the minimum quantity of inputs in order to produce the maximum feasible quantity of outputs. Relative means that firm performances are evaluated according to the technological frontier defined by the best practices. When data envelopment analysis (DEA) is applied, such a frontier is built on the basis of actual observations of firms' input/output combinations joined to a standard set of a priori assumptions.

More specifically, DEA uses mathematical programming and estimates a technology set $T^\star$ (i.e., a characterisation of the input-output combinations that are assumed to be feasible) according to the so-called minimal extrapolation principle. This means that, in a setting where K firms use N inputs (vector $x = (x_1, ..., x_n)$) to produce M outputs (vector $y = (y_1, ..., y_m)$), a technology set T^* is the smallest subset of $R^N_+ x R^M_+$ that contains the data and meets some technological assumptions.

The most important assumptions in basic DEA models are those related to (i) the free disposability of inputs and outputs, (ii) the convexity, and (iii) the typology of the returns of scale. Such assumptions are well summarised and explained in Bogetoft and Otto (2011). Free disposability means that firms can produce fewer (outputs) with more (inputs). Convexity implies the practicability of any weighted average of feasible production plans. Returns to scale refers to the fact that some rescaling of production is possible: the two extreme assumptions are the so-called constant returns to scale (CRS) and variable returns to scale (VRS). According to CRS, any feasible production plan can arbitrarily be scaled up or down, while according to VRS, no rescaling is possible.

Figure 15.1 shows the technology sets under the assumptions discussed above (with CRS and VRS) for a production process with 1 input and 1 output and 6 firms (A, B, C, D, E, and F).

The frontier is the boundary of the technology set and the relative efficiency can be defined as the distance of a given DMU to the frontier. Basic DEA models are based on radial Debreu-Farrel (Debreu 1951; Farrel 1957) measures of efficiency. More specifically, in an output-based radial efficiency model, the measure of efficiency is the amount of necessary proportional expansion of

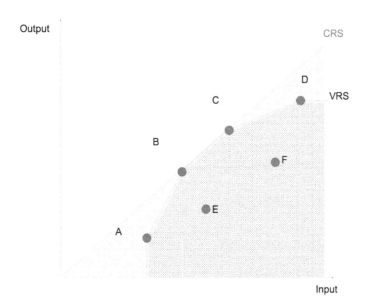

Figure 15.1 CRS and VRS DEA technology sets

outputs to move a DMU to the boundary of the DEA technology set. In input-based radial DEA models, the measure of efficiency is the amount of necessary proportional reduction of inputs to move a data point to the boundary of the DEA technology set.

With an output orientation (that will be adopted in the application presented later) the efficiency of firm i (θ^i) can be described as follows:

$$\theta^i = \theta\big((x^i, y^i); T^\star\big) = max\{\theta \in \mathbb{R}_+ \mid (x^i, \theta y^i) \in T^\star\} \tag{15.1}$$

Given the assumptions discussed above on the characteristics of $T^\star$, Eq. (15.1) consists in solving for each DMU i the following linear programming problem (assuming VRS):[1]

$$\max_{\theta, \lambda^1, \dots, \lambda^K} \theta$$

$$s.t. \quad x_n^i \geq \sum_{j=1}^{K} \lambda^k x_m^k \qquad n = 1, \dots, N$$

$$\theta y_m^i \leq \sum_{J=1}^{K} \lambda^k y_m^k \qquad m = 1, \dots, M \tag{15.2}$$

$$\lambda \in \mathbb{R}_+^k \wedge \sum_{j=1}^{K} \lambda^k = 1$$

Given that $T^\star$ (and consequently the frontier) is built on the basis of actual observations, it is important to check first for the presence of outliers. Firms differing significantly from the rest of the sample may have a negative impact on the estimation of the technology set by impacting the evaluation of the sample under examination (Bogetoft and Otto, 2011). Different approaches can be adopted to identify outliers: from a simple scatterplot analysis to more sophisticated ones. In our application we apply a data cloud method.

A further important concept in DEA models is that efficiency may be biased. Bogetoft and Otto (2011) provide a concise and clear explanation of the issue and of how to tackle it. The estimated technology set $T^\star$ is (by definition) a subset of the real but unknown T. This implies that DEA scores are computed over a smaller set, whose size depends on the sample. As a result, estimated efficiencies are sensitive to sampling selection and may be larger than the real ones (i.e., this is the bias). Unfortunately, the bias cannot be computed directly since the distribution of the true efficiency (i.e., the efficiency based on the true unknown technology T) is unknown. A possible procedure to correct this bias is to assume that θ^{ib} is the b bootstrap replica estimate of the true efficiency θ^i. In this way the bootstrap estimate of the bias can computed as follows:

$$bias^{i\star} = \frac{1}{B}\sum\nolimits_{b=1}^{B} \theta^{ib} - \hat{\theta}^{i} \qquad (15.3)$$

and a biased-corrected estimator of θ^{i} is given by $\tilde{\theta}^{i} = \hat{\theta}^{i} - bias^{i\star}$. Simar and Wilson (1998) and Simar and Wilson (2000) develop and describe in a comprehensive way how to bootstrap the DEA frontier, compute biased-corrected efficiencies, and estimate confidence intervals for bias-corrected scores.

As abovementioned, DEA basic models such as the VRS output-oriented efficiency model described by Equation (15.2) are useful to measure the distance of observed input-output combinations to the frontier. However, it may be even more relevant to identify what are the determinants of inefficiency rather than just estimating them. As explained in Badunenko and Tauchmann (2018), it is common in the extant literature to combine DEA to second-stage regression analysis where DEA efficiency scores are included as dependent variables. In many applications, the second stage is generally performed through either OLS regression or tobit regression (the latter does not neglect the bounded nature of DEA scores). However, Simar and Wilson (2007) argue that the estimated DEA efficiency scores cannot be treated as independent observations since they are computed from the same data sample (i.e., serial correlation problem). In order to solve this problem, they developed two parametric bootstrap procedures (i.e., algorithm #1 and algorithm #2). While algorithm #1 excludes efficient DMUs (i.e., DMUs with a score equal to one) from the second-stage analysis, algorithm #2 relies on bias-corrected efficiency scores and considers all the DMUs in the regression analysis. In both the procedures, standard errors and confidence intervals for the coefficients of efficiency determinants are estimated through a parametric bootstrap procedure (more details are provided in the methodology section and in Appendix A). In our application to European NUTS2 regions, traditional tobit approach is compared to truncated regression and to the abovementioned algorithm procedures.

A DEA application to estimate the relationship between air transport and regional development

Production process, dataset, and research hypothesis

The base idea of our model is that a significant relation exists between air transport and regional development and in turns GDP generation. This belief derives from the previous literature where such connection has been deeply investigated. As presented in Mukkala and Tervo (2013), Florida et al. (2015), and Adler and Volta (2017), several studies provide evidence of the connection between air transport activities and regional development. For example, aviation has been recognised as a determinant of agglomeration economies (Rosenthal and Strange, 2001, Glaeser et al., 1992), of population and employment growth (Bloningen and Cristea, 2012; Green, 2007), of international trade (Button et al., 2015), and of FDI flows (Fageda, 2017). The issue of the direction of the causality between aviation and economic development with controversial results has been largely discussed in the literature.[2] Although we recognise the importance of the direction of the causality, we underline that the purpose of this contribution is not to discuss it (this would require at least an entire *ad hoc* chapter) but simply introduce DEA and show a relatively simple empirical application. Such application is therefore built on the literature mentioned above that suggests that aviation may help economic development. When assessing the impact of air transport on economic growth, the literature describes four main components: (i) direct impacts, (ii) indirect impacts, (iii) induced impacts, and (iv) catalytic effects (Graham, 2003; ACI, 2004). Direct impact captures the pure effect of airport activities. Indirect impact refers to the level of employment and income generated by the suppliers of airport activities. Induced impact is generated by the spending of incomes of employees directly or indirectly connected to the airport. Finally, the catalytic effect measures the employment and income generated in the economy thank to the contribution of the airport to business productivity and to attractiveness for economic activities (e.g. investments and tourism).[3]

The aim of our model is to empirically address the question whether air transport service provision have an effect on European NUTS 2 regions' economic development. The analysis is based on a panel of 270 NUTS 2 European regions observed for 11 years (2005–2015). Our model tries to incorporate the connection between aviation and regional economic development in the production process depicted in Figure 15.2.

We consider a regional-level production process that generates the single output GDP by using two inputs: capital stock (Capital) and economically active population (Labour). We notice that the application of benchmarking analysis (parametric and non-parametric) to countries and regions (treated therefore as DMUs) as well as the use of GDP as an output of their production

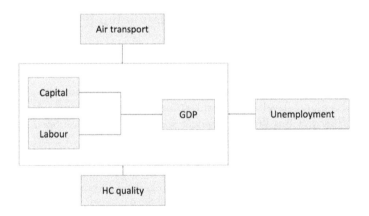

Figure 15.2 NUTS 2 regions' production process

process have been largely used in the previous literature.[4] The simple production process described may then be influenced by some environmental factors that are neither inputs nor outputs of the production process, but are expected to exert an influence on regional transformation of capital and labour into GDP. More specifically, we consider (i) a measure of air transport services provision (Air transport) represented by the total scheduled seats by NUTS 2 region, (ii) a measure of human capital (HC) represented by the ratio of the population with tertiary education, and (iii) the unemployment ratio. The unit of measures and the sources of the data are provided in Table 15.1, while descriptive statistics at sample level are shown in Table 15.2.

The capital stock variable (Capital) is not directly available at NUTS 2 level. We approximate it by starting from country level values provided by

Table 15.1 Variables in the dataset

Variable	Description	Unit of measure	Source
Input			
Capital	'govern.'+'private'+' public-private' Capital Stock	Billions of constant 2011 int. $ (PPP adjusted)	Authors' elaboration on IMF data
Labour	Economically active population 15–64 years	Thousand	Eurostat
Output			
GDP	GDP by NUTS 2 regions	Million euro PPS	Eurostat
Environmental factors			
Air transport	Total scheduled seats by NUTS 2	Number	Authors' elaboration on OAG data
Unemployment	Unemployment rates by NUTS 2 regions	Percentage	Eurostat
HC	Population aged 25–64 with tertiary education	Percentage	Eurostat

Table 15.2 Descriptive statistics

Variable	Obs.	Mean	Std.dev	Min	Max
Capital	2,970	149	143	2.7	1,142
Labor	2,970	885	716	14	5,802
GDP	2,970	51,978	57,055	1,047	619,466
Air transport	2,970	5,962,977	14,117,420	0	123,282,100
HC	2,970	0.26	0.09	0.07	0.70
Unemployment	2,970	0.09	0.05	0.02	0.37

the Investment and Capital Stock Dataset of IMF. These values have been weighted by regional population to obtain a capital stock input value for each of the NUTS 2 regions in the dataset. It is important to note that between the determinants of efficiency, air transport is the main variable of interest. We notice that there are two main reasons why air transport is not considered as an input of the production process shown in Figure 15.2. First, according to the benchmark theory, a correct evaluation of DMUs' performance requires a common production process in terms of inputs and outputs used. In fact, not all the NUT 2 regions have airports. Second, regional air traffic may be considered (at least partially) exogenous and determined by airport/airline management choices.

Our starting research hypothesis is that air transport positively affects the regional efficiency in GDP generation (hypothesis #1). Concerning the other determinants included in the analysis, we expect that human capital education positively affects efficiency (hypothesis #2).[5] Finally, unemployment is expected to affect negatively efficiency (hypothesis #3). Moreover, we look at a possible interaction effect between air transport and human capital: air transport efficacy may be related to the level of HC. Finally, to allow for NUTS 2-size effect related heterogeneity (Badunenko and Tauchmann, 2018) in the link between air transport and regional efficiency, we include in the analysis also the interaction term between the air transport variable and the size of the NUTS 2 expressed in terms of logarithm of the population.

Methodology

We start our analysis by investigating year by year the presence of outliers applying the data cloud method described in Bogetoft and Otto (2011).[6] Consider the combined matrix containing all the observations $[X\,Y]$ where X is the $K \times n$ matrix of inputs and Y the $K \times m$ matrix of outputs. The rows of the matrix can be considered as a cloud of points in the space $\mathbb{R}^n_+ \times \mathbb{R}^m_+$ characterised by a volume that can be measured through the determinant (D) of the matrix. When removing one or more NUTS 2 regions from the data sample, the cloud volume may variate. Observing the cloud changes when observations are removed from the sample is an effective way to identify the outliers. As an example, assume that $D^{(i,j)}$ is the determinant after removing observations i and j. The ratio $R^{(i,j)}$ between $D^{(i,j)}$ and the original determinant D will be smaller than 1 when i and j are outliers while close to 1 if not. When r observations are removed, different combinations of $r < K$ observations lead to different values of the ratio R. In this regard, we are interested in the combination of r firms that minimise the value of R or, more specifically, in the combination of r firms having $\log \dfrac{(R^r)}{R^r_{min}} = 0$. Figures 15.3–15.4 show ordered pairs of $(r, \log \frac{(R^r)}{R^r_{min}})$, where r is the number of observations removed from the sample and the log of the ratio is used as indicator of isolated small values.[7] The r values on the horizontal axis with isolated low points give an indication of r outliers, while a dashed line is drawn between the points just above 0. Therefore, we have a group of outliers where the dashed line is significantly above 0. In the case of our dataset, Figures 15.3–15.4 show several peaks of the dashed line despite the year under analysis. Generally, the last relevant peaks are consistently around 5–7 observations removed (r) per year. The outliers detected by this approach tend to be the same across the years. To ensure consistency in the analysis we removed from the sample the same regions. Eight

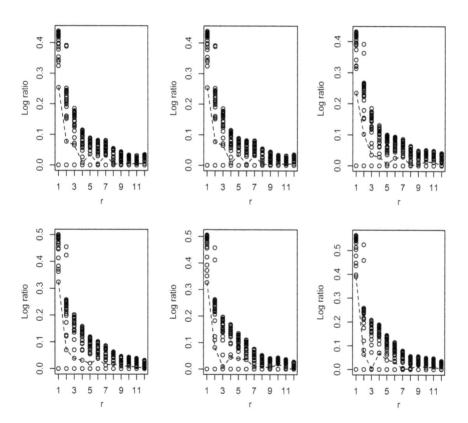

Figure 15.3 Outliers' detection for years 2005–2010

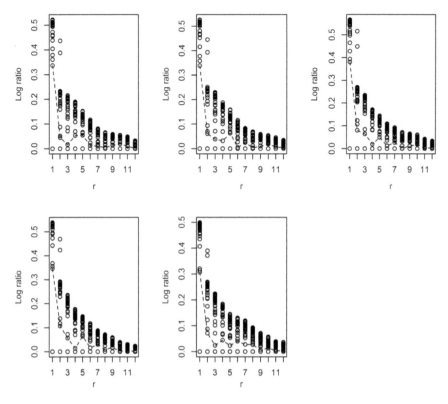

Figure 15.4 Outliers' detection for years 2011–2015

NUTS 3 regions have been detected as outliers: ITC4-Lombardy, FR10-Île de France, UKI3-Inner London (West), ES61-Andalusia, ITF2-Molise, PL12-Mazowieckie, ITG1-Sicily, DE21-Oberbayern.

Once that outliers have been removed, we computed the output-oriented Farrel efficiency measure assuming variable returns to scale as described earlier. Efficiency scores take value equal to one if the observation is fully efficient, or larger than one if inefficiency is detected by the model.[8]

Once computed the efficiency scores (θ^i), we run a second-stage analysis to investigate the determinants of inefficiency in GDP generation according to the following Eq. (15.4):

$$\theta^i = \beta_0 + \beta_1 HC^i + \beta_2 AIR^i + \beta_3 UNEM^i + \beta_4 SIZE^i \\ + \beta_5 HC^i \times AIR^i + \beta_6 SIZE^i \times AIR^i + \varepsilon^i \tag{15.4}$$

Eq. (15.4) is estimated through four different empirical models. More specifically, following Badunenko and Tauchmann (2018), we compare the results from (i) tobit estimation, (ii) truncated regression (truncreg), (iii) Simar and Wilson algorithm #1 (SW1), and (iv) Simar and Wilson algorithm #2 (SW2). Despite the fact that also OLS regression is largely used in the literature, we do not run an OLS regression. Indeed, such approach does not ensure that the fitted value of the efficiency scores will be higher than or equal to 1 (the same applies to the expected value and to the mean value). Such theoretical problem is overcome in both the tobit and the truncreg estimations. In Appendix A, Simar and Wilson's approach is deepened and the steps of the two algorithms are specified.

DEA results

The average efficiency score for each year and the NUTS 2 deemed as efficient are presented in Table 15.3. The average efficiency level is almost constant and relatively high (i.e., low efficiency) over the period analysed. More precisely, an average efficiency score around two indicates that European NUTS 2 regions should double the output in order to reach the technology frontier, all things being equal. Moreover, considering the sample size (262), the frontier is spanned by a relatively small group of regions (only 11 to 13 regions are efficient). Seven NUTS 2 regions (BE10-Région de Bruxelles-Capitale, DE60-Hamburg, ES30-Comunidad de Madrid, ES51-Cataluña, FI20-Åland, LU00-Luxembourg, SK01-Bratislavský kraj) consistently define the frontier resulting fully efficient in all the years analysed. Most of these regions appear in the top European position in terms of GDP and/or GDP per capita and are usually considered among the richest regions in Europe (we recall that some important regions are not included because they were identified as outliers). In this sense, the results sound reasonable. Furthermore, some other recognised rich regions (e.g., CZ01-Prague, DE71-Darmstadt, ITI4-Lazio) are efficient in more than one year according to Table 15.3.

Table 15.4 shows the biased-corrected efficiency scores for the year 2015. Despite by definition the biased-corrected scores are different from the unit (i.e., no fully efficient observations), the most efficient NUTS 2 are similar to the ones obtained according to traditional DEA model.

Table 15.5 compares the results of the second-stage analysis using the four different estimation approaches. To compare the models, we use the year 2015 (i.e., the most recent one in the dataset).[9] When analysing the results, signs, and significant levels are generally similar across the different models. However, the coefficients' magnitudes exhibit some differences. As explained earlier, there are conceptual and technical differences between the estimation approaches. According to Simar and Wilson (2007) the tobit estimation erroneously

Table 15.3 Average efficiency scores and efficient regions by year

Year	2015	2014	2013	2012	2011	2010	2009	2008	2007	2006	2005
Average efficiency score	2.029	1.972	1.997	1.983	1.991	1.981	1.951	1.911	1.895	1.883	1.926
Efficient NUTS 2											
1	BE10	BE10	BE10	BE10	BE10	BE10	BE10	BE10	BE10	BE10	BE10
2	CZ01	DE60	DE60	DE60	CZ01	CZ01	CZ01	CZ01	BG41	BG41	BG41
3	DE60	DE71	DE71	DE71	DE60	DE60	DE60	DE60	CZ01	CZ01	CZ01
4	ES30	ES30	ES30	ES30	DE71	DE71	DE71	DE71	DE60	DE60	DE60
5	ES51	ES51	ES51	FI20	ES30	ES30	EL30	EL30	DE71	DE71	DE71
6	FI20	FI20	FI20	HU10	ES51	ES51	ES30	ES30	EL30	EL30	EL30
7	IE02	HU10	HU10	ITI4	FI20	FI20	ES51	ES51	ES30	ES30	ES30
8	LU00	LU00	LU00	LU00	HU10	HU10	FI20	FI20	ES51	ES51	ES51
9	RO32	RO32	RO32	PL22	ITI4	ITI4	HU10	ITI4	FI20	FI20	FI20
10	SK01	SK01	SK01	RO32	LU00	LU00	ITI4	LU00	HU10	HU10	HU10
11	UKI4	UKI4	UKI4	SK01	PL22	SK01	LU00	RO32	ITI4	ITI4	ITI4
12	-	-	-	UKI4	SK01	-	SK01	SK01	LU00	LU00	LU00
13	-	-	-	-	UKI4	-	-	-	SK01	SK01	SK01

Table 15.4 Biased-corrected efficiency scores for most efficient regions (year 2015)

	NUTs 2	Score
1	UKI4	1.088
2	DE60	1.092
3	DE11	1.118
4	RO32	1.118
5	DE71	1.129
6	BE10	1.132
7	CZ01	1.136
8	ES30	1.153
9	ES51	1.153
10	HU10	1.157
11	PL22	1.194

Table 15.5 Estimated coefficients of efficiency determinants (year 2015)

Variable	Tobit	Truncreg	SW_alg 1	SW_alg 2
HC	−2.0895	−1.8608	−1.8608	−2.8910
	(0.0002)	(0.0023)	(0.0020)	(0.0001)
Air transport	0.2011	0.2434	0.2434	0.2388
	(0.0175)	(0.0047)	(0.0068)	(0.0329)
Unemployment	3.0673	3.1838	3.1838	4.1079
	(0.0000)	(0.0000)	(0.0000)	(0.0000)
Size	0.0631	0.0407	0.0407	0.0079
	(0.4189)	(0.5999)	(0.6087)	(0.9371)
Air transport × HC	−0.0090	−0.0047	−0.0047	−0.0207
	(0.8417)	(0.9247)	(0.9233)	(0.7436)
Air transport × size	−0.0154	−0.0184	−0.0184	−0.0183
	(0.0106)	(0.0026)	(0.0038)	(0.0218)
Constant	1.6933	1.9248	1.9248	2.9127
	(0.1239)	(0.0803)	(0.0880)	(0.0402)

Legend: p-values in parentheses

considers full efficiency. Differently from tobit, truncreg does not consider efficient observations. However, truncreg results might be spurious due to the fact that standard errors are incorrectly estimated. SW models have been run with 2000 bootstrap replications. As expected, SW1 presents the same coefficients of truncreg, because it works on standard errors and confidence intervals only. In SW2 bias-corrected efficiency scores are used as a dependent variable in the second-stage regression.[10]

According to our results, hypotheses #2 and #3 are verified. Indeed, unemployment has a positive and statistically significant coefficient, while HC exerts a negative effect both alone and combined with air transport. It is instead less straightforward to quantitatively interpret the coefficients related to air

Table 15.6 Marginal effect of air transport on efficiency (year 2015)

Tobit	Truncreg	SW_alg 1	SW_alg 2
−0.019	−0.015	−0.015	−0.021
(0.0000)	(0.0006)	(0.0006)	(0.0001)

Legend: p-values in parentheses

transport that is our main variable of interest. This can be done through the average marginal effect of air transport on regional GDP efficiency (Table 15.6).

The impact of air transport on inefficiency is negative for all the models suggesting that, according to hypothesis #1, air transport has a positive impact on NUTS 2 ability of generating economic growth.

Given the similarities between the approaches, we focus our analysis on the SW2 results (i.e., the most rigorous and statistically advanced approach). Table 15.7 shows the estimated marginal effect of air transport for each year (i.e., 2015 value corresponds to the one presented in Table 15.5). The average marginal effect over the period is -0.028, decreasing from -0,029 in 2005 to -0.021 in 2015. Despite the small decrease over the years, the estimated effect is always negative (i.e., positive effect on efficiency) as well as statistically significant.

Once an average positive impact on efficiency is identified, it is possible to analyse the possible existence of heterogeneity of such effect (Badunenko and Tauchmann, 2018). Indeed, the average outcomes of Tables 15.6–15.7 may be the result of heterogenous effects depending on specific regional characteristics. In this regard, Figures 15.5–15.7 show the estimated marginal effects of air transport on inefficiency by (i) HC, (ii) region size, and (iii) its respective own value for three years – namely 2005, 2010, and 2015 (results do not change consistently when other years are considered).

Looking at year 2015, Figure 15.5 shows a constant effect of air transportation both qualitatively and quantitatively with respect air transport itself. The same applies to HC with the exceptions of extreme values of HC where the effect tends to lose its relevance. Results are similar when looking at 2010 and 2005, where the positive effect of HC is slightly decreasing (as HC increases), but still relevant for low HC levels. When looking at size, the result suggests that air transport's positive effect on efficiency is a prerogative of highly populated NUTS 2, while the effect tends to reduce as the population is lower until it loses its relevance when the population is not sufficient. This suggests that airports located in areas with lower population density (e.g., some secondary airports) may not be as beneficial as one can expect for the regions that host them.[11]

Conclusions

This chapter provides an example on how to apply DEA analysis in order to study the connection between air transport and regional development. Previous

Table 15.7 Annual marginal effect of air transport on efficiency (2005–2015)

2005	2006	2007	2008	2009	2010	2011	2012	2013	2014	2015
−0.029	−0.028	−0.031	−0.031	−0.033	−0.031	−0.030	−0.028	−0.027	−0.022	−0.021
(0.0000)	(0.0000)	(0.0000)	(0.0000)	(0.0000)	(0.0000)	(0.0000)	(0.0000)	0.0000	(0.0000)	(0.0001)

Legend: p-values in parentheses

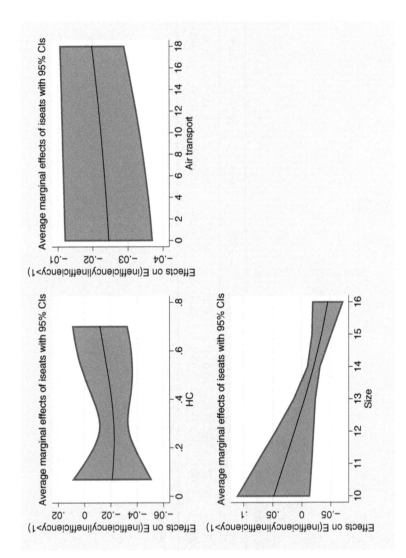

Figure 15.5 Effect heterogeneity year 2015

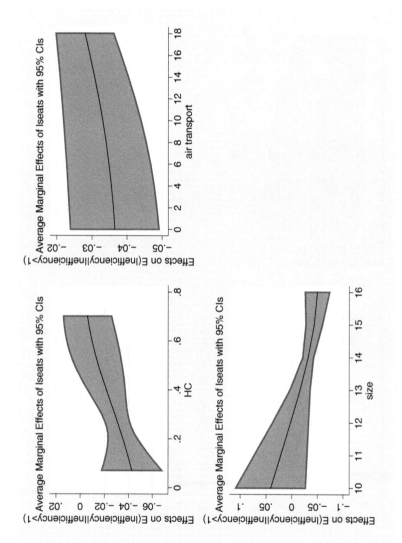

Figure 15.6 Effect heterogeneity year 2010

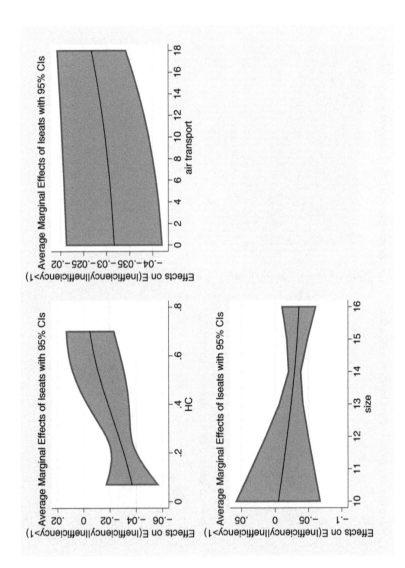

Figure 15.7 Effect heterogeneity year 2005

literature suggests that aviation can help regional economic growth. In this regard, we empirically analyse whether air transport service provision affects positively the generation of gross domestic product (GDP) at European NUTS 2 level. The analysis is based on a panel of 270 NUTS 2 European regions observed for 11 years (2005–2015). After a summary of the main assumptions and issues related to DEA methodology, the production process under investigation is presented together with the research hypothesis. Then, a detailed application of DEA is provided with outlier detection, bias corrections, comparison among different second-stage approaches, and analysis of heterogeneity. Our results show that aviation positively affects the efficiency of GDP generation of European regions. Furthermore, our analysis suggests a positive relationship between efficiency and human capital quality, while an expected negative impact of unemployment on regional efficiency. However, the positive effect of aviation is not homogeneous across regions. Our results show that aviation tends to lose its positive influence on GDP generation when population is relatively small.

Notes

1 Under CRS assumption the term $\sum_{j=1}^{K} \lambda^k = 1$ is neglected.

2 The seminal paper of Aschauer (1989) points out that the demand-side economic development may determine needs and services raising the question of the direction of the causality between air transport and economic development. In this sense, the results from the existing studies are still controversial and dependent on the area and the period of analysis (Manello et al., 2017).

3 See Baker et al. (2015) for an extensive review of papers dealing with the estimation of such effects.

4 See for example Henderson and Russell (2005), Badunenko et al. (2008), Mallick et al. (2016) Simar et al. (2017), Athanassopoulos (1996), Masternak-Janus and Rybaczewska-Błażejowska (2017), Ghosh and Mastromarco (2013), and Henry et al. (2009).

5 An indicator of human capital has been considered as well by Mastromarco and Ghosh (2009) and Arazmuradov et al. (2014) as a determinant of efficiency.

6 For a comprehensive explanation of the data cloud method see Wilson (1993) and Wilson (2008).

7 A value equal to 0 indicates that the specific combination r is minimising the ratio (i.e., maximise the reduction of the volume) and should be isolated from other values of $\log \dfrac{(R^r)}{R^r_{min}}$.

8 Stata *teradial* command has been used. See Badunenko and Mozharovskyi (2016) for more details.

9 Results are similar when comparison is made on observations of other years of the sample.

10 We use 1000 replications for the bias correction bootstrap as in Badunenko and Tauchmann (2018).

11 We thank an anonymous reviewer for this comment.

12 As highlighted in Badunenko and Tauchmann (2018), the assumption of independent ε^i implies that their algorithms are not suitable for panel analysis. This is the reason why also second stage analysis is performed separately year by year.

References

Adler, N., & Volta, N. (2017). Spatial catalytic effect of aviation. COST Workshop on Air Transport and Regional Development: Case Studies on Core Regions. November 2017, Dublin City University.

Athanassopoulos, A. D. (1996). Assessing the comparative spatial disadvantage (CSD) of regions in the European Union using non-radial data envelopment analysis methods. *European Journal of Operational Research*, 94(3), 439–452.

ACI, 2004. The social and economic impact of airports in Europe. ACI-Europe and York Aviation.

Arazmuradov, A., Martini, G., & Scotti, D. (2014). Determinants of total factor productivity in former Soviet Union economies: a stochastic frontier approach. *Economic Systems*, 38(1), 115–135.

Aschauer, D. A., 1989. Is public expenditure productive? *Journal of Monetary Economics*, 23, 177–200.

Badunenko, O., & Mozharovskyi, P. (2016). Nonparametric frontier analysis using Stata. *The Stata Journal*, 16(3), 550–589.

Badunenko, O., & Tauchmann, H. (2018). *Simar and Wilson Two-stage Efficiency Analysis for Stata* (No. 08/2018). FAU Discussion Papers in Economics.

Badunenko, O., Henderson, D. J., & Zelenyuk, V. (2008). Technological change and transition: relative contributions to worldwide growth during the 1990s. *Oxford Bulletin of Economics and Statistics*, 70(4), 461–492.

Baker, D., Merkert, R., & Kamruzzaman, M. (2015). Regional aviation and economic growth: cointegration and causality analysis in Australia. *Journal of Transport Geography*, 43, 140–150.

Blonigen, B., & Cristea, A. C. 2012. Airports and urban growth: evidence from a quasi-natural policy experiment. National Bureau of Economic Research. Working Paper 18278.

Bogetoft, P., & Otto, L. (2011). *Benchmarking with Dea, Sfa, and R* (Vol. 157). New York: Springer Science & Business Media.

Button, K., Brugnoli, A., Martini, G., & Scotti, D. (2015). Connecting African urban areas: airline networks and intra-Sub-Saharan trade. *Journal of Transport Geography*, 42, 84–89.

Debreu, G. (1951). The coefficient of resource utilization. *Econometrica*, 19, 273–292.

Fageda, X. (2017). International air travel and fdi flows: evidence from Barcelona, *Journal of Regional Science*, 57(5), 858–883.

Farrell, M. J. (1957). The measurement of productive efficiency. *Journal of the Royal Statistical Society, Series A*, 120, 253–281.

Florida, R., Mellander, C., & Holgersson, T. (2015). Up in the air: the role of airports for regional economic development. *The Annals of Regional Science*, 54(1), 197–214.

Ghosh, S., & Mastromarco, C. (2013). Cross-border economic activities, human capital and efficiency: a stochastic frontier analysis for OECD countries. *The World Economy*, 36(6), 761–785.

Glaeser, E. L., Kallal, H. D., Scheinkman, J. A., & Shleifer, A. (1992). Growth in cities. *Journal of Political Economy*, 100(6), 1126–1152.

Graham, A. (2003). *Managing Airports: An International Perspective*. Cheltenham: Edward Elgar.

Green, R. K. (2007). Airports and economic development. *Real Estate Economics*, 35(1), 91–112.

Henderson, D. J., & Russell, R. R. (2005). Human capital and convergence: a production-frontier approach. *International Economic Review*, 46(4), 1167–1205.

Henry, M., Kneller, R., & Milner, C. (2009). Trade, technology transfer and national efficiency in developing countries. *European Economic Review*, 53(2), 237–254.

Mallick, S., Matousek, R., & Tzeremes, N. G. (2016). Financial development and productive inefficiency: a robust conditional directional distance function approach. *Economics Letters*, 145, 196–201.

Manello, A., Scotti, D., & Volta, N. (2017). European regions and air routes' dismissal risk. COST Workshop on Air Transport and Regional Development: Case Studies on Core Regions. November 2017, Dublin City University.

Masternak-Janus, A., & Rybaczewska-Błażejowska, M. (2017). Comprehensive regional eco-efficiency analysis based on data envelopment analysis: the case of Polish regions. *Journal of Industrial Ecology*, 21(1), 180–190.

Mastromarco, C., & Ghosh, S. (2009). Foreign capital, human capital, and efficiency: a stochastic frontier analysis for developing countries. *World Development*, 37 (2), 489–502.

Mukkala, K., & Tervo, H. (2013). Air transportation and regional growth, which way does the causality run? *Environment and Planning A*, 45, 1508–1520.

Rosenthal, S., & Strange, W. C. (2001). The determinants of agglomeration. *Journal of Urban Economics*, 50, 191–229.

Simar, L., & Wilson, P. W. (1998). Sensitivity analysis of efficiency scores: how to bootstrap in nonparametric frontier models. *Management Science*, 44(1), 49–61.

Simar, L., & Wilson, P. W. (2000). A general methodology for bootstrapping in nonparametric frontier models. *Journal of Applied Statistics*, 27(6), 779–802.

Simar, L., & Wilson, P. W. (2007). Estimation and inference in two-stage semi-parametric models of production processes. *Journal of Econometrics*, 136: 31–64.

Simar, L., Van Keilegom, I., & Zelenyuk, V. (2017). Nonparametric least squares methods for stochastic frontier models. *Journal of Productivity Analysis*, 47(3), 189–204.

Wilson, P. W. (1993). Detecting outliers in deterministic nonparametric frontier models with multiple outputs. *Journal of Business & Economic Statistics*, 11(3), 319–323.

Wilson, P. W. (2008). FEAR: a software package for frontier efficiency analysis with R. *Socio-economic Planning Sciences*, 42(4), 247–254.

Appendix A

As already discussed in the introductory section, Simar and Wilson's (2007) approaches assume that the DEA efficiency scores are computed against an estimated frontier and not with respect to the true frontier. As a result, DEA scores are biased towards one (finite sample bias). Hence, Eq. (13.4) cannot be estimated straightforwardly and θ has to be replaced by $\hat{\theta}^i$. Consequently, it is not true that ε^i are statistically independent across regions. To address the issue, Simar and Wilson assume a data generating process (Eq. (13.4)) in which ε^i are – conditionally on regressors of Eq. (13.4) – independently,[12] truncated normally distributed with $\mu = 0$, σ and left-truncation at $1 - z^i \beta$. Hence, in their data generating process θ^i cannot be smaller than unity and full efficiency occurs with zero probability. This is why algorithm #1 excludes efficient DMUs from the analysis, while algorithm 2 computes bias-corrected DEA scores. More specifically, algorithm #1 steps are as follows (see also Badunenko and Tauchmann, 2018):

1. Get DEA efficiency scores from the dataset built with the original observations.
2. Use maximum likelihood (ML) estimation on the J $(J < K)$ inefficient DMUs to obtain coefficient $\hat{\beta}$ and variance parameter $\hat{\sigma}$ by a truncated regression (left-truncation at 1) of $\hat{\theta}^i$ on the determinants z_i.
3. Get a set of B bootstrap estimates $(\hat{\beta}^b; \hat{\sigma}^b)$ by looping over the following steps B times
   3.1 For each DMU $i = 1,...,J$, draw an artificial error $\tilde{\varepsilon}_i$ from the truncated $N(0,\hat{\sigma})$ distribution (left-truncation at $1 - z_i\hat{\beta}$).
   3.2 Compute artificial efficiency scores $\hat{\theta}_i$ as $z_i\hat{\beta} + \tilde{\varepsilon}_i$ for each DMU $i = 1,...,J$.
   3.3 Run a truncated regression with left-truncation at 1 of $\hat{\theta}_i$ on z_i to get ML, bootstrap estimates $\hat{\beta}^b$ and $\hat{\sigma}^b$.
4. Compute confidence intervals (CI) and standard errors (SE) for $\hat{\beta}$ and $\hat{\sigma}$ from the bootstrap distribution of $\hat{\beta}^b$ and $\hat{\sigma}^b$.

Algorithm #2 steps are instead as follows:

1. Like algorithm #1.
2. Like algorithm #1.
3. Obtain, for all the K DMUs, a set of B_1 bootstrap estimates $\hat{\theta}_i^b$
4. For each DMU k compute a bias-corrected efficiency score $\hat{\theta}_i^{bc}$ (see Eq. (13.3))
5. Get ML, bootstrap estimates $\bar{\bar{\beta}}$ and $\bar{\bar{\sigma}}$ by a truncated regression (left-truncation at 1) of $\hat{\theta}_i^{bc}$ on z_i.
6. Obtain a set of B_2 bootstrap estimates $(\bar{\bar{\beta}}^b; \bar{\bar{\sigma}}^b)$ by looping over the following steps B_2 times
   6.1 For each DMU $i = 1,...,K$, draw an artificial error $\bar{\bar{\varepsilon}}_i$ from the truncated $N(0,\bar{\bar{\sigma}})$ distribution (left-truncation at $1 - z_i\bar{\bar{\beta}}$).
   6.2 Compute artificial efficiency scores $\bar{\bar{\theta}}_i$ as $z_i\bar{\bar{\beta}} + \bar{\bar{\varepsilon}}_i$ for each DMU $i = 1,...,K$.
   6.3 Get ML, bootstrap estimates $\bar{\bar{\beta}}^b$ and $\bar{\bar{\sigma}}^b$ by a truncated regression (left-truncation at 1) of $\bar{\bar{\theta}}_i$ on z_i to.
7. Compute CI and SE for $\bar{\bar{\beta}}$ and $\bar{\bar{\sigma}}$ from the bootstrap distribution of $\bar{\bar{\beta}}^b$ and $\bar{\bar{\sigma}}^b$.

For further details see Simar and Wilson (2007) and Badunenko and Tauchmann (2018).

Index

Abayasiri-Silva, K. 120
accessibility 200, 216–22; in econometric studies 192–3, **193**, **194**
Acemoglu, D. 11
ACI (Airport Council International) 50, 70, 71, 77, 78, 133, 160, 290
Adams, P. 114, 143
Adelman, I. 110, 122
Adler, N. 6–7, 22, 250, 251, 252, 257, 289
Africa 66, 70, 135, 144
agglomeration 13, 15, 110, 273, 289; and WEBs 48, 49
aggregated models 121, 123
Aguirregabiria, V. 238, 239, 240
Aigner, D. 269
air connectivity 3, 26–44; *see also* connectivity
air transport 9–25; CGE models 108–28, *116–17*; cost-benefit analysis 93–107; econometric approaches 20–2, 175–201; economic evaluation 131–2, 150; and GDP; *see* GDP; input-output approach 66–92; and regional development 66–72; DEA application for 286, 289–303; SFA 272–5, 280
Air Transport and Regional Development (ATARD) 1–8
aircraft certification standards 157, 158, 162, 170; movements 188; noise and emissions 166, 168, *168*, *169*; size in game theory for 250, 253
airfares, game theory for 250, 252, 253; EU-Israel agreement 253–4, 256–7, 259; El Al 259, **260**, 261; results 262, 264, 266
airlines/airline industry 249; entry games in 226–48; European 240–1, **241**; full-service carriers 233, 234, 238; in game theory 253, 254, 256; Israel case study **257**, 258, 259; results 262, 264, 265;

legacy carriers 254, **257**, 259, 264, 265; low-cost; *see* low-cost carriers; USA 234, 239, 259
airports 133–4, 188; accessibility 200, 216–22; Australia 114, 119, 133, 134, 196; connectivity 28–33, 34–7, 51; *see also* air connectivity; economic impact studies 17–19, 66; Europe 71, 81, **82**, **83**, 132–3, 133, 218; Italy 217, *217*, 218; London 115, *116*, 118, 133, 134, 146; social cost studies 161, 162; *see also* Milan airports; input-output model 72–84, 88; Japan, Haneda 114–15; noise and emissions 166, 170; as producers in game theory 258; slots 250, 252–3; social costs of emissions 156–7, 159–60, 170; USA 52–6, 69; *see also* aviation; infrastructure
Airports Commission 49, 115, *116*, 133
Akbulut, G. 186
Alam, S. 27
Alamdari, F.E. 251, 255
Alderighi, M. 27
Alers, T. 134
Allroggen, F. 28, 72, 186–7, **190**, **199**
Anas, A. 111, 113
Anderson, S.P. 251, 254
Andrew, A. 78, 87
Antunes, A.P. 6
Apulia 6, 217–22, *217*
Arazmuradov, A. 274
Arellano, M. 191
Armington. P.S. 123
Arrow, K.J. 110
Aschauer, D.A. 46, 67, 177
Asia 37, 40, 66, 70; *see also* China; Hong Kong; Japan; Korea
ATARD (Air Transport and Regional Development) 1–8
attributes 208, 209–12, 215

Australia 132, 134, 135, 136; CGE
  modelling 114, 119, 120; econometric
  studies 176, 180–1, **181**, **198**, **199**; remote
  and regional 196, **197**; market, demand
  modelling 252
Austria 1, 193, *195*
aviation 51–6, 84–8, 275; econometric
  studies 186–7, **187**, **188**, **189**; and GDP;
  see GDP; *see also* air transport; airports

Bachmann, C. 112
Badunenko, O. 289, 295, 298
Bailey, R. 78, 87
Bajari, P. 230, 233, 234, 235, 238, 239
Baker, D. 20, 26, 196, **197**, **199**
Balistreri, E.J. 120
Baltaci, N. 186
Banister, D. 110
Bannò, M. 26
Baranzini, A. 162
Barnhart, C. 250
baseline scenario 249, 253, 262
Bateman, I.J. 161
Batey, P.W. 76, 77, 80–1
Battese, G.E. 272, 274, 275, 276
Baum, H. 145
behaviour modelling 202–25
Behrens, K. 121
Bel, G. 24
Belotti, F. 276
Ben-Akiva, M. 204, 207, 208, 251, 254
benefits; *see* CBA; net benefit; welfare
Benell, D. 72, 178, **179**, **198**
Benkard, C.L. 239
Berdica, K. 39
Bergantino, A.S. 6, 203, 215, 216, 217, 218,
  221, 222
Bernardo, J.E. 160
Berry, S. 226, 227, 228, 230, 231, 232–3,
  239, 241, 243
Betancor, O. 4, 96
Bhaumik, P.K. 252
bias 186, 215–16, 219; in data envelopment
  analysis 288–9; and entry games 232
Biehl, D. 67
Bilotkach, V. 20, 191, **191–2**, **199**
Bjorn, P. 230
Black, I.G. 251, 255
Blair, P.D. 72
Blake, A. 149
Blevins, J.R. 239
blocking strategy 210, 212
Blonigen, B.A. 21, 26, 196, 273, 289

Boardman, A. 131
Bogetoft, P. 271, 275, 286, 287, 288, 292
Bogulaski, C. 238
Bontemps, C. 6, 230, 231
bootstrap estimate of bias 288–9
Bover, O. 191
Bresnahan, T. 226, 227, 231, 232
Britton, E. 78, 84
Bröcker, J. 22, 108, 111, 112–13, 138,
  139, 141
Brueckner, J.K. 20, 26, 177, 181–2,
  183–4, 196–7, **198**
Brugnoli, A. 196
Bruinsma, F. 68, 77, 84–5
Buckley, P.H. 112
Bulwien, H. 133
Bunditsakulchai, P. 112
Burfisher, M. 131
Burghouwt, G. 26, 27, 51
bus services 219, *220*, 221
business establishments, number of
  191, **191–2**
business travel 180–1, **181**, **198**
Butler, S.E. 69, 77, 80, 85, 87
Button, K. 84, 179, **198**, 273, 275, 289–90

Calatayud, A. 26
Cameron, A.C. 205, 207
Campante, F. 16, 21, 26, 196
Campos, J. 4, 96
Canada 86, 135, 178, **198**
capital in DEA 290, *290*, 291–2, **291**
Caplin, A. 254
Capurso, M. 203, 216, 217, 218, 221,
  222
cargo 182, 192–3, **198**
cars, travelling to airports in 218, 219,
  220, 222
Cascetta, E. 210
Catalano, M. 6
catalytic effects 77–8, 81, 84, 145, 290; and
  WEBs 45, 49–50, 56
Cattaneo, M. 27
causality 86, 275, 290; and employment
  193, **194**, *195*, 196; and investment
  17, 20–2; *see also* Granger-causality
  analysis
CBA (Cost-Benefit Analysis) 4–5, 93–107;
  evaluation 130, 131, 133–4, 135,
  138–44; interpretation of results 147;
  optimising 148–50; and WEBs 45,
  50, 145; certification standards 157,
  158, 162, 170

CGE (computable general equilibrium) models 5, 110–18, 150; availability of models 146–7; evaluation with 108–28, 130, 138–40, **140**; and air transport *116–17*, 134, 135–6; comparisons 131, **131**; optimising 148–50; interpretation of results 147–8; issues 121–2, 140–4; and policy 108–28, 135–6; and WEBs 50, 145

China 3, 35–42, **38**, **40**, **41**; econometric studies 176, 186

Choi, J.H. 30

choice, consumer 203–22

Ciliberto, E. 230, 234, 239

Cleeren, K. 226, 233, 238, 239

Cobb-Douglas (CD) 187, 270, 274

Cockburn, J. 109

Coelli, T.J. 269, 271, 272, 274, 275, 276

Cohen, J.P. 47, 48

competitors/competition 6–7, 12–13, 253; with airlines and rail 251, 252; and entry games 226–31, 233–4, 236–42, 244; and game theory 249–51, 253–9, 262–6; and liberalisation 120–1

computable general equilibrium; *see* CGE

congestion 113, *116*, 118, 250

connectivity 3, 26–44, 145–6; and airport accessibility 217; in econometric studies 188; and economic growth 21–2, 26; supply chain perspective 51; *see also* air connectivity

ConnUM (Connectivity Utility Model) 3, 28–42

constant returns to scale (CRS) 287, *287*

consumer surplus 258, **263**, 264–5, **265**

consumers 203–8, 252, 258

contexts in SP surveys 215, 217–18

Cooper, A. 50

core-periphery model 14–15

cost game theory for 250, 251, 254–7, 259; regional, measurement of 101–4; of trade 15–16; *see also* social costs; transport costs

Cristea, A.C. 273, 289

Cristea, A.D. 21, 26, 196

cross-border effects 95, 97, 98, 104, 105

curfews 119, 132, 159

data cloud method 271, 275, 288, 292

data collection 85, 218–19

data envelopment analysis (DEA) 269, 271, 286–306

dataset in DEA 286, 292

Davies, R. 120

de Dios Ortúzar, J. 202

de Haan, J. 47, 67

De Jong, G. 258

De Maio, L. 122

De Melo, J. 110–11

de Oliveira, A.V.M. 238

De Rus, G. 93, 131, 147

DEA (data envelopment analysis) 269, 271, 286–306

Debreu, G. 110, 287

Dehnen, N. 161, 165

Dekkers, J.E.C. 161

demand, modelling 251–2

dependent variables **198–9**; Benell & Prentice study 178–9, **179**; Bilotkach study 191, **191–2**; Brueckner study 181–2, **183–4**; Button & Taylor study 179; Goetz study 177, **178**; Green study 182, 185–6, **185**; in SP studies 209, 210–11; deregulation 114, 135, 264; *see also* liberalisation; open skies

Derudder, B. 186, 193, *195*, **199**

Dervis, K. 110

destinations in econometric studies 179–80; Bilotkach study 191, **191–2**

Diao, X. 111

Dings, J.M.V. 157, 161, 163, 164, **165**, 167

Dinwiddy, C. 141, 142

direct air connectivity 28–30, 35–7, **38**, 8–9

direct effects 75, 76, 88, 95

direct impact 74, 77, 78–80, *78*, **82**, **83**; in cost-benefit analysis 104; and economic growth 290

disaggregation 139, 147

discrete choice 208–22

distribution of income and wealth 143–4

distributional impacts 121

Dixit, A.K. 120, 121

DMU (decision-making unit) 269, 286, 287–8; outliers 271; production process 290–2

Dobson, G. 250, 254

Domencich, T. 202

Doyme, K. 252

Drake, R.L. 69

Dreze, J. 141

Duchin, F. 85

Dunn, A. 238–9

Dusek, T. 70, 79, 81, **82**, **83**

Dwyer, L. 109, 111, 149

dynamic effects 226–7, 238, 239; in CGE
111, 114; in input-output methods 85

EASA (European Union Aviation Safety
Agency) 158, 159, 163–4
Eberts, R.W. 46
econometric approaches 6, 20–2,
175–201, 203; entry model 226, 227, 230
economic growth 67, 273, 290, 303; and
connectivity 21–2, 26; and public capital
46–8, 59; *see also* growth
economic impacts 50, 110, 111
effectiveness, firms' 286
efficiency 7; and DEA 286–8, 289, 294–5;
heterogeneous effects 298, *300–2*;
results 295, 298; and SFA 269, 272, 275;
results 276–80
efficiency scores in DAE 289, 294, 295;
results 295, **296**, 297, **297**
efficient designs 210, 212–14
EIA (Economic Impact Analysis)
5, 130–1, 132–3; air transport
policy 108–9, 134–5; analysing the
technique 137–8; for aviation tax 136;
and catalytic impacts 50, 56, 145; and
employment 142; limitations 108–9, 150;
see also EIS (economic impact studies);
Vein, L. 238
EIS (economic impact studies) 69–72;
airport investment 17–19; on
airports 66, 88; *see also* EIA (Economic
Impact Analysis)
El Al 259, **260**, 261, **261**, 266; *see also* Israeli
airlines
Elbehri, A. 120
emissions 156–7, 159–63, 164, 170;
Bergamo airport 166–70, **167**, **168**, **169**;
monetary value 164–5, *165*; *see also*
environmental issues; greenhouse
gases
employment 141–2, 150, 273, 289, 290; and
causality 193, **194**, *195*, 196; econometric
studies **198**, **199**; Benell & Prentice
179, **179**; Bilotkach study 191, **191–2**;
Brueckner study
181–2, **183–4**; Button & Taylor
179–80; Europe 192–3, **193**, **194**; Goetz
177, **178**; Green 182, 185–6, **185**;
Percoco study 186–7, **187**, **188**, **189**;
game theory model 265, **265**, 266; in
input-output models 74, 75, 76, **82**, 87;
airports 77, 78–80, *78*, *79*, *80*
enplanements 179–80, 181–2, **183–4**

entry games 226–48; of complete
information 227–32, 238–9;
of incomplete information 234–8,
239–40; *see also* game theory
environmental factors 271, **273**, 291, **291**
environmental issues 156, 170, 258; in
input-output studies 86, 88; and rail
travel 252; *see also* emissions; noise;
pollutants
EU; *see* European Union
Euro-Mediterranean agreement 7, 253,
265, 266
Eurocontrol 157, 159, 161, 163, 164,
165, 167
Europe 1–2, 3, 4, 6–7; airports 6,
217, *217*, 218–19; EIA 132–3; EIS
81, **82**, **83**; impact studies 71; London
115, *116*, 118, 133, 134, 146; Milan;
see Milan airports; social cost studies
161, 162; CGE modelling 118–19, 131;
econometric studies 21, 197, **198**, **199**;
destinations 179–80; Mukkala & Tervo
study 192–3, **193**, **194**; Van de Vijver et al
193, *195*, 196; EIS 66, 70, 71, 81, **82**, **83**;
entry games 6, 240–4; game theory
253–8, 262–4, 265; networks 250; GDP
impact of aviation 19; input-output
method 86; legacy carriers in 259;
NUTS2; *see* NUTS2 regions;
regulation 158–60; Trans-European
Transport Network (TEN-T) 95; see also
by name of country
European Aviation Safety Agency; *see* EASA
European Union 11–12, 14–15, 16;
econometric studies 176, 186;
Euro-Mediterranean agreement 7,
253, **265**, 266; income disparities 9;
infrastructure and growth 68;
modelling demand 252; open skies
262, **263**; policy 22–3, 68; project
approval 97; publications 158, 159, 160;
evaluation 129–40, 146–51; and air
transport *116–17*, 134, 135–6; of air
transport infrastructure 69–72; CGE
models 108–28, 130, 138–40, **140**;
comparisons 131, **131**; difficulties
140–4; optimising 148–50; and WEBs
144–6; *see also* CBA; CGE; EIA
Evangelinos, C. 161
ex-ante 76, 129
ex-post 76–7, 175
explanatory variables **198–9**; Benell &
Prentice study 178–9, **179**; Brueckner

study 181–2, **183**–4; Button & Taylor study 179–80; Goetz study 177, **178**
externalities 5–6, 143, 150; social costs 156–74

FAA 69, 70, 71, 132, 163–4
Fageda, X. 21, 273, 290
fairs; *see* airfares
Farrell, M. 287
Farrow, S. 141
Federal Aviation Administration; *see* FAA
Ferbrache, F. 109
Fernald, J.G. 47
final demand 73, 74, 75
Findlay, C. 26
firms 15, 227–8; in DEA 286–8, 289, 294–5, 298; inefficiency 294–5, 298 *see also* DMU
Florida, R. 20, 196, 289
Foggia airport 217, *217*
Forsyth, P. 5, 49, 70, 71, 87, 108–9, 110, 114, 119, 135, 136, 144, 145, 149
fractional factorial designs 210–12
France 1, 193, *195*
free trade agreements (FTAs) 37, 40
frequencies in game theory 250–3, 256, 258–61; results of analysis 262, 264–5
frontier analysis 7, 170; in DEA 286, 287–8, 289, 295; stochastic 7, 200, 269–85
full factorial design 209–10
full-service carriers (FSC) 233, 234, 238

game theory 6–7, 249–68; *see also* entry games
Garcia, A. 253
Garcia-Palomares, J.C. 39
GDP (Gross Domestic Product) 289–90; and DEA 290, *290*, 292, 294–5, 303; econometric studies 188, **198**, **199**; Europe 192–3, **193**, **194**; and SFA 273, **273**, 276, 280
general equilibrium 109, 122, 138, 139, 140–1, 150
generalised method of moments (GMM) 191, **199**
Germany 1, 71, 118–19, 133, 134, 136; econometric studies 186, 187–8, **190**, 196, **199**
Geurs, K.T. 27
Ghobrial, A. 249–50
Ghosh, S. 274

Gillen, D. 3, 47, 70, 79, 135, 145, 240
Gillingwater, D. 70, **80**, 86
Givoni, M. 161, 162, 163
Glaeser, E.L. 51, 273, 289
global open skies **263**, 264, 265
GMM (generalised method of moments) 191, **199**
Goetz, A.R. 176, 177, **178**, **198**
Goolsbee, A. 233
governance and development 11–12
government revenue, shadow price of 150
government surplus 258
Graham, A. 69, 70–1, 290
Graham, D. 145
Graham, D.J. 109
Gramlich, E.M. 46, 177
Grampella, M. 5, 157, 162–9, 170
Granger-causality analysis 180, **181**, 186, 192–6, 197–8, **198**, **199**
Green, R.K. 20–1, 177, 181, 182, 185–6, **185**, **198**, 273, 289
greenhouse gases (GHG) 136, 138, 143, 156; standards for 159–60; *see also* emissions
Gregan, T. 135
Grieco, P.L.E. 226
Griffiths, W.E. 275
growth 273, 275, 289; econometric study 177, **178**; *see also* economic growth
Grubesic, T.H. 27
Gualtieri, G. **82**, **83**

Hahn, F. 110
Hajargasht, G. 275
Hakfoort, J. 70
Hansen, M. 250, 251, 254, 256
Hansman, R.J. 19
Harback, K. *116*, 118
Harberger, A.C. 110
Harker, P.T. 252, 254
Harris, J.M. 156
Harris, R. 109, 120
HEATCO Project 96, 156, 161, 165
hedonic prices method 161
Heggie, I.G. 67
Hensher, D.A. 113, 209, 210, 212, 214, 215, 252, 255
Herfindhal index 226
Herndon, S.C. 160
Herte, T. 120
Hess, S. 203, 216, 217, 218, 221, 222
Heuer, K. 70, **82**, **83**
high-speed rail 28, 251, 252

Hill, T. 209, 210, 211
Hinsch, H. 70, 79
Hiramatsu, T. 111, 113
Hirte, G. 111, 112, 113
Hitomi, K. 112
Ho, C.Y. 239, 240
Holgersson, T. 20, 196
holiday travel 180–1, **181**, **198**; *see also* tourism
Holmes, N.S. 161
home market effect 13–14
Hong, S. 252, 254
Hong Kong 35, **36**, 37; vulnerability analysis 39, 40, **40**, **41**
Horridge, M. 120
Hosoe, N. 121
Hossain, M. 27
Huang, J.C. 161
hubs 66, 70, 79, 115; and connectivity 26, 27, 33, 34, 37; econometric studies 182, **183**, 185–6, **198**; in entry games 239; and game theory 250, 251, 254, 256–7, **257**; Israeli market 259, **260**; and WEBs 51, 52, 53, **54**, **55**, 56
Huderek-Glapska, S. 3, 5, 70, **82**, **83**, 85
Hudson, E.A. 111
Hujer, R. 71, 73–4, 75, 76
Hulten, C.R. 46
human capital (HC) 278, *290*, 291, **291**, 292; analysis of results 297, **297**, 298
Hummels, D. 16
Hurlin, C. 193

ICAO 157–8, 158, 159, 162, 163
impact 45, 123, 130–2, **131**, 175; in CGE 108; and CBA 139, **140**, 142; econometric approaches 175–201; on economic growth 290; EIAs fail on 133, 134–5, 137–8, 150; *see also* EIA; EIS
income in input-output models 74, 75, 76; airports 77, 78, 79, **83**; areas of concern 84–8; as indicators 87
indirect connectivity 30–4, 38–9
indirect effects 74, 76, 88, 95; ways of calculating 86, 87
indirect impact 77, 80–4, **82**, **83**; and CGE 111; in cost-benefit analysis 104; and economic growth 290; issues with 87–8
induced effects 74, 75, 76, 88; of airports 77, 81, **82**, **83**; ways of calculating 86, 87
induced impact 290

industry sectors and connectivity 53, 55–6, **57**, **58**, 59
inefficiency 294–5, 298; in SFA 270, 271, 274, 276, 280; results 278, 279, 280
inefficient projects 86
infrastructure 48, 66–72, 273; CGE for 114–18; in input-output studs 84–5, 87; and WEBs 51–6, 59; *see also* airports
input-output model 3–4, 18–19, 66–92, 137, 145
inputs 15, 66; in DEA 286–7, 288, 290–2, *290*, **291**
integration 95, 98
international trade 180–1, **181**, **198**, 273; aviation, as determinant of 289–90
international travel 180–1, **181**; *see also* tourism
InterVISTAS 77, 134, 259
investment 9–25, 48; as catalytic effect 290; CGE models for 108–28; and WEBs 45
Ireland 2, 193, *195*
Ishutkina, M. 19
Israel 6–7, 253–8, 262–4
Israeli airlines 262, **263**, 264, 265; *see also* El Al
Israeli market **216**, 258–64, **260**
Italy 1, 6, 217–22, *217*; econometric studies 186–7, **187**, **188**, **189**, **198**; *see also* Milan airports
Ivanova, O. 112

Japan 114–15, *116*, 180–1, **181**
Jenkins, G. 133
Jenkins, G.P. 97
Jensen, R.C. 75, 86
Jia, P. 233
Johansen, L. 110
Johnson, M. 135
Jorge-Calderon, D. 105n, 134
Jorgenson, D.W. 111

Kalaitzidakis, P. 67
Kalyvitis, S. 67
Kamble, S.D. 118
Kamruzzaman, M. 20
Kanafani, A. 249–50
Karakaplan, M.U. 275
Kazda, A. 70
Keen, M. 150
Kenya 135, 144
Kiernan, L.J. 69, 77, 80, 85, 87
Kim, E. 111, 112, 113
Kincaid, I. 51

Klophaus, R. 145
Knight, B. 23
Knowles, R.D. 109
Kokot, S. 71, 73–4, 75, 76
Konan, D.E. 120–1
Korea 35, **36**, 37
Korzhenevych, A. 161, 164
Kroes, E.P. 162
Krugman, P.R. 9, 14, 145
Kulendran, N. 180, **181, 198**
Kulmer, V. 113
Kumar, R. 231
Kumbhakar, S.C. 269–70, 272, 275
Kuo, C.-Y. 97
Kupfer, F. **82, 83**
Kutlu, L. 275

labour 14–15, 290, *290*, **291**; *see also* wages
Lagneaux, F. **82, 83**
Lakshmanan, T.R. 97
Lancaster, K.J. 203–4
Lavandier, C. 161
Lederer, P.J. 250, 254
Lee, L.F. 272
legacy carriers 254, **257**, 259, 264, 265
Leontief, W. 72, 73, 77, 85
Lerman, S. 204, 207, 251, 254
Lewicki, P. 209, 210, 211
liberalisation *116*, 120–1, 132, 134, 135–6; and economic impact studies 70–1; in game theory 252, 253, 255, 258; *see also* deregulation; open skies
Limão, N. 98
LIML method 188, **199**
Liu, X. 26
Liu, Y. 113
Lobo, P. 160
Lofgren, H. 112
London 275, 276; airports 115, *116*, 118; evaluation of 133, 134, 146
Louvière, J. 210
low-cost carriers (LCC) 233, 234, 238, 241; in game theory 253, 254, 257, **257**, 259; results 262, 264, 266
Lu, C. 157, 161, 162, 164, **165**, 167
Luke, R. 70
Lukovics, M. 70

McFadden, D. 202, 204, 207
Mackie, P. 110
Madden, J. 72
Madio, L. 217
Magnac, T. 230

Malighetti, P. 27
Malina, R. 72, 81, **82, 83**, 186–7, **190, 199**
Mamruzzaman, M. 196, **197, 199**
Mamuneas, T. 47
Mandel, B. 41
manufacturing 182, 196, 197, **199**
Marianov, V. 251
Marin, P.L 120
market design 252–3
market share, game theory for 250, 251, 252; EU-Israel agreement 253, 255, 256, 257, 259; El Al's 259, **260**, 261; results **260**, 261, **261**, 262, 264–5
markets 233; entry games for 226–8, 231, 232–7, 245; airline sector 238–44, **241, 242, 243, 244**, 245; complete information 227–8; game theory for 249–68; Israeli market **216**, 258–64, **260**
Martini, G. 5, 6
Maskus, K.E. 120
Mastromarco, C. 274
Matisziw, T.C. 27
Matsumoto, H. 26
maximising unconfounding design 211
Mazzeo, M.J. 226, 233, 239
Meeusen, W. 269
Meißner, M. 215
Mellander, C. 20, 196
Melo, P.C. 49, 109
Mercenier, J. 108, 111, 112, 138, 139, 141
mergers 239–40, 251
Merkert, R. 20, 196, **197, 199**
metropolitan standard area 179
Mexico 11
MFP (multifactor productivity) 52–6, 59
Miguel, C. 129
Milan airports 5–6, *158*, *167*; case study 166–70, **167, 168, 169**; noise 166–70, *168, 169,* **169**
Miller, R.E. 72
Mills, G. 133
Mira, P. 238
Mishan, E.J. 133
Miyagi, T. 112
Miyazawa, K. 73
MMRF (MONASH Multi-Regional Forecasting) 114
mobility of workers 14–15
Monderer, D. 253
Montalvo, J.G. 84, 85
Morawska, L. 161
Morikawa, T. 208

Morrell, P. 157, 161, 162, 164, **165**, 167
Morrison, S. 134, 254
Morrison Paul, C.J. 47, 48
Mukkala, K. 186, 192, 193, **193**, **194**,
    198, 289
multi-modal connectivity 34–5
multiple equilibria 228, 229–31, *229*,
    233, 245
multipliers 74, 75–6, 77, 80–1; in EIAs 137;
    specific airports **82**, **83**; ways of
    calculating 86, 87
Munnell, A.H. 46, 67

Nadiri, M. 47
Nalebuff, B. 254
Nash, C. 22
Nash equilibrium 229, 238, 250
natural advantage and development 11–12
Navrud, S. 161
negative externalities, social costs of
    156–74
nested logit framework 206–7, **206**,
    219, **220**
net benefit 130, 131–2, **131**, 150; CBA for
    138, 139; and CGE 111, 140–1; EIAs fail
    on 134–5, 137–8; *see also* CBA; welfare
Netherlands 1, 133, 136
NetScan model 27, 29
network carriers 253
network effects 239
network quality models 27
networks, game theory for 249–50
new economy employment 179–80, **198**
New Zealand 180–1
NextGen 118
Niemeier, H.-M. 5, 7, 18, 49, 69, 70, 71, 84,
    85, 86, 87, 88, 133
Nijkamp, P. 67
Nitzsche, E. 111
Njoya, E. 5, **116**, 121, 135, 144
noise 132, 149, **158**; in SFA 269, 270, 280;
    social costs 156–9, 160,
    161–4, 170; Bergamo airport 166–70,
    168, *169*, **169**; monetary value 165–6;
    see also environmental issues
non-stochastic environmental factors
    271–2
North America 176; *see also* Canada; USA
Norway 2, 4, 186
NPV 99, *100*
NUTS2 regions 192, 193, 269, 273, 280;
    efficient regions 278, **278**, **279**; and
    regional development 286, 289, 290, 303;

data for 291–2; results 295, **296**, 297,
    297, 298
Nwaneri, V. 143

Official Airline Guide (OAG) 163, 164, 166;
    entry games studies used 240
O'Kelly, M.E. 251
OLS regression analysis 177, 178, 179, 181,
    197–8, **198**
open skies 252, 258, 262, **263**, 265; global
    263, 264, 265; *see also* deregulation
optimal designs 210, 212–14
ordered choice models 226
Orme, B. 215
Otiso, K. 27
Otto, L. 271, 275, 286, 287, 288, 292
outliers 271, 275; in DEA 288, 292–4,
    293, *294*
output 15, 66, 72, 73, 77; in DEA 286–7,
    288, 290–1, **291**, 292; in SFA 269–71,
    270, 273
output orientated technical efficiency 269
output-efficiency model 288–9, 294
overall connectivity, China's 38–9

Paleari, S. 27
panel data 272, 280
partial equilibrium 109, 120, 138, 140–
    1, 150; and evaluation of externalities 143
Partidário, M.R. 129
passenger transport costs 16
passengers in econometric studies 178–9,
    179, *195*, 196, **198–9**; Bilotkach study
    191, **191–2**; Brueckner study 181–2,
    183–4; Button & Taylor study 179–80;
    Green study 182, **185**; Mukkala & Tervo
    study 192–3, **193**, **194**; Percoco study
    186–7, **187**, **188**, **189**; game theory for
    251–4, 256, 258–9
    results 262, 264, 266
PATH (path aggregation theorem) 41
Pearce, B. 144
Peeta, S. 113
Pels, E. 22, 256
Percoco, M. 186–7, **187**, **188**, **189**, **198**
Pereira, R.H. 121
Pesendorfer, M. 235
Pfähler, W. 72, 76, 81
Phaneuf, D.J. 156
physical node-to-node measure 41
Pischner, R. 73
Pitt, M.M. 272
Pleeter, S. 18

policy 118, 132, 134–6, 136–7; and airport accessibility 221–2; and CGE 108–28, 136; discrete choice models for 216–22; European 22–3, 68
pollutants, social costs of 156, 159–60, 170; *see also* environmental issues
population 273, 289, 298, 303; in econometric studies **178**, **198**; Allroggen & Malina studies 188, **190**; Green studies 182, 185–6, **185**
Prentice, B. 72, 178, **179**, **198**
prices 250, 251, 252; game theory for 253–4, 256, 262, 264, 265
producer decisions, modelling 249–50
producer surplus 258, **263**, **265**
producers 252
production process 286, 290–2, *290*
productivity 51–6, 59, 79, *79*
products/services as outputs 286
profit and entry games 226, 227–38; airline sector 238–9, 241, 242, 244; game theory for 250, 252, 253, 256, 258; results 262, 264, 265
profit shock 227–31, 234–5, 237, 244
project definition in CBA 97–8
Proost, S. 2, 9, 12, 22, 23
public capital 45, 46–8, 59
public service obligations 249
public transport 217, 218, 219, *220*, 221; *see also* bus services; rail
Puga, D. 22, 98
Püschel, R. 161
PwC (UK) 115, *116*, 118, 136, 146

quality of service and game theory 251, 255
Quinet, E. 129

rail services 28, 251, 252; for Apulian airport system 218, 219, *220*; and connectivity 34, 188; in econometric studies 188, 192, **198**
Ramirez, J.V. 162
Ray, A. 142
Redding, S.J. 17, 20
Redondi, R. 26, 51
regional development 11–15, 17–22; DEA application for 286, 289–303; econometric approaches 175–201; and game theory 249–68; input-output approach 66–72, 88–9; SFA for 272–5, 280
regional economic growth 273, 303; *see also* growth

regional economic theory 2–3, 9–25
regions cost-benefit analysis for 93–107; and decision criteria 99–101, *100*, *102*; measurement of benefits and costs 101–4
regression analysis 186–92, 197–8, **198**–**9**; OLS 177, 178, 179, 181, 197–8, **198**; 2SLS 181, 197–8, **198**, **199**
regulation 118–21, 252; of emissions and noise 157–60, 170; *see also* deregulation; liberalisation; open skies
regulators 249, 252, 253
Reiss, P. 226, 227, 231, 232, 233
Requate, T. 156
research hypothesis in DEA 286, 292, 297–8
returns to scale 12–13, 287; variable (VRS) 287, *287*, 289, 294
revealed preference (RP) 202–3, 216, 218
revenue and game theory 254, 255, 256, 257, 262
Rietveld, P. 67, 68, 77, 84–5, 161, 162, 163
risk assessment analysis 160–1
Roach, B. 156
roads 188, 192, **198**, 218, 219
Robinson, J. 11
Robinson, S. 110, 112, 122
Robson, E.N. 112, 113
Rodríguez-Núñez, E. 39
Rodrik, D.A. 98
Romp, W. 47, 67
Rose, A. 141
Rose, J.M. 213
Rosen, H.S. 251, 258
Rosenthal, S. 49, 273, 289
Roson, R. 120
route allocation 134
RP; *see* revealed preference

Sampaio, R.M.B. 6, 233, 238
sampling 203, 214–15
Samuelson, P.A. 112
Sándor, Z. 213
Sarmiento, S. 2
Scarf, H.E. 110
Schipper, Y. 161, 162, 165, 250
Schläpfer, F. 223
Schlumberger, C.E. 134
Schmidt-Dengler, P. 235
Schürmann, G. 160
Schwab, R.M. 46
Scotland 193, *195*
Scotti, D. 5, 7

Sebestyen, T. 112
Seim, K. 226, 234, 235
Sekmen, O. 186
services 197, 286
SFA (Stochastic Frontier Analysis) 7,
    200, 269–85; limitation 271; and
    regional development 272–5
shadow price 141, 142, 150
Shahrokhi Shahraki, H. 112
Shapley, L.S. 253
Sheard, N. 20, 196
Sheldon, R.J. 162
Sheng, D. 252–3
Shoven, J.B. 108, 110
significance 130, 131–2, **131**, 134–5
Simar, L. 289, 295
Simon, H.A. 203
simulated estimator 231–2
slots (airport) 250, 252–3
Small, K.A. 251, 258
Smilowitz, K. 251
Smith, P. 50
Smith, V.K. 161
SNPV 94, 99, 100–1, *100*, *102*, 105
social costs of negative externalities
    156–74; Bergamo airport 167–70, **168**,
    169, **169**
social welfare 97; in CBA 93–4, 95,
    99–104; in game theory studies 252,
    253, 258, **263**; analysis 264–6, **265**;
    see also welfare
society and air transport 93; and CBA
    94–5, 99, 104
socio-economic effects, model for 72–84
South America 66, 70
SP; *see* stated preference (SP)
Spain 1, 5, 12, 193, *195*
spatial CGE models 111, 112, 113, 115
spatial spillover effects 186, 187, **189**
spillover effects 51–6, 186, 187, **189**
Staglin, R. 73
standard entry game 227–8
standard ordered choice models 226
stated preference (SP) 6, 162, 202–25
static entry games 6
static models (CGE) 111
Steer Davies-, Gleave-. 259
Steiner, M. 215
Stern, N. 141
Stiglitz, J.E. 120, 121
stochastic frontier analysis; *see* SFA
Strange, W.C. 49, 273, 289
Sturm, J.E. 47
subsidies 111, 119, 133, 193, 249
surveying 208–16, 218–19

Sutton, J. 226
Swan, W. 257
Sweden 193, **195**
Syverson, C. 233
Szyld, D. 85

Tamer, E. 227, 230, 234, 239
Tarr, D. 110–11
Tauchmann, H. 289, 295, 298
Tavasszy, L.A. 112
tax 67–8, 118–19, 132, 136; in input-
    output models 77, 80; social
    opportunity cost 150
taxi services 218, 219, *220*
Taylor, L. 122
Taylor, M.A. 27, 39
Taylor, S. 179, **198**
Teal, F. 141, 142
TEN-T 95–6
Tervo, H. 186, 192, 193, **193**, **194**, **198**, 289
Thisse, J.-F. 9, 12, 23
Thissen, M. 110
Thomopoulos, N.A. 94
Thurlow, J. 111
Thurstain-Goodwin, M. 110
time, value of 221
time-varying efficiency 272, 274
Torija, A.J. 160
tourism 118, 119, 121, 144, 290; CGE
    studies 111, 136, 141, 149; and
    connectivity 37, 38, 40; econometric
    studies **187**, **188**; game theory
    258, 265–6, **265**; and liberalisation
    135, 137; measuring benefits 149; and
    natural advantage 2, 10, 19; net value
    of 81, 84; in regional economic theory
    17, 19, 20, 23; and transport costs 17;
    see also holiday travel
trade 15–16; international 180–1, **181**,
    198, 273, 289–90
Train, K. 207
trains; *see* rail services
trans-border effects 96
Trans-European Transport Network
    (TEN-T) 95–6
translog 270–1, 274, 276
transport 122, 202; CGE for 111–14;
    see also air transport
transport costs 12, 13–16, 17–22; in CGE 112
Tretheway, M. 51
Trivedi, P.K. 205, 207
Truong, T.P. 113
Tscharaktschiew, S. 111, 112, 113
Turner, M.A. 17, 20
Tveter, E. 186

Ueda, T. 115, *116*, 134
UK 2, 3, 9, 49, 131, 132; econometric studies 180–1, **181**; London airports 115, *116*, 118; evaluation of 133, 134, 146; Scotland 193, *195*; tax 118–19, 136, 146
unemployment 7, 278; in DEA *290*, 291, **291**, 292, 297
urban economics 9, 12
urban growth in econometric studies 177
USA 1, 11, 16, 134, 135, 226; airline industry 234, 239, 259; airports 52–6, 69; connectivity and productivity studies 52–6; deregulation 135; econometric studies 177, 197, **198–9**; Bilotkach study 191, **191–2**; Brueckner study 181–2, **183–4**, 185–6, **185**; Button & Taylor study 179–80; trade and travel with Australia 180–1, **181**; and economic development 20–1; economic impact analysis 132, 133; economic impact studies 66, 69, 70, 71; entry games for 232–3, 234, 239, 245; game theory analysis 250; input-output method 86; modelling of congestion *116*, 118; public capital spending 46
utility function 203–5, 219, 286
utility-based connectivity measures 41

Van Assche, A. 120–1
van Den Broeck, J. 269
van Seventer, D.E. 120–1
Van der Straaten, J.W 161
Van de Vijver, E. 26, 186, 193, *195*, **199**
Van Wee, B. 27
variable returns to scale (VRS) 287, *287*, 289, 294
variables in econometric studies 175, **198–9**; Allroggen & Malina studies 187–8, **190**; Baker, Merkert & Mamruzzaman studies 196, **197**; Bilotkach study 191, **191–2**; Mukkala & Tervo study 192–3, **193**, **194**; Percoco model 186–7, **187**, **188**, **189**; in SFA dataset 273–4, **273**, **274**, 275; results 276, **277**; in SP studies 209, 210–11; *see also* dependent variables; explanatory variables
Vaze, V 250
Veldhuis, J. 27

Venables, A. 110, 145
Venables, A.J. 48, 50, 51, 59, 98
Venet, B. 193
Vickerman, R. 109, 144
Volta, N. 7, 218, 289
vulnerability analysis 39–40, 41
Vuong, Q. 230

wages 14–15, 191, **191–2**, **199**
Walras, L. 110
Walrasian general equilibrium structure 110
Walters, J. 70
Wang, H.J. 272
Wang, J. 27
Waters, W. 130
WEBs (wider economic benefits) 3, 45–65, 151; in CGE models 109, 110, 144–5; and input-output model 88–9; *see also* wider economic impacts
Wedel, M. 213
Wei, W. 250
Weisbrod, G. 69
welfare 45, 59, 150; and CGE 111, 119, 131, 139, 141; and CBA 45, 59, **140**; net benefit 108, 123; *see also* social welfare
welfare maximisation 87, 88
West, G.R. 75, 86
Whalley, J. 108, 110
wider economic impacts 104, 120; CGE for 109–10, 113, 122; *see also* WEBs (wider economic benefits)
willingness-to-pay 203, 214–15, 223; and social costs 161, 162
Willumsen, L. 202
Wilson, K. 180, **181**, **198**
Wilson, P.W. 289, 295
Winston, C. 135, 254
Witlox, F. 186, 193, *195*, **199**
worker mobility 14–15; *see also* labour

Yamaguchi, K. 114, *116*, 120
Yanagizawa-Drott, D. 16, 21, 26
Yang, X. 186
Yao, S. 186
Yu, L. 113

Zeigler, P. 26–7
Zhang, A. 3, 26, 28, 51
Zhang, P. 113
Zhang, Y. 3, 26, 27, 28, 29, 30
Zhu, Z. 26, 27, 28, 30, 31, 34, 37

Lightning Source UK Ltd.
Milton Keynes UK
UKHW020754010822
406672UK00006B/791